IT ALL BEGAN

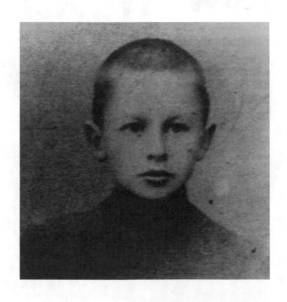

COLUMBIA UNIVERSITY PRESS
NEW YORK

How it all began

Nikolai Bukharin

Translated from the Russian by George Shriver

Introduction by Stephen F. Cohen

Columbia University Press
Publishers Since 1893
New York   Chichester, West Sussex
Translation copyright © 1998 Columbia University Press
Introduction and Afterword © 1998 by Stephen F. Cohen
All rights reserved

Library of Congress Cataloging-in-Publication Data
Bukharin, Nikolai Ivanovich, 1888–1938.
[Vremena. English]
How it all began / Nikolai Bukharin : translated by George Shriver.
p.   cm.
ISBN 0–231–10730–7 (alk. paper)   —   ISBN 0–231–10731–5 (pbk.)
I. Shriver, George, 1936–   .   II. Title.
PG3476.B776V7413   1998
891.73'42—dc21   97–38428

Casebound editions of Columbia University Press books are
printed on permanent and durable acid-free paper.
Printed in the United States of America
c 10 9 8 7 6 5 4 3 2 1
p 10 9 8 7 6 5 4 3 2 1

Contents

Introduction

Bukharin's Fate

STEPHEN F. COHEN

I wrote [the prison manuscripts] mostly at night, literally wrenching them from my heart. I fervently beg you not to let this work disappear. . . . Don't let this work perish. I repeat and emphasize: *This is completely apart from my personal fate.* Don't let it be lost! . . . *Have pity!* Not on me, *on the work!*

—BUKHARIN PRISON LETTER TO STALIN, 1937

Manuscripts do not burn. —MIKHAIL BULGAKOV

The history of this novel is almost certainly unique—even in the dismal twentieth century with its mountain of literature written by people doomed by politics. Normally we would be deeply moved by the tragic fate of the book and its author, but they are products of the Soviet experience, about which most of us have little if any such sentiment. Imagine, therefore, the history of *How It All Began* apart from its geography and politics.

A once beloved founding father is falsely accused of terrorism and treason against the state he helped create and is arrested by the bloody despot who now rules it. Tormented in prison for a year and completely cut off from the outside world, he is forced to stand trial and publicly confess to having been a vile enemy of the political ideas and aspirations to which he had devoted his life and had symbolized for almost twenty years. Two days later he is shot in a secret execution cell, his place of burial never discovered. His entire biography is excised from the nation's official history, his name lingering only in the epithet "enemy of the people."

Unknown to anyone except the despot and a few jailers, who are themselves soon shot, the victim managed to write four book-length manuscripts during his year in prison, even while being coerced into his scripted role at the show trial. Uncharacteristic of a man so absorbed with contemporary politics and theory, the last manuscript was an unfinished novel about his childhood. But because his name continues to be anathematized by the despot's successors, all his prison writings remain buried in secret state archives for more than half a century.

Eventually a leader untainted by past crimes comes to power determined to repudiate the tyrant and undo his political legacy. In order to achieve this, he must fully exonerate the martyred founding father, who immediately becomes a cherished historical figure and symbol of long-awaited change. Rumors circulate about his prison manuscripts, but four more years pass before they can be retrieved from the despot's classified documents. Finally they are published in the martyr's homeland, but by now the vast state he helped found has broken apart, even its name discarded. As new troubles spread across the land, only a few citizens any longer care about a founding father whose political creation no longer exists.

Bulgakov was wrong: Manuscripts do burn, and many did in Stalin's Soviet Union. Some examples are well known and especially lamented. In the bureaucratic language of an official investigation, it is reported that the last prose fiction of Boris Pilnyak, arrested with him in 1937, "has not been preserved." Several unpublished works by Isaac Babel and the great scientist Nikolai Vavilov suffered the same fate. Not even Lenin's letters were safe, a number of important ones evidently having been destroyed along with his old comrades who had received them. But we can never know how many manuscripts, eminent correspondence, government documents, photographs, films, and even paintings perished in the bloody years from 1929 to 1953, when Stalin's regime tried to repress anything that deviated from its falsification of almost everything.

Some were lost indifferently in the crude haste of millions of arrests, searches, and confiscations; others were frantically discarded by their owners in fear of such nocturnal visits; but many more were systematically destroyed by the terror regime. From the central Lubyanka Prison in the late 1930s, "a soot-stained chimney . . . sprinkled Moscow with the ash of incinerated manuscripts."[1] Scores of incinerators no doubt were also flaming in provincial Lubyankas throughout Russia and the other Soviet republics. Later Stalin's political police and its successor, the NKVD and

---

[1] Vitaly Shentalinsky, *Arrested Voices* (New York, 1996), p. 285. The fate of Soviet writers and their manuscripts during the terror years, as revealed in archives, is the subject of this valuable book.

KGB, destroyed masses of paper when Hitler's armies approached in 1941, again when Nikita Khrushchev's revelations threatened the *organy* in the 1950s, and once again, now shredding instead of burning, after the failed putsch against Mikhail Gorbachev in 1991.

And yet a great many forbidden manuscripts and other materials did survive Stalin's long reign of terror and its aftermath. Some were saved in secret acts of private courage—by relatives and friends of victims who took the great risk of hiding poems, letters, and photographs for decades. But most were actually "preserved forever"—as they were often stamped—by the terror apparatus itself, buried in the ever swelling archives (*vaults* seems a more fitting word) of the NKVD and of the chief terrorist, Stalin. There is no satisfactory explanation for why the "Boss," as his top henchmen called him among themselves, allowed so much incriminating evidence to be preserved—Was it his seminary education or his self-ordained role as "greatest scholar on the planet"?—but for this, if nothing else, the nation could be grateful.

An authentic despot has the personal power to make time for what truly interests him, no matter how petty it may seem. Amid all the political, economic, and social upheavals of the Soviet 1930s, Stalin received and at least scanned an enormous volume of confiscated materials, commonly scrawling on them the instruction "Send to the archive" or, more evocatively, "Let all this 'material' lie deep in the archive."[2] Thus did his personal papers grow year by year and decade by decade into a vast and long impenetrable repository of forbidden history and culture.

In *How It All Began*, the reader is holding one of the most remarkable manuscripts to have survived those years. Its author, Nikolai Ivanovich Bukharin, was only one of Stalin's millions of victims, but his fate was special.[3] Barely twenty-nine years old when the Bolsheviks took power, he was the youngest, most genuinely popular, and perhaps most interesting intellectual member of the Communist Party leadership that forged the new Soviet state during the years of revolution and civil war from 1917 to 1921. Lenin, with whom he had a periodically feuding but essentially son-like

[2] These instructions in Stalin's handwriting are on documents that I have seen. For the leader's voracious reading, see Robert C. Tucker, *Stalin in Power* (New York, 1990), pp. 51–52. With Tucker's first volume, *Stalin as Revolutionary*, this is the best biography of Stalin, including his role as architect of the terror.

[3] In some sections of this essay I have borrowed from two of my previous writings on Bukharin and his times: Stephen F. Cohen, *Bukharin and the Bolshevik Revolution: A Political Biography, 1888–1938* (New York, 1973 and 1980); and my introduction to Anna Larina, *This I Cannot Forget: The Memoirs of Nikolai Bukharin's Widow* (New York, 1993), pp. 11–33.

relationship, called him the "golden boy of the revolution," the "favorite of the entire Party," and its "biggest theorist." Those special tributes alone were more than enough to doom him in Stalin's terror, which swept away virtually the entire original elite of the Soviet Union.

But it was Bukharin's role in the 1920s that would make him Stalin's most important purge victim in the 1930s. In 1921, after four years of draconian political and economic measures that helped win the civil war but left the economy in ruins and the Party's own constituencies in rebellion, Lenin introduced a fundamental change of course known as the New Economic Policy, or simply NEP. Until Stalin abolished NEP in 1929, it was, to use language popularized later in Soviet history, the first era of Communist liberalization or, as would be said during Mikhail Gorbachev's reforms of the late 1980s, the first perestroika.

Though the NEP 1920s were far from democratic, compared to the decades of despotic terror, bureaucratic tyranny, and deprivation that followed, they were for many citizens a "golden era" in Soviet history. Private enterprise and market relations were officially encouraged, especially in peasant agriculture, small-scale manufacturing, and retail trade. The Communist Party maintained its repressive political monopoly, but while permitting much more social, intellectual, and cultural diversity than would ever again be the case until the Gorbachev years. By the mid-1920s the economy had largely recovered, civil peace had been restored, and Moscow had become a leading cultural capital of Europe.

Lenin created NEP, but after the leader's death in 1924, as his heirs on the ruling Politburo and Central Committee split into factions warring over power and policy, Bukharin became its greatest interpreter and defender. Regretting his own extremist views during the civil war, he now warned repeatedly against the abuses of power inherent in the Party's political monopoly and ideological zealotry—great policy leaps beyond the people's wishes, warfare actions against society, rampant bureaucracy and administrative caprice, economic monopolism, and elite privilege. He advocated instead conciliatory policies to encourage both the private and state sectors to evolve into socialism in mutually beneficial conditions and without further bloodshed. He called this philosophy and program "socialist humanism."

Henceforth Bukharin's political fortunes and historical reputation were linked inextricably to NEP. From 1925 to 1928 he and Stalin led the Party's pro-NEP majority against the several Left oppositions headed by Leon Trotsky, Grigory Zinoviev, and Lev Kamenev. And when Stalin himself turned against NEP at the end of the 1920s, for a draconian kind of rapid industrialization based on forcing the country's 125 million peasants into state-run collective farms, Bukharin's adamant protests put him at the head of the so-called Right Opposition—the last great struggle inside the Communist Party against its ascendant general secretary.

Even before Stalin's ruthless measures of 1929–33 had left perhaps 10 million peasants dead or enslaved in a vastly swollen Gulag of forced labor camps, Bukharin presciently understood their "monstrously one-sided" intent—and their consequences. Evoking "Lenin's Last Testament," he protested that socialism could not and must not be achieved through "military-feudal exploitation" of the country's peasant majority. "Stalin's policy is leading to civil war. He will have to drown the revolts in blood." The outcome, he warned, "will be a police state."

Bukharin's prophetic opposition, undertaken on the eve of the nation's most fateful and ultimately irreversible turning point after 1917, would never be forgotten in Russia or forgiven by Stalin. In late 1929, as catastrophe unfolded across the land, the new Stalinist majority stripped Bukharin of all his leadership positions—member of the Politburo, editor of the Party newspaper *Pravda*, and head of the Communist International. Once the Party's co-leader and most authoritative ideologist, Bukharin saw his ideas and policies denounced as "anti-Leninist" and "rotten liberalism." He no longer had any real power or influence over political events, though he remained a nominal member of the Party Central Committee and later served as editor of the government newspaper *Izvestia* until his arrest on February 27, 1937.

Bukharin was not seen again publicly until March 2, 1938, when the last and most spectacular Moscow Show Trial opened in a glare of international media attention. (The eleven-day trial made worldwide headlines, though news of Bukharin's execution, on March 15, was overshadowed by Hitler's march into Austria.) By now Stalin had falsely condemned all Lenin's other co-leaders as covert enemies of their own cause, but none as completely and grotesquely as he would defame the "favorite of the entire Party." Bukharin's defense of NEP, special relationship with Lenin, and lingering personal popularity still were the greatest reproach to the official cult of Stalin's infallibility, which had grown in almost direct proportion to the rural holocaust caused by his leadership.

Twenty-one defendants sat in the dock, several of them prominent old Bolsheviks, but for Stalin it was the inquisition and confession of Bukharin that really mattered. After only the first day, the Stalinist press made clear the trial's purpose and preordained verdict: "Bukharin sits there with his head bowed low, a treacherous, two-faced, whimpering, evil nonentity who has been exposed . . . as leader of a gang of spies, terrorists, and thieves . . . This filthy little Bukharin." As the pseudo-judicial proceedings moved toward their inexorable outcome, Stalin, through his mouthpiece-prosecutor Andrei Vyshinsky, leveled an exceptional accusation against Bukharin: "The hypocrisy and perfidy of this man exceed the most perfidious and monstrous crimes known to the history of mankind."

For many years to come, Bukharin's trial would be an enthralling and emblematic mystery of twentieth-century politics, the subject of philosophy and fiction: Why had he—indeed, all the illustrious old Bolsheviks put in the dock—confessed to preposterously false charges? (Not a few foolish Western observers, it might be remembered, from foreign Communists to the American ambassador in Moscow, actually believed the charges, or said they did.) Perhaps the most popular explanation, elaborated in Arthur Koestler's famous novel *Darkness at Noon*, argued that Bukharin, morally bankrupt and sincerely repentant for his past opposition, willingly confessed as a last service to Stalinism.

In fact, Bukharin did not really confess, as was clear even from the edited transcript of the trial published at the time in the heavily censored Soviet press. Forced to participate in the grotesque spectacle, if only in the hope of saving his family, his tactic was to accept personal responsibility for Stalin's general indictment while denying all its specific charges: "I plead guilty to . . . the sum total of crimes committed by this counterrevolutionary organization, irrespective of whether or not I knew of, or whether or not I took a direct part in, any particular act."

Lest anyone failed to understand that the second part of that statement negated the first, Bukharin went on to discredit his whole "confession" (and allude to the torment being inflicted in Stalin's prisons) with a simple aside: "The confession of the accused is a medieval principle of jurisprudence." As for the crucial charges that he had plotted to assassinate Lenin and commit other terrorist acts, overthrow the Soviet government, and betray the country to fascist Germany and Japan, he flatly and repeatedly rejected them: "I do not plead guilty . . . I do not know of this . . . I deny it . . . I categorically deny any complicity."

Indeed, if Bukharin's presence in the dock was a capitulation to Stalin, his conduct there was a last struggle against Stalinism. Taking on his assigned role as representative of a martyred Bolshevik movement, he tried to show—through double-talk, code words, evasion, and digressions— that the criminal accusations were really political falsifications and the doomed Bolsheviks actually the revolution's true leaders whose non-Stalinist conceptions of socialism were being eradicated. Stalin's bullying prosecutor and judge, panicked by Bukharin's "acrobatics" and refusal to follow the jailhouse script, tried to frighten him from "following definite tactics . . . hiding behind a flood of words . . . making digressions into the sphere of politics," but he persevered day after day. In his final statement he again "confessed" to the indictment but then, according to a foreign correspondent in the courtroom, "proceeded . . . to tear it to bits, while Vyshinsky, powerless to intervene, sat uneasily in his place."

By the 1960s, several Western historians had reexamined the published transcript and concluded that Bukharin's trial, "degrading as it was in many respects, may fairly be called his finest hour."[4] In the Soviet Union, however, it took much longer, including three and a half decades after Stalin's own death in 1953 and five subsequent leaderships, to overturn the court's verdict. After a struggle at high levels, Bukharin was fully exonerated and restored to official honor at Mikhail Gorbachev's insistence in 1988, a year marking both the fiftieth anniversary of his execution and the centenary of his birth. The subject of popular biographies, novels, and films, his historical reputation continued to grow in public esteem right up to the end of the Soviet Union three years later.[5]

The Soviet judge who formally reopened Bukharin's case files in 1988 remarked, "He was a fighter to the end, despite the conditions in which he found himself." It has always been possible to imagine those terrible conditions, but only recently have terror-era archives begun to reveal more about what happened to him during the year between his arrest and execution. Even today, however, *more*, not everything, is the correct word. Despite the opening of many former Soviet archives, access to two of the most important ones remains highly restricted and much of their historical material yet to be declassified.

The NKVD archive, which contains most of the records from the "investigation and interrogation" of Bukharin in prison, is still under the control of its Russian successor organization. Special permission is required from the ministry in order to see any of its files, for which no catalogue or other inventory is made available. Even when shown a large quantity of documents, as I have been, one cannot be sure they are complete. Probably they are not, but the archive is so vast and its history so long and secretive that not even Lubyanka's current staff seems to be certain.

---

[4] Anonymous reviewer of George Katkov, *The Trial of Bukharin* (New York, 1969), in *Times Literary Supplement*, January 29, 1970; and, similarly, Tucker's introduction to Robert C. Tucker and Stephen F. Cohen, eds., *The Great Purge Trial* (New York, 1965), pp. ix–xlviii.

[5] See the surveys of Soviet public opinion on historical figures reported in the *New York Times*, May 27, 1988; and *Moscow News*, no. 44 (1990).

Incongruous as it may seem, the Russian Presidential Archive, where Stalin's enormous personal archive is kept, is even more inaccessible. Sometimes called the Kremlin Archive, it passed in 1991 from Gorbachev's control to Boris Yeltsin's. Some less significant holdings have been transferred to open repositories. But none of its unique remaining materials, not even remote historical ones, can be seen except on instruction of the president or his chief of staff. Nor does this zealously guarded citadel of secrets make known a list of its full holdings, though we have learned they include the original typed stenograph of Bukharin's trial with handwritten "corrections" by Stalin and his hanging judge, Vasily Ulrikh.[6]

An often unanswered question therefore haunts surviving members of a victim's family and historians: Do missing materials confiscated during Stalin's terror still exist? Are they preserved somewhere in those once "top-secret" and still reticent archives, were they bureaucratically mislaid or privately stashed elsewhere, or did they "burn" many years ago? Where, for example, are Bukharin's own personal papers, a large and rich collection accumulated during an extraordinary life of revolution, power, and writing? Immediately following his arrest in February 1937, NKVD men hauled away a "mountain of paper" from his Kremlin apartment, the truck "overflowing" with materials, including unpublished manuscripts, photographs, letters from Lenin, and other historical documents.[7] None of it has ever been found.

Consider two subsequent examples. During his year in prison Bukharin wrote several (evidently revealing) undelivered letters to his wife—one of them, dated January 15, 1938, and reprinted in this book, was found fifty-four years later; the others are still missing. When his trial finally began, all the proceedings were filmed and sound-recorded on Stalin's orders by NKVD cameramen. Those reels might tell us what actually happened in the courtroom, but they have disappeared. Indeed, it is astonishing that not a single frame of film or photograph showing the faces of the defendants at this most infamous political trial of this most visual century has ever been made public.[8]

Nonetheless, archives have now told us more about Bukharin's fate,

---

[6] An important but relatively small part of the original transcript has been published and analyzed by Yuri Murin, once a senior archivist at the Presidential Archive. See *Novaia i noveishaia istoriia*, no. 1 (1995): 61–76; and *Istochnik*, no. 4 (1996): 78–92. As I write, however, the full transcript, some fifteen hundred typed pages, remains inaccessible.

[7] Larina, *This I Cannot Forget*, p. 336.

[8] The only trace of the reels is a thirty-minute newsreel about the trial, *Verdict of the Court—Verdict of the People!*, shown briefly in Moscow theaters in 1938 and preserved in an archive. It shows the defendants only fleetingly and only from behind.

however grudgingly and fragmentarily, than we ever expected to learn. He spent his last year "dangling between life and death" in Stalin's top factory of false confessions, Lubyanka Prison, fully in the hands of NKVD "investigators" who were under pressing orders to "prepare" him for the trial. Bukharin immediately understood, as he wrote to Stalin from prison, that "they can do with me here anything they want."[9] Except when taken through always dark corridors to an interrogation room, he was confined in a tiny cell harshly lit around the clock by a naked bulb, alone for months but periodically with a cell mate who was actually an informer. Interrogations to extract his testimony for the script being dictated and constantly enhanced by the Kremlin Scenarist usually began late at night and continued into the early morning hours.

For three full months Bukharin adamantly refused to "confess"—that is, to play his designated role at the trial—despite prospects of physical torture, threats against his family, and shattering face-to-face confrontations with his cherished young protégés who had been brutally beaten into giving lurid testimony against him. Asked to make admissions that "contradict my whole life, my entire being," as he also wrote to Stalin, Bukharin refused "to slander myself out of fear or for other analogous reasons." But on June 1 he capitulated and began inventing "testimony," probably because he learned that the country's top military commanders had now been arrested and forced to sign statements incriminating him. If those armed and tough men could be taken and broken so quickly, there would be no way out for him. The "other analogous reasons," most fearfully the fate of his family, became inescapable.

According to an unconfirmed report, the reels were destroyed on Stalin's orders. Several photographs alleging to be of Bukharin and other defendants at the trial have been published, but none are convincing and some are clearly miscaptioned. Scores of paintings done by Bukharin since childhood (as readers of the novel will learn) are also indicative. Only ten were recovered, from relatives and friends, when his surviving family was freed in the 1950s. Two more were found in 1996—one folded in old newspapers in a Moscow apartment; the other, having been anonymously held and sold, in the American state of Oregon. Discovering them at this late date is reason enough to continue the search for other Bukharin materials even today, as is the recent discovery of dozens of caricatures he drew at Politburo meetings in the 1920s. They were uncovered in 1995—in the private papers of Kliment Voroshilov, a top Stalin crony and vicious persecutor of Bukharin in the 1930s, who died in 1969.

[9] Unless otherwise indicated, direct quotations from Bukharin in Lubyanka and my account of his prison circumstances are from his letters to Stalin itemized in note 10 below, his letter to his wife that appears at the end of this book, or a few other written communications by Bukharin and his jailers preserved in the NKVD and Presidential archives.

For the next nine months Bukharin went along with the Lubyanka inquisitioners, but while haggling stubbornly over the terms of his confession. At first he tried to limit his "crimes" to a history of "theoretical mistakes" and "political opposition," but those concessions were far from what was needed. Finally he agreed to take on the part of leader of the "counterrevolutionary criminal bloc," but he continued to be vague about specific misdeeds. His tenacious recalcitrance may have been one reason why the trial was postponed at least twice. On several occasions high-level emissaries from Stalin—notably the NKVD chief, Nikolai Yezhov, and the prosecutor, Vyshinsky—came to deal personally with him. Among other things, they promised he would live if he played the role well. Bukharin desperately wanted to believe them but he never really did, and repeatedly asked to be given poison, "like Socrates," instead of being shot.

Always a fragile personality—"soft" and "artistic," according to people who knew him—Bukharin was already debilitated by months of persecution and a hunger strike undertaken before his arrest. Unlike so many other victims, including the army commanders, he seems not to have been physically tortured in prison. But all the other agonies inflicted in Lubyanka—over his family and closest friends, his impending trial, his historical reputation—were enough to leave his "soul shattered and in torment." His "grief and boundless anguish" brought on episodes of "hallucinatory delusions," even an occasional loss of vision, and though he seems to have always revived, his "physical and spiritual strength [were] weakening." (There are hints he may have been given drugs to calm or manipulate him.)

Those rare glimpses of Bukharin's condition in prison are from four letters he sent to Stalin from his cell between April and December 1937.[10] Of all the documents found in archives, they are the most painful to read. Two might be interpreted simply as the pathetic pleadings of a completely broken man. Filled with lachrymose professions of "true devotion" and "enormous love" for his persecutor, along with fantasies of being freed to live under a pseudonym, they assured Stalin, "I acknowledge myself to be entirely yours" and "I would be ready to carry out any of your demands."

---

[10] All four—dated April 15, September 29, November 14, and December 10—are in the Presidential Archive. One is twenty-two pages long, another barely two. Even before his arrest, Bukharin wrote many letters to Stalin, or "Koba" as he usually called him, partly as a precaution. As he explained to a childhood friend in 1936, the novelist and journalist Ilya Ehrenburg, "I have to write. Koba loves to receive letters." Quoted in Joshua Rubenstein, *Tangled Loyalties: The Life and Times of Ilya Ehrenburg* (New York, 1996), p. 153. It is possible that he wrote more than these four letters to Stalin from prison.

But the long, densely rambling letters can also be interpreted more complexly, particularly in light of other evidence that Bukharin remained "a fighter to the end," as part of a cruelly inequitable negotiation.

Throughout his imprisonment Bukharin tried desperately to "bargain" (*vytorgovat*) with Stalin, whom he had known well for many years, but without enraging his now tyrannical suspicions, envies, and personal cult. The Lubyanka prisoner had only one thing to offer: his willingness to satisfy Stalin's profound need for his participation in the macabre trial. The Kremlin Inquisitioner, on the other hand, had unconstrained power of life and death over Bukharin's large family, most ominously over his twenty-three-year-old wife, Anna Larina, whom Bukharin, at almost forty-six, had married three years earlier; their infant son, Yuri; and Bukharin's thirteen-year-old daughter, Svetlana, by a previous marriage. In return for going through with the trial, Bukharin wanted assurances of their well-being.

Assurances were given, but falsely. Bukharin went on trial in March 1938 without knowing that his wife and son had been taken from their Moscow apartment nine months earlier, Anna to begin a twenty-year journey through Stalin's prisons, labor camps, and Siberian exile, and Yuri a two-decade odyssey under another family name through foster homes and orphanages. Reunited only in 1956, both survived to be present at Bukharin's 1988 rehabilitation, but probably not for the reason he had imagined. Many "wives and children of enemies of the people" were summarily shot in the 1930s, but Stalin kept some alive in case they were needed for future trials; spouses made handy co-conspirators, and sons and daughters grew into adult defendants. (Svetlana was not arrested until 1949.) The tyrant died, at seventy-three, before he could invent lethal scenarios for all of them.

But we now know that Bukharin was also bargaining for something else, second in importance only to his family. It, too, only Stalin could grant. A man for whom politics had always meant writing—his publications numbered in the hundreds[11]—Bukharin wanted permission, exceedingly unusual in that place of debasement, to write in his cell: "I simply would not be able to survive here if not permitted to use paper and pen." Stalin must have interpreted the letter as Bukharin intended, "I would not be able to play my role," and gave the order. Knowing it could be reversed at any moment, the Lubyanka author tried to ensnare his captor in what

---

[11] Most are listed in Sidney Heitman, ed., *Nikolai I. Bukharin: A Bibliography* (Stanford, 1969); and T. N. Kamzolova, ed., *Nikolai Ivanovich Bukharin: ukazatel literatury* (Moscow, 1989).

he was writing. Bukharin's letters carefully apprised Stalin of his projects, even proposing he write a preface for one of them. As weeks turned into months, and tightly handwritten pages into large manuscripts, Bukharin more and more wanted his prison writings to survive him: "*Have pity*! Not on me, *on the work!*"

Those writings are the most remarkable discovery of our archival investigation into Bukharin's Lubyanka fate. In barely one year, while constantly being interrogated and tormented about his family and the next ordeal that awaited him, this middle-aged intellectual, so often said to have been weak, found the moral and physical stamina to write four books (the equivalent of about fourteen hundred typewritten pages)—a study of modern politics and culture, a philosophical treatise, a thick volume of thematic poems, and this unfinished novel about his childhood in prerevolutionary Russia.

Exactly how Bukharin managed to write the manuscripts in those circumstances is left to our imagination. The only other person who probably knew was a shadowy thirty-five-year-old Lubyanka officer directly in charge of interrogating and preparing him for the trial, Captain Lazar Kogan; not long after, he, too, was arrested and shot. An educated and soft-mannered man who had begun his NKVD career specializing in intellectual cases, he must have been specially chosen for Bukharin's. Kogan was, of course, a loyal agent of the terror—he was awarded an Order of Lenin in murderous 1937—but his few surviving traces suggest a complex relationship with his famous victim during their months together in Lubyanka.[12] Hoping to help her husband, Anna Larina was allowed to meet Kogan once and thought she saw "unspeakable remorse in his eyes." Whatever the full truth, he provided his prisoner with writ-

---

[12] The traces include the protocols of Bukharin's interrogations, a few Lubyanka internal documents written by Kogan, several notes and one letter to him from Bukharin, and the childhood memories and family possessions of Kogan's daughter, who lives today not far from Moscow. Kogan knew, of course, that Bukharin was innocent, but nonetheless could write the following lines to his own daughter on her ninth birthday in August 1937: "My dearest little daughter! I congratulate you on your birthday. I kiss you warmly. Live and grow with our sunbathed country—the only, most beautiful Soviet country. In our country, everything is for you. And your papa lives and works for you. And the Order of Lenin is for you and for all the children. Grow and be a worthy daughter of your country and its leader, Comrade Stalin. Papa." When I brought Bukharin's widow and Kogan's daughter together in 1993, Anna Larina said of her husband and his Lubyanka interrogator, "Both of them were victims." On the other hand, Anna Larina, despite her years of suffering, was an exceedingly compassionate person. Nothing special can be read into Kogan's own fate. Almost all his NKVD colleagues also were shot.

ing materials and books, boosted his morale, and watched the manuscripts grow.

Unless more documents are uncovered, perhaps Kogan's own files, all we can know with certainty is that Bukharin wrote mostly at night and early morning, sleeping sporadically in the harsh light that blurred his vision, working without a typewriter, sources he needed, or even a reliable supply of paper, using the backs of used sheets when he ran out. We should not be too surprised. It was the same Bukharin who then appeared at the show trial so carefully planned by Stalin and found ways "to tear it to bits."

When Bukharin was taken to be shot, three of his prison manuscripts evidently were still in his cell, including this novel, the other having been confiscated months before. All four, along with almost everything else he wrote in Lubyanka, were sent by his jailers, acting on standing orders and their own fearful instincts, to the Kremlin Boss. It is not known whether Stalin read them carefully, but he certainly looked at them. He then buried them deep in his personal archive, the deepest archaeological recess of the Terror Era. They were excavated, at my initiative, fifty-four years later, in 1992. The novel was published separately in Moscow in 1994, the manuscripts on politics, culture, and philosophy, with selections from the poems, in two volumes in 1996.[13]

The role I unexpectedly played in this saga was an outgrowth of my biography of Bukharin, first published in the United States in 1973 and eventually in the Soviet Union in 1989, and my close personal relationship with his widow and son from the time we first met surreptitiously in 1975 in pre-glasnost Moscow. While researching that book from afar, I came across vague reports that Bukharin had written some kind of manuscript in prison, as indeed he hinted at the trial, but neither I nor his family, who were still living with an official stigma, could learn anything more for many years.[14] Only in 1988 did an aide to Gorbachev, who had read and publicly remarked on my book, tell me privately that not one but four such manuscripts existed in closed archives.

On behalf of Anna Larina, her artist son Yuri Larin, and myself, I began

---

[13] Nikolai Bukharin, *Vremena* (Moscow: Progress Publishers, 1994); and Nikolai Bukharin, *Tiuremnye rukopisi*, 2 vols., ed. Gennadii Bordiugov (Moscow: AIRO-XX, 1996).

[14] During his years in power Nikita Khrushchev may have learned about Bukharin's manuscripts from Politburo investigations into Stalin's terror against the Party; if so, he kept them secret. In the early 1960s Khrushchev seemed to be inclined to rehabilitate Bukharin, but for various reasons, including his own complicity in Bukharin's persecution and arrest, he never took the step. Under Leonid Brezhnev, who ruled from 1964 to 1982, all such investigations and revelations were ended.

asking for the manuscripts. Gorbachev, although sympathetic to the request, was already locked in a bitter political struggle with Communist Party opponents who resented his revelations about Soviet history and particularly about those kinds of "Party documents." Nonetheless, I still was optimistic in 1991 that he would soon authorize release of the manuscripts. Suddenly, however, with the end of the Soviet Union and his own office, Gorbachev no longer controlled any of the archives.

In 1992 Anna Larina, now almost eighty and ill with cancer, and I took a different approach. Believing that the Bukharin family was the legal and moral heir to his works, and had a juridical right in the "new, democratic Russia" to examine all files related to his case, she formally named me her proxy and requested that relevant archives give me full access to the materials. To our surprise, the former NKVD/KGB archive, under the Ministry of Security, responded promptly and more or less positively. My work in that storehouse of historical horrors soon began.

I quickly learned, however, that not even the top archive officials of the new Russian state could authorize access to the Presidential Archive, where the manuscripts and other essential materials were held. It could be done only by someone at the highest levels of the Yeltsin government. Nor was it a good political moment. The end of Communist rule had diminished public interest in all the Soviet founding fathers, and the new government seemed interested only in archival documents that would discredit Gorbachev and enhance its upcoming trial of the Communist Party. The prison writings of a martyred founding father embraced by the last Soviet leader served neither purpose.

Advised by a Russian friend, I identified a person who might have the power and inclination to help. In July 1992, ironically during the opening session of the Communist Party trial, I cornered one of Yeltsin's closest and most influential associates. Though not a politician with any sympathy for the Soviet founding fathers, he knew of Anna Larina through her best-selling 1988 memoir and was moved by her desire to learn everything about her husband.[15] That person deserves our public gratitude, but I still do not feel free to name him, even though he has since left Yeltsin's side. Within a few minutes I was in his government office while he spoke on the telephone to archive administrators, and within a few weeks photocopies of the four manuscripts were in our hands. Another large batch of related materials soon followed, just before that archive's doors again slammed shut.

[15] After serialization in a mass-circulation journal in 1988, Anna Larina's memoirs were published in full as *Nezabyvaemoe* (Moscow, 1989). The English-language edition is entitled *This I Cannot Forget*.

Thus were Bukharin's widow, son, and daughter, the historian Svetlana Gurvich, able to encounter him anew across an enormous chasm of time and suffering. For Anna Larina, who died in 1996, there was just enough time left, with the help of family and friends, to ready her husband's last writings for publication in his homeland.

Readers of *How It All Began* may wonder about Bukharin's other prison manuscripts. Political in overt ways that the novel was not, they had to be written on a razor's edge between what he desperately wanted to say—to the despot and to posterity—and the desperate plight of his family. Like his later courtroom statements they must be read on two levels, the outwardly conformist and inwardly polemical, for the non-Stalinist meanings embedded in obligatory Stalinist ritual. Also unlike the novel, the other manuscripts were very much of their time, the 1930s, a decade already unfolding in the catastrophic ways that would shape the rest of the twentieth century.

Once inside Lubyanka in 1937, Bukharin was given almost no news of the outside world, but by the time of his arrest Hitler and Mussolini were in power, their military ambitions clear, and the Spanish Civil War under way. With those developments on his mind, Bukharin completed the first prison manuscript, *Socialism and Its Culture*, at an astonishing pace, evidently within four weeks of being permitted to write, partly because it was the second part of a larger work begun before his arrest to be called *The Crisis of Capitalist Culture and Socialism*. The first volume, *The Degradation of Culture and Fascism*, was among the papers taken from his apartment and never found, but the nature of the overall project is clear. For Bukharin, "culture" meant modern civilization; fascism was its mortal crisis and socialism its only possible salvation.

Forced to stand trial as the last original Bolshevik, Bukharin was also the last great antifascist of the Soviet 1930s. Alone among Soviet leaders, he had worried about fascism as a new phenomenon and special menace ever since the early 1920s. By the mid-1930s that worry had grown into profound alarm: not only was Hitlerism in power and ever more virulent, Stalin was speaking publicly of the Nazi Führer as merely another capitalist dictator with whom he could do realpolitik business. (Bukharin no doubt knew of Stalin's secret diplomacy, already under way, that would lead to the Nazi-Soviet Pact of 1939.) Right up to his arrest, Bukharin used all his remaining personal authority and political positions to urge, in passionate articles and speeches, that the Soviet Union put itself at the head of the antifascist struggle and collective European security.

A leading twentieth-century Marxist and Soviet founding father, Bukharin remained loyal, even in Lubyanka, to Marxism and the Soviet

Union. In addition, Stalin's modernizing goals, however brutally pursued, were his as well. But Bukharin knew, as he had made clear before his arrest, that the Stalinist regime, much like Hitler's, was growing into an "omnipotent 'total state' that de-humanizes everything except leaders and 'super-leaders.' " *Socialism and Its Culture* tried to overcome that nightmarish paradox. It argued effusively for the "humanist" potential of the Soviet system while pleading with the despot for its humanization, even a "transition to democracy," so that the nation could play its essential antifascist role. Bukharin believed deeply in those historic Soviet missions, even while knowing they were being terribly deformed under Stalin, and a final opportunity to testify on their behalf was another reason he agreed to stand trial.

Though he hoped *Socialism and Its Culture* would reach a world "at the crossroads of history," it was, in effect, a book-length policy memorandum to Stalin. Its urgent importance for Bukharin was clear from letters to Stalin begging him to save the first volume and publish both quickly, under a pseudonym if necessary, with a preface by the Kremlin leader. (What better way to wed Stalin to Bukharin's policies?) Here, too, Bukharin failed. Seventeen months after the trial, Stalin's pact with Hitler helped unleash world war while leaving Soviet borders virtually defenseless when Nazi armies came in June 1941. But if we still honor a handful of political figures who understood the dangers of appeasement and fought it, we might add their counterpart in Lubyanka to the list.

By his seventh month in prison, September 1937, Bukharin had largely completed a second manuscript, a collection of poems of "universal scope" entitled *The Transformation of the World.* Though outwardly "chaotic," he explained in his last letter to his wife, the collection was based on a "plan." Most of the nearly two hundred poems were reflections on previous centuries—particularly their great thinkers, cultural figures, and rebels—and an epic telling of Soviet history from 1917 to the 1930s, culminating in the ongoing "struggle of two worlds," socialist humanism and fascism. In that respect, the second manuscript was an expansive poetic rendition of the first. Whatever the literary quality of the poems—expert Russian opinion is mixed—they are of compelling interest.

Carefully dated with the time of composition, the poems were written during the months when Bukharin was being intensely pressured for the false testimony Stalin demanded. Composed after midnight, when he was returned to his cell from those nocturnal interrogations, they can be read as a chronicle of his emotional state and a quest for spiritual escape. Two sections of the volume, one entitled "Lyrical Intermezzo," are especially moving. Along with autobiographical themes that reappear in the novel, they express his intense love for Anna, longing for their brief life together, and yearnings to be free. For a biographer or any historian of the terror, they are an unexpected view into the soul of a condemned man.

By then Bukharin seems to have understood that he was doomed, which meant the antifascist manifesto would not be published, and to have begun thinking about his posthumous legacy. He had already started another "big" project, *Philosophical Arabesques*, now considering it the "most important thing" and his most "*mature* work." Even though he lacked most of the books needed for such a wide-ranging treatise (Kogan apparently gave him a few from the prison library and from his own collection), it was full of erudition and remarkably precise references. It, too, was written very quickly, because "much of it was in my head."

This third prison manuscript mattered greatly to Bukharin for at least two reasons. In 1921 he had published a philosophical work, *Historical Materialism*, that immediately became a canon of international communism. Translated into many languages, it established him as a major Marxist thinker and the Party's "biggest theorist." Stalin could not really obliterate that reputation, but serious intellectual and political challenges to Marxism, in addition to the theory and practice of fascism, had arisen since 1921. The still proud and intellectually ambitious Lubyanka inmate wanted to respond to those challenges and complete his long-standing project of bringing nineteenth-century Marxism fully into the twentieth century.

Something else equally personal was on Bukharin's mind. In 1922, while exalting him as the movement's best theorist, Lenin had added a biting caveat, as only a father figure can: Bukharin "has never studied and, I think, never fully understood dialectics." Since dialectical understanding was thought to be at the center of Marxist theorizing, Lenin's paradoxical qualification rankled and lingered. (Most of all, it reflected generational differences between the two men: Lenin's Marxism was imbued with nineteenth-century German philosophy, particularly Hegel, and Bukharin's with early twentieth-century sociology.) Now on the eve of his own death, in a last discourse with his dead leader and revered friend, Bukharin undertook, as "Ilich [Lenin] recommended," a book that would be "*dialectical* from beginning to end."

Whether or not Lenin would have approved, the result was anything but conformist. When *Philosophical Arabesques* was published in post-Communist Russia, an eminent Moscow philosopher noted the "illusions Bukharin shared with many Communists of that time" but emphasized his "secret polemic with Stalinism." The "tragedy of this manuscript," he continued, was in having been kept hidden for so long:

If the ideas Bukharin developed in this manuscript had been made known even in the 1950s or 1960s, they could have led to a fundamentally new Marxist philosophical vision. The kind of philosophy Bukharin outlined here was not the same as the Stalinist version of Marxism, a Marxism crucified. . . . Many themes first raised and discussed by Bukharin were new for Marxist philosophers even in the 1960s! And the people who kept this manuscript under lock and key . . . are guilty not simply of degrading Marxism, which was transformed into ideological solder, but of a barbaric attitude toward . . . culture, and not only Russian culture.[16]

History often inflicts cruel ironies on its most engaging victims. Bukharin finished his solitary Lubyanka effort to redeem Soviet Marxism just as Stalin's regime was celebrating the twentieth anniversary of the Communist revolution, overnight on November 7–8, 1937. Five nights later he began this unfinished novel. The first seven chapters were written by mid-January 1938, when he thought the trial was about to begin and his time had run out. Another postponement, to early March, allowed him to write fifteen more.

Readers should remember that even the twenty-two chapters in this book, which take Nikolai "Kolya" Petrov (Nikolai "Kolya" Bukharin) to about age fifteen and Russia to the eve of the failed revolution of 1905, a kind of dress rehearsal for 1917, are themselves unfinished. No professional writer, which Bukharin certainly was, would consider any major work complete without revisions, even further drafts. Bukharin had neither time nor paper for such perfections.[17] All his prison manuscripts were written not only at an astonishing pace but with almost no corrections. Misled into believing that they would be given to his family, he expected his elderly father, a great lover of literature (as readers will learn) to "polish the poems and the novel." When we finally retrieved the manuscripts half a century later, a decision was made to publish all of them unedited, if only to honor the circumstances in which he wrote them.

How It All Began was written as an autobiographical novel, but it is virtually a memoir. None of the people are invented or really disguised. In addition to the later world-famous Kolya Petrov-Bukharin, for example,

---

[16] See A. P. Ogurtsov's foreword to Bukharin, *Tiuremnye rukopisi*, vol. 2, pp. 5–28.

[17] Thus, in the prison letter dated April 15, Bukharin begged Stalin to return the antifascist manuscript to him so he could make revisions and corrections and eliminate the repetitions "inevitable in such a method of writing." It was not returned to him.

four of the main characters became people well known in Moscow political society after 1917: his father, Ivan; his brother, Vladimir ("Volodya"); and his first cousins, Nikolai and "Manya" Yablochkin, who were actually Nikolai and Nadezhda Lukin—he by then a prominent Bolshevik revolutionary and historian, and she Bukharin's first wife. Elderly friends and members of Bukharin's extended family who were still alive when the novel was obtained in the 1990s were amazed by how exactly he had portrayed those people. (They would share his fate under Stalin in one way or another, as I explain in the afterword to this book.)

Above all, little Kolya Petrov of the novel is fully recognizable in the legendary Nikolai Bukharin of Soviet history. The Russian Huck Finn ("Kolya's hero") with a classical education, who dismayed his mother and grandmother by already knowing "everything he's not supposed to," grew into the most iconoclastic and intellectual member of the Soviet leadership. The boy who fell in love with painting became the revolutionary who ruefully admitted having had to choose between art and politics. The impish and athletic schoolboy "monkey" was still walking on his hands and springing from trees over courtyard walls in the 1920s and 1930s, now for the amusement of an ailing Lenin and Maxim Gorky. And Kolya's childhood passion for assembling menageries wherever the family migrated remained with Bukharin everywhere he later lived, from Moscow's Hotel Metropol to the Kremlin, their abandoned denizens still running wild after his execution.

Even the writing of this novel, the only one he ever undertook, can be traced to the literary enthusiasms young Kolya inherited from his underachieving but beloved father. ("He goes out to buy sausage and comes back with a canary.") Though the most surprising of his prison manuscripts, it is consistent with the Soviet leader who wrote extensively about literature and culture, gathered the best writers around the newspapers he edited, and repeatedly did what he could to protect three of Russia's greatest and most endangered poets—Osip Mandelstam, Boris Pasternak, and Nikolai Zabolotsky. Nor is little Kolya's raucous humor uncharacteristic of the zestful man later renowned as a Kremlin caricaturist and punster. He never stopped telling the novel's story of his hapless Latin teacher, a native Czech, who translated the proverb "Life is short; art is long" for his Russian students as "The belly is short, but the thing is long."

We might wonder how Bukharin recalled those distant childhood years in such detail after decades of political upheaval and his own wide-ranging travels and activities. His memories had been refreshed by romance earlier in the 1930s, when he, his brother, their father, and even cousin Manya/Nadezhda related their life stories to his new wife Anna. But

Bukharin gives us an additional explanation in the third chapter: "Children, like grown-ups, have their superstitions, prejudices, heartfelt dreams, ideals, and unforgettable incidents in life, which are stored in the memory forever and which suddenly, at terrible or tragic moments in life, come swimming into consciousness, surprisingly vivid, in full detail, down to the wrinkles in somebody's face or a spider's web illuminated by the evening sun." Lubyanka, of course, was such a terrible and tragic moment.

We cannot be certain, however, how far Bukharin hoped to take his story and Russia's, though clues strongly suggest that he wanted the novel to encompass or culminate in 1917. In his next to last prison letter to Stalin, he said it was to be a "big novel," which presumably meant in scope and content and thus including "The Great Revolution." There is also the somewhat enigmatic title Bukharin put on the manuscript, *Vremena*, whose Russian meaning suggests an unending process of time linking the past, present, and future. In the Soviet Marxist imagination, the revolution of 1917 was a kind of nexus between Russia's previous history, ongoing developments, and Communist future.

In grappling with Bukharin's title, I bear responsibility for the liberty taken here. If translated literally into English—as "Times," "The Times," "Seasons," or "Ages"—*Vremena* would lose its resonance and simple elegance. Evocative equivalents—inspired, for instance, by the prison poem "River of Time" or similar passages in the novel—lack the political edge Bukharin intended. And so, after consultations here and in Moscow, and much uncertainty, I settled initially on "In Those Times" but finally on *How It All Began.* It is not a perfect rendering, but the verb is faithful to the chapters he managed to complete and the pronoun and adverb to his larger intent.

Why did Bukharin choose to write about the beginning of his life at its very end? Working on a previous prison manuscript, he had assured Stalin that it "calmed me somewhat"; memories of childhood and a loving family may have eased his adult sorrows. But the contents of *How It All Began* hardly suggest that emotional escape from Lubyanka was its primary purpose. For that, he might have written exclusively about his lifelong passions for nature or art, which are secondary themes of the novel. A political man to the end, Bukharin chose autobiography as his last subject for a political reason.

By 1937 entire generations of Russian revolutionaries, Bukharin's in particular, were being massacred in Stalin's terror, their biographies and ideals criminalized in the name of their own once-sacred cause. Though isolated, Bukharin witnessed firsthand the fate of his contemporaries, having been brought face to face with childhood friends who also were being tortured into falsifying his life and their own. For his sake and theirs, he wanted to leave behind a personal testimony of how it had really been—a testament to the idealism that had led them as young students to become Marxist radicals in tsarist Russia—and how, he still hoped, it might be.[18] An unembellished memoir would have been too dangerous and less likely to survive; a novel must have seemed the safest approach and, after the strain of composing three rigorously aesopian manuscripts, the freest.

As a result, *How It All Began* was the least self-censored of Bukharin's Lubyanka manuscripts, though it too was laced with anti-Stalinism. Even under a pseudonym and without its specific family history, the novel could not have been published in the despot's Soviet Union. Multicolored pictures of pre-1917 Russia, sympathetic portrayals of doomed classes, and humanistic characterizations of future Leninists were already forbidden. And writers were being shot for less literary sedition than Bukharin's fleeting mirror images of Stalin's regime in its considerably paler tsarist predecessor.

No NKVD censor or interrogator would have overlooked, for example, the contemporary parallels with a tsar tightening "all the screws in the terrible system of power"; with a predecessor "officialdom, the chinovniks of all varieties . . . thick-headed, arrogant, and 'patriotic,' the kind who threw the word *Yid* around contemptuously"; or with an old regime that promoted people "who seemed to have been born for police interrogation, provocation, and torture chambers" and under which the "best heads are cut off, the flower of the nation, as though by a mowing machine."

Certainly no one in Stalin's Russia would have been permitted to say, as does one of Bukharin's characters long before it actually happened, "You have transformed your party into a barracks. . . . You have killed all freedom of criticism among yourselves and you want to extend this barracks to include everything and everyone." And most Soviet readers, with their instinct for interpreting what could not be written, would have guessed that the author of such lines was somewhere in a successor to those tsarist prisons where "behind thick walls, interrogations went on, uninterrupted, through the nights."[19]

----

[18] On the eve of his arrest Bukharin had his wife memorize a kind of last testament. Full of despair about the present, it was optimistic about the cleansing "filter of history" and "a future generation of Party leaders." See Larina, *This I Cannot Forget*, pp. 343–44.

[19] Other telling polemics against Stalin appear in the novel. In chapter 4, for example, Bukharin attributes the slogan Stalin had used against him in 1928–29, "There are no fortresses Bolsheviks cannot storm," to a tsarist military officer. And in chapter 20 he refutes the charges that he had conspired to assassinate Soviet leaders by having his Leninist cousin reject terrorism on Marxist principle.

For today's readers, however, the importance and pleasures of *How It All Began* lie not in its polemic with Stalinism but in its intimate portrayal of Russian society and a characteristic family on the eve of a great upheaval. I am too close to the manuscript, and too lacking in literary judgment, to comment on Bukharin's achievements, but several Russian readers have already done so. The literary scholar Boris Frezinsky has praised Bukharin's "outstanding writer's memory for all of life's details," his "lush and vivid language," and his "panorama of social, political, and artistic life."[20] The venerable children's writer and poet Valentin Berestov ranks the novel among the "best accounts of childhood in Russian literature." Other readers, including historians, single out its description of everyday existence in the empire's remote provinces, particularly Bessarabia, re-creation of the sights and smells of old Moscow, and portraits of Russia's half-impoverished lower-middle classes, from which so many revolutionaries sprang.

Indeed, *How It All Began* may be the most authoritative firsthand account we have of how and why so many of tsarist Russia's best and brightest young people had already defected on the eve of the twentieth century's most fateful revolution. It is this that Bukharin wanted us to understand—how they began to identify with the "lower orders of society," to "look at the world from the bottom up instead of from the top down," and why "this world of misery entered [their] soul forever"; how "sedition had crept" into the homes of loyal tsarist parents and why boys privileged to study at an elite gimnaziya[21] embraced the "gleaming weapons of Marxism." Bukharin's own story was to stand for all his boyhood contemporaries who soon would be swept into power by a revolution they so wanted and who, twenty years later, would be destroyed in its aftermath.

Bukharin probably knew that the twenty-second chapter, where the manuscript of the novel breaks off, would be his last. Reliving the death of his youngest brother three decades before, he wrote: "The sooner it's all ended, the better." But it was not yet the end of his novelistic alter ego. Immediately after sentencing Bukharin to death, Stalin demanded another humiliating ritual, a formal plea for mercy. Bukharin wrote two, on March 13 and 14, 1938, the first perfunctory but the second an elaborate profession of complete political and psychological repentance: "The former Bukharin has already died; he no longer lives on this earth. . . . Let a new, second Bukharin grow— let him even be called Petrov." Whether or not Stalin already knew the ruse, they were, of course, one and the same Kolya. He was shot the next night.

[20] See Frezinky's introduction to the Russian edition, *Vremena*, pp. 3–20.

[21] gimnaziya—elite high school with emphasis on classical education, especially Latin and Greek.

Translator's Preface

On the Spelling of Russian Names

I have generally followed the more familiar and readable system of transliteration, omitting diacritical marks to indicate soft signs, hard signs, and so on, and in most cases using *y* rather than *i* or *j*, or *-ii* or *-ij* (thus Dostoyevsky, not Dostoievskii or Dostojevskij). In some cases a standard spelling in English is preferred, for example, Leo Tolstoy (not Lev Tolstoj). Names of tsars are usually Anglicized. Titles of books or periodicals are sometimes given in the Library of Congress form of transliteration as an aid to readers wishing to locate them in a library catalogue.

Russian Nicknames and Middle Names (Patronymics)

Russians' middle names are based on the father's first name; the middle name is called a patronymic. Thus a man whose father was Ivan will have the middle name Ivanovich (short form, Ivanych), and a woman whose father was Ivan will have the middle name Ivanovna (short form, Ivanna). Also, various nicknames or variations on a person's first name are widely used in Russian culture. An English-speaking reader encountering such a nickname for the first time might think a new character had been introduced when in fact the reference was to an already familiar character. The list below is intended to help avoid such confusions.

MAIN CHARACTERS/ NICKNAMES

Nikolai Ivanovich Petrov (alter ego of Nikolai Bukharin)/Kolya, Kolyushka, Kolyechka, Kolyun

Kolya's Father—Ivan Antonovich (or Antonych) Petrov/Vanya, Ivanushka, Vanyechka

Kolya's Mother—Lyubov Ivanovna Petrova/Lyuba, Lyubochka

Kolya's Oldest Brother—Vladimir Ivanovich Petrov/Volodya,
   Volodyushka
Kolya's Next Oldest Brother—Andrei Ivanovich Petrov/Andryusha,
   Andryushka
Kolya's Aunt (Mother's Sister)—Marya Ivanovna Yablochkin/Manya
Kolya's Cousins:
Daughter of Mother's Sister—Marya Mikhailovna Yablochkin/also,
   Manya
Son of Mother's Sister—Nikolai Mikhailovich Yablochkin/also, Kolya
Kolya's Uncles:
Husband of Mother's Sister—Mikhail Vasilyevich Yablochkin/Misha,
   Mishka
Brothers of Kolya's Father:
Yevgeny Antonych Petrov/Zhenya
Dr. Mikhail Antonych Petrov/Mikhalushka, Misha, Mishka, Monkey
Dr. Georgy Antonych Petrov/Yegor, Zhorzh
Friends of the Family (the Slavyanskys):
Father—Anton Ivanovich Slavyansky/no nickname
Mother—Natalya Dmitryevna Slavyanskaya/Natasha
Son and Kolya's Close Friend—Anton Antonovich Slavyansky/Tosya
Art Teacher—Mikhail Samoilovich Kellat/Mikhal Samoilych

   In chapters 15 and 20 I have used the full name Kolya Yablochkin (or
Nikolai Yablochkin), rather than just "Kolya," in the hope of avoiding
confusion with Kolya Petrov, the chief protagonist of most other chapters.
Kolya Yablochkin and his sister Manya (modeled on Bukharin's first wife,
also his cousin) figure prominently in chapters 15 and 20, while Kolya
Petrov is absent from these chapters.
   In real life "Kolya Yablochkin" was Nikolai Mikhailovich Lukin, a party
member since 1904, prominent Soviet historian and member of the Academy of Sciences, author of outstanding works on the French Revolution,
the Paris Commune, and modern European history. Perhaps Bukharin
devoted so many pages to his cousin, demonstrating "Nikolai
Yablochkin's" crustiness and strong commitment to Marxism and high-
lighting the abuse his cousin's father had inflicted, in the hopes of sparing
Lukin from repression by arousing some sympathy in Stalin. (Stalin's
father, of course, had also been a child-beater.)

Notes and Glossary

I have added some footnotes to explain or comment on passages that
might be obscure to the general reader. Where a note is directly repro-

duced from the Russian edition, I have so indicated. A glossary has been included in the back of the book, providing more information on many of the names and terms that occur in Bukharin's text. The glossary is based in part on notes (or commentary) by Boris Frezinsky in the Russian edition. See Nikolai Bukharin, *Vremená*, with introduction and commentary by B. Ya. Frezinsky (Moscow: Progress Publishers, 1994).

Some Comments on Bukharin's Text

Boris Frezinsky, in the Russian Edition, cites one passage in Bukharin's novel that seems to him "the only place in the novel where the real circumstances of time and place during its writing are discernible."

In chapter 17, however, Bukharin has one of his characters, Natalya Slavanskaya, make an observation that surely applied to himself as well. She expresses the certainty that if her physically fragile son Tosya were to live long enough, he would "join the revolution." But, she adds, "one's fate here [i.e, as a revolutionary] is virtually known in advance . . . *Few survive in this walk of life, even in the event of victory*" (emphasis added—G.S.).

Another passage, in chapter 19, though it does not hint at Bukharin's own fate, seems to be a comment on the hierarchical bureaucratic caste that had created a cult of personality around Stalin, whose victim and prisoner Bukharin was as he wrote this novel, waiting for death in a cell in the Lubyanka. Bukharin seems to give a socio-historical explanation for the unjustified power and arrogance of a nonentity, an "empty quantity" (like the Grand Duke Sergei Aleksandrovich Romanov). He writes:

> In real life one's "place" (or social position) actually adorns the person to a considerable extent, even when essentially there is no person present. The "place" enters and fills the personal emptiness, and the common herd, educated in the spirit of religious deference to hierarchy, may well kneel to this emptiness, which has swollen to vast proportions solely because of its "place." In fixed and frozen hierarchies of the caste type, such hereditary fetishes maintain themselves on the strength of historical traditions, whose roots go deep into the soil of economic existence.

Bukharin, indirectly and perhaps even unconsciously, may have aimed the above passage on "place" and "person" at Stalin and his entourage. It is entirely consistent with Trotsky's explanation—with which Bukharin was undoubtedly familiar—that the power and political influence acquired by Stalin, whose individual personality was quite "mediocre" or "empty," resulted from his place at the head of the bureaucratic hierarchy.

Chapter 1

Kolya Petrov was born at the end of the eight-
ies of the last century in Moscow, on Bolshaya
Ordynka—that is, in the Zamoskvorechye
district, in a building belonging to the Aleksandro-Mariinsky Zamoskvorechye Merchants Association. This building was designated an "Academy"
according to the inscription carved in gold letters on a signboard black as
soot. The Ordynka was quiet, measured, and orderly, a solid citizens' street.
Here stood the houses of the Zamoskvorechye merchants, one-storied and
two-storied, with cleanly washed windows, sometimes of plate glass. In the
backyards were stables, with carriage horses and coachmen of enormous
dimension, the darlings and favorites of the well-rested, pink-complexioned,
ample merchants' wives. The bakery shops gleamed with their big gilded
imitation loaves hanging high and visible from afar, respectfully inviting the
public to come in and buy a *kalach* (a wheatmeal loaf), a cookie, or a bun
sprinkled with moist grains of sugar. Throughout the area, golden-domed
churches, it seemed, had planted themselves firmly in the ground for centuries to come—there was the church of the great martyr St. Catherine, of
St. George Neocaesarius, of the Parasceve of the Pentecost, of the Assump-
tion of the Mother of God, and of the Trinity in Luzhniki. The mellow
chiming of their bells resounded morning and evening, and the shuddering
waves of sound would roll, subsiding, all across the town.

The poor, the "shirtless ones"—factory hands, cobblers, carpenters, servants, and yardmen—huddled in cellars or lean-tos hidden out back in the
far corners of the yards; they looked out at the sidewalks from below street
level through the dusty, dirty eyes of cellar windows, whose grime gave off
a flash of rainbow now and then. But these black pits and gloomy hollows
did not distract the gaze of the higher orders, who sped along in their
sleighs over the squeaking snow as the rosy-fingered dawn would gild the

steeples of the churches and melt the dark-blue ice patches of the frosty early morning.

It was a quiet street. No crush of carriages or horsedrawn trams, no noisy din, no squabbling or fighting. In the winter, when the stern frost would lock down everything with its piercing icy breath, the street would be completely covered by clean, hard-packed snow; along the edges of the street, by the squat, dumpy little figures of the curbstones, the snow would form small pyramids where the yardmen wearing their brass nameplates had shoveled it into heaps. Fires crackled at the street corners, horsecab drivers strutting around them self-importantly, wearing their big, thick gloves; they warmed themselves by the fire, beating their arms across their chests and dancing to relieve their frozen, benumbed feet swaddled in footcloths. Occasionally a policeman would come up, head covered with a hood, icicles dripping from his whiskers all hoary with frost. With a whoop the merchants' trotters would sweep by, raven-black or dappled beauties puffing and snorting, and the eye barely had time to catch the fast-moving blur of legs, the carriage rug of fur, the mighty backside of the coachman, and the portly figure of the well-fed merchant. Smoke from the chimneys rose straight up, and all the houses seemed to be puffing out curly columns, which gradually faded and disappeared in the clear and frosty air.

In the summer things were livelier and more cheerful: hanging around the gates were the neighborhood kids, the yardmen, the servants, the factory hands; they chewed seeds and flashed their teeth, laughing and cursing at one another, covering the ground with the shells of sunflower seeds; in the evenings couples crushed against one another in secluded entranceways of buildings or on benches out of view; now and then some drunken man would come running by, all torn and disheveled, with a crowd of "enforcers of order" rushing after him, their voices carrying all up and down the street; the little boys flew kites ("dragons" and "black monks") and climbed with the agility of monkeys up on the roofs, chasing pigeons: tumbler pigeons, solid-colored, or mixed black and skewbald. Peddlers with trays on their bellies supported by thick leather straps stained with salt marks sold warm, thick kvass made of pears; they also sold pies, dumplings, ice cream, and sunflower seeds; around them swarmed a noisy crowd of boys, licking their lips and fingering their copper coins. There, too, children's games would be played—the arguments, shouts, and general uproar of the players disturbing the sleepy stillness of the merchant's quarter. Only rarely would organ grinders wander into this neighborhood, and when they did, the street would echo with the squeaking, penetrating sounds of the rickety instruments.

It was different in other neighborhoods like Serphukhovki, Kozhevniki, and Babyi Gorodok, where things were dirty, loud, drunken, and poor. In kennel-like quarters, half-naked children swarmed amid worn and dirty scraps of cloth; the dank odors of the latrine, of mold, of sour cabbage, and of hides pervaded; in the cellars and the tiny, leaning huts, where the plaster was peeling and falling off in whole chunks, and in the wooden peasant houses, all the little cagelike rooms were jammed full with people, poor working people on the verge of destitution: laborers and factory hands, who were considered the bad ones, the desperadoes; artisans and petty "master craftsmen"—shoemakers, box makers, glassworkers, carpenters; the peddlers who sold things from their trays; laundry women, women hired by the day; and professional beggars. All these filled the cellars, attics, and littlest closets to overflowing, and on holidays would flood out onto the street or go choke on the fumes of the taverns and beer halls with their red and blue signs: "Beer Garden" or, in quaintly shaped lettering, "Friends Get Together Tavern." Here waiters dashed about in dirty clothing, white only in name, and all hell broke loose as a "machine" played, glasses clinked, an accordion rent the air, and yearning, sobbing songs were heard. This motley crowd of many faces sang, brawled, drank, roared, embraced, had fist fights, kissed, and wept.

The churches were filled with people. In front of the gilded icons the hot wax candles burned brightly. There resounded the basses and the still lower basses of the archdeacons, whom the staid merchants had selected, those lovers of heavenly harmony, the big-bellied elders of the church and honored members of the congregation. The basses made the air shake with their mighty roar. In the parts of the church reserved for the choir, the choristers sang in good order—the lads had shaven heads, pale faces, firm mouths; the grown-ups looked puffy and slovenly. But the music of Bortnyansky was exultant, and the canticles were borne aloft to God the omnipotent, the omniscient, the omnipresent. The merchants' wives in their silk dresses stood in front, their jackets and skirts rustling, crossing themselves with their pink, plump little hands. Their husbands prayed devoutly and staidly. Spread out behind them were a host of hangers-on: old women dressed in black, God-fearing gossips, guardians of the family hearth and procuresses, aunts, nieces waiting for bridegrooms and growing numb from boredom and fat, mistresses, and household servants.

Here, too, stood the government officials, the *chinovniks*, and their wives. And in the rear in a thick crowd, standing and on their knees, were the common people, exhausted, awaiting consolation from God, the source of all good, for salvation from the Savior. But the Savior remained silent and only looked out sadly through the lamplight upon the bowed bodies, the bent backs, the heavy sighs of the hapless and deprived . . .

The neighborhood boys joked with one another, not without fear. They moistened their fingers to try to put the candles out. The candles would sputter, and the girls and boys would snort, and laughter would overcome them, despite the threatening glances of the elders. Here and there lovers would exchange glances. On the church's porch sat beggars, cripples in sorry rags and scraps of clothing, with stumps instead of arms and legs, with bloodshot eyes, with cataracts, with eyelids inside out, the halt and the blind, and the holy fools, the fools for God's sake. Importunately they pressed forward with their wounds, their pus, their stumps, their humped backs for all to see, and in whining voices with self-deprecating refrains they begged for single kopecks or five-kopeck pieces, which clattered as they fell into the torn hats and caps on the plates of stone. Faith in the Heavenly King was strong, as well as in the earthly one, the tsar, our little father, who at the same time was tightening ever so tightly all the screws in the terrible system of power then still in the hands of the great landowners.

In the homes of the wealthy parishioners much still remained from the harsh strictures of the priest Sylvester's *Domostroi*.* The power of the man of the house was pretty fierce. These men were big shots, fat cats who sometimes were rolling in millions, dealers in fabrics, fish, tea, meat, lard, lumber, tar, leather, and hides; the owners of big taverns, town houses, and market places.

Their practical business life was in the Trading Rows, the Moscow equivalent of London's "The City": they sat there in their high-vaulted "barns" and dimly lit offices, counting, weighing, and measuring, exaggerating and deceiving, drinking tea from the saucer or sending their "boys" for sour cabbage soup, the favorite drink of those times.

Meetings on business matters were held there, too, or else in select taverns, accompanied by open-topped pastries, meat, fish, and vegetable pies, roast piglet, caviar, sterlet, mushrooms, and vodkas of all kinds. And at home, under a mask of propriety, in the stuffy air of the living rooms, dining rooms, and bedrooms, behind the heavy blinds and curtains, amidst a heap of quilts, down coverlets, and featherbeds, trunks, bins, and chests, icons, lamps, and pillows, life went its own way with muffled dramas and tragedies, which occasionally surfaced in the form of a flaming scandal or sometimes—a fountain of blood. Merchants' wives whose flesh was troubled slept with coachmen; young women, out of longing, threw them-

---

*On *Domostroi* and Sylvester, see glossary.

selves on the necks of the better-looking salesmen or shop assistants; "himself" arranged to have on the side some "madamoiselles" from among the French; the sons, forgetting all shame, would fall into a life of debauchery—is there any shortage of secrets that could be told by the alcoves and spare rooms in those heavy merchants' houses? Still, over everything there hung the heavy hand of the master of the house, and more than one cheek felt its cruel touch!

From among the merchants, one or another individual would establish ties with elements of the illustrious landowning nobility who had fallen on hard times. In Russia, too, a process was under way such as had gone on in France and other countries. And this was looked upon as no different than the Sodomite kingdom by the zealots of traditional piety, who in Moscow had their main citadel on the Rogozhsky.*

The heraldic shields of olden days needed to be gilded anew, and the power of money, that great procuress, through the church and through marriage, brought renewed luster to the heraldic emblems and titles, as merchants' blood flowed through the blue veins of the old aristocratic families. Merchants' daughters had already appeared in the halls of the Moscow Assembly of the Nobility, where they shone with their precious jewels and rosy complexions among the pale, elegant, and overly refined grandes dames of the ancient Russian nobility: the upstarts kept gaining in strength, and more than one distinguished gray head of the finest breeding was seen to fawn upon a figure wearing a caftan and boots that squeaked.

As for the bearded ones, they, too, began to change: they struggled into frock coats, hired governesses for their children, learned languages, received instruction in music and dancing, and sent their sons to the *gimnaziya*.

In Russia there had already begun to arise from among the *kulaks* (the "tight-fisted ones") and the *prasoly* (the "old salts") an enlightened Russian bourgeoisie, future counterparts of Maecenas, captains of a growing native-Russian industry: the Morozovs and the Mamontovs, the Shchukins and Chetverikovs. And no matter how much the prophets of the old nobility, who sang in elegant French the praises of Byzantium and the Asiatic way—no matter how much they wanted to strengthen and retain their hold on the great estates, which kept slipping away through their fingers, estates with many-columned palaces, liveried footmen, linden-tree alleys, and the peaceful life—money kept loosening the soil, like

*Even today the main church of the Old Believers is located there. [Note from Russian edition.—Trans.]

a mole, undermining the foundations of the old order, eating away like rust on the abutments.

The Ordynka Street school, where Kolya Petrov was born, consisted of two large buildings: one fronting on the street; the other, a three-storied building, set back on the grounds. The school itself was housed in the first building, and in the second lived the families of the teachers, although on the top floor there was a manual arts classroom: here the graduated adult girls were taught needlework.

The merchants who had built the school gave their due to the spirit of the age: as if to say, we're not backwoods people; we're all for book learning, too!

The school was spacious, the parquet floors gleamed, massive portraits of the tsars looked down from the walls. The children of the lower middle classes, petty officials, artisans, yardmen, all the little people of the city, filled the classrooms, made noise in the hallways, and sat at the desks with ink-stained hands. Very rarely did any of the school's benefactors visit it, and when they did everyone stiffened with fear.

For the most part the school lived its own life, distinct and apart. The teachers were usually former seminarians who had undergone the standard regimentation of the seminaries, but there were others. Among those others was Kolya's father, Ivan Antonych (Vanya) Petrov. He was a typical *raznochinets.* When he had been only four his father had died—after losing at cards, not long before his death (from "galloping consumption"), the few assets he still owned, leaving his wife with a slew of kids and pockets empty but for the holes.

Kolya's grandmother, with borrowed money, had opened a sewing shop and herself began to sew; nevertheless little Vanya from the age of ten had to earn the cost of his school lessons. He was a good student at the *gimnaziya*, his talents were not small, but his was a soft and yielding character—although at the same time he was cheerful and gregarious. Throughout his youth Vanya had worked to earn money for the family to support his mother and brothers. At the university he was friends with activists of the People's Will and might perhaps have been drawn into the revolutionary movement. But an almost anecdotal incident put a stop to that: one day as he was getting ready to go to a political meeting, his mother, an energetic woman with the face of an old dissenter, hid his shoes and trousers in a trunk, under lock and key—and that was the end of it! It was an ultimatum of action. In addition, tears started to flow, with talk about

*raznochinets—a member of the intelligentsia not of noble birth (plural, *raznochintsy*).

the fate of the family and all the other things that go on in such cases. The
mild-mannered Ivan Antonych made his peace. And thus ended his revolutionary career. In those years he had a romantic affair as well: he fell in
love with a certain young woman, a beauty and a revolutionary, and his
love was reciprocated; she called him "dearest Zhano" (or "Jeannot," from
Jean, the French equivalent of Ivan). But then something happened that
was forever after kept secret; the only thing known was that for several
weeks "Jeannot" had lain in bed with a nervous fever and had come within
an inch of dying, but he had managed to pull through and recover. Later
the young woman met with him several times, but soon afterward went off
and got married. Nothing more was known to anyone, and no matter how
one might try to pry the secret out of Ivan Antonych, he would lapse into
silence and you couldn't get a peep out of him; only in his eyes little fires
would blaze up, then quickly die out, and wrinkles would stand out on his
brow as deep as trenches . . .

He graduated as a mathematics major, but literature was his real passion: he knew an enormous number of poems by heart, loved to recite
poetry and read it aloud (and he read extremely well).

He would catch someone unawares, grab them by the collar, and start
in:

"See this? If you want, I'll read it to you. It's a marvelous piece, you
know, absolutely charming. Just listen."

"Ivan Antonych, excuse me, another time. Really, I'm so busy right
now."

"No, no, wait! It'll only take a minute—"

And he would make his victims sit down and listen no matter what.
And they would listen: Ivan Antonych, to be sure, read well.

As for politics, he stopped thinking about it. Alexander the Peace
Maker,* that crude heavyweight of a man with his broad, thick beard, who
boasted of how much he loved simple, truly Russian food—cabbage soup
or kasha—and who didn't forget about Russian drinking either, kept tightening the fist of his gendarmerie, and it was not for such natures as Ivan
Antonych's to dive into the deeps of the underground.

But he did read a little, and sometimes liked to blurt out radical
remarks. He didn't believe in God and treated the clergy with irony,
though not with malice. In general, he was not capable of malice: he would
flare up, then his anger would die away; he had to be regularly "reheated"
for angry feelings to stay alive. In his life he was not a systematic person,
but he was kind. There was a saying about him, "Ivan Antonych goes out

*Tsar Alexander III.

to buy sausage and comes home with a canary." Still, he had a sharp tongue in his head, and sometimes he liked to tease people close to him, accumulating some enemies in this way. However, these were rare exceptions, because on the whole Ivan Antonych was thought of as the life of the party. He was of average height, thin, almost frail; his eyes were large, gray, kind, and intelligent; he had an aquiline nose and looked like the Christ of the ancient Russian icon painters, except that he went bald early in life. When he was teased about this he didn't take offense but headed off his tormentor; pointing at his bald skull and speaking in the language of the Holy Scriptures he would say: "And from his loose and lascivious ways there grew a bald spot on his head." But this was nothing but bravado, for in reality dear old Ivan Antonych was celibate to a fault. He belonged to that rather rare type of man whom women chase after, although he himself was not shy, and sometimes he was rather free with them, at least in words.

He knew quite a lot about the most varied subjects and could talk endlessly about the pistils and stamens of flowers, about butterflies and beetles, birds and fish, the moon and stars, Heinrich Heine, geometry, or the roots of words. He had a cheerful, light-hearted, ironical cast of mind. He had made a first-rate study of the Bible at one time, and in conversation with the school priests and deacons he would recite to them from memory great mountains of biblical indecencies, sowing confusion and dismay among his interlocutors. Because of this kind of thing he was sometimes even dubbed "the Antichrist."

He met his future wife, Lyubov Ivanovna, at work: she was a teacher at the same school. She had been a sweet, slender blonde with a turned-up nose—a lively and intelligent person. There was something half childlike in her face. In no way could she have been called beautiful, or even pretty. But there was such an attractive air about her, her figure, her clear, intelligent (though not large) eyes, the lively play of her mouth, that Ivan Antonych fell in love with her at first sight and soon married her following all the proper procedures of marital law.

Lyubov Ivanovna came from a military background. Her father had been an officer. But her mother was from Poland, from a family with the old revolutionary tradition of the Polish gentry (the Szlachta, jealous of its rights against the monarchy). She was viewed as a renegade for marrying a Russian, and an officer at that, even if she did it for love; her action stirred up terrible indignation among her kinsfolk.

On the other hand, the Russian side of the family had no sympathy for her and saw in her only an offshoot of the rebellious Polish race. In the end it was more than this energetic and intelligent woman could stand. She began to suffer from severe depression (melancholia) and lost her sanity, passing into the care of her daughters. Lyubochka graduated from the Institute for Girls of the Nobility but from the very start had to earn her own bread by the sweat of her brow: her father had died, her mother had gone mad, and the young woman was left to her own devices, as were her sisters. Now, although she was of the social group called the *raznochintsy*, she was not about to get involved in revolution and was always extremely restrained in voicing opinions: over her head there always hung the madness of her mother, whose mind was haunted by arrests, house searches, executions. She resolved to keep out of politics—firmly, once and for all. Hers was a strong-willed character, and she had great tenacity, which was very hard to imagine when one looked at that naive, half-childlike little face.

Out of this marriage there came a first-born child, little Kolya. And after him, like mushrooms—one smaller than the next—came others . . .

At the age of four Kolya already knew how to read and to print. His parents loved him to an extraordinary degree, took pride in him, showed everyone how he was reading and writing and how well he drew horses and Christmas trees, houses and birds. In the quiet winter evenings, when the light outside the window turned dark-blue and the flocks of jackdaws with their sharp, guttural cries would settle on the school building roof, scolding each other, calling back and forth, then falling silent; when the noises of the street died down and in the sky, green stars began to burn; when the icy cold grew fiercer and traced on the window glass its quaint, fantastic patterns of unknown ferns and unfamiliar crystal flowers, in the Petrovs' small apartment the kerosene lamps with their glass hoods would be lighted, and after tea the skinny little fellow would recite from memory Lermontov's "The Merchant Kalashnikov":

Above great Moscow, golden-headed,
Above the white-stoned Kremlin walls,
From distant steppes, from mountains dark,
Chasing off the dark gray clouds,
The scarlet dawn ascends the sky.
A woman shaking out her golden curls . . .

The guests were amazed and shook their heads. Then his drawings and doodlings would be shown, and his reading ability demonstrated—he didn't go syllable by syllable, but in complete sentences, from one full stop to the next. But Kolya would soon tire of this business and instead would drag the guests off to see his birds. Ah, this was a whole world to itself, so interesting you could live in it for hours on end. In the child's room a net had been stretched across a window space and behind the net on an arrangement of dry branches there fluttered goldfinches, titmice, blue tits, linnets, bullfinches, and waxwings. In the evening they were already asleep, having gone off into the corners, puffing up their delicate feathers and hiding their heads under their wings. The noise of guests arriving wakened them; they looked around, surprised, with their flashing black eyes, flew up, and began to beat against the windowpanes, but Kolya, considerate keeper that he was, would quickly pull the guests away from the area and lead them out of the room: as if to say, I've shown you the birds and that's enough . . .

Sometimes the guests and the Petrovs would sing together. Their songs included "Bystry, kak volny" (Quick as the waves), "Iz strany, strany dalyokoi" (From a far-off, distant land), and the traditional student song *Gaudeamus igitur*. But when Ivan Antonych would try, with his ungodly off-key singing, to start in on something more radical, such as "The reason we drink from the bitter cup is / That every *shtof**unit is sealed with a seal, / With the two-headed eagle of Russia," then Lyubov Ivanovna would give him severe, meaningful looks and Ivan Antonych would obediently be still. His wife would very tactfully lead the guests over to the little upright piano and begin to play a Schubert serenade or some romances popular at the time, such as "Gazing at purple sunset rays, / On the banks of the Neva we stood . . ." or "Don't feel sorry for Hassan / In his ancient tattered rags." Duets or trios would be formed. Ivan Antonych, with equal enthusiasm and just as brutally off key (he loved to sing but simply had no ear for music), would join in on these new melodies, forgetting completely about his *shtof.*

Sunday for Kolya was a real holiday. And this was not only because his mama and papa, whom he idolized, stayed home with him the whole day, unlike on weekdays when they were always away at work and he was left in the company of an old nanny. There was another reason. On Sundays in Moscow the bird market was open. It was called the "Truba," being located on Trubnaya Square, near Tsvetnoi Boulevard. No sooner had Kolya opened his eyes on Sunday than he would run barefoot to his father in the bedroom, get under the covers with him, and, snuggling up, start to beg him ingratiatingly.

"Vanya"—he called his father that, the way his mother did—"Vanya, are we going to the Truba?"

"It's freezing outside today. Where can you go in weather like this?"

"Dear Vanya, dearest, let's go. I won't freeze. I'll put on my hood—"

---

*shtof—an old Russian unit of liquid measure, 1.23 liters.

The pleadings were so insistent that Ivan Antonych, exchanging glances with his wife and smiling, would finally give in. They'd wrap Kolya up, and wrap him some more, then off they'd go.

What a joy it was! They would take a horse cab to the Truba. And what you couldn't find there! All kinds of birds, squirrels, fish, bear cubs, fox cubs, meal worms, water beetles, mosquito grubs, cages, nets, traps, dogs, all kinds of special feed, jars and bottles, aquariums—and all this was overlaid with the chattering of many voices, the twittering, whistling, and singing of the birds, and the hubbub of the motley crowd. There were loiterers here, too, and thieving pigeon snatchers with cages under their arms; ragged urchins, who darted in and out, using two fingers to whistle piercingly; drunks with terrible bruises, blue-gray noses, and brown, puffed-up faces, like apples that were rotting. And there were bird lovers of all classes and social estates, experts who could determine by signs invisible to the uninitiated the merits of one or another specimen. There were speculators and second-hand dealers; high school and university students; and hunters in sheepskin coats from the villages surrounding Moscow. And all of them seethed in a solid multicolored mass and stirred about like a pile of worms crowded for space, with every part of the collective body in motion. The sellers knew the Truba regulars perfectly well, and there were no tricks or cross-examinations: after all, the regulars knew their way around in these matters. Ivan Antonych also knew what was what, and young Kolya, "Little Robinson," as his family jokingly nicknamed him, had an excellent knowledge of the feathered kingdom: the bird books of Brehm and Kaigorodov were already permanent fixtures on his desk.

When they had fought their way through the thick crowd, in which Kolya felt lost among the maze of legs and couldn't see where they were going until they arrived at the booths or carts of the vendors, they bought new birds, put them in small temporary cages, and, numb from the cold, trundled home in a sleigh. Trembling with joy, Kolya would take hold of the little red handles and open the doors of the cages to let the new arrivals out. Then he would sit for hours, without stirring, and watch his feathered friends . . .

But now spring was coming. The snow on the streets was melting. The sun kept shining brighter. Beside the wooden pavements muddy-brown rivulets were running, gurgling, and leaping playfully. The schoolchildren went outside the gates of the academy and quickly mastered the art of sailing paper boats. They launched them on the water in the gutters and these flotillas then sailed all the way down to the Moscow River, tipping from side to side to the eager cries of the watching children. Along the sides of the buildings the earth grew bare and dried out. They began to play Russ-

ian children's games—knucklebones, skittles, and others. The buds in the
school's little garden began to swell. Unhealthy, yellow-faced old women
crawled up out of the cellars, where the night watchmen, the porters, the
cleaning women, and the yardmen lived, to warm themselves in the cheerful sunlight, to breathe a little fresh air, to sit on the steps.

The first lemon yellow butterfly of the season flew by. Flies appeared on
the sides of the walls warmed by the sun. The buds on the lilac bushes
burst, and before you knew it the birch tree was covered with a net cap of
light-green, sticky baby leaves. In the garden you could smell the earth,
and you could walk without galoshes. Living things came creeping out of
every nook and cranny. And Kolya darted about the gardens, examined
every tree and fence, dug in the ground, and gathered caterpillars and
cocoons. He loved the smell of the earth, the rotting leaves, the wet twigs.
And what a joy it was when a butterfly would hatch from a cocoon, crawling out all wet and helpless, with its wings folded and hanging down like
little rags! And then before your eyes those wings would straighten up and
grow: the butterfly would force air into the little "ribs" and the wings
would stretch out like an umbrella being raised—they seemed actually to
grow as you watched them.

Kolya would get so wrapped up in this that he forgot about everything
else. And his first burst of rage, the first foul language to come from his
lips, had to do with this passion of his.

It happened this way. One spring day he caught a ground beetle in the
school garden. He fiddled around with it for a long time in spite of its foul
odor, then enclosing it tightly in his hand, he began running home.

"Kolya! Where are you going?"

A young woman was calling him, the teacher of the sewing class.

"A ground beetle. See?"

"And what is that? Come on, now, show me! Show me!"

He showed it to her.

"Ugh, how disgusting! And how awful it smells!"

At one blow the young woman crushed Kolya's treasure under her heel
. . . He shuddered all over, his eyes filled with tears: it even seemed to him
that it hadn't been just an everyday garden variety but a big, dark-blue
Crimean ground beetle, vivid and mysterious, the kind he had dreamed
about. His indignation knew no bounds. He stood stock still and stared
the woman right in the face—she who had no idea of the worldwide significance of the crime she had just committed—in a kind of frenzy he
cried out, his voice cracking:

"Bitch lady!"

He remembered this phrase, "bitch lady," the rest of his life.

But now from the village of Makarovo, where the Petrovs went in the summer to stay at a dacha, carts began to arrive. Beds, baskets, pots, pillows, featherbeds, everything was piled upon them, and the two wagons dragged themselves back at a walk over the eighty versts they had come. The Petrovs traveled by train to the town of Bogorodsk, then took a wagon for the last twenty versts to the place where they spent the summer: the teachers had summer vacation, and Kolya's father could now devote his free time to the young boy.

The village of Makarovo, where the Petrovs rented a peasant hut, a traditional Russian *izba*, from the local sexton, Ivan Ivanych, was typical of the Bogorodsk-Glukhovo region. Here there were large forests and marshes. At that time the forests were still wild and untrammeled, and bears still roamed in the vicinity of Makarovo, sometimes ripping into the peasants' cows. Legends abounded, about how Uncle Mitry or some other "uncle" had driven off a bear with a bast basket. There was one old peasant known by the nickname "Bear's Leftovers," whose whole face had been torn and disfigured by the tender paw of "Mikhail Ivanych Toptygin."* They would show you the place in the forest where a bear had been startled by a group of girls gathering berries; in its surprise it had soiled itself and run away. Berries there were in plenty—strawberries, blueberries, huckleberries, gooseberries, whortleberries, and others. There were also plenty of mushrooms. But there was not plenty of land for the peasants, and what land they had was poor and loamy. The clumps of earth turned over by their wooden plows would turn yellow in the sun like the bones of something dead. Life in the village was pretty slim pickings.

Sorry little huts, covered with old, blackened straw, stood in two rows leading up to the country churchyard, where the parish church stood, with the village priest's house alongside it. Not far away was the sexton's hut. The peasants lived a hard life, full of sweat, toil, need, and—on holidays—vodka. Their extra earnings came both from seasonal work and from labor on weaving machines in their cottages, on material contracted out to them by intermediaries. Barefoot, dirty, ragged, half starving five- and seven-year-old girls were already being trained for work on the primitive looms, and from dawn to dusk they wove and wove without stopping in order to earn an extra kopeck. The peasant mothers were both working themselves and remorselessly keeping the pressure on their own children, amidst filth, bedbugs, roaches, and a heap of disintegrating rags. Competition from the mighty textile plants located nearby had driven the pay down to a pittance. A sword hung over the peasant's head, while the pushy, greedy contractors gathered

*The full Russian name fancifully assigned to bears.

in a rich harvest. There was no prospect of relief from poverty for the peas-ants, whose sighs could be heard by night: "If only the Lord would take us!"

In the middle of the village stood an iron-roofed tavern, tilted slightly to one side. Alongside it, in a heavily trampled-down area, the village assemblies were held, a handier way of keeping the people supplied with drink. Inside it, on Sundays, they drank away their last half-kopecks, and from it the tavern keeper's underlings would throw out carousers who got rowdy. This too, ordinarily, was where meetings were held by the ring-leaders of the organized brawls, or rumbles, when village turned out against village, and they fought with savagery, turned into beasts, with great bloodshed, both bats and stakes being brought into play.

In the country churchyard stood the small gray house of the village priest. Around it was a small garden with big lilac and jasmine bushes. The bushes grew in such a way that the house itself was almost invisible and only its white shutters showed through the leaves and branches. The parish was wretched and impoverished, and the priest's entire family lived in poverty, afflicted moreover, as many families in the village were, by con-genital syphilis: eloquently testifying to this were the nasal speech, the lumpy noses, much eaten away, the pallor of the faces, the scrofula and stuttering of the children, always covered with sores, suffering from rick-ets, with chronic colds and runny noses, spindly-legged and sickly . . .

In the morning, after waking and rubbing his eyes, Kolya ran down to the river with his father. They walked on narrow logs laid over the swampy wetland, trying not to fall in: the swamp made smacking and sucking noises, trembled and gurgled, and bubbles came up from under the logs; even the hummocks were unsteady under foot. Finally they came out on solid ground along the shore of the river, by a small deep pool. The wil-lows draped their silvery branches in the water. The large, old alder trees shaded the pool, where under the sunken logs crayfish nested and sleek, fat eelpout lay in hiding; over the water flitted dark-blue damselflies, their tiny wings vibrating tremulously; a dragonfly would launch itself from a dry branch and, making a headlong circle through the air, quickly return to its favorite spot.

Kolya and his father sat down on the grass. On the riverbank the grass was cold, still wet from the morning dew. The sun played through the leaves; little slivers of light scampered across the mirror of the water. Silence. Only the warbler *pyenochka tyenkovka*, chasing through the green foliage for midges, steadily kept up its ringing cry: tyen, tyen, tyen! It was scary to slip into the cold water. But both father and son, after sitting on the bank for a while, went in, splashing and snorting—and they didn't want to get back out. The sun climbed higher. The grass dried off. The meadow flowers gave off honeyed aromas. Sitting on a lungwort plant were golden-green sap chafer beetles, who had tapped into the plant's fragrant juices. On the bank, in the damp soil, mole crickets were astir, creeping out of their intricately chambered burrows. A yellowish fly hung motionless in midair, its tiny wings going in place so fast they couldn't be seen—and suddenly with a hum it disappeared.

But it was time to go home, have some tea. And then—into the forest. What riches! Kolya opened his eyes as wide as they would go: he had such a yearning to absorb into himself all the multiplicity of life that in endlessly varied forms unfolded there before him. Squirrels leaped through the spruce trees, sailing through the air and skillfully catching and clinging to branches garlanded with cones. The orioles sang back and forth, as though playing on flutes. The jays kept up their hoarse and furious cry, the turquoise mirrors of their wings flashing in the thickets. The magpies chattered in the shrubbery like quarrelsome vending women at a bazaar. And among the emerald pillows of moss, where here and there a brambleberry or the beads of a whortleberry showed red like drops of blood, the little brown caps of boletus mushrooms stood out. Flitting among the flowers were machaon and "king's mantle" butterflies and forester moths, while golden beetles took refuge on field asters. In the evenings hawkmoths hummed around the flowers into which they lowered their long proboscises.

Wasn't this the life! "Little Robinson" would busy himself for entire days with the luxuriant gifts of nature: from pine bark a kind of cork board could be made for preparing butterflies and beetles, according to all the proper rules, to be added to his collection; from the same bark, tapered floats for fishing could be devised; nets could be made out of wire and gauze; and excellent fishing lines could be woven out of horsehair. For the time being Ivan Antonych helped with everything; he himself collected specimens for the herbarium and was genuinely carried away with the work: for days on end he wandered about with his head uncovered, and the gleam of his bald spot was evident everywhere. He was highly knowledgeable about grasses and flowers, insects and birds; and his stories roused his son's curiosity more than ever: Oh, if only he had a death's head moth! If only he could find a harpie caterpillar, with its little flags!

When the moon rose, Kolya took his seat on the church porch with his friends among the neighborhood boys and waited: on the sand-covered village square, goatsuckers (nightjars) would fly in and land, mysterious gray nocturnal birds, with enormous black eyes and the noiseless flight of down-soft wings. Oh, if only he could catch a live goatsucker!

And so the Petrovs' summer went by. Toward autumn they traveled back to Moscow: once again the wagons were loaded with housewares and kitchenware, and the little horses with measured pace, heads hanging, made their way back from the village of Makarovo to the "first city of the throne,"* to the quiet of Bolshaya Ordynka Street.

*"first city of the throne"—that is, Moscow, Russia's first capital. St Petersburg, built by Tsar Peter the Great, was the capital from 1712 until the Russian revolution. In 1918 Moscow was made the capital again.

Chapter 2

The Petrovs' neighbors in the school building were the Yablochkins. Mikhail Vasilyevich Yablochkin was married to Lyubov Ivanovna's sister, Marya Ivanovna, and was considered the head of the school, the senior teacher. He was a tall, handsome man but suffered from a serious heart ailment. He had an aquiline nose, slightly curly black hair, and was very thin, sort of a mixture in type between a Georgian and a strict Old Believer, a *kerzhak*. In his black eyes and jaundiced, sickly-looking face there was something deathly and deadening: the dull glow in those eyes spoke of an inner rust that was eating away at him and ravaging his organism. He was eternally ill. Constant little heart attacks tormented him. He was hot-tempered and irritable, and at the same time was frightened of his own irritability. His childhood had not been of the brightest: his father, a village priest, a huge man with an enormous nose, had the reputation of a terrible despot who had driven his beautiful, intelligent, but unresisting wife to the grave.

This "man of God" had been terribly bossy, miserly, and grasping; he was harsh and abrupt with the peasants and ferocious toward his wife and children. He knew how to make use of his position in the community and had a flourishing farm operation going, with fruit orchard, raspberry patch, and small bathhouse. Nor was he ashamed of charging ever higher fees for his priestly services. After his wife died he lived with his servant girl, torturing her just as he tortured everyone in the family. He beat his children and "kept order" in the household according to the backward and patriarchal prescriptions of the *Domostroi*. He trained Mikhail for the priesthood, turning him over to the seminary with all its charms: rote learning of Greek and Latin, apologetics and homiletics, moral theology and unbridled corporal punishment, plus the bestial manners of the sem-

inarians themselves. Having passed through this school, the already sickly
boy emerged with his health completely ruined. He didn't become a priest
but instead went to a teachers' seminary, from which he graduated. The
beatings he endured at home and at school aroused no protest in his heart,
nor did they give rise to a rebellious and critical nature. He was not gifted
enough for that and did not possess the necessary native vitality. On the
contrary, he devoutly believed in the existing spiritual and secular hierarchy and was more than reliable in all respects. All the progressive and revolutionary ideas of the age went right past him: he read nothing that might
disturb his limited and screened-in mind.

In his entire outward aspect, in the way he walked, sat, read, and spoke,
in all his gestures, and in his facial expressions one felt a certain deathly
tiredness, as though he had swallowed some foul poison which had
affected him for life and for which there was no cure. He walked slightly
hunched over, listlessly putting one long, thin, storklike leg in front of the
other. He spoke slowly, stretching out his words. His favorite gesture was
one of hopelessness accompanied by a set phrase, or constant refrain,
repeated in a sing-song way with mournful intonation: "Everything
around here is somehow not right." That concept of "not right," however,
had no relation to criticism from the standpoint of higher principles—he
never rose to such heights; no, it always referred to some petty everyday
matter; "Nikeshka" (Mikhail Vasilyevich liked to use old-fashioned nicknames*) didn't buy the right kind of firewood, the cook hadn't made the
right soup, the tablecloth hadn't been put on the table right, the heating in
the rooms wasn't right, and so on. He was eternally displeased with something. But he was satisfied with the social order and the principles on
which it was based; he was devoted to it, not out of fear but "good conscience." For all that, this weak, sickly, and limited individual had inherited from his father the characteristic traits of a despot, made all the more
unbearable in combination with the perennially failing state of his health.

In contrast, his wife was a very intelligent woman. She was much more
beautiful than her sister: her dark, thick chestnut braids, sable brows, large,
radiant, intelligent eyes, and sweet smile made her sometimes extremely
alluring. Was it her beauty that had won Mikhail Vasilyevich's heart? Perhaps so. At any rate, she knew that her future spouse was not indifferent
to her sister, Lyubochka, for it was only after a refusal from the latter that
he turned his attention to Marya. Be that as it may, after several years,
when Marya Ivanovna had already borne three children, their family life—
not the one seen in public, not the one that was manifested in a show of

*Nikeshka—old-fashioned nickname for Nikolai.

well-being, with everything smoothed over and licked clean, but the one that went on in reality, starting from the marital couch, the real family life that Tolstoy was so repelled by—the Yablochkins' family life became a thing of hellfire and damnation. How many tears Marya Ivanovna shed in secret, concealing her true self from everyone, how many thoughts she rethought, what strength of will, tact, and restraint she displayed not to reveal her sufferings by word or gesture or even a trembling in her voice—of all this no one had any idea. Only the children, much later, guessed at much of it—they who had loved her as one can love only one's mother. For the sake of the children, Marya Ivanovna accepted all her torments and stayed with this husband, who on top of everything was jealous of her—jealous in a crude and stupid way, as only thick-headed people lacking inner cultivation can be jealous, for despite all their malice they are aware of their own inadequacy.

Mikhail Vasilyevich understood perfectly well how superior his wife was to him in all respects; inwardly, because of his respect for rank and authority, he was even impressed by the fact that Marya Ivanovna in her day had graduated with honors from her institute, earning a "cipher," the highest mark of excellence, and that some sort of highly placed personage, someone just short of her August Highness,* had presented the award. Not only had Marya Ivanovna been educated at an institute, from which she had acquired a magnificent command of languages—as had all her sisters, incidentally—she also read a great deal and had a very broad perspective on things. Thus she and her husband really had nothing in common. Nevertheless—such are women!—she felt sorry for him, she worried about him when his health grew worse, and she yielded to him in all things. Only in one respect was she unable to yield: when he raised his hand to the children. And he did beat—beat unmercifully, with a belt—his firstborn, who was also named Kolya, a thin, sickly, rather intelligent boy, who grew up like a hunted wolf cub, full of hatred for his father, to whom he stubbornly offered resistance on every applicable occasion. At these times the mother would rush to her son's defense, forgetting everything else. And the rest of the children—two daughters—would cry, holding onto their mother's skirts . . . The scene usually ended with Mikhail Vasilyevich having a mild heart attack, and then Marya Ivanovna would run to get his medicine, send for the doctor, and for several days in a row would self-sacrificingly tend to the ailing despot. During those days the windows would be closed and the blinds lowered. The overpowering smell of medications filled the dark rooms. Everyone walked on tiptoe. Marya Ivanovna, doing her own

*The tsarina.

and her husband's work at the school for days on end, would not be able to sleep at night.

And so the months and years went by.

The storm would start usually over a trifle. It often happened this way: after a meal that had passed in complete silence, which oppressed everyone, including the irritable Mikhail Vasilyevich, he suddenly couldn't stand it any longer and, casting his deathly eye upon his son, who was gloomily bent over his plate, would toss off some incendiary remark—and an entire scene would begin, as when the fuse to a powder keg is lighted.

"Nikolai, why are you hunched over like that?"

"No reason."

"What do you mean, no reason? Straighten up."

Silence.

"I am speaking to you! Do you hear me or not?"

Silence.

"Are you going to listen to your father?"

"No."

"What did you say? Repeat that, please! Repeat that!"

"No."

"Ah, that's what you're like! You rotten little—"

And Mikhail Vasilyevich would leap from his chair, his napkin still in his collar, hands trembling. Kolya would bounce away from the table like a springy rubber ball. Marya Ivanovna would rush to her husband:

"Misha, Misha, calm down. Misha, for God's sake, don't get so upset—"

But he was already beside himself.

"So you too, you're taking this bastard's side! A fine bunch you all are!"

And roughly shoving his wife aside, he would rush after his son.

Kolya would take refuge behind tables and bedsteads with the swiftness of a haggard little wolf cub, then he would run from room to room, knocking over chairs and stools, using them to barricade himself as he went, to block his father's way, and slamming doors he would rush through the dark hallway and disappear down the stairway leading outdoors.

But it also happened sometimes that the father would catch the boy. And then he would squeeze him between his knees, pull his pants down, and mercilessly slash him with his belt. This gave him a strange kind of satisfaction: he would release his anger this way, his own feeling of inadequacy, his lack of worth, his alienation from everyone else, his illness, his impotence. But after administering the punishment he would clutch at his chest. His heart would pound, then subside, and then suddenly seem to stop. He would barely be able to crawl to the sofa—a heart attack had already brought him to the verge of the universal end all mortals meet.

And now there ensued that phase in the Yablochkins' life when for several days the whole apartment would be turned into a gloomy sickroom.

These scenes, in one or another variation, were periodically repeated in the Yablochkin family as though by a law of nature. How many times already had Marya Ivanovna, with all her remarkable tact and caution, approached her husband and tried to have a serious discussion with him on the question of child rearing. But he would turn upon her that vicious, deathly-angry gaze that boded no good, and she, afraid to upset him more, would back away. No arguments on a higher plane—citing Pestalozzi, Comenius, and other luminaries—had any effect or, if they did, it was the effect of a red rag on a bull, and poor Marya Ivanovna bore not the least resemblance to a toreador. And so it would be that Mikhail Vasilyevich lay there for weeks in the dark, curtained-off study, propped up by pillows and surrounded by medicines.

It also happened that Marya Ivanovna, doing the work of two people at the school, putting herself at everyone else's disposal, keeping up all the appearances, remaining smiling and outgoing as usual, at home would lock herself up in her bedroom, to be alone, to sob out her inconsolable grief. Her nerves were unable to bear the strain: this constant tension, the constant necessity to *faire bonne mine au mauvais jeu*, in the midst of the inevitable gossip, the sidelong glances, and sometimes the sharp and piercing allusions—because everyone knew, as the neighbors responded to the sounds reaching their ears—all this had its effect.

This, then, was the situation the Yablochkin children grew up in. Kolya Yablochkin, a boy advanced beyond his years, quite consciously nurtured and cultivated within himself a fierce hatred for his father, and he learned quite early to observe and detect everything that was negative in life and in social existence. Manya, the older daughter, a thin little girl with thin little legs, with beautiful, black, velvety eyes, was the incarnation of sorrow: even then they called her *Mater Dolorosa*. She suffered deeply over the persecution of her brother, whom she loved very much, and over the tears of her mother, whom she idolized, and over the illness of her father, for whom she felt terribly sorry. A quiet girl—she was a year and a half younger than her brother and a year and a half older than Kolya Petrov— she read a great deal, and even at her tender age was tormented by the problems of relations among people: Why did her mother have to suffer when she was such a good person? Why did her father have to persecute her brother? Was this either just or fair? Why did God allow it—when God is supposed to be kind and good? Hundreds of questions like these swarmed in that little head covered with black hair, looking out on the world with mild, sad eyes. She wept over *Uncle Tom's Cabin*, Dickens, the

Bible, and Gogol's *Taras Bulba* when Ostap was being tortured. She hunted for answers to her questions everywhere—and found none. Even her mother, her dear and beloved mother, who knew everything and understood everything—even she, with the answers she gave, could not bring reassurance and calm to her child's troubled soul.

Manya was Kolya Petrov's only friend. Kolya's brother, Volodya, was still small, even smaller than Kolya himself. Manya, on the other hand, although a full year and a half older than Kolya, liked to wander about the garden with him, hunt for cocoons, and have conversations with him on the most varied subjects. To her, everything in the Petrovs' lives was interesting and different: they didn't have fights and arguments, everything was cheerful among them; they had what the Yablochkins didn't have. The contrast in their ways of life had its effect. Becoming absorbed in a different atmosphere and by different interests, Manya was able simply to rest and recover from the unending jabs and thrusts piercing her soul and tormenting her in her accustomed domestic surroundings. And so they would go around together, climbing fences and trees, stripping the bark from the logs lying in the school's backyard, and digging in the ground . . .

"Kolya, look here, what a strange-looking worm!"

"That's not a worm; it's a caterpillar. The larva of a poplar moth."

"It looks just like a stick."

"Yeah, they're all that way. It's mimicry."

"So, Kolya, what are you going to be when you grow up?"

"I'm going to major in natural science. Papa promised to buy me the *Atlas of Butterflies* by Kholodkovsky. Know it?"

"No."

"It's got such great pictures! It's got everything, everything. I'll show you. It even has the 'death's head.' "

A pause.

"Uncle Vanya never beats you?"

"Never."

"And you don't cry?"

"No. Only I did cry last Sunday. We didn't go to the Truba."

"Say, don't you feel sorry for Jesus the way they crucified him?"

"Yeah, I do."

"And didn't you cry over it?"

"Yeah, I did."

"There you see! And you said you never cry!"

"Well, but that's different. They crucified him. Of course you feel sorry when someone's being hurt."

A pause. Manya is thinking something over. Her thoughts give her no rest and they break through the flow of attention to other interests. It's hard for her to sort things out in this chaos. Reflectively, she moves her long, thin fingers, the fingers she already uses to play simple pieces on the piano. (She loves music with a passion.) But she says nothing more.

"Manya, come on over to our place."

"All right. Only I have to ask Mama."

"Okay. But hurry up. Will you come?"

"If they let me. And Mama—most likely she'll let me."

Kolya goes home with his loot: caterpillars, leaves (to feed them), cocoons. He distributes all this among various boxes. Manya comes running in, all happy and aglow: they had let her come over so quickly! For the umpteenth time Kolya shows her his collection. Evening comes. The sun goes down. The flocks of jackdaws circle and make their commotion. Pressing their noses against the window glass, the children watch the dying embers of the day. Soon the "chiki-ftiki" arrive. (That's what they called the "hunters" and "golden-tongued ones" who dumped the academy's garbage out into the barrels.) The "chiki-ftiki" would do their work, and you could hear them cursing one another. It got dark. Kolya and Manya sit down at the little children's table in his room and drink tea from tiny cups that Kolya's grandmother had given him. Manya plays housewife.

But soon it all comes to an end. In the doorway appears Ivan Antonych; he strokes Manya's little head:

"Manya, your mama has sent for you."

The children run into the kitchen. There stands the Yablochkins' cook: "The lady says you have to come home now. Time to go to bed."

And Manya goes home, a sadness transforming her little face.

Ivan Antonych begins to tease his little son. He has a bad habit that Lyubov Ivanovna protests against every way she can, but without results: Kolya's father is teaching him all kinds of "foolishness" that he doesn't understand but that is riotously funny when it comes out of the mouth of a babe. Thus Kolya pompously declaims:

A man without a woman
Is like an engine without steam
Valves missing from a clarinet
Or a pistol you can't aim

"Well, now, Kolya! Try it again!"

"A man without a woman—"

"Vanya! Stop it! What foolishness this is! Kolya, that's enough—"

"But Papa taught it to me."

"I know Papa did. You'd do better to take a look at your new book. *Kot-Murlyk*" (Meower the Cat).

"Where is it? Where from? A new one?"

"Yes, a new one."

"Did you buy it?"

"Yes, just today. It's got really good pictures."

And Kolya rushes over to his mother, who is looking at her husband meaningfully, full of reproach. Ivan Antonych laughs to himself in his beard: he never goes so far as to get into a fight with his wife.

Meanwhile Kolya was already engrossed in his new book. In general he read everything that came his way. He learned to read virtually by himself, with help from his father, from the blocks with words and letters that he played with. Then came the primer that Tolstoy wrote when he took his great interest in pedagogy. This was followed by Tolstoy's *Reader* in its yellowed covers, and after that came all the rest. A favorite of Kolya's was Kaigorodov's *From the Feathered Kingdom*. Brehm's bird book was also there, with its heavy, fat volumes, like monuments to a higher wisdom. But of all the books there was one for which Kolya had a special passion, one he cherished the most, one he read and reread and read again, although by then he knew every line. It was not *Robinson Crusoe* or *Captain Grant's Children* by Jules Verne; it was *The Adventures of Huckleberry Finn* by Mark Twain. Huck was Kolya's hero, and he delved into the adventures of this naughty fellow with all possible enthusiasm . . .

It shouldn't be thought, however, that the Petrovs' life, with its modest joys and modest dimensions, proceeded without any friction. This could not be said. Still, it wasn't within the immediate family that the sphere of conflict lay. It was in the life of the school, with its special interests, problems, tasks, the whole web of interpersonal relations connected with work and daily life, which were sometimes very tangled and complicated, for all their pettiness. Here was a seething cauldron of passion and self-interest, ambition and honor, vanity and light-mindedness, haughtiness and arrogance, pride and envy, virtue and weakness. And strange as it may seem, the poles of attraction among the various groups and individuals at the school were the heads of the two families that were so closely connected with each other: the Yablochkins and the Petrovs. What caused Mikhail Vasilyevich and Ivan Antonych to clash? Perhaps somewhere in the deepest, darkest abyss of the subconscious there still resided those ancient conflicts, hidden away and never allowed to surface, over Ivan's wife, Lyubochka, who had once been the object of Mikhail's attentions but who had chosen to marry Ivan instead. But even without this aspect of things, the two men had sufficient reasons for conflict. One of them was a seminarian, not of the type that hissed disapproval but "quite the contrary"; the other was a university student. One was an Orthodox son of the church, devoted to the existing order; the other, to whatever slight extent, was still a man over whom the freedom-loving aspirations of the age had hovered, brushing him with their wings. One was dark, gloomy, and cold; the other cheerful, gregarious, and light-hearted. One was the man in charge; the other was a subordinate, but one who did not in any way acknowledge the authority of his "leader."

Given this state of affairs, it was not at all surprising that disputes arose between them, and not just once or twice; these were sometimes of practical relevance, sometimes completely senseless, flaring up now here, now there, and often over completely incidental matters. And to these two heroes their colleagues would attach themselves like iron filings to a magnet, and they would gossip, incite, egg on, flatter, pour flames on the fire, spread slander, hash over every little detail, and pass judgment—that is, they would do everything that is done, repetitively, millions of times with deadly monotony, in the philistine, quasi-intellectual circles of petty officialdom. Thus, in the inner depths of the school a great war between the mice and the frogs was going on, sometimes blazing up as a serious conflict that would become a scandal throughout the school, at other times smoldering at hidden, underground levels, like a fire in a peat bog when sometimes the only indication is the smell of burning and the tiny, barely noticeable curls of smoke making their way up from deep in the ground.

One day Ivan Antonych stopped in at someone else's classroom during a recess.

"Ivan Antonych!" the sound filled the classroom. The kids quieted down, but they weren't frightened: Ivan Antonych didn't have the reputation among them of being a bogeyman or a "thunder and lightning" type.

Ivan glanced at the blackboard. There, in big chalk letters, were the Russian words: *konava, kon,* and *babki stoyat na konu.**

"Who wrote this?" Ivan Antonych asked.

"Ivan Palych!" dozens of voices answered as one.

"So you write *kanava* with an *o?*"

"Yes, Ivan Antonych. That's what Ivan Palych[†] told us."

"You'll be writing rubbish, kids. He couldn't have told you such foolishness. This *kon* here has nothing to do with *kanava.*"

---

*Kon is "the kitty" or "the stake" in a game of chance, such as in the Russian game *babki* (knucklebones). The sentence means: "The knucklebones were at stake." *Konava* is a misspelling of the Russian word for "ditch," *kanava.*

[†]Ivan Palych is a colloquial form of "Ivan Pavlovich."

"But Ivan Palych explained it to us."

"Then your Ivan Palych explained rubbish. And you tell him I said so."

The boys began looking around and laughing. They looked at one another and snorted. Snorted and turned away. One listened in total incomprehension, absent-mindedly digging into his nose. Another, in more lively fashion, had already laid his notebook on his desk, pulled a hard rubber eraser and quill pen out of his pencil box and diligently, with his head to one side, even sticking his tongue out to help in the effort, was erasing and correcting, changing the *o* to *a* and removing all traces of the ill-advised *kon*. A third, who didn't care one bit how you spelled *kanava*— spell it with the ancient Russian letter *yat'* for all he cared—had filled his mouth with a cookie and was chewing with concentration and wondering why they had put so little sugar on his cookie when Volodka Vasilyev over there had so much on his! A fourth pinched the backside of his neighbor, who gave him a kick as hard as he could under the desk. In a word, each was busy with his own affairs. Yet the impact of Ivan Antonych's remarks was considerable.

Nor did he limit himself to this passing slight: his philological zeal required him to go further. He had the reputation, besides, of a man who gets carried away, a troublemaker, and a mocker.

In the teachers' room there was already considerable animation. Mikhail Vasilyevich was restlessly pacing from one corner to the other on his long, stork's legs, his face green, grasping at his sunken chest with a thin, ascetic hand. The priest, Father Voskresensky, short and chubby, with a prematurely gray, divided beard, little pig's eyes, and little braids that swung next to his cheeks, was blinking his eyes expectantly and was about to slide under the table from his big easy chair because of his great weight. Ivan Palych was sitting, as red in the face as any boiled crayfish, and didn't know where to look or what to look at. The rest of the teachers whispered among themselves: Mikhail Vasilyevich, having heard about the incident, had already made a declaration to the assembled teachers that he would not permit any teacher's authority to be undermined and would give Ivan Antonych a reprimand for his tactlessness. The latter, suspecting nothing, flew into the teachers' room with a cheerful expression on his face and, without pausing, went right over, put his hand on the shoulder of Ivan Pavlovich, who had lost his bearings completely, and launched an offensive:

"I say old man, you aren't starting to go batty, are you? You don't really write *kanava* with an *o*, do you?"

Silence.

"Listen, gentlemen! This Ivan Palych of ours! He's teaching the boys to spell *kanava* with an *o*! Says it's derived from *kon*. A-ha-ha-ha! What do you think of that? A new era in the history of Russian grammar! The penetration of our Russian knucklebones into Western European linguistics!—"

"Ivan Antonych, your behavior . . . Your behavior . . . In front of young children . . . You allowed yourself to use the word *rubbish* . . . This is . . . This is—"

"What 'This is'? Teachers should teach grammar, not promote illiteracy."

"Here now! You are taking liberties— this is an inappropriate presumption."

"What do you mean, I'm taking liberties? Surely you know that the root of the word *kanava*—"

"How dare you! How dare you!"

"Don't yell. The root of the word *kanava* is the same as that of *kanal*. It's a foreign root, not Russian. If you want me to, I'll show you right now—"

"Well now, of course, you learned such things at the university . . . But I must reprimand you . . . You are undermining authority . . . You are instituting . . . Why, you have an obligation—"

"Mikhail Vasilyevich, if I may, it is *you* who has the obligation—"

"I know very well without you what obligation I have—I would ask that you not try to tell me—"

"You have an obligation to see to it that the right things are taught. Ivan Palych, excuse me, but weren't you telling these kids a bunch of baloney? Tell the truth now, wasn't it a lot of bunk?"

"Well, Ivan Antonych, but, if you please, where does the *v* in *kanava* come from?"

"Well, if *kanava* comes from *kon*, how would you get a *v* from that? It's a case of *lucus a non lucende*."*

"But wait! How dare you ridicule a member of the teaching staff in front of the youngsters! You are corrupting the school!"

"And how dare you shout at a member of the teaching staff!"

Ivan Antonych then stormed out, slamming the door of the teachers' common room so hard that the glass in it tinkled.

That evening in the Yablochkins' apartment there was an eerie silence; the children were in dismay: Mama and Papa had locked themselves up in the office, two hours had gone by, and they hadn't come out. Kolya Yablochkin kept demonstratively quiet. Manya started to steal up to the

---

*The Latin means "brightness from the unbright"; used ironically to suggest faulty logic behind an apparently clever deduction.

awesome door to the inner sanctum but suddenly took fright and turned back. What, after all, might you hear or find out? Poor Mama: what if Papa was berating her? Or maybe Papa had died, and Mama too . . .

Bitter tears welled up in Manya's eyes: she felt infinitely sorry for her mama; she already imagined her lying there, not breathing, eyes closed, turning cold—"Mama, dear Mama!" the little girl wanted to shout. She wanted to rush to the door and bang on it with her little fists, to make sure her mother was alive, that her eyes were open, that, as ever, she was warm, loving, alive; that she could press her little head to her mama's breast and forget everything in the world, all the nasty and the bitter . . . But little Manya, swallowing her tears, got hold of herself and waited.

Behind the secret door a conversation in low voices was going on. One voice was shaking in anger, squeaking, full of barely contained hatred, constantly broken by fits of coughing and weakness of the heart. The other was gentle, soothing, reassuring, the kind of voice an experienced doctor with a good bedside manner uses to speak with a patient who is seriously ill.

"This is disgraceful! This Ivashka is ruining the whole school for me."

"Don't get upset, Misha. Just don't let it upset you. Ivan Antonych can see for himself that he was tactless. And you can also tell Ivan Palych that in cases when he's not sure, he can at least look things up in Grot's book on the Russian language."

"Just listen to you! As if that was the issue! When what it is, is some sort of—why it's a case of insolence. After all, what am I to him? Am I his superior or not? It's not him but me who has to answer for the school—"

"Of course, Misha. But this incident is not a case of—God knows what. There's no need to make so much of it. It's true that Ivan Antonych is thoughtless, but he is, as you yourself know, a good teacher."

"What kind of teacher! A troublemaker. A smart aleck, that's all. I'm going to write to the school administrator tomorrow—this school isn't big enough for the two of us. These blabbermouths from the universities—"

"Wait, Misha. At least don't rush into anything."

"I've already told the other teachers: it's either him or me. I can't get along with this chatterbox, this . . . this swine!"

"All right, all right, Misha, do what you wish; you know best. Only don't let it upset you. Here, take this and try to sleep—take it, please—calm down—I'm going to say good-night now. Be well."

After giving her husband his medicine, Marya Ivanovna went out ever so quietly. She emerged from Papa's gloomy den to the general joy of the children. At last!

That same evening Ivan Antonych unexpectedly blurted out to his beloved Lyuba:

"I'm going to leave the school."

"What are you talking about? What's happened? Come on, tell me, Vanya."

"There's nothing I can do with that blockhead."

"What blockhead are you talking about? Be serious, please, don't talk in riddles."

"It's obvious what blockhead. Yablochkin. What's wrong with you, now? Couldn't you guess?"

Then, laying it on thick and sparing none of the details, Ivan Antonych told the story of *kanava* with an *o* and the scene in the staff room. He, Ivan Antonych, was standing guard at the portals of proper grammar. It was impermissible that the children be taught God only knows what. On top of it all, this Yablochkin had the audacity to shout at him!

"But, Vanya, wait, you'll have time—"

"The doorbell! Who the devil is ringing our bell at this ungodly hour?"

Through the kitchen, as it turned out, there had come to call on them another teacher, Dmitry Dmitryevich. Not very tall, and with deep pock-marks—the traces of smallpox he'd suffered in childhood—with eyes pink from continual drinking, with a servile smile on his gaunt face, this small fidgety man was somehow completely gray, as if he hadn't washed in a year, neither his teeth nor his shoes nor his clothing.

"I wanted to drop in just for a minute, Ivan Antonych."

"But please, have a seat. Lyuba! Give Dmitry some tea."

"No, thank you, Lyubov Ivanovna! Ivan Antonych, just for a minute. I just wanted to tell you . . . I wanted to pass along . . . to share with you . . . as a colleague—"

"What are you getting at, Dmitry Dmitryevich?"

"Well, you see, when you left—"

"Left where?"

"Why, when you left the teachers' room—"

"Oh? What about it?"

"Well, Mikhail Vasilyevich announced to us all that he was going to send a request for your dismissal to the school administrator—he said—"

"So that's how it is!"

"Actually that's all there is. Please forgive me, Ivan Antonych. I considered it my duty as a colleague to warn you—to bring it to your attention—we are all outraged, the best among us, that is—the teachers value you highly—among us you—"

"Why, thank you—I didn't expect—"

The guest began to take his leave, but for a long time he couldn't get his feet into his galoshes, either because he was really having difficulty or because he was deliberately prolonging the process to listen in on how Ivan Antonych would react in talking with his wife about this "information from a colleague." Finally the galoshes were on, the door opened, the warm air formed little clouds by the cold entranceway, the little brass bell tinkled as the door closed again—Dmitry Dmitryevich was gone.

"Lyuba, did you hear that? What a scum!"

"That's enough, Vanya. You don't really know Mikhail Vasilyevich. You can't view him as you would a healthy person. Today he lost his temper, but tomorrow he'll think better of it—"

"But why do they put such people in charge? After all, a school is not a poorhouse or a hospital!"

"He's not a bad teacher."

"You're ready to speak up for anyone, Lyuba. What do you want me to do, turn the other cheek like a good Christian? But I'm not his little errand boy. And tomorrow in front of everyone, after he's told them all he's going to kick me out, I'm supposed to crawl in front of him? Hell, I'll show him Kuzkin's mother! I'll pull that ignoramus's nose!"

"Vanya, enough of this. You're being so impulsive. You're not being serious. You have to think this over, not throw yourself headfirst off the bridge. And if you're going to leave the school, you have to think about finding another position. What about the children? Where are we going to find a place for them? You have to think about that, too, a little. We're accustomed to this place; we've put down roots here. And to talk about leaving raises all sorts of questions, starting with where we would live. You haven't even thought about that—"

"I can always find a job."

"Where did you get that idea?"

"I'm telling you, I can."

"No, Vanya, you can't do things this way. What a lot of stuff you've been talking. I beg you not to get so hot under the collar. You're a regular dynamite fuse this evening."

Lyubov Ivanovna kissed her husband's brow. He in turn kissed her small, intelligent hand, which had already ceased to be such a tiny, child-like thing, like a doll's hand, as in earlier days when they used to go for walks in the Sparrow Hills . . .

Around ten in the evening Marya Ivanovna came to see them. It was obvious that she was upset but was holding herself in as much as she could.

"Lyuba, I want to have a word with you?"

"And I with you. I was about to come see you."

"Mikhail Vasilyevich has decided to write to the school administrator tomorrow. Do you know about all this?"

"Yes, I do. And Vanya, too, wants to leave."

"What are we to do?"

"We've got to put the brakes on. What do you think?"

"Yes, I think so too. I've already tried to talk Misha out of it, but he's still simply beside himself. I'll try to talk to him again tomorrow. Right now he's resting. It's so hard on all of us, Lyuba, all this."

Just then through the door could be heard the cheerful singing voice of Ivan Antonych. In a voice shamelessly off key, he was trying to render the roulades of Offenbach's *Beautiful Helen of Troy.*

Three goddesses began to feud
One evening high upon a hill
"Evoë"—they spoke as one—
"Who is the fairest of us all?"

The sisters looked at each other in silence. They smiled. Through the door the singing went on with no letup.

O gods, no doubt you are amused
When our fates go upside down,
When our lives go flying upside, upside down.

Ivan Antonych had switched to another aria. His voice played for a long time with the "upside, upside down," and at last, content with its successes and achievements, fell silent. He came in all revived and cheerful to where the sisters were—with a look on his face as though nothing had happened.

"Ah, you've come to visit, fairest Marie. How beautiful life is. One's very soul sings."

"Do you really find life so beautiful?"

"Indeed."

"You're a very lucky man, Ivan Antonych. I envy you, Lyuba. With him around you'll never be bored."

"Yes, angel of my soul, I am not the boring type. And how, pray tell, is your precious health?"

"Well, it's all right; I can't complain. But I have to be going. My Misha is bedridden again, Ivan Antonych—well, good-bye, Lyuba. Good-bye, Ivan Antonych."

"Sleep well. And may you in your dreams walk tree-lined alleys, smell jasmine, and kiss whoever is dear to you."

"Enough out of you, you joker. Good-bye."

The wise sisters on that occasion warded off the unraveling of fate. But disputes continued, one after another: over the selection of books for the teachers' library, the length of the teachers' pay period, the interpretation of one or another impersonal pronoun or verbal root, or relations with the employees—in a word, there were always incidents or influences enough to start a new conflict. At the school two opposing parties came into existence, with a small "marsh" of neutrals between them. There were deserters to one side or the other, and spies; also incendiaries, and the starters of whispering campaigns, as well as reconnaissance experts, informers, and provocateurs—the whole assortment of individuals and social forces that always, like froth or dross, arise in the process of a real struggle and that grow like topsy when petty squabbling reigns in place of genuine conflict. And there are cases in which squabbling passes over and develops into genuine conflict, and vice versa . . .

Lyubochka finally insisted that Ivan Antonych, as a preventive measure, should find himself another position, against the time when it would become truly unbearable to go on living this way. The search for such a position, to the great surprise of Ivan Antonych, who imagined that his lovable nature would be met with open embraces everywhere, continued for quite a long time. And Ivan Antonych suffered both the piercing of his self-esteem and outright humiliation until at last he received an appointment as an assessor of taxes in the province of Bessarabia.

One fine evening when the children and some of the teachers were playing in the school's little garden, Ivan Antonych suddenly appeared on the porch in a new uniform, sewn with patterns of gold braid, and ceremoniously announced like a deacon from a pulpit: "I'm off to serve the Fatherland."

Farewell to the school, farewell to the garden, farewell to Manya. How glad Kolya was, but he also came very close to crying.

Chapter 3

Bessarabia, where the Petrovs found themselves after a long and difficult journey, presented itself to their eyes in the form, not of the comparatively large and cultured town of Kishinyov, which even non-Muscovites, who had never left their little country lanes such as Bended Knee, Savior of the Sands, or Savior of the Blockheads—even they knew Kishinyov because of Pushkin's adventures there.* No, for the Petrovs, Bessarabia presented itself in the form of the small and dirty county seat of Byeltsy, whose very name rang with cruel irony, for Byeltsy was famous above all for its impassable black mud.† There was a veritable sea of this viscous, sticky stuff flooding even the main street, Church Street, over all its "vast expanse," to the immense satisfaction of entire herds of pigs, who in various poses were enjoying life to the fullest: some were lying up to their ears in the foul-smelling liquid, closing their straw-colored eyelids in sweet languor, only occasionally making a lazy movement of the ear; others were wandering around with playful grunts, shaking the ball-shaped lumps hanging from their tails; still others scratched their backs against a ramshackle palisade fence, squealing voluptuously. In a word, this was truly hog heaven.

The land in and around Byeltsy belonged to extremely wealthy families of landed aristocrats, the Krupensky family and the Kantakuzen princes. They owned virtually entire country districts. The Moldavian peasants, sunburnt, looking like Gypsies, dark, thin, and unkempt, lived a difficult

---

*Aleksandr Pushkin, the first great poet of Russian literature, was exiled by the tsar in 1820–23 to Kishinyov, capital of Bessarabia, which he wrote about in his narrative poem *Tsygane* (Gypsies) and elsewhere.
†In the town's name, the Russian root *Byel-* means "white."

life: maize, watermelons, sunflowers, small fruit orchards were the source of their meager incomes, which were chipped away at from all sides by taxes and other assessments and by rent, which was triply inflated by the "pushy Jewish rental agents," who let the land out to the peasants at ungodly prices. Not just meat but even bread were excluded from the normal diet of the peasant: he had to thank the Lord on High and the powers that be on earth for the one and only national dish of Moldavia, *mamalyga*—a crude porridge made from kernels of maize; it was pressed and squeezed by one's fingers for a long time before being inserted in the mouth. The same kernels were used for other "treats."*

In the midst of the hot, bare steppes were small villages with white huts—and you would also come across entire little hamlets where the Jewish poor lived; these unfortunate paupers, with eyes hollowed out by trachoma, with bodies devoured by fleas, lived on whatever sorry crusts they could get. Working at petty handicrafts or hiring out as horse-cab drivers or engaging in miserable retail trade, in which the entire stock would consist of a few packs of matches, little flasks "for the photogenic," balls of thread, and a few hundred needles, they somehow contrived to exist and at the same time to be fruitful and multiply with extraordinary robustness, although all their starving offspring would run barefoot through the streets covered with scabs, insects, and mud, displaying by their outward appearance how much Jehovah cared for his chosen people. To make up for it, their wealthy and important kinsfolk were prospering: as renters, as greedy, pitiless, and insolent moneylenders, as large-scale merchants and traders, who owned stores in Byeltsy and carriage-renting businesses, goods warehouses, and offices. They had their own fine, clean houses, and their children attended elite schools in Kishinyov or Odessa. They were the keepers of the Covenant, and the places of honor in the synagogues belonged to them. All the other Jews regarded them with God-fearing respect as wise men (*khokhem*) who knew how to make their way in the world and who had been rewarded by the mighty Adonai (the Lord) for their orthodoxy and piety.

Russians in the town of Byeltsy were represented primarily by the officialdom, the chinovniks of all varieties: the police superintendent, the military commander, the officers, the excise duty officials, the treasury officials, the police, the gendarmerie, priests, judges, the warden of the prison, government doctors, and so on—these were all Russians, and usually Russians of a rather specific kind: thick-headed, arrogant, and "patriotic," the

*The author names other Moldavian dishes made from maize, but they have been omitted here.

kind who threw the word *Yid* around contemptuously and scorned the Moldavians, too; the kind who were confirmed thieves, drunkards, and card players, who spent days and nights on end at the green felt tables, with vodka, cognac, packs of cards, chalk to mark down the score, and other accessories of the Russian chinovniks' way of life. "Beat in the Jew's mug" was the patriotic slogan of the Cossack officer, the prison guard, the military commander, and any Russian chinovnik in general. And their children were raised in a corresponding atmosphere, with nasty little ditties always on their lips, such as "*parkhaty**Yid, crucified on a pile of shit." It was considered the proper thing, one's patriotic duty, and an act of daring to make fun of the Jews. The wealthy Jews bought their way out of this—there were many ways of doing so. Therefore they were treated with some consideration; sometimes Russians would even endure their company, spitting distastefully when their backs were turned.

But when it came to the small fry, the lesser folk of the Jewish hamlets—they, in the eyes of the Russian civilizers, occupied a place in the hierarchy of living things much lower than pigs and backyard dogs. This Great Russian caste of chinovniks behaved like some kind of aristocracy, though they had none of the aristocratic virtues, so petty-provincial and miserable everything was among them, including in cultural respects. This environment was like a black sucking swamp, like a dreadful quicksand, which either dragged the new arrival down into its depths, remaking him in its own likeness and image—that is, transforming him into a bribe taker, a drunkard, and a compulsive card player, imbued with patriotism of the police-chinovnik type and the habits of a colonializing cur—or else, sooner or later, it would reject him as an alien to be ostracized, fashioning a web of gossip and slander around his name in order to justify the act of ostracism.

These were the surroundings in which Ivan Antonych Petrov, with his household and household possessions, found himself. The Petrovs settled on the outskirts of the town, at the very end of Church Street, in the little house of the Stanevich family. The master of the house, Ivan Yegorych Stanevich, a Moldavian, was a simple, semi-literate man, who lived on the income from his house and his fairly large orchard. He himself was always digging in the earth—and invariably the flash of his well-worked spade was visible from some part of the orchard: at one moment he would be turning up the earth around the apple or apricot trees, at another he'd be working on straightening up the pathways, at another he'd be digging ditches or putting in new seedlings. He had no hired help, but instead

---

*The word *parkhaty* is an insulting adjective.

from early morning till late in the evening he busied himself in the orchard, repairing the fences, putting braces under tree limbs, whitewashing the walls, putting new shingles on the roof, trimming the bushes and branches with his big gardening clippers. He was a strong, solid old man, well groomed and well knit, wearing a beard black as coal with a sprinkling of salt. His wife, Katerina Ivanovna Stanevich, in outward appearance was the classical type of older Moldavian woman: her big black eyes had been thought of as fiery once, but now they were dimmed and surrounded by yellow-brown, wrinkly skin; her large Roman nose curved down toward a sharply pointed chin; around her thin old neck two folds of skin stretched out like wattles. In fact, in her entirety—skinny, lean, and wrinkled—she resembled nothing so much as a turkey well on in years. She was forever smoking *papirosy** in the rough and ready way of an inveterate tobacco hound. Her powerful native intelligence and considerable experience of life really set her apart. It was not Ivan Yegorych, but Katerina Ivanovna who wore the pants in the Stanevich family.

They had three grown-up children. The sons had finished secondary school. Pavel Ivanovich, the elder, was a handsome man with black eyes and strikingly regular features, who wore a luxuriant beard and a thick beaver hat; he worked in Kishinyov as a teacher at the local *gimnaziya*. Vasily Ivanovich, the younger son, worked in Byeltsy for the treasury office. He too was a handsome man, not crushingly so, but in a fashionable, hairdresser's kind of way. There was something of the butterfly in everything about him: his dark, curly, always pomaded and carefully styled hair; his neatly trimmed and parted beard, brushed smoothly to either side; his fancily tied bow tie; and even the way he walked, all aflutter like a true Papillon. Their sister, Yelizaveta Ivanovna, a marriageable young woman with burning, fiery eyes, would have been beautiful if not for her exceptionally prominent, aquiline nose, which added a somewhat too masculine touch to the subtle, exquisite features of her face. She was tall, lithe, and shapely, a slender young palm tree. Aside from her overlong nose she had one other defect, which gave her no end of worry: an overpoweringly strong body odor. The poor young woman tried in every way to dispel it with perfume, and she constantly perfumed herself, to the point of distraction: in front of the mirror in her little room stood an entire array of little flasks and bottles, and at any moment she might resort to the most varied aromas in an attempt to drown out her own scent, which caused her no little torment. The younger Staneviches were a modest and soft-spoken crowd. To be sure, it was said that Pavel Ivanovich had a weakness for

---

*The Russian type of cigarette with a cardboard mouthpiece.

drink. But he lived in Kishinyov, and besides there's always some kind of gossip!

In general the Petrovs had no grounds for complaint about their land-lords, and very good relations were established between the Petrovs and the Staneviches from the start.

For the children—for Kolya and Volodya—the main thing was the orchard and garden. Spreading out around the town were steppelands, corn fields, hills, and salt flats. No woods at all, not even clumps of trees. But the orchard was rather large, and most important, nearly all the trees in it were new, not the kind found in Moscow or Makarovo. Here there grew apricot, peach, cherry, and plum trees. The white acacias were huge with their heavy, gnarled, and wrinkled trunks; and then there were the luxuriant evergreen thuja trees with their thickly spread mass of resinous, aromatic twigs and branches. And there were ash trees and beeches. And entire thickets of rose bushes, from whose flowers people made jam and sherbet, the favorite treat in Bessarabia, something unknown in Moscow. And beyond the fences—a neighboring vineyard, where fragrant, luscious grapes were ripening.

All this was strange and new, as was the world of animals—birds, insects, mammals. In the orchard itself, where Kolya had soon climbed over or around all the trees, bushes, paths, and fences, he discovered incal-culable riches, such as one could only dream about in Moscow. Those round holes in the ground, carefully covered on the sides with spiderwebs, were the homes of poisonous tarantulas. The tarantulas could be flooded out of their holes with water, but there was another way to catch them: with a ball of wax tied to a string. The ball was lowered into the hole, and the tarantula, when jostled by the wax, would bite into it with powerful jaws; then you would reel it in like a fish from the river . . .

Ever so quietly Kolya would steal up to his mother's dresser, slide the drawer open, and gnaw bits of wax off his mother's wedding candles, kept there as mementos, along with waxen *fleurs d'orange*. Who would have thought these reliquaries would end up being used to catch the dreadful poisonous spiders of Bessarabia?

There were other holes, steep ones—black field crickets of a kind that didn't exist in the Moscow region. It took a long time to track them down and wait for them to come out of their holes, and, holding his breath, Kolya waited for that favorable moment, at which time he would quickly block the entrance with his hand.

On the fat-leaved lilac bushes, grown thickly together, sat green beetles that gave off a distinct odor—the Spanish fly.

On a blackened old fence, covered by a colorful mosaic of tiny mosses, a huge nocturnal butterfly had tried to hide itself. This was the largest butterfly or moth in Europe, a kind of saturnia, shaggy and mysterious-looking, with a nocturnal eye like that of a peacock and a wing span like that of a flying squirrel.

In a tall tree, a walnut, the covers of whose fruits smelled of iodine and made one's hands turn black, a shrike had built its nest, and the boy had climbed like a monkey to that dizzying height: there was a place where, for a second—just one second—he had to support himself with the sole of his shoe against a barely noticeable little bump on the bare tree trunk in order to reach up and catch the next branch. If he had slipped it would have been good-bye cruel world! But Kolya made it: he knew all those acrobatic tricks so well. A shiver had passed over his scalp for a moment, but no matter; it all worked out!

High in the sky golden bee-eaters circled. Crawling on the lilac flowers were huge red-headed wasps, twice the size of hornets. In the evenings you could hear the buzzing and humming of beetles and the sound of them knocking against the walls of the terrace: rhinoceros beetles, reindeer beetles, copras. There were so many you couldn't list them all. It took Kolya's breath away, this new world where everything was so much bigger, brighter, more colorful than in far, far distant Moscow . . .

In another respect the Petrov boys found themselves in a situation totally new to them. In Moscow they had lived like hothouse plants, closely watched over and attended to—they never went anywhere outside the school garden by themselves. They were well mannered, obedient, properly brought up "model children." How surprised the Staneviches were, both young and old, that Kolya and Volodya, amid the abundance of fruits of the earth sprouting forth in the orchard, never picked a single cherry or plum or even a lovely, juicy peach! No temptations could break down these children's goodness and decency. But alas! All this eventually evaporated: in Byeltsy the children found themselves in the street, which, like the new acquaintances they made, had its own special brand of morality, a code of derring-do and mischief, and its own kind of educational process. Still, the change in the boys' behavior did not happen overnight.

At first, Lyubov Ivanovna decided to take a hand in Kolya's training and education on a regular basis. She even had the idea of giving him religious instruction, based on the notion that "that's how things should be." She herself was not particularly religious, although she protested against her husband's constant anti-religious jibes. One fine day a number of newly purchased booklets appeared, beginning with "The Holy Story," which had entertaining pictures that captured Kolya's imagination: an angel with a sword driving Adam and Eve out of Paradise; Noah's Ark breasting the stormy waves in the midst of the Great Flood; the splendid Joseph being sold into slavery by his brothers; the prophet Jonah being swallowed by an enormous whale; poor, unfortunate Job sitting in nothing but rags with his arms outstretched to Heaven; the tiny Moses lying in a basket among the reeds on the River Nile. Many other interesting pictures and stories were in this book. His mother began giving Kolya lessons, making him first read a prayer in preparation for his studies: "O Lord most merciful . . ." But that was as far as the virtuous undertaking went. It turned out that Lyubov Ivanovna was pregnant. Ivan Antonych, while slicing the bread, would intone:

"You have a swelling, a *gorbúshka.*"

"You'll soon have a son—Andryushka."

And sure enough Andryushka appeared in the world, with a wail and a howl, which was no small surprise to Kolya, who began to wonder about his parents' gift of prophecy. New cares and worries came to preoccupy the young mother, and the children found themselves at liberty, completely free of restrictions: a boundless freedom, new friends, the streets, the fields, the orchards, new games and adventures burst into their lives and transformed them in an entirely new way.

Next to the Staneviches' house was the house of the widow of a Moldavian priest, Ciorescu. She was a big, burly, black-browed, black-eyed woman, and she walked as though her greatly enlarged belly was constantly getting in her way. She was extraordinarily good-natured, extraordinarily illiterate, and extraordinarily hard-working. She kept a little orchard, received a pension, sold apples, gooseberries, and pears, and was taking care as well as she knew how, that is, wasn't taking care at all, of her two children: Volodya, whom the Petrovs dubbed "Volodya Sosedsky" (the neighbor's Volodya); and little Tanya, with her small black eyes and eternally dripping nose, which she never stopped wiping with her tiny little, always dirty hands. Volodya Sosedsky was two years older than Kolya Petrov but was just barely beginning to read letter by letter, and Kolya felt, inwardly, terribly triumphant when a reading contest was organized one day. He read a little story in a masterful way, swiftly and with expression. But Volodya Sosedsky, to whose lot fell Tolstoy's "The Shark," stuttering and stumbling with every step, sounded it out, virtually letter by letter: "Our sh-shi-ip—Our ship—sa-ai-sai-il-led—sailed—by—the—sh-sho-or-ore—by the shore." At once Kolya's authority rose tremendously among all the neighborhood "brethren" . . .

A Jewish boy named Levka proved to be another good friend. He was thin, red-headed, and freckled, very lively and spry. The Petrov boys were drawn to him right away, and he enriched their store of knowledge with amazing tricks. He could turn his eyelids inside out. These turned-out eyelids were bright red, like blood; he would run around with them like that, frightening all the children. He knew how to make peculiar guttural sounds, a skill he quickly taught Kolya and Volodya. They mastered this art to perfection despite the protests of their mother, who called them "idiotic noises"—but her authority as a mother had nearly disappeared. Levka knew how to pass a string up his nose, then spit the end out of his mouth, and "saw" it back and forth. He also could swallow spent bullets, which he found near the town's military barracks. Like him, the Petrov boys would "saw" through their noses and swallow bullets. Then they would watch carefully to see when the bullets came out, checking their feces, and rejoiced when a bullet reappeared in the world, having completed its cycle as it was supposed to. In a word, Levka was an all-around expert.

Another boy also held a leading place in the crowd of neighborhood kids—Vanka Nesterov, the son of a Russian carpenter, who was well informed on the occult secrets that were grouped under the general heading "where children come from."

Finally, there were two other girls who were close neighbors, the two daughters of a "rural dean": Sanya, who had big, blue eyes that looked out on the world with surprise, and her older sister Lena, who because of her age didn't really fit in with the children. Sanya's beautiful, yearning eyes always seemed to have a sty on them, but to Kolya Petrov it seemed that these sties made the thoughtful face of this quiet, affectionate girl even lovelier than ever.

Kolya and Volodya spent almost all their time in the orchard or on the streets. Kolya was quick and agile, had gaps between his teeth, and played the boss, gave the orders, and urged his younger brother on. Volodya, with his large, honest, innocent eyes, was ready to do anything for his brother.

"Volodka, quick! Run and get some water! We're gonna flood the gopher out of its hole! Hurry!"

"Here I go!"

Rushing and tripping, Volodya ran to get the water.

"What, you only brought half a bucket?!"

"Sorry, Kolya, I'll get another."

Once again Volodya compliantly ran for more water and got back in time to see the poor little gopher, completely soaked, trembling all over, its tiny body shivering and shaking, looking like a wet rat. A discussion started on whether the little creature might have some disease, and how to disinfect it.

"Volodka, bring a box!"

"Right away!"

Kolya remained at his post keeping watch: although he by no means shied away from dirty work and knew better than anyone else how to track down and catch all the interesting creatures; still, when a complex operation was being carried out, the supervisory functions fell to him, and Volodya, touchingly naive, would invariably subordinate himself to his older brother.

And thus the time went by, day after day, month after month. When the heavily perfumed clusters of white acacia flowers were blooming, all the kids in the neighborhood could be found sitting up in the trees like flocks of monkeys, furiously devouring the flowers. Where had all their good behavior gone? From the apricot and cherry trees, the boys would take bits of gum in their teeth, right off the bark, and spend entire days chewing it; it was dark-red and hard, or yellow and amberlike, and hung in frozen drops like wax from a candle; after a rain it would be all soaked and watery, having no taste—Kolya tried it all out with his own teeth. Nor was he averse to feasting on cherries or knocking down an enormous, dark-blue pear, with a touch of bluish gray on it, peeking out from among the curling green leaves, or shaking an apricot tree to bring down some of that ripe, sweet, sugary fruit, whose pits could, besides, be made into excellent whistles.

As for the gooseberries, my Lord! They weren't even given a chance to ripen: no sooner had the sour little beads of berries begun to swell where the flowers had been than the kids pounced on them, despite all the shouts and warnings of the grown-ups; they fell upon them like voracious locusts and picked the bushes clean. And how many tiny displays of cunning there were: when a big branch on an apricot tree was unintentionally broken it was immediately tied back in place, then the wound and its bandage were smeared with dirt, so that all outward signs of the crime were obliterated— go ahead, take a look, find it if you can!

Children, like grown-ups, have their superstitions, prejudices, heartfelt dreams, ideals, and unforgettable incidents in life, which are stored in the memory forever and which suddenly, at terrible or tragic moments in life, come swimming into consciousness, surprisingly vivid, in full detail, down to the wrinkles in somebody's face or a spider's web illuminated by the evening sun. The world of childhood is vast and multifarious. But with every day it grows bigger; the naive eyes of the child are wide open to everything; and little souls devour with tremendous avidity all the colors and sounds, the light and the shade, and all new forms and objects as they make their way into the secret caverns of existence or stroll through its sunlit meadows and woods.

Kolya, too, had his own special little dream, an ideal, a guiding star. It was the mystery-shrouded "fire butterfly." It was not listed in any atlas. It had neither a Russian nor a Latin name. The entomologists did not know it. But it was the point of concentration for all his childhood dreams. It was his equivalent of the Firebird, a thing of Paradise, unattainable but always desired, almost like Maeterlinck's fantastical Bluebird. And the most amazing thing was that Kolya actually saw it several times. One day it fluttered by quite close, and skimming along smoothly on its fiery red wings, like a mysterious apparition, it disappeared behind the black shingles of the neighbors' rooftop. Choking with excitement, Kolya ran home, shouting like a madman:

"Papa, papa! I saw a fire butterfly!"

And a flood of stories poured out . . .

But they never managed to catch the fire butterfly

There were other marvels to make up for it.

Once Kolya was sweeping the palisade fence with his eyes to see if some rare nocturnal butterflies might not have chosen to rest for the day in the shadowed chinks of its wood. Suddenly he heard the song of a bird, an unfamiliar "Pah-prrooh, pah-prrooh." He froze. His heart pounded. Varicolored, fiery circles began to swim before his eyes. What could it be? Silvery, opalescent wings gleamed. They were flashing tremulously from the dense webs of foliage in the giant white acacia trees. They were strange and mysterious, like the wings of a seraphim. How many times in his dreams had Kolya seen rose-colored flamingos flying across a dark-blue sky or heard miraculous French horns sounding from the bright blue abyss of heaven . . . And now something magical had suddenly descended on its wings in reality, in his waking state. And it was somewhere there, just within reach. Again the peculiar sound was heard . . . Fascinated and bewitched, Kolya, like a lunatic in a trance, made his way along the side of the fence, stepping cautiously in the direction of the sound. Wasn't it really some kind of miracle? All his thoughts ran together in his head, thousands of them. What kind of bird could this be? How could this happen, that it came to be there? Why, no one would believe it! Was he just having a dream? Kolya wanted to pinch himself, but both hands were occupied: though drenched with sweat they firmly clung to a mass of soft feathers—and no force on earth could have torn those tightly clenched fingers from the miracle bird!

The secret was quickly explained: somewhere on the other side of town there was a bird fancier whose Egyptian dove had flown away from home. It was almost tame enough to sit on your hand, and thus had fallen into the clutches of our little rascal. Nevertheless, the memory of what the young boy experienced, the sweet perturbations of the heart, the unusual nature of the event—all that lived on.

Another time, among the wide variety of plunder Kolya brought home—mole crickets, black field crickets, rhinoceros beetles, and other things—he dragged in a big green caterpillar with red stripes and a gold horn at the end of its tail. This was a joy known only to a few—it was the caterpillar stage of a "death's head," a marvelous huge moth with a golden skull on its back, the only moth or butterfly that makes a sound, the king of all our European moths and butterflies! How many conversations, hopes, and expectations ensued! The expectations were long in being realized: the death's-head cocoon had to lie there for two whole years before a strong, slender butterfly would come fluttering out of it, a butterfly that robbed beehives. Like the legendary Egyptian thief, it stole into the pyramids of the bees to steal the tasty treasure of their kingdom! They fed the caterpillar potato leaves, as was suggested, put soil in a box, and placed it there with all "the comforts of home." And soon, within a few weeks, a large, brown cocoon, the color of the gum from the cherry tree, was lying there. When incautious fingers touched it, it would move, but Kolya would turn into a regular wild beast if he saw some "fool of a boy" or girl display excessive curiosity and disturb his precious possession.

The little box with the cocoon stood like a small silver shrine in a monastery where the remains of a saint were preserved. In general Kolya defended most fiercely that part of the glassed-in porch where he had a genuine temple of zoology, a holy Ark of the Covenant, the key to which he invariably kept in his right-hand trousers pocket. The only thing missing was a sign saying *Eingang verboten!* (Keep out!) But even without this, everyone knew how zealously Kolya protected the dwelling place of his deity, and to avoid tears, reproaches, and terrible scenes, they stayed away from his sanctum sanctorum. And what didn't Kolya have there! Cages hung with the various birds he had caught with his own traps and snares. Jars with tarantulas who tended to devour one another, so that there emanated from the uneaten parts of the corpses a repulsively nauseating odor. In larger jars, where preserves had been kept and which he had obtained from the kitchen, he kept those entertaining creatures, the mole crickets, which made intricate passageways in the soil, digging with their strong and spadelike front legs; in the evenings they would make a muffled chirring sound, similar to that of the goatsucker bird in its springtime mating area. The enormous green "blacksmith beetles" crawled slowly on the window frames and among the flowers, moving their long thin whiskers with wise determination, as though feeling their way in the world, testing their path, considering, reflecting . . .

This whole zoo was constantly being replenished. And it had an affiliated subdivision out in the yard: huge boxes in which there sat a merlin, and next to it the Egyptian dove, and then some "little owls" (*Athene woc-*

tua), and other feathered creatures. Cats were the enemy. The Petrov children hated them and were ruthless toward them, showing no mercy: they were considered personal enemies.

Sometimes the merlin would jump out of its box and, dragging its broken wing behind it, would hop about the yard and for some reason jump on the back of the beautiful, peaceful peacock. This would send the peacock flying about in terror, bearing its strange rider on its back . . .

One morning Kolya was wakened by cries: "Kolya, Kolya! How awful! How wonderful! Oh God! Oh, damn!" There in the hallway stood the elderly nurse holding something in her hand that was still alive though pierced through with a needle—the death's-head! Kolya rushed to where the cocoon was: the door was open, the cocoon was empty, all that remained of it was a shell. It was a good thing that the pollen on the moth's wings had not been rubbed off. The moth was carefully hidden away, and during the night it was necessary to put it to sleep with ether: it squeaked in its tiny voice, beat its wings, and for a long time refused to die. Kolya came close to crying. There was nothing to be done, though, for otherwise all its beauty would have been lost. The next morning Kolya printed out a letter to his grandmother: "Dear grandmother! Come visit us. I have a death's-head. Kolya."

That's how the swiftly flowing time went by. After an entire day, when the children had been roaming around in every corner of the orchard, after playing Cossacks and robbers and other games, the exhausted children would sit on the steps with Ivan Yegorych or their father or Katerina Ivanovna. The black shapes of the giant walnut trees were sharply etched against the clear sky at sunset. On a dry branch at the very top of one of the trees a screech owl suddenly appeared and soon emitted its piercing cry: couk-vau, couk-vau. A line from a poem, "Owls in the valley were calling back and forth," swam into Kolya's consciousness. The moon rose and the stars appeared. Lights went on in the house. Lyubov Ivanovna could be heard washing the baby's bottle—a device produced by the Sokhlet company for feeding a new infant. Large beetles bumped against the windows. The weary youngsters went to bed and in their dreams saw butterflies of fire, imaginary birds, and enormously fascinating books; thousands of other innocent eyes caressed their souls with their enchantments . . .

But, alas, the boys were soon fated to taste the fruit of the tree of knowledge of good and evil, the same tree on which long ago a perch had been found by the biblical serpent, the one who succeeded so well in tempting Eve, that innocent ancestress of us all. The serpent took the form of Vanka Nesterov, who one day initiated the boys into the secret of human reproduction, with all the details. Volodya took it with indifference. But Kolya really flew into a rage. He held out for a long time, arguing that maybe things worked that way with other people, but the idea that his mama and papa engaged in anything like that—well, other people could believe what they wanted, but as for him, he knew it wasn't possible. And yet the worm of doubt gnawed at his soul. For a while he wanted to put the question squarely to his parents, but he couldn't bring himself to do it. Later he started remembering that during Bible story lessons his mother had been very clumsy in trying to explain what in fact that commandment meant which said: "Thou shalt not commit adultery." And what kind of nonsense was written in the Scriptures where it tells the husband to cleave unto his wife and let their twin flesh become one. He knew the words perfectly well but never understood their hidden meaning. Hadn't this meaning, filthy and frightening as it was, been revealed in the explanations given by Vanka Nesterov? And why wouldn't it be so, when Vanka claimed that he himself had seen these foul things going on in his own family, talking about his own father and mother? Besides, even dogs, for example, mate or breed or whatever you call it. After all, their own dog Byelka . . .

Bewilderment and suspicion grew like a rolling ball of snow. Kolya began to be always on the alert. And then there occurred a scene that was really remarkable in its way. It was late in the evening. The doors to his parents' bedroom were open. Kolya and Volodya were lying side by side in their room. They couldn't sleep. Hundreds of thoughts and images were astir in their minds, buzzing around in their heads like a swarm of mosquitoes on a quiet summer night. Silence. Then suddenly in the midst of this silence Volodya's little voice could be heard:

"Hey Papa, you know, Vanka Nesterov told us that Stepan loves with (*lyubaetsa*) the girls."

"Not 'loves with' (*lyubaetsa*) but 'fucks with' (*yubaetsa*)," Kolya corrected him, then lay there shivering, waiting for an answer. The question had been posed point-blank.

In his parents' bedroom there was dead silence. Followed by some barely audible whispering.

"Aha!" thought Kolya. "You fell into the trap, my turtledoves. That means it's all true! That means you do it, too! And it means you've been fooling us all this time. Well, what the—think I'm gonna believe you anymore? Just wait and see!"

After that Kolya placed all grown-ups under suspicion. He watched their every move. He was suspicious of them even when there was nothing to be suspicious about.

One day his mother said something to her husband offhandedly, *en passant*:

"Say, Vanya, did you know that in a few days Aunt Sonya is having her jubilee?"

"Is that right?"

"Why yes—on Tuesday."

"Mama, what is *jubilee*?"*

For some reason Lyubov Ivanovna let Kolya's question slip past unheard.

"Aha!" the boy decided. "We know what it is."

Another time Lyubov Ivanovna came under even worse suspicion. She was washing her face and brushing her teeth. Kolya noticed there was blood coming from her gums: her toothbrush had a touch of blood on it.

"Mama, why is there blood on your toothbrush?"

His mother said nothing.

"Aha!" Kolya decided. "We're wise to you! Of course you're bleeding if you—"

At that time Kolya of course had not heard of Freud. But he began diligently constructing entire theories, of the most fantastic kind, in the spirit of those children's notions about sex that the fashionable founder of psychoanalysis has reported to the world in such detail . . .

At any rate, all trust in grown-ups, including his parents, had been undermined once and for all. Besides, Kolya felt especially offended by his parents because they, his loved ones whom he had trusted in all things, had practiced deception so basely, so unscrupulously. His feeling of insult at their hands and his disillusionment with them were experienced with special pain and strong emotion which hid itself in the deepest, the bottommost level of his soul. Kolya did not understand how his friends—Vanka, Volodya Sosedsky, Levka, and others—could take such an indifferent attitude toward all this, even treat it with laughter.

Only later did he himself begin to feel interested in these things and begin to listen with curiosity to all sorts of stories on the subject, stories not distinguished by either indifference or chasteness of spirit. Gradually these stories drew him into that very special world. He even stopped getting into fights when the boys would tease him with off-color ditties, such as:

Kolya, Kolya, Nikolai
Took a girl into a barn up high,
Poked and poked but got nowhere
Spent ten kopecks—on air.

*The word "jubilee" in Russian is *yubilei*, which Kolya mistakenly connects with the vulgar verb *yubat*, or *yebat* ("to fuck").

Or other products of the bad-boy oral tradition. He began to avoid any contact with those terrible creatures called "girls." To deal with them seemed somehow shameful and embarrassing. He ceased to view them in a simple, straightforward way. His soul had been poisoned by this street-smart sexual enlightenment. But he kept all this—all his questions, doubts, wonderings, guesses, and theories—as a deep, dark secret from anybody else. He buttoned up all the buttons of his soul in this department and, with animal cunning, avoided any reference to the subject on the part of the grown-ups. Sometimes it all seemed to him a savage night-mare, a terrible dream. He remembered Moscow, remembered Manya, remembered how they had played together, what pure, simple, good rela-tions there had been. What would Manya think if she knew what he, Kolya, was carrying around now in his heart? Dear, sweet Manya! Where are you? How good things were then . . . And Kolya saw before him the sad, sweet eyes of his childhood friend.

Chapter 4

Ivan Antonych's civil service career was drab, depressing, and without prospects; in general it fit him like a saddle on a cow; the specific circumstances of this remote borderland region, and the stifling, corrupt world of provincial officialdom went against his grain; he often felt nauseated by the intrigues, the backstabbing, the bribe taking, the very physiognomies of his "colleagues," the craftiness and stupidity, the bowing and smiling and servility. There was no way he could get into his head the subtle philistine wisdom lodged in the old Russian saying, "If you live with wolves, then howl like a wolf." The nature of his work was such that he had to see to the payment of taxes and duties, commercial documents and certificates, compile reports to the Department of Revenue, and file charges. With his complete lack of talent as an administrator, his gentle personality and humane sociability, no effort was required for others to wrap him around their finger. He feared this like the plague and therefore often adopted the pose of the stern, unbending official. But this pose would dissipate in a moment, like smoke. His honesty and uprightness quickly became common knowledge. No one offered him bribes—they couldn't bring themselves to try. Among themselves, the other officials made fun of him, viewing him as something in the nature of a *yurodivy* (a holy simpleton) or just a plain fool. However, they did not resort openly to this latter formulation out of their inner respect for Moscow and for his university education: for these people Moscow was an intimidating source of power, a force to reckon with, and a university diploma was something akin to a rank in the civil service, an honorary title or order, which inspired involuntary respect. They couldn't bring themselves to insult Ivan Antonych in public—say, at the club or while a guest at someone's home. His mocking tongue was already famous and it was dangerous to cross swords with him in that arena; if luck was not with you, he would plant an epithet on you that you couldn't wash off no matter how much eau de Cologne you used. So people were cautious with him; they stayed on their toes in his company.

Periodically certain people came to see Ivan Antonych on business—so-called commercial intermediaries, advocates for the owners of stores or businesses that had been shut down, representatives of the commercial caste. They usually came in a group: Raful, a Jewish elder, wearing his Orthodox *peisy** and a large, uncombed beard, gray and greasy; his red eyes, forever watering, were wasting away, and his eyelids, stricken by trachoma, were shot to pieces; swollen, dark-blue veins stood out on his skinny arms; his gaunt body, in a long, soiled gaberdine, always seemed to be trembling from the weakness and infirmity of age; his scratchy voice seemed to know how to hit only two notes: pathos and supplication. But to a large extent this was a pose developed over decades of subservience to the flock of carrion crows—the chinovniks. On the Jewish streets Raful was considered a *khokhem*, a man of authority, whose counsel was listened to even by the very wealthy Jews. They gave him the respect they felt was due his experience of life and his tenacity, and because of the penetrating, insinuating mind of this old man, who in outward appearance was feeble and pathetic. With Raful there usually came a man named Schneiersohn, a solid man whose nose had been almost completely eaten away by syphilis; all that remained of it were some pink lumps full of holes that seemed to have been tied into one awful knot; his whole face was covered with a network of tiny red veins; he was constantly blowing his nose, giving off a foul smell from the depths of his ailing nasopharyngeal regions, a smell that even garlic could not overcome; Schneiersohn always spoke much more firmly and confidently than Raful; he didn't have to hunt for words and didn't have the beaten down look Raful had. However, this squarely built, self-confident man did not by any means enjoy the same confidence among his own people as the soft-spoken Raful. A man named Pinkhensohn would also come, dressed in the Jewish fashion in a jacket, collar, and tie, but he usually limited himself to brief or passing remarks.

The Russian trader Ryabinin bore himself apart. His face was strikingly similar to the Old Believers' archpriest Avvakum or Nikita Pustosvyat: a hawk's beak; cold, piercing eyes that for some reason looked yellow, which would stare without blinking at his interlocutor; an ascetic, pockmarked, almost pitted face; skinny hands, reminiscent of digging hooks; a soft step,

---

*Peisy are long curled or braided sideburns, which have religious significance, worn by certain Jewish groups, such as the Hasidim.

"pantherlike," like that attributed in medieval epics to Svyatoslav; his long caftan in the old Russian style, the kind that was dear to the hearts of the Old Believers—indeed, Ryabinin was one of those Old Believers. They knew how to make their way in business, and in them the virtues of ancient piety were an expression of miserliness in commercial dealings, moneygrubbing, and acquisitiveness, as with the pious Protestants of Western Europe or the heroes of Moscow's Rogozhskoye Cemetery, the center of Old Believers' commercial capitalism. Ryabinin represented the Russian faction among the trade delegation: he frequently came with his Jewish colleagues but kept himself apart; he liked to enter separately from the back porch, demonstratively underlining his special position, as if to say, "Please don't confuse me with those others, the Jews."

Ivan Antonych was probably the only one of the Russian chinovniks in Byeltsy who spoke with the Jewish representatives in a humane way and did not show any favoritism toward the Russian element. In Ivan Antonych's family there was absolutely none of that repulsive nationalistic gutter talk that declined the nouns *Jew*, *Jewess*, and *Jew-child* in all the cases of the Russian language. And this very circumstance created a peculiar atmosphere around Ivan Antonych. It was said behind his back that he "pampered the Jews" or was a "Jew lover." And in his presence condescending smiles appeared, as if to say, "We know your weakness—but what's to be done? It can't be helped." He was regarded as a defective person, not all there, one who didn't quite measure up from the point of view of that full-blooded patriotism which saw the trampling of "aliens" as the honor and glory of the Russian Empire. Actually, the souls of the chinovniks did not rise to such abstract heights. With them everything was really much simpler, more elementary and crude. Sycophantic in relation to their superiors, the chinovniks were able to feel themselves masters of the situation mainly in relation to "outsiders," and they took pleasure in this. In relation to the Jews, they had *carte blanche*; the Jews were simply objects that had been turned over to them, the chinovniks, for wholesale pillaging, much as "property" was defined under Roman law—*jus utendi et abutendi*.*

A Jew could be pulled by the beard; he could be beaten; he could be insulted and made a mockery of; bribes could be taken from him—and you could get away scot-free with all these things. If there was any protest, it was easy to find as many witnesses as desired who would swear under oath that "the Yid" was completely in the wrong: after all, they would say, it's no accident it was the Jews who killed Christ . . .

*"The right to use or abuse" (as the owner wishes).

The interests involved in such cases were banal and petty, and stank to high heaven. Any event might take place in the world, kingdoms collapse, crowns fly from royal heads, great discoveries be made, heroic feats accomplished. All this went unnoticed past the green felt card table—the focal point, the point of intersection for all the ideals, aspirations, heartfelt dreams, and lustful desires of the local chinovniks. "To have a go with the cards," "to play a little vint," "to throw down a glass of something," "to have a little snort with something to snack on"—such phrases seemed to exhaust nearly all spiritual needs and requirements.

The cream of Byeltsy officialdom consisted of such people. In their front ranks was the military commander Vasily Semyonovich Petushkov. Small, pot-bellied, and barely fitting into his uniform, which, despite all the tailor's craft and art, failed to conceal the comical corporeality of his figure, Petushkov was so much like Krylov's frog who saw the bullock that it was laughable.*

Whether he was walking or sitting at a card table or commanding soldiers or strolling on the boulevard hand in hand with his wife, whether he was sober, drunk, or just a little tipsy—it didn't matter; he constantly puffed himself up, strutted about, and tried to look important, which only made his neck become an apoplectic red and his hefty wattles turn as purple as any good Ukrainian beet root. On top of all that he had a thin, squeaky little voice that was shrill and hoarse at the same time, as unpleasant a sound as a naughty boy scraping glass with a fork. He was nothing but a belly on short, little legs, stuffed into a uniform, with a sword at his side, plus a red face and angry, malicious gray eyes. This arrogant, puffed-up belly saw the essence of creation in a glass of "macao" or "cognac, yes, you know, with a lemon twist." His wife was half again as tall as this warlike hero. Her frame, the immense rounded forms of her body, would press and spring, at any point on her mighty torso, against the unfortunate outer shell of her clothing, which seemed to groan under the pressure of this unrestrainedly expanding flesh. When Petushkov would stroll pompously, hand in hand with his other half, along the walkways of Byeltsy's sorry little boulevard, planted with ash trees and rose acacia, he looked like nothing more than a uniformed accessory to this grand dame's *toilette*. She strode along like an ever-so-fertile Cybele, the Phrygian mother of the gods, with hips and thighs whose very dimensions were testimony to a higher race of being. Nevertheless, this highly respected family had produced no offspring, although whose fault that was remained unknown.

*In Krylov's fable the frog puffed itself up, trying to look as big and strong as the bullock.

Petushkov was especially close friends with Colonel Korshunov, a drunkard, brawler, and lover of fisticuffs. This Korshunov "beat in the mugs" not only of Jews but of his soldiers as well, and he had the reputation of a desperado when it came to cusswords. From the drill field outside of town his loud and thundering use of foul language even reached the ears of those in the Staneviches' home. His presence was feared in mixed company. For his own part, he obviously felt that his swashbuckling, barbaric rudeness gave him some kind of originality, setting him apart from the general mediocrity around him, and he took pride in his unbridled soldier's gruffness, making very much a point of it. He was a tall man, with a face that looked like it was shaped by an axe, reminiscent of ancient idols carved from wood. In the middle of his face stood a meaty, reddish-violet nose; his eyebrows stuck out like rumpled, bushy feathers; and the graying red hair of his mustache concealed a mouth from which wafted the foul fumes of sour wine and tobacco.

He regarded his chubby little friend and colleague Petushkov half contemptuously, half protectively. When it came to Petushkov's spouse, however, he was transformed; he would gallantly click his heels together, so that his spurs rang, and bend with agility to kiss her hand, invariably receiving in reply a kiss on one of his short sideburns, which were as thick and well-clipped as the brushes used to clean lamps. Korshunov, a regular visitor at the local house of prostitution and a notorious debaucher, thought about women generally in the most vulgar terms, and on this point the worthy colonel's thinking was strikingly similar to that of his orderly, Ivan. Looking at Madame Petushkova, he would think: "Yeah . . . There she is like a hen with her rooster . . . A regular butterfly in her prime . . . Yeah, there's something you can get hold of . . ."

His imagination went no farther than these thoughts about "her prime" and "something to get hold of." But one could by no means draw the conclusion that the worthy colonel never went any farther than kissing her hand. Not by any means could he be numbered among the purely Platonic natures and anemic romantics of the type with "beautiful souls." As a military man he was accustomed to taking fortresses by storm and he was very good at doing so, especially since in this provincial hen's kingdom the choice of roosters was not very large. At any rate, Korshunov's measurements were much more in keeping with those of Madame Petushkova than those of her lawful micro-spouse.

"Basil! Oh, Basil!" the madame addressed her spouse using the French equivalent of Vasily.

"What, darling?"

"Why is it that the colonel hasn't been seen among us for so long?"

"What do you mean? I just saw him today down at the club."

"Basil!"

"What's up, little gal?"

"You should at least have invited some guests over. You're always saying, 'At the club this' and 'At the club that.' While I—"

"What guests am I supposed to invite?"

"Why, all of them—"

"Who's all of them?"

"Well, there's Korshunov."

"Hmm—okay. Who else?"

"Khinkulov . . . Well, whoever you know, invite them—"

"For tomorrow?"

"Yes, tomorrow, why not? Otherwise it's so-o bo-o-oring! Lord God!"

"Okay. But you take care to look after the cards, the *balyk*,* the cognac, and all that. You're the past master with that stuff, as I see it."

In the evening Petushkov comes up to Korshunov, who, without his uniform coat on, with a billiard cue in his hand and chalk dust all over him, has his whole huge body stretched out so that he is practically lying across the billiard table. He has one leg sticking out behind him and he's trying to sink a double in the middle pocket. He still has some command of the language, but not by far the gift of a Cicero. As for the steadiness of his hand, the systematic lubrication of the spirit, which always got him into such a rage and dredged up such unheard-of expletives, suggested that the colonel was fairly overburdened with strong drink.

"Hello, Colonel—"

"Hmm—my pleasure—wait a minute—I'm just—double in the center pocket! . . . Oh, damn! Missed again! Why are you talking to me, moving my arm? Vasily Semyonych—what the hell?"

"Pardon me, Colonel. I had a personal message from my wife."

"Oh. At your service!"

"To tell the truth, she just can't live without you."

"Get along with you, Vasily Semyonych."

Korshunov is obviously embarrassed. He's afraid someone's going to pull a dirty trick on him: might there not be serious content behind this joking conversation, and with serious consequences? But what the hell! What jokes the Devil plays. Here today, gone tomorrow. Let the loser weep, Korshunov thinks to himself. Where's that from? Oh yeah, some opera—three cards—three cards—

Nevertheless, no serious conversation ensued.

*Cured fillet of sturgeon.

"The wife asks you to visit us tomorrow."

"With pleasure."

"You know how it is. We'll have a go at the cards. We'll have a drink and something to snack on. Everything'll get better somehow. Oh, but, you know, I've completely lost track of my wife—"

"That's a great failing on your part," said Korshunov, suddenly sobering up for some reason and putting on the coat of his uniform. "A great failing, Vasily Semyonych. The Lord God gave you this kind of happiness, and you—"

"Well, here you are handing out compliments to my wife—ha, ha, ha!—but none for me, Colonel. So shall I say that you'll be there?"

"I thank you. I'll be there without fail."

"I have the honor, then, to take my leave!"

"My pleasure—"

Korshunov left the clubhouse, whistling "Dark Eyes":

Eyes as black as coal, eyes as bright as fire,

Eyes miraculous, full of beauty fair

How I love those eyes

How I loved those eyes

Unlucky was the day

I fell in love with you

He was pleased with his life, himself, cards, Petushkov's wife, Petushkov himself, the club, Byeltsy, and everything in the world. He looked forward to the renewal of relations with the magnificent madame, who evidently longed for him so touchingly.

All right! he thought to himself, and as for that milksop, they ought to bring a ladder to rescue him . . .

Such was Korshunov, that never dejected representative of the Christ-fearing warrior caste.

In Byeltsy there was another dashing and handsome Cossack officer by the name of Kutulov. A black-browed, fun-loving young fellow and a fine dancer, Kutulov drank, brawled, and engaged in debauchery, although in the depths of his soul he did not have the same cold, calculating meanness of Petushkov or the rude and crude soldier's cynicism of Korshunov. He had some inclinations that were not bad. But they had long ago been drowned in the black pool of a drunken, aimless way of life. One day, after losing absolutely everything at cards, Kutulov suddenly found himself on the edge of the precipice: he had no means with which to pay off his debts. His honor as an officer, the honor of the uniform, of the regiment, and so on, would be held up to scorn and ridicule. He prepared himself to settle scores with life, and did so more than once in fact, stroking the smooth, cold barrel of his revolver and touching his lips to it. And undoubtedly he would have taken the road to oblivion had he not suddenly found another way out: he got married. He married a very wealthy, aristocratic lady, one of those of whom they say "she has preserved the remnants of her former beauty"; the fact was that he married her for her money. His conscience hardly even bothered him: if he hadn't paid his debt at cards to his drinking buddy—that would have been the supreme transgression; whereas to sell himself for money, as long as the sale was sanctified by the Holy Church and there was a marriage license to prove it, that was not considered reprehensible. "What a fool," some said. "Fine fellow," said others.

But things turned out to be more complicated than people had thought or gossiped about. Yekaterina Agafovna, Kutulov's wife, was a personality of a much higher type than all the ladies of the town, the wives of husbands and lovers of lovers. In her youth she had been very beautiful. She still had large, dark eyes, although they had lost their former glow, had grown tired and dim; there also remained her sable brows, her chiseled features, elegant nose, and fine figure. But everything had yellowed, faded, gone to seed, for, alas, she was already past forty. She was educated, well-read, played beautifully on the piano. And in total contrast to the philistine ladies of Byeltsy, she had excellent taste. She dressed with refined simplicity. The *interieure* of her home, which stood apart, was distinguished by its noble, though expensive, modesty: there was nothing flagrant; the tasteless impudence of the newly rich was nowhere to be seen; a carefully considered elegance was evident everywhere. Kutulov himself realized that his wife stood a head taller than he. He saw that she loved him madly, with all the love of a woman who already had one foot in old age, the last fiery, troubling love of her life. But, alas, she was old. She was old. No matter how Kutulov twisted and turned, he could not bring himself to be a true husband to Yekaterina Agafovna. For her part, she would spend the night weeping, and during the day she would sit with the heavy blinds closed, jealous and suffering, suffering and jealous. Sometimes Kutulov, who bore no resemblance whatever to a martyr, would run from the house and indulge in wild bouts of drinking and dissipation and, after thus debasing himself, would return home, half ill, with clothes torn and the suggestion of bruises on his person. At the club on one occasion he went so far as to nearly become involved in a senseless duel; he was saved by Ivan Antonych Petrov, Kolya's father, who happened to be there and who took the nearly unconscious Kutulov back to the Petrov home.

For three days Kutulov stayed at the Petrovs'—sleeping it off—before he was back to his old self from a condition of complete physical and moral intoxication. In order to return him to his domestic deities with greater tact and delicacy, when delivering Kutulov back to Yekaterina Agafovna, who had been informed in a timely way about the whereabouts of her prodigal spouse, Petrov brought Kolya along; in this way it would be easier to avoid heart-rending conversations, interrogations, and possibly unpleasant scenes, for which on the whole Ivan Antonych had no stomach. Kolya was amazed by the whole set of circumstances at the Kutulovs, and by Yekaterina Agafovna, with the perennial look of sadness in her eyes. The air in their living room was suffused with a kind of subtle aroma, gentle and pure. But for some reason it seemed to Kolya that it smelled like a funeral parlor, and looking at Yekaterina Agafovna, he thought of a painting by Kramskoy, *Inconsolable Sorrow*, which he remembered well from reproductions . . . Several days later Kutulov committed suicide.

Doctor Khinkulov was one of the luminaries in the constellation of the Byeltsy chinovniks: in the presence of ladies they called him "the ladies' doctor"; in male company he was called "the community stallion." He was distinguished by what was termed, in the language of Saltykov-Shchedrin,* a "Guards officer's willingness to work," and he truly enjoyed great success among representatives of the fair sex who were suffering from boredom in Byeltsy; the absence of epaulets on his shoulders was made up for by more substantive items. He was a husky, well-fed, pink-complexioned fellow, of indefinite ethnic origin: whether he was Armenian or Greek or came from the province of Tambov was not clear. He regarded himself as Russian and on major holidays demonstratively attended Russian Orthodox services. His facial features were large and expressive. Especially pronounced was his nose: big, meaty, an excellent subject for "nosology." He had lively eyes, like black olives; not the kind clouded over by Oriental languor and voluptuousness; rather, they reminded you of bustling black cockroaches, going in all directions at once. His voice was like the trumpet of an archangel. He could drink any amount of vodka without ever getting drunk. His attitude toward Jews was one of bigoted contempt, but he loved having wealthy Jews as patients because they paid a handsome fee; also, he was not squeamish about having his pleasure with good-looking Jewish women, and he would expatiate on such exploits shamelessly in the company of so-called studs; as for his adventures with the Russian ladies, he preferred to remain silent about those.

Around these luminaries there revolved satellites, who were often created in the image and likeness of their idol, although of course each had his or her own individual features; only the smallest of small fry in the

*On Saltykov-Shchedrin, see glossary.

world of the chinovniks was so faceless that individual differences disappeared. In fact, everything being relative—as the familiar truism has it—it is possible to find both distinctive features and the so-called divine spark in everyone and everything. One need only alter one's perspective, that's all.

But let us return to our heroes. At the Petrovs' home we find a distinguished official from the department of excise taxes, Dolivo-Dobrovolsky, a man with an enormous, fan-shaped, gray beard, greasy strands of hair parted in the middle, and wildly protuberant eyes, as though he had a thyroid condition. He bore a surprising resemblance to a large, green frog, which amazed the Petrov children, amazed them so much that on one occasion little Volodya, impelled by some impassioned urge to penetrate the inner frog's nature of this strange adult, blurted out, while looking him straight in the eye: "Kolya says you're a large frog—really—"

There followed the silence of the grave and a dumbfounded batting of the eyelids. Kolya bolted for the children's room, like a dog breaking from its chain, then ran to find his mother, to report on his brother's utter tactlessness. The visitor, however, disregarded the incident. What was most special about him was his air of importance, which was summed up symbolically in his beard. When he raised a glass of vodka to his lips, it was a sacramental act. When a piece of *balyk* was being directed toward the same destination, it was done at such a momentously gradual pace, in such a drawn-out, ceremonious way that even this ordinary operation seemed to be filled with inner meaning. This same manner, full of pomp and circumstance, was used in everything he did: whether it was to walk, sit, take a deck of cards in hand, note down losses at cards, look for his walking stick in a corner of the vestibule, or put on his hat and cape; it was all done with feeling, with interpretation, with deliberation, not as ordinary mortals do.

His colleague Mikhailov was the complete opposite, having none of this mannered and theatrical staidness: he was a fine straightforward type, no slouch at hitting the bottle, and could sit at cards three nights in a row without wearying. He was a man who lacked any central sources of restraint; as he saw it, the world was his oyster. But to do him justice, it must be said that he did not take bribes or behave contemptuously toward others.

Mikhailov's corrupt "liberalism" was so far advanced that he openly lived with an "illicit" wife and even had had a lovely little daughter with her, which the ladies of Byeltsy, with looks of disgust on their faces, would whisper about among themselves.

The crafty army paymaster and the unctuous local priest, who could talk for hours about the virtues of Holy Father Ioann Kronshtadtsky,* completed the picture of this world of civilian officials, military men, and clergy in the town of Byeltsy, anno Domini 189–. To this lovely bouquet of flowers should be added the commander of the stockade, who raised tumbler pigeons, the sharp-tongued principal of the school, and numerous other civil servants of lesser rank: the secretaries, desk chiefs, clerks, and other bureaucratic gnats who swarmed into and over the eyes, ears, nostrils, and hands of the population and under whose "guardianship" that population was fleeced and picked clean.

Ivan Antonych was obliged, one way or another, to maintain relations with all these people. And not only because it was unavoidable, in view of his official position and despite his own wishes and desires, that he move in these circles, thrash in the toils of this net of objectively formed social relations; it was also because, by his very nature, he was incapable of being a granite-hard type, a Child Harold a la Byron, or a Buddhist monk. On the contrary, even in moments of heartache, Ivan Antonych sought to be out in the world, among people, so as to forget himself in the thick of humanity and discover some sort of further impulse toward life. He preferred to run away from sorrow rather than wallow in it or "suffer through it." People in general, in this respect, are very much like dogs. Dogs can be divided into two categories: some of them, when they've been hurt, will head for the pack; others disappear into the forest to lick their wounds in solitude and eat some sort of healing grasses known only to them; only much later, gaunt but recovered, they return to their owner's yard. Ivan Antonych was like the dogs of the pack, the first category. He literally could not live without people. And since there were no other people he could be among (aside from the circles he was obliged to move in), he was drawn more and more into the stupid philistine life of parties in the evening, drinking, eating, and playing cards. This soon got his wife into a state of worried perplexity.

"Lyubochka," he would say, "we're having guests tomorrow—"

"Vanya, for heaven's sake! We just had guests day before yesterday."

"Well, but you know, it would have been awkward to say no."

In Ivan Antonych's life the phrase, "It's awkward," played an exceptionally important role. It was "awkward" for him to reprimand a subordinate who had erred. It was "awkward" for him to cut short someone who was being insolent; it was "awkward" not to go to some drinking party to which he had been invited; it was "awkward" not to drink down the

*On Ioann Kronshtadtsky, see glossary.

umpteenth glass of vodka or to join in at a game of cards; it was "awkward" for him to refuse to invite guests over if they suggested it. In short, "awkward" became for him a kind of categorical imperative of behavior in a fairly large part of his life, a part that had a tendency to grow and grow.

"Listen, Vanya, we don't have anything in the house."

"Do come up with something, Lyubochka. After all, it would be awkward, embarrassing—"

"I don't even have any money."

"That's nothing. I'll borrow some."

"Vanya!"

"Well, please now, fix everything up just right. A little cognac, some *balyk*, some caviar, some wine, some mushrooms, and so on."

"Again you want to have it your way. Where is all this getting us? What for? You're being sucked down into this local swamp. Yet you yourself said—"

"Leave it be, Lyuba. How am I going to say to them, 'Don't come.' You know it yourself: it would be awkward—"

And Ivan Antonych drew up a list of all the victuals and drinks, hors d'oeuvres and dishes, hot and jellied, wines, vodkas, fruit liqueurs, everything that gave life around there its glory, if you could call it that. Strange as it may seem, he began to derive some special satisfaction from the brilliant impression he seemed to make on his guests by having such a variety of good things to eat and drink. He began to enjoy the role of the gracious host, and he preferred to sit down to meager meals for a week so that he could afford lavish treatment for guests whom, in the depths of his soul, he did not and could not respect. But when they were at his house, drinking, eating, playing cards, praising him for his hospitality, he sincerely thought that these were all good friends and wonderful people. He completely forgot at that moment that all these fine friends, once they went out the door, would immediately start gossiping about him, backbiting and speaking ill of him, calling him over and over a "Jew lover" and a "fool for Christ's sake"; he would forget that they were thick-headed, dull-witted, conniving, unscrupulous people. A cloud of half-drunken, rosy illusion would come over him, and it was not without pleasure that he wafted in this airy cloud. Even the children could not help noticing the change in him and the mounting anxiety of their mother, who after tactfully playing the role of welcoming hostess, after the feasting was over, would fall into gloomy reflection; sometimes she would even weep to see her beloved Vanyechka, who didn't have much tolerance for spirits, spit up the previous night's ham into the brass basin or lie motionless on the bed with a headache, groaning and vowing that this was "the last time." The children even came up with a satirical formula: "Mama's a proud aristocrat; Papa's a 'bread-and-salt' Russian"—a formula that Ivan Antonych himself would laugh at sincerely in a momentary fit of self-criticism. But no matter how he vowed, "This is the last time," it always turned out to be the precursor to the next "last time."

People in Byeltsy were awaiting the arrival of a certain important inspector from Kishinyov. Soon this figure actually appeared and took up residence in the Stanevich home, no less, where of course the Petrovs were living: the room had been recommended by Pavel Ivanovich Stanevich, who lived in Kishinyov. The new arrival—Vasily Ivanovich Knyazhnin—had a proud and majestic bearing, which was an expression of his highly qualified importance, the kind that always distinguishes graying senators and other high-ranking lackeys in their fancy livery. He had a grand and stately way of walking and used rounded gestures, full of dignity. His face—gray, pale, and powdered—was like a flattened mask of stone or like a death mask, the *facies Hyppocratica*; on either side of this stone mask there flowed carefully combed and brushed muttonchops in the style of Tsar Alexander II, plus a goatee parted just as carefully down the middle. His watery eyes expressed contemptuous indifference and indifferent contempt. In addition to all this, Vasily Ivanovich played the flute, a diversion he engaged in with great passion every morning, and with even greater passion he played the card game vint.

For three days and three nights in a row the wild card playing went on. Vasily Ivanovich didn't even have time to amuse himself with his flute. The rooms looked like all hell had broken loose: everywhere there were bottles, unemptied glasses, cigarette butts, chewed cigar ends, empty or half-empty cans of sardines, pieces of lemon, decks of cards, scraps of paper, and pieces of colored chalk. By the mornings the air had become so suffocating that the guests, who seemed glued to their card tables, had to be removed almost by force, so that the rooms could be ventilated. Tottering, the honorable gentlemen would make their way, like shell-shocked soldiers, into the yard, where shivering from the morning cold, they would stare at the sky that was growing pale and in which the stars could be seen barely twinkling; they saw to their natural needs, then returned once again to poisoning themselves, others, and the air with cognac, tobacco, and the heat of the game.

Soon everything had turned blue again, and in the ocean of tobacco smoke all that could be discerned were vague, humanlike forms, and brief outbursts could be heard:

"Grand slam."

"Two no trump."

"Listen, but what about the queen?"

"Pass."

"More cognac? How about another glass—"

"I ca-a-an't—hiccup—y'unnershtan—I ca-a-an't—"

Wine-stained tablecloths, ashes, filth, traces of vomit, universal swinery—all this had to be cleaned up and washed up—and it fell to the lot of the female half of the race.

Vasily Ivanovich's visit of inspection was drawing to an end. With his face half-swollen, dark bruises under his eyes, which had become quite glassy, like those of a sleeping burbot, Vasily Ivanovich, conscious of duty fulfilled and with some winnings in his pocket, set off for Kishinyov to report to his superiors that everything was fine, couldn't be better, in the region entrusted to him, only that Petrov, it seems, is soft on the Jews, caters to them, or so it is asserted by the voice of the people, and the voice of the people, as everyone knows, is the voice of God. *Chaque sot trouve toujours un plus sot qui l'admire* (A fool always finds an even greater fool to admire him), says an old French proverb. Vasily Ivanovich was a model fool, a 24-carat fool bearing the official stamp and seal, and the fools of Byeltsy, being even greater fools, had every reason to prance around on their hind legs in his presence and to gaze with utter servility into his blank, mindless eyes, expressive of nothing. Thus both sides turned out to be quite pleased with each other, both the ones being admired and the ones doing the admiring. A fool of a different order was that "bread-and-salt" Russian, the hospitable Ivan Antonych, the naive eccentric who in the provincial capital of Kishinyov was depicted by his "dear friend" Vasily Ivanovich as the only blemish on the resplendent surface of the Byeltsy sun.

As for Ivan Antonych, he hadn't the slightest suspicion of things turning out this way. Besides, he was ill for about three days as a result of the genteel way in which they had spent their time together. He lay with a wet towel on his head, drank fish oil from sardine tins, groaned and moaned, cursing everyone and everything in the world, until at last the illness passed and he was himself again.

Such was the upshot of the provincial tour of inspection.

Ivan Antonych's affairs at work proceeded middling well. He felt no zeal for his work at all. At certain times reports had to be compiled, and this compilation was usually put off, so far as possible, until the last few days. To make up for it, in those last few days everything was turned on its head. Lyubov Ivanovna would do half the work, while Ivan Antonych restlessly paced up and down, throwing his hands up in dismay, giving himself over to mournful reflections out loud, on how he absolutely did not understand how so little time could be left. To assist in copying over the report a "secretary" would show up, a young man named Dzyub, who had an enormous Adam's apple on an otherwise skinny neck, which was covered with pink, red, and yellow pimples, well known by the name *boutons d'amour* (love bumps). One could hear the scraping of the pens, going full tilt, and the report would be completed on time after all, to the no small delight of Ivan Antonych Petrov.

Perhaps this process of collective authorship gave Kolya the idea of becoming a writer. But a writer of interesting books. Not reports. At that time he was reading the most varied things: Bret Harte and Korolenko, Dickens and Leo Tolstoy, *Murylka the Cat* and the books from Posrednik Publishers about Marcus Aurelius, Epictetus, and Sakyamuni; the Gospel and the erotic poems of Mirra Lokhvitskaya, Heine, and Garshin—all this the young boy devoured like a pie filled with the most varied ingredients.

However, after his lessons in sexual enlightenment, after the lying of adults had grown in his mind into a fact of monstrous enormity, into one of the principles of life, Kolya no longer asked other people about anything: he wanted now to get at everything with his own mind, because he no longer believed in any explanations from his parents. "Once having lied, who will believe you?" as is said in the writings of Kuzma Prutkov, the unforgettable poetaster and Assaying Office director.

Among the various products of the printing press to be found in the Petrovs' home was an anthology called *Pearls of Russian Poetry*. Of all the poems in the anthology, Kolya had two favorites. The first was Lermontov's translation of Goethe's "Über allen Gipfeln ist Ruh" (or, as Lermontov had it, "The mountaintops sleep in the darkness of night").*

Kolya's other favorite poem was Maikov's "Trial of Johann Hus."† He read the poem over dozens of times and could say it by heart:

> At the assembly, at Konstanze,
> The theologians in holy session,
> After condemning Johann Huss,

---

*Bukharin mentions Goethe's poem twice, perhaps suggesting sympathy with its attitude toward approaching death. An English version of Goethe's poem might go as follows:
> Over all the hilltops, peace rests.
> In all the treetops,
>   hardly a rustle escapes.
> The birds in the woods
>   have grown still.
> Wait just a little. Soon you
>   will be resting too.

†John Huss, or Jan Hus (1371–1415)—national hero of the Czech people, whose ideas laid the basis for the Czech Reformation. He was condemned as a heretic by the Council of Constance and burned at the stake.

devised for him a worthy death.
In lengthy speech a black-robed doctor
Discussing all the forms of torture
Proposed to all those gathered there
To break him on the wheel of fear.
His heart, the source of evil, would
To a pagan wild-dog pack be fed,
And his tongue, the instrument of ill,
Be pecked to bits by crows from hell.

Kolya, "Little Robinson," was filled with a dull, burning hatred for the "theologians," not understanding at all why they had to deliver John Huss to such a cruel death. The poet's irony in regard to the theologians made it obvious that they were no good at all—scum, rubbish. Wasn't it the theologians, the Scribes and Pharisees, who had condemned Jesus and, along with the Roman soldiers, crucified him? They say "the Jews" killed Jesus. But wasn't Jesus himself a Jew? Wasn't his mother, Mary, a Jew? Didn't it say in the Bible that Jesus was "of the House of David"? But David had been the King of the Jews. And biblical history—that was all about the Jews. No, here too the grown-ups were up to some trickery. It's true that Papa always laughed at the Holy Scriptures. But why, the boy wondered, did he take me to church if he thought it was all nonsense?

Then there arose in vivid detail in Kolya's mind the scene on the night before Christ's Holy Resurrection when his father took him to the impressive church service while all the bells pealed. Off in the distance you could already see the enormous bonfires where, in honor of God risen from the dead, they were burning barrels smeared with tar. But alas, Kolya never got to hear the hymns of triumph being sung—on the way he nearly drowned when he stumbled into a ditch full of mud and pig's manure. He suddenly found himself up to his waist in the foul-smelling mire, with his shoes stuck in the mud. He lost his galoshes, and barely managed to get himself out, then spent all the rest of the night trying to scrape off and wash off the muck, working away at his new dress shoes, which were crusted over with the vile stuff, and his stockings and his trousers. Yes, he would remember that Easter night all right!

"But if Christ was good," Kolya continued to ponder, "why do people who believe in him act the opposite? He told us to love everyone—but what do they do? Christ was for the poor—but what attitude do these Christians take? There's some sort of trickery and deception here, too. And what about that Sakyamuni? He left his life in the palace, threw it all away, good for him! And what about Epictetus? He was a slave, but what a wise man! And the convict in Dickens's *Great Expectations*—why he was a thousand times better than all the rich people—"

Thus, on all sides, Kolya felt surrounded by riddles: as he saw it, there were snares, deceptions, traps, nooses, and trip wires set out by the grownups all around, and he had to part the bushes ever so carefully to expose all this trickery.

Of all the things he read, Kolya especially liked Heine. The boy would nestle in a corner of the sofa with his little book of Heine's poems. He would swallow bitter tears and a lump would rise in his throat as he read the author who is called "the last of the Romantics, the king of nightingales and poets."

There was Edith, with a neck like a swan, walking amidst the corpses and blood at Hastings Field. Kolya imagined, down to the tiniest details, the strands of her hair blowing in the wind, the wounds and the blood. He sees the distracted eyes of the swan's-necked maiden, he hears the repulsive shriek of the corpse-eating ravens, he can make out the three cuts of a sword to which the unfortunate maiden presses her lips. . . .

And then there was Heine's poem about Don Ramiro, with his voice from beyond the grave answering his beloved Clara: "You it was that called me here." A cold chill comes over Kolya. He hears the hollow voice of the deceased Ramiro. What shame that Doña Clara now must feel! And what a scoundrel, that rotten Don Fernando! Kolya felt infinitely sorry for Ramiro, and his tears flowed silently upon the precious book.

And the young knight Olaf, what a splendid fellow! The king had placed his headsman by the door, but Olaf, in the very face of death, sang a passionate song in praise of life, the stars, the flowers . . . And the king, what a worthless person he was, the villainous wretch!

Then there was *The Slave Ship*:

Van Keuck sits in his supercargo's cabin
And calculates in his accounting book
Estimates the value of his shipload
Figures out the profit that he took.

Kolya pictures the poor Negroes in chains and the foul mugs of Van Keuck and the ship's captain, and right away his hatred wells up and his little fists are clenched.

What a joy it was, on the other hand, when the son of the learned rabbi, Gabriel de Saragossa, tweaked the nose of the pretty young daughter of the Spanish alcalde! What a marvelous piece that was from Heine's *Hebraic Melodies*. Kolya wanted to read this bit of wonder to all the fools who went on and on about "the Yids," the way the pretty young daughter had done.

And what about William Ratcliffe? Kolya's heart sank as he repeated the lines: "O why is your sword all bloody, dear Edward!"—the Scottish song of Margaret, gone mad.

And then there was Almanzor and Witzli-Putzli.* They got what they deserved, those greedy stinking Spaniards. It was an entire discovery for him, the fact that in Heine's poem "Witzli-Putzli" the Christians were called God-eaters. Yet if during Communion the real body and the real blood of Christ were actually in the bread and wine, what a foul thing it was! That was worse than eating humans! And how was it that no one noticed? The boy's mind kept working with effort, as though heavy boulders were being rolled from one place to another . . . Another thing that was said in Heine was that the doctrine of the Trinity was in conflict with the multiplication table. Well, wasn't that so? What kind of nonsense it all was. Even Mama couldn't find a way to explain how the Son of God, within eternity, is born from the Father, and the Holy Ghost, existing from before eternity . . . The hell they're born! And the hell they come from! The simple truth is that it's all nonsense served up with Lenten oil. More trickery, and what trickery this time! Made-up fairy tales—and nothing more. And in the Holy Scriptures, first God created light, and then the sun, moon, and stars. If so, where did the light come from? Or here's another: one of the prophets asked God to make the sun stand still. But in geography it's said that the earth goes around the sun. That means the Scriptures were talking a lot of rot. It says that a fish called a whale swallowed Jonah. But the whale is not a fish; it's a mammal. And there's no way it could swallow a man; it has a very narrow throat. The earth started out as just a ball of fire. But in the Scriptures, Adam and Eve appeared within a week: they would have been well done, indeed, the darlings, in that fiery Garden of Eden! In scientific books it says that the earth has existed for many millions of years, but in the Scriptures to get from the Creation of the world to the birth of Christ took exactly 5,508 years. Yet there are archaeological digs of human dwellings from more than ten thousand years ago. No, it was all stuff and nonsense.

Thus Kolya, through the exertions of his own mind, arrived at a state of the most thorough disbelief. His thoughts were sometimes quite naive; nevertheless they had a solid base in natural science, while irony and ridicule served as a lubricant.

Of course childish arguments were also tacked on, along with the standard blasphemies of naughty children.

*The title of Heine's poem "Witzli-Putzli" distorted the name of the Aztec god of war, Huitilopochtli.

"Oh yeah, and can your God make a stone heavier than he can lift?"

The other kids would freeze, dumbstruck . . .

"And maybe your God can punish me if I say he's an idiot, a no-good, and a turd?"

Kolya's friends' eyeballs were already up on their foreheads.

The blasphemies kept growing: all the specifics derived from enlightenment now came crashing down on the head of God, the unfortunate and much maligned deity, but He evidently was really powerless if He allowed such terrible things to go unpunished.

Among the books in the Petrov household was one, either by Mamin-Sibiryak or by Nemirovich-Danchenko, about the northern lands. Kolya was attracted to it by the illustrations but also by the luxurious binding, with gold imprint and black enamel in various patterns and designs. And for some reason the idea entered his head that if he began to copy this book over afresh, it would be like a new work, his own, Kolya's. Just try to explain it: this boy already understood that there is no God, but he had faith that a copied work would be original! And he believed strongly, too. From his father's office he took entire reams of paper, lined for official government use, then concealing himself and hiding away, he spent hours copying out the book. He tossed spoiled sheets of paper behind the sofa, where heaps of trash had soon piled up. Over these his conscience soon began to gnaw at him: after all, he had stolen the paper. And would Epictetus or Marcus Aurelius have stolen? Kolya's scalp, beneath his head of hair, began to sweat from his secret shame over the stolen paper.

One day he was caught by surprise in the midst of his authorly preoccupations by the elderly nanny, whose job it actually was to look after the infant Andryusha, but who kept an eye on Kolya and Volodya too.

"You, Kolya, what are you doing there?"

"Composing a book."

"Lord! Look at all that paper! Where did you get all that?"

"For a book you always need paper."

"Oh yes? And what in the world are you writing?"

"I told you, I'm composing a book."

"My saints! And how in the world are you composing it?"

"That's easy. Out of my head."

"Is that your father's paper that you've taken? Did you ask him?"

"Oh, dear nanny, don't say anything. I took a little. I won't anymore—"

The nurse promised not to tell. But what if she had known that crammed in behind the sofa there was ten times more paper—sheets that had been started but then got messed up. How to get rid of all that trash?

Where could Kolya throw it? It was a vast problem over which Kolya's little brain fretted in vain, tortured by the knowledge of the transgression which he was sure would be discovered by someone at any moment.

Such was the peculiar form in which the literary aspirations of Kolya Petrov first manifested themselves in childhood.

Chapter 5

She appeared on the Byeltsy horizon all of a
sudden, like lightning, like a falling star, like
a meteor. She was a charming flaxen-haired
young woman, with deep blue eyes like violets; with a tender countenance
like the petals of the gentlest rose in the Staneviches' garden; with golden
braids twined round her head, like bright, entrancing rays of sun; with a
sweet smile like springtime; with the lightness of step and innate grace of
the fairest of nymphs. She had just graduated from one of the St. Petersburg institutes, and having some distant relatives in Byeltsy, she chose to
flutter down there like some butterfly that has just hatched from its
cocoon, with all the radiance of its brightly colored little wings, from
which life had not had time to rub off the primordial beauty with its
grubby hands. Her name was Yelena Vladimirovna Klevanskaya, and she
was living through her nineteenth spring. Everything about her was amazingly natural. She was a living, fluttering refutation of the French saying:
Pour être belle, il faut souffrir.

Her behavior in Byeltsy (and she appeared at the Staneviches, with
whose daughter, Yelizaveta Ivanovna, she soon became fast friends) created
a genuine furor. Besides her purely external attractiveness, she possessed
other merits: she was not the naive and helpless type, like Gretchen, for
whom Faust's every utterance had the ring of a pastor's virtuous instructions. She was lively as mercury, educated, and witty, and she had a
worldly, but not overdone, polish of the kind that allows one to feel confident and not be especially shy when out in what is called society. In a
word, she won universal recognition within a few days, and like planets
around a heavenly body, all the prominent personages of the intelligentsia
and officialdom in Byeltsy, both young and old, civilian and military,
began to revolve around her. As though in keeping with some law of grav-

ity, people broke out of their accustomed orbits and started to move along new trajectories. The Stanevich home was filled with noise and chatter, laughter and good cheer. The universal pursuit of Yelena Vladimirovna created a kind of bustling, crowded crush: not only were men coming there in droves but so were bouquets of flowers, boxes of candy, bars of chocolate, fine prints, and statuettes—every kind of souvenir that could be brought to the feet of this angelic girl by her numerous admirers.

Visiting the Petrovs just at that time was Lyubov Ivanovna's stepsister, whom everyone called Aunt Lyalya, or Auntie Lyalka. She was still young, rather interesting, very intelligent, and distinguished by a virtual absence of philistine prejudices. Despite her youth she had lived through a very severe drama of the soul. When she was still plugging along at her institute, she had become involved in a platonic romance: the two young people loved each other very much, but he always held himself at a certain respectful distance. The reason for his deference and reserve, and the story behind it, came out after several years, which had been filled with the deepest love on either side. And the revelation took the form of a truly dark tragedy. One fine day, this man, who was still quite young, this object of her passionate devotion, suddenly—and for no apparent reason—went out of his mind. Then it came out that he went mad because of *lues*,* which he was secretly being treated for all along. Whether this was a "gift of inheritance" from his parents or the result of some earlier sin remained unknown. At any rate, he knew about the illness and suffered terribly within himself. That was the reason for his strictly platonic attitude toward his beloved. Whether he hoped to be cured of the illness or whether he lacked the courage to forsake women entirely or whether he was preparing to reveal his terrible secret to her—all this remained unknown: he died as he was, without saying a final word of farewell.

Auntie Lyalka, after learning all this from his sister, her friend at the institute, veered off course like a bird that has been shot on the wing. Her heart bled. She came close to having a nervous breakdown at the time. Hunters know of such cases: a duck that has been wounded on a meadow will suddenly tremble, then fly straight up, seem about to fall, but somehow will right itself and manage to fly off over the horizon into the unknown distance; perhaps somewhere far away it will collapse, becoming a meal for a hawk; or perhaps it will recover, perhaps the wound will close, and only sometimes make itself felt as a dull ache, a physical reminder of the past.

That was what poor Auntie Lyalka was like. With her copious head of curls, she betook herself to far-off Bessarabia in order to still the sorrow in

*Latin for syphilis.

her heart. Here her relatives treated her with great care and consideration. Yelizaveta Ivanovna, the young Stanevich daughter, fell completely in love with her, and the boys simply adored her, especially Kolya, not only because she brought him from Moscow a bow-and-arrow set with an excellent metal quiver, with which he pranced around dashingly while riding a hobby horse and wearing his hat at a jaunty angle, but mainly because Auntie Lyalka talked with the boys as though they were grown-ups, logically and without making baby talk. She could see quite well that Kolya understood much more than people thought he did. And so she began to heal; sometimes she was even cheerful, and as often happens with people after experiencing great shock, she put on an appearance of light-heartedness and even flirted a little. Pavel Ivanovich, the Staneviches' older son, was already looking at her in a tender way with his velvety, burning eyes and strutting around her like a cooing male pigeon around a female. Watching unobtrusively, the elder Staneviches saw, partly with joy, partly anxiety, that something was going to happen (although probably nothing would) . . .

And then Yelena Vladimirovna appeared on the scene. Every axis was realigned. Auntie Lyalka got her suitcases together and, no matter how they pleaded with her, went off to Moscow: either she didn't want to be in second place as a woman or the juxtaposition of genuine light-heartedness and cheer to the kind that she put on, in which a tiny bitter tear, somewhere in the depths of the soul, was always trembling—that contrast was perhaps too painful for her. At any rate she would not give in to any protestations, imprecations, or attempts at persuasion, and she disappeared just as suddenly as she had come.

The reign of Yelena Vladimirovna was established as a solid and unshakable monarchy.

The friendship between Klevanskaya and Yelizaveta Ivanovna Stanevich developed quite naturally, of its own accord. They were similar in age and interests, and they had the same dreams. The girls often invited Kolya into Yelizaveta Ivanovna's little room. Everything there was strange and marvelous to him: the neatly made bed, the little toiletries table with the mirror, the tiny cut-glass bottles of perfume, the decorative rug hanging above the bed, the room-dividing screens painted with peacocks and birds of paradise, the entire atmosphere of something unusual, closeted off, inaccessible, completely special. The girls poured out their affections on the young boy, sometimes even kissed him, drowned him in perfume, and made fools of themselves trying to get him to recite poetry for them.

This strange mixture of suppressed eroticism and inclinations toward motherhood had a gently lulling effect on Kolya. He sank into a kind of fog filled with the aromas of Yelizaveta Ivanovna's multifarious perfumes. In this fog he could hear the girls' cheerful voices: the brunette's rapid chatter and the blond's chesty contralto. Their white teeth flashed; their black and dark-blue eyes laughed merrily. Kolya felt shy, but it was pleasant for him to be sitting in this girl's room. And so they didn't have to ask him twice: he showered a veritable flood of verses—a goodly number of which he already knew by heart—down on the heads of his listeners fair.

"Kolya, please. 'The mountaintops . . .' "

And he recited Goethe's poem in Lermontov's translation. After the final sighing line: "Wait just a little, you too / Will be resting soon," a melancholy silence followed. Then, "How about something from Fet now. Kolyechka, Sweetheart, come on."

"Well, what? Do you want 'I have come to you with a greeting'?"

"Okay. That one first, and after that do 'Whispering, a timid breath.' "

"All right, if that's what you want."

Kolya got himself into a more comfortable position in a corner of the crazily colored couch, among the pillows. The light from the kerosene lamp with its frosted glass shade, and from the two candles burning on the dressing table in front of the looking glass, barely reached to where he sat. He filled the order for Fet. But Kolya was not fond of Fet, regardless of the fact that Yelena Vladimirovna liked him enormously. (She obviously had not been exposed to the teachings of Pisarev;* the orientation at her institute had been in quite a different direction.)

"If you want, I'll recite something for you from Heine."

Then with his small voice trembling from emotion, he recited "Hastings Field." He came to these lines:

Her neck was graceful as a swan's
Beautifully white and slender and fair
And our King Harold, now resting at Bowes,
At one time had loved her with passion,
Loved her and kissed and embraced her,
Then fell out of love and just left her . . .
Days followed days, years followed years
Till the sixteenth year had gone by—

At this point the girls grew silent, their chests rose and fell, and tears welled up in their eyes.

After the final verse, when Edith was brought the corpse of her beloved and when

*A harsh critic of Fet.

The monks softly whispered a prayer

the girls were on the verge of crying. In the dark of the room Kolya was wiping away tears himself with the sleeve of his jacket, so that no one would notice. For several minutes he was physically unable to say a word.

Sometimes Kolya would read them a story out loud: from Chekhov's *Tales of Many Colors* or Gogol's *Evenings on a Farm near Dikanka*. From the latter he read them "A Terrible Vengeance," and he felt as though his own hair was standing on end when the evil magician's giant head kept growing . . . And the girls sat still, frozen with terror.

Then they began to pull Kolya about and shower him with candies, and the next day they rang all the bells in his honor, telling everyone how well he read and what an extraordinary youngster he was. Ivan Antonych beamed. Lyubov Ivanovna smiled. Kolya got as red as a beet and ran away to seek relief from the extravagant praise, though he felt flattered by it all, and in fact felt as though he was soaring in the skies. He found himself standing alone, in a luxuriant growth of goosefoot. He looked at the sky and thought—he didn't know what he thought.

Once after one of these evenings Yelena Vladimirovna, in a fit of tender emotion, gave Kolya a present of the best thing she had (so she said). It was her album from the institute, a beautiful album, with magnificent paper and an expensive stamped leather binding. It gave off a fragrance of absolutely extraordinary perfume. Almost all the pages were filled with lines of verse and the comments of her girlfriends at the institute, her teachers, her acquaintances in St. Petersburg, naive drawings, wishes for her happiness, quotations from prominent people, homemade translations from English and French poets, whose content was sometimes very much in the high-society vein, for example, "Arise now my glad-hearted ladies and lords."

These "ladies and lords" were being invited to participate in a highly refined elk hunt. In the depths of his soul Kolya was extraordinarily proud of this gift from this delightful girl. The album became his most treasured possession, and, like the protagonist in Pushkin's "Miserly Knight," he would sit in a corner for hours looking over his treasure, leafing through the pages of the album, knowing its contents already by heart. Yet among all the various outpourings, poetry and prose, one little line in particular brought Kolya up short. It was nestled unobtrusively off in a corner and briefly but clearly stated: "Remember Moiseika." That was all, no signature or anything. Kolya was already enlightened enough to understand what an inscription like this could mean, how full of significance it was despite its brevity. In his heart something snapped.

Was this precocious childhood jealousy? Hardly. For Kolya had never experienced the kind of childhood infatuation which the biographies of many people tell us about. But there must have been some element of jealousy, some early shoots of that feeling, apparently, because he felt hurt and annoyed that there was something secret between Yelena Vladimirovna and this unknown "Moiseika."

Meanwhile, the universal courting of Yelena Vladimirovna continued: there was a constant crowd of people, as before; guests were always filling up the Staneviches' home, and Yelena Vladimirovna flourished; she glowed, she sparkled, she dazzled with her wit. Even Anton Ivanych—who was devoted to his Lyubochka from his head down to his heels, who in the realm of tender feelings belonged entirely to his wife, *mit Haut und Haar*—even he would liven up visibly in the presence of this young woman and, with bravado and a passionate expression on his face, declaim some lines from Lokhvitskaya:

I yearn for sultry summer joys
In darkness with the candles out

Or he'd recite some risqué verses, such as:

Give me a woman, a wild, wild woman.
I'll wind myself around her like a love vine.

In reply to this everyone laughed in unison; sometimes they'd even applaud—these pompous specimens of Byeltsy officialdom. Kolya was always irritated when his father mixed with the Byeltsy chinovniks: he already understood their real attitude toward Ivan Antonych. He loved his father very much; he loved his mocking of everything sacred; he loved his masterly skill at reciting; loved the things he knew, the stories he told; and he simply loved him as the dear, kind father he was. He suffered when his father had nausea after the usual drinking bout. He could not tolerate these guests, with the exception of the debauchee Mikhailov, who could make splendid drawings of castles on the Rhine from days of yore and who taught Kolya how to do humorous drawings: for example, "troika on the other side of a hill," in which there was visible over the top of a hill a coachman's whip but the troika could not be seen; or "sentry behind a guardhouse," where instead of the sentry you saw a bayonet sticking out from behind the guardhouse; or "horses lying down," which, if looked at from the right angle, showed them galloping fiercely. There were many other tricks on paper that Mikhailov showed him.

By this time Kolya had stopped associating with girls. Yet he did "have dealings" with Mikhailov's daughter; they went for walks together, swung in the swings, and played. She was a fine, smart gal, but people looked at her askance because she was "illegitimate." Kolya knew about this; he observed how people treated her (no one ever invited her to visit), and seeing something in her that was unusual, he made an exception in her case to his new rule of not associating with girls. Once he brought her to his home and spent the whole day with her, so that it caused great alarm at the Mikhailovs': they thought she had gotten lost or that gypsies had stolen her. And all along she was having a fine time in Kolya's company.

Then—and here was a strange thing!—in regard to Yelena Vladimirovna, Kolya developed a feeling that the guests who came to see her were unworthy of her; they were stupid, petty, banal. It gave him an unpleasant feeling to see her playing the coquette and flirting, skimming about like a fish in water, among all these not-so-witty wits and respectable swine, dressed up in frock coats, jackets, and striped trousers. Of course, the Staneviches were all right. But the others? And how was Yelena Vladimirovna able to keep from being bored by listening to the same thing over and over again: the same witticisms, the same anecdotes, the same comments, accompanied by the same old gestures, smiles, and laughter?

It seemed to Kolya that this was an entirely different Yelena Vladimirovna, not the one that sat in Yelizaveta's room and listened to poetry. There everything was tender and subtle and beautiful and good. But here there were wineglasses and affectations and, above all, stupidity. There arose in Kolya's soul a vague desire to do something unpleasant to this "bad" Yelena Vladimirovna, so that only the "good" one would remain. Not that there was any plan or clear thought or rationally chosen, conscious goal. He didn't have an inkling of any such thing. Instead he was impelled half unconsciously, not realizing it; he was moved by an undefined impulse, a dark yearning arising from the depths of his childish soul. It seemed to Kolya that he was standing guard over that beloved room of Yelizaveta's and everything connected with it, that he was standing guard over the real Yelena Vladimirovna, that in knightly fashion he was defending her against all the "male dogs in heat" sneaking up from every side. For all his youthful enlightenment, there was no way Kolya could grasp the fact that all these attentions were pleasing to the young society girl from St. Petersburg. To his naive mind Yelena Vladimirovna's behavior among the guests was something abnormal, something he might have called, if he had known Hegel, inconsistent with the Idea, not real and not rational. But, as is easy to guess, he did not then know Hegel. Nevertheless, although he didn't think it, he felt that this Yelena Vladimirovna was not genuine, was false, not the one constituting her true essence.

All these fragments of half-formed thoughts, images, sensations, and urges were resolved one fine day in quite a surprising manner. There was a "gathering of all the units" at the Staneviches, and as usual in such cases, Yelena Vladimirovna was lavishing her smiles upon one and all. And Kolya was right there watching, with the precious album in his hands. Suddenly, like the boy in Chekhov who says, "Hmm, but I know," he opened the album, found the line of writing that bothered him, and read aloud: "From the album of Yelena Vladimirovna: 'Remember Moiseika.' " Far from everyone present, of course—if anyone at all—had much of an idea what this was all about. On the other hand, Yelena Vladimirovna knew very well. She exploded. She jumped up from the table and rushed at Kolya, grabbing for the album. He was out of the room in a flash, the girl running behind him. In fact she was swifter than the proverbial doe. But she couldn't jump walls or fences. And after clearing two walls in a hurry, Kolya was already out of her range. The chase ended.

The result of this outburst was quite unexpected for Kolya. Apparently "Moiseika" played a much more important role than he had imagined. It seemed he had a stuck a sharp needle into the real Yelena Vladimirovna herself, into the very one that sighed and grew sad as she listened to Heine's romantic verse. And this most secret part of herself had been exposed to public ridicule and desecration by the bad boy Kolya. Thus there ended forever the evenings in Yelizaveta's room. Yelena Vladimirovna did not try to seize the album again; she politely greeted the boy when she saw him, but never again asked him to recite poetry. As it turned out, she soon received some sort of telegram from St. Petersburg and traveled off to the northern capital, leaving all her courtiers and suitors like so many fish out of water. All that remained of Yelena Vladimirovna was the album.

But fate soon made up to Kolya for this loss. Some people from Moscow arrived all of a sudden in Byeltsy—the Slavyanskys. Mrs. Slavyansky, née Gorodetskaya, or as Ivan Antonych used to call her, "Natashka Gorodetskaya," was an old friend of his, the sister by blood of that very same beauty of a revolutionary with whom Ivan Antonych had had such a tragic romance before he got married. Natalya Dmitryevna was an outstanding woman in every respect, and not just, of course, on the pitiful scale of Byeltsy: in her outward appearance, her strength of will, her intelligence, her exceptionally good education and broad cultural horizon. Her husband, too, was a highly educated person; but he could barely drag his legs along, being a very sickly, delicate, and nearsighted man. His frail figure, with an enormous head, with glasses on a small nose, and an unruly shock of always rumpled, light-colored hair, which would not submit to the civilizing effects of the comb, made quite a sharp contrast to his wife. With them they had brought their little son Tosya (Anton). He was, to put it bluntly, a phenomenal child. Thin and weak, the same age as Kolya Petrov, frighteningly nearsighted, already wearing huge eyeglasses with powerful lenses, he was physically a copy of his father. But he was so well-read, knowledgeable, intelligent, and sharp-witted that he exceeded anything that could be expected of a boy at that age.

The Slavyanskys' appearance on the Byeltsy horizon brought a fresh human stream into the Petrovs' lives: all at once here were real people for a change! Old memories flooded in upon Ivan Antonych, and the advanced thinking of Moscow, with all its ideas and interests, swept in like a fresh breeze clearing out a foul aroma. Lyubov Ivanovna was also extraordinarily glad: now she could have conversations at last like a human being and get a break from the turbid dullness of provincial chinovniks. The poor woman, whose life had been entirely taken up with the infant's swaddling clothes, with cooking, housekeeping, guests, her worry and alarm over her impractical spouse, had simply been yearning for just plain lively conversation. But Kolya was probably happiest of all, because for the first time he had a companion who not only was in no way inferior to him but in many respects far outstripped him. At first Kolya was surprised by this, but he quickly came to acknowledge Tosya's superiority.

In their very first conversation, as the two boys were strolling quietly in the orchard, exchanging sentence fragments and scrutinizing each other, it came out that Kolya did not know who Uriel Acosta was. In his soft but steady voice Tosya gave Kolya an entire lecture about that stubborn-minded rationalist thinker. It also came out that Tosya was reading Swift— whereas Kolya had not even sampled him. Kolya started to explain to Tosya the secrets of procreation—but Tosya, in the same thin voice, calm and even, told him in a generalized way about reproduction by cell division and by budding or grafting, things that Kolya hadn't been able to figure out with his own head, and which he certainly hadn't heard from the other boys. Heatedly Kolya rushed on to expound on the subject of his birds and butterflies. But Tosya responded with tales of his work with a microscope and how remarkable the infusoria were. The farther you went in the forest, the more wood you found. It turned out that Tosya knew German and French and could speak those languages rather well, whereas Kolya hadn't the slightest notion about them. But when the soft-voiced Tosya began to sing in Italian (the motif, *La donna e mobile*, was one well known to Kolya), our hero was stricken once and for all. To be sure, Tosya didn't know the world of plants and animals as well as Kolya, he didn't know how to paint and draw, he couldn't run or climb trees, or catch tarantulas or flood marmots out of their holes . . . But Kolya was simply crushed by Tosya's book knowledge, and it seemed to him that there lurked behind Tosya's enormous, pale, and fragile brow inexhaustible mountains of every kind of wisdom.

Within a few days the two boys had become bosom buddies, spending all their time together. What Tosya liked about Kolya was what he himself lacked. And Kolya already worshipped outright at the feet of Tosya's intelligence: his friendship with Tosya became for Kolya a genuinely holy thing; he was ready to do battle with dragons on behalf of his delicate but sagacious little friend. Tosya had a surprisingly literary way of speaking: he spoke as if he were reading; every sentence was clearly set off and did not resemble children's speech in the slightest, let alone the usual conversation of grown-ups. Tosya was distinguished by a vivid and subtle wit, a brilliant ability to pounce on his opponent and cut him to ribbons with the sharp steel of logic and make a mockery of him the way Pisarev did—and all this without raising his voice: quietly, evenly, calmly. A very distinct impression was created by this contrast between the biting intensity of the content and the calm, dispassionate, even disinterested manner. All the grown-ups would smile and think secretly to themselves, where does this frail child get all this from? To judge by his thoughts, however, he could not be treated as a child: he was just a small and very wise grown-up, a superintelligent dwarf, wearing large glasses through which peered unblinking porcelain eyes. This hypertrophy of the mind, however, cost Tosya dearly: within a few years, not yet a man, he died of a brain disorder. But that happened later. At this time he was alive and became Kolya's friend; but Kolya, while he loved him with all his heart, always felt a vague anxiety about his friend, the kind people feel for a rare, irreplaceable treasure.

The Slavyanskys were sitting at the dinner table at the Petrovs on their closed-in porch. Tosya was with them. Lyubov Ivanovna, as always, was fussing about the samovar, cleaning the cups, stacking the dishes, setting out on the table bread, meat, jam, sherbet. Outside the glass enclosure it was already pitch-dark. Only the nocturnal moths were tapping against the glass in their effort to get to the light; they would come diving out of the darkness, run into the glass, then flutter upward, working their little legs ever so quickly and flapping their little wings, then they would fall down and start up again with their labor of Sisyphus. Wasps had gotten into the jam: one was already done for; others were barely able to get out, all smeared with the sticky jam and half paralyzed, like incurable invalids. The lamps were burning brightly. Around them and on the ceiling, where there shone patches of light, little beetles, golden-eyed, and midges were circling, knocking against the lamps or the ceiling and falling on the tablecloth . . . How quiet and pleasant it was there on a late summer's evening.

"So actually how are you getting along here, Ivan Antonych?" Natalya

Dmitryevna asked. "You haven't told us anything very clearly, after all. But then, it never was possible to get anything sensible out of you."

"That's the way to tell him, Natalya Dmitryevna. It will do him good," Lyubov Ivanovna chimed in.

"Oh, *Natalie*." (He used the French version of her name.) "How are we getting along? Well, we're alive, not dead—we chew our bread—quiet and easy as we go."

"Well, you know, that's not saying much, not enough for us to understand. What kind of people do you have here?"

"Nothing special, like people everywhere: two holes at the end of the nose, and the legs grow out of the same place they do for everyone."

"Quit playing the fool, Ivan Antonych."

"He's always like that, Natalya Dmitryevna! Was he really like that before, too? You know, for us it was different in Moscow: of course there was a lot of empty-headedness there, but at least there was some axis, but here there's none. It's cards today and cards tomorrow and cards the day after. That's the meaning of life. Meanwhile, I've still got children on my hands—but, to tell the truth, I don't know how to get out of this situation."

"Playing cards apparently helps Ivan Antonych develop his mathematical abilities," Tosya suddenly put in, with his thin little voice, not realizing he was inserting a sharp needle.

"Tosya, don't butt in where you're not asked!"

"I was only commenting, Mama, that cards can also have a positive aspect and, taking that aspect into account, Ivan Antonych can relate to them in a way that is not negative at all." (Kolya had told Tosya about life in Byeltsy.)

After listening to this discussion, Ivan Antonych was blushing. What a child! Lyubov Ivanovna, despite all her power of self-restraint, was taken by surprise and was unexpectedly and visibly disturbed. Kolya felt both suffering and joy. Tosya sat with a face of porcelain and porcelain eyes, like a fragile doll, and nothing registered on his countenance. He just sat there like a little Buddha. Natalya Dmitryevna didn't know what to do.

Slavyansky had come to a standstill somewhere behind the samovar: there wasn't a sign of him.

"Tosya, don't talk foolishness!" Natalya Dmitryevna said at last, in a rather uncertain voice.

"To talk foolishness, Mama, would mean to get upset. But it is harmful for me to get upset. As everyone knows, I inherited Papa's iron constitution."

"Listen, Anton," Slavyansky's high-pitched voice could suddenly be heard. "Come on over here. Let's go for a little walk."

"If the problem of fathers and sons is so sharply posed that my presence is injurious for you or for someone else, Papa, I will fulfill your wish out of a feeling of elementary love for my fellow man."

Tosya got up, grabbed Kolya by the hand in passing, and disappeared with him out the door.

A pause.

The awkward silence lasted about five minutes.

Finally Ivan Antonych made a breach.

"The lads must be brought back. What a phenomenon you have there, Natalya Dmitryevna; your Tosya, Lord save us, is a phenomenon! What did you nurse him on? . . . Kolya, Kolya! Bring Tosya back here! Hurry up!"

The boys came back and sat down. Tosya was in his place again. Exactly as he had been before being exiled, as though nothing had happened. And, indeed, had anything really happened? Ivan Antonych still didn't understand: was it in a dream that this youngster had told him off? Was such a child possible in general? Perhaps that wasn't at all what had been said. Perhaps everyone had placed their own adult interpretation on those words. But no, that was exactly what he said . . . Still (Ivan Antonych thought to himself), why am I getting upset over what a child says?

"And so, Natalya Dmitryevna, you seriously want to know how we live here?" Ivan Antonych turned to a third person to change the subject. "Do you remember Herzen's description of a provincial town in 'Memoirs of a Young Man'? That's what it's like here. A government office, the twentieth day of the month, men wearing orders and medals. Then after work, something to drink, some snacks, and cards. The majority take bribes. But what is surprising in this? What revelations, tell me please, would you want after Herzen? After Saltykov-Shchedrin? Even after Gogol? In the end, they described it all."

"What about the local color?"

"Of course there is that. There's the barbaric treatment of Jews, and partly of Moldavians too. But I think you know that perfectly well without my telling you. The peasants toil by the sweat of their brow, don't get enough to eat, survive on *mamalyga*, and, on days off, drink vodka like all good Orthodox Christians. The Jews in their little hamlets suffer from trachoma and live on nobody knows what or how. You know, it's like the anecdote where everyone manages to scrape up a bite to eat by borrowing from somebody else. I sometimes wrack my brains trying to figure out how this impoverished mass survives—but they do—they are fruitful and multiply and fill up the earth. They are being fleeced, and on top of that, they are yanked around by their beards. You know something about Bessarabia from Pushkin. But that was Kishinyov, after all, not Byeltsy.

Say, but why aren't you drinking your tea? Lyubochka, pour her some tea, for heaven's sake!"

"Thanks, but don't fuss over us, Ivan Antonych."

"Well then, besides Byeltsy, there's also Skulyany, Faleshty, and all the other small towns. I sometimes have to go to them in the line of duty. Such sights there—you'd never get tired of looking at them."

"All right. And what about you? What are you going to do, Ivan Antonych?"

"What can I do? Complain? Who to? Draft some proposals for reform? I neither want to nor can I. What kind of a reformer am I? Besides, you know, it's absolutely useless. Nothing would come of it but unpleasantness. This government work, speaking truthfully, has become repulsive to me. God grant that I can remain simply an honest person in this job. They're digging holes for me to fall into. Just because I won't take bribes or use foul language against the Jews. Nice, isn't it?"

"Not much that's good in the situation."

"Not much at all. Not like it was in Moscow. What times we had, eh, Natalya Dmitryevna? Remember? But there you have it. Man proposes but God disposes. Only somehow he disposes in an awfully stupid way . . . You know, it would be better if you and Anton Ivanych told about Moscow and 'Piter' (St. Petersburg). Lord knows, that would be something far more interesting. If only I had taken some sort of Hannibal's vow the way Herzen and Ogaryov did. But I, as you know, never did that—"

The time came for stories about Moscow. And they really were more interesting. The Slavyanskys told about the coronation of Tsar Nicholas II and the Khodynka disaster;* after that, all hopes for change disappeared like smoke; the government crackdown on dissent became fiercer than it had been under Tsar Alexander III. They said that a student friend of Ivan Antonych's, a certain Raspopin, who had almost drawn Ivan Antonych into revolutionary activity, had died in Siberian exile; that in the progressive circles of the intelligentsia the Marxists had multiplied ("amazingly energetic, but such narrow people"); that in literature a group of Symbolists had appeared, cultivating the French decadent poets but at the same time flirting with Vladimir Solovyov's followers; that in philosophy, the tone was also being set by mystics and idealists and that Lopatin had taken over the journal *Problems of Philosophy and Psychology*; that things were going hard for all the Narodniks and their old traditions; not only were the Marxists pecking away at them but also they were under attack from the "ultramodern" Europeanizing bourgeois elements; that a new theater was

*On Khodynka, see glossary.

coming into existence in Moscow with the support of some of the more enlightened merchants; that there was great ferment among the intelligentsia in general—things were not like they had been in the old days; that a terrible intolerance was developing and bitter verbal battles were being fought . . .

In a word, the Petrovs' guests brought down on the heads of their hosts a world of ideas as far removed from the paperboard world of Byeltsy as heaven from earth. The disparity was so tangible that even Ivan Antonych, with all his recollections of former times, by no means understood everything Natalya Dmitryevna was relating. The break from their past life had been too great, and life evidently had been moving on too swiftly and intensively. Kolya looked blank. Some humorous satirical verse from the institute that Auntie Lyalka had taught him swam into his head:

Buckle, Mill, Comte, and Kant
They're all easier to read
Their "substance" easier to grasp
Than you, my friend, to understand

Who the above-named persons were, or what "substance" was, Kolya of course did not know. But his ignorance and the feeling of complete mental impasse made these verses into a symbol for all this incomprehensible abracadabra, this devil-only-knows-what gibberish, and would come to him whenever he heard big words and phrases that had no meaning for him.

Ivan Antonych had somehow grown serious. The very nature of the conversation ruled out his usual way of clowning around and practicing his light-minded, frivolous *façon de parler*. Also, the presence of Slavyansky, whom he had just met for the first time, restrained him: Natasha (he thought) knew him backward and forward, but what would this eternally serious, bespectacled gentleman, who probably never in his life understood a joke or did anything naughty, what would he think? Why, he didn't even know how to toss back a glass of vodka; he was repressed. He was bound to come up with some thought like: "So this is the kind of friend Natasha has!" Such was Ivan Antonych's thinking. And so he became subdued, reined in his tongue, and adopted a serious tone, more suited to the occasion. Besides, it was interesting for him to have a heart-to-heart talk with the Slavyanskys: the way of life in Byeltsy had not entirely pounded all his real needs and interests out of him, and he spoke the honest truth when he said that this government work, with all its accompanying relationships and consequences, had become profoundly repulsive to him.

The conversation meandered. Tosya was beginning to nod, and soon his little face, with its washed-out pallor, exhaustedly and painfully dropped onto the table.

His mother looked at him with sad eyes.

"It's time for us to go, Ivan Antonych."

"Ah, stay a little longer! It's been ages!"

"No, it's time," Natalya Dmitryevna was resolute. "Anton Ivanych, let's go!"

She got up.

"Bring the lanterns, or the devil will break someone's leg. Kolya! Run get the lanterns! Let me see you home."

"You don't have to. Don't trouble yourself, for heaven's sake."

"No, you're going to drown in this mud here. Little Kolya almost drowned once hereabouts—"

The Slavyanskys went off, and suddenly Kolya felt empty and alone within himself, even though his mother and father and little Volodya were still there.

Chapter 6

Around Byeltsy there were steppes, fields of corn, rolling hills, and here and there patches of saline soil. The little Reutsel River flowed through like a winding ribbon. Over the steppes the wind blew last year's tumbleweed, those bushes which, like light brown woven balls, would roll along, bouncing and trembling, flying headlong across the unbounded expanse. The gophers stood as still as tiny pillars, whistling now and then, and swiftly disappearing down their holes when a human being appeared or the ominous shadow of a hawk swept by. Immediately beyond the edge of the town were some sprawling barracks, their whitewashed sides looking stark, and off to the side stood the stockade, surrounded on all sides by high brick walls, its crude squares and rectangles inspiring fear with their dry geometric simplicity. Above the fort, as though in mockery, flocks of cheery, multicolored pigeons were always soaring, swooping, diving, playing against the dark-blue sky: the chief of the stockade was a great pigeon fancier and especially prized snub-nosed, opaline, tumbler pigeons.

The river was a small one; in the heat, when cracks appeared in the exhausted land and the steppes turned reddish-brown, like cloth made out of camel's hair, the river dried up, and instead of a continuous silvery ribbon there were only occasional foul-looking pools. Not many fish could be found in the river, but to make up for it, crayfish abounded on the bottom. Locally they were called *skoiki*. No bush or tree grew on the river's banks, which were cut by long narrow gullies through which small streams would flow in the spring, bubbling to form a dirty yellow froth. The large stretches along the river were overgrown with tall weeds: thistles, burdock, goosefoot, jimsonweed, and wormwood. It was fairly difficult to get through these thickets; on the other hand, it was an ideal place for goldfinches, greenfinches, warblers.

Kolya sometimes longed for the forest at Makarovo. The Staneviches' orchard was so familiar to him, down to its very last twig almost. And then one day his father announced: "Tomorrow, we're going to the forest!"

Oh Lord, what a wonderful thing to hear! The forest was a long way off, maybe twenty versts. A large company gathered for the trip: Yelizaveta Ivanovna Stanevich, the Slavyanskys, the elder Staneviches, Mikhailov and his daughter, Tanya, and two treasury employees—they and Mikhailov had brought guns and dogs along—to hunt for ducks and bustards. They hired several Jewish drivers, whose phaetons each were harnessed to a pair of nags—and the persistent ringing of their harness bells announced the passage of this grand cortege beyond the borders of the small provincial town, so wearing to the eye of the beholder.

The weather turned out superb. A breath of freshness and coolness filled the early summer morning. Small, pearl-white, gentle groups of clouds swam by on the infinite deep blue sky. Merlins sailed over the fields, stopping short in midair, their wings flapping as their sharp eyes sought their prey. Gophers ran across the road, swinging their hind ends awkwardly. Corncrakes were trying to outdo one another with their ripping, piercing cries, as though naughty boys were maliciously tearing sheets. Now here, now there, a quail would sound off from its hiding place in the light, silky, rippling grasses. There was the smell of wild flowers and wormwood: the steppes had not turned dry that year; it had been rainy—rainier, they said, than any year the old-timers could remember. Life was flourishing in all its diversified fullness . . .

The sun rose higher; it began to get hot. The horses already were starting to sweat and kept slowing down to a sleepy pace, from which the blows of the whip and the coachmen's shouts would rouse them. Clouds of horseflies, gadflies, and other biting insects were swarming over the poor animals, no matter how hard they shook their heads or waved their tails. Their coats were covered with spots of blood from the stinging bites, and bumps were welling up. The harness bells were jingling. A cloud of yellow dust stretched back behind the phaetons . . .

Everyone was glad they'd soon be seeing something new, instead of the same old rooms and trees and fences that they always saw. Yelizaveta Ivanovna, under her breath, was singing a Moldavian song:

Spune, spune, Moldovane
Inde drumu la fokshani
Shi kasutsa mititik
Shi nevasta frumushik

Shi barbatu natereu
Yakuloi suflitu neu?*

The hunters rode together and, anticipating the pleasures of the hunt, exchanged preliminary considerations on the subject.

"So what do you think, are the smaller bustards out in force?"

"No, I don't think so. Not hot enough yet."

"What about the greater bustards—think there'll be any?"

"Devil only knows. Sometimes they're there in flocks as many as two hundred, sometimes there's nary a one. Sometimes the frosts catch them so that the peasants come along and kill them with sticks or drive them off to their barnyards like tame geese. When their wings get frozen."

"What about ducks?"

"Along the river in the reeds I think we'll find them: both mallard and teal. We'll come across partridges, too. My Rex is a specialist in them: he'll get you down to them so well you couldn't want better—"

"Ha, ha, ha! What good will it be if he 'gets you down.' "

"Never mind the wisecracks. You know what I mean. You're a hunter, aren't you? Or is hunter's vodka the only thing you know about?"

"Well, that's a good thing, too. Out in the fresh air. And what about the cognac, did you bring it?"

"What would we do without cognac? Of course we brought it. After all, you know—ha, ha!—we're hunters, too."

"And did you bring a net or a game bag?"

"I brought my paws."

"Come on, now. Don't worry. We won't come home empty-handed."

The dogs were yearning to leap out and start the chase. Their eyes were burning and they fidgeted constantly. Swift kicks sent them back to the carriage floor, and the kicks were accompanied by shouts and sometimes unprintable obscenities. The Slavyanskys were riding with the Petrovs, except for Kolya and Tosya, who were with the Staneviches. Tosya was staring at everything with dismay through his thick glasses, like some small Martian suddenly finding himself on Earth.

"What's that over there?"

"That's corn. Did you think it was palm trees?"

"And that thing? Flying over there? All silvery!"

"That's a harrier."

---

* These verses are transliterated from the Cyrillic form of the Moldavian alphabet imposed by the tsarist authorities after the Russian conquest of the area in the late nineteenth century. The spelling in Romanian, which is based on a Latin script, would be somewhat different.

"What does it eat?"

"Mice, beetles, grasshoppers."

"Kolya! Look! What a beautiful bird! All blue!"

"There's as many of those as you'd want around here. That's a roller. Heck, it'd be better if we got to the forest."

"Kolya," the elder Stanevich addressed the boy. "I forgot to tell you: this morning I cut down a root-digger with my shovel."

"What root-digger? What did it look like?"

"Well, it was reddish-brown, with black spots. About the size of two gophers."

"It must have been a hamster. Why didn't you show it to me? When you cut it did you kill it?"

"Well, it was still alive."

"Ivan Yegorych, be a good friend, please, and show it to me. Why in the world did you kill it? You could have taken it alive."

"What would I need *that* for? Trash that it was! Ruining everything in my orchard, and I'm supposed to feel sorry for it?"

The barouche in which the Petrovs were riding with the Slavyanskys had its own conversation going.

"Natalya Dmitryevna, don't you think it's really bad for Tosya to read so much? Such very early mental development—it's quite unusual—doesn't it frighten you?"

"Well, of course, but what can I do? There isn't an ounce of rational pedagogy involved—I know that myself. I really can't deal with it all, Lyubov Ivanovna. The trouble is he's physically so weak, so weak—just the thought of it makes me shudder—he doesn't like to play children's games, and he really isn't able to: he can't run, or swim—and then, he's always with grown-ups. So he compensates for it with his world of books. Of course, such one-sidedness is dangerous—I've suggested to Anton Ivanych so many times to take him to Rossolimo,* but—"

"Of course, of course," Slavyansky began to squeak, "it's a bad thing. On the one hand, it's bad that there isn't equal development of all his functions . . . and probably that's . . . um . . . dangerous. On the other hand, there you see him, he's just like Henry Thomas Buckle. It's almost four years now that he's been . . . um . . . writing in . . . um . . . classical Greek. And he's been growing up fairly well—"

"That's my Anton Ivanych for you: on the one hand, on the other, and for a third thing. And what's the conclusion? To waver back and forth and ruminate like Hamlet? And then it's going to be too late. Can you believe

---

*On Rossolimo, see glossary.

this: not long ago I took a book away from Tosya—by John William Draper.* Imagine that: an eight-year-old boy reading Draper! And, you know, there was so much grief and crying I had to give it back."

"Well, you know, I even worry about our Kolya."

"Oh, now he's a different story: you have a regular little live wire there! He's an expert at everything."

"You don't know, Natalya Dmitryevna. I can't keep track of the children. They've become real street urchins now. They've been initiated into everything. Vanya and I were trying to think about how to approach the question of—the sexual question. And it turns out, they already know all about it. Learned it on the streets."

"There's nothing so awful about that, Lyuba. Enough of this idea of keeping children locked up! Let them learn to swim—"

"You talk like that because you're so light-minded. You yourself taught Kolya a bunch of foolishness. You never stopped to think about when it's all right to say something and when it's not. When it comes to good sense in such matters, God surely shortchanged you."

At that point the foremost carriage, with the hunters, suddenly came to a halt. What was it? Men with guns and dogs were getting out. It turned out that a flock of partridges had just flown across the road: the birds had been bathing in the dust and flew right out from under the horses' hooves.

"We're going to start off from here, Ivan Antonych. It's about five versts to the forest, no more than that. You make yourselves to home there; the woods isn't that big; we'll find you."

"All right."

"Aren't you going to wish us 'neither feather nor fur'?"

"How's that? Come again."

"My dear man, it's totally obvious that you are 'young and fair, and haven't been to Saxony.' "† Mikhailov began to chortle. "It's a hunter's saying for good luck. But excuse us, asking you for a blessing like that is like asking for milk from a billy goat. Adieu! Please look after my daughter well.

"O what a duty, Dear Creator,
To be a dad to a grown-up daughter."

Mikhailov began roaring this song in his rough bass voice, till the Petrovs and Slavyanskys involuntarily broke into smiles. And off the

---

*American popularizer of scientific subjects; author of *Human Physiology* (1856), *History of the Intellectual Development of Europe* (1863), and *Thoughts on the Future Civil Policy of America* (1865).

†A line from a popular song.

hunters went. Tosya and Kolya got out of the Staneviches' carriage and went to sit with Tanya, and the carriages moved off toward the forest, which soon appeared as a strip of blue, like a bank of fog, in the distance.

And then at last the cool of the forest was blowing in their faces and the carriages rolled under an arch of mighty green branches, flashing with emerald specks of light. The horses stopped. The coachmen quickly unharnessed them and led them into the cool shade, where the tired horses immediately began using their teeth to strip the leaves off branches, and switching their tails in a melancholy way, with the muscles all over their bodies quivering and shuddering, they began to chew on the rich, sweet grass.

In the forest a triumphant, concentrated silence reigned. Enormous trees—oaks, beeches, hornbeams, and the trunks of wild cherries—like colossal pillars supported a magnificent ceiling of foliage, through whose thickness, in bright splashes, sportive and playful, pierced the cheerful life-giving rays of the sun. Everywhere under foot were soft pillows of moss and silken grasses, strewn with wreaths of flowers. In the solid vault of the forest overhead, here and there showed dark-blue spaces of open sky from which floods of gleaming light fell upon the small forest clearings. In the shadows, among the mighty, moss-covered trunks and roots, which seemed like great intertwining serpents that had frozen still when they entered the earth, a little brook was gurgling, almost invisible beneath the clumps of ferns, which spread their shapely patterned greenery every-where.

"Over here, over here!" several voices began to shout at once.

"Here's a good place for a picnic. A really good place! Isn't that so?"

Ivan Antonych got excited.

"Natalya Dmitryevna! Yelizaveta Ivanovna! Katerina Ivanovna. Come here. Lyubochka, you give the orders, please."

Everyone, including the carriage drivers, set about transferring to the chosen spot all the various appurtenances of a picnic: tablecloth, samovar, food, bottles . . .

"Only, please, if possible, be sure not to leave any paper on the ground," with an ingratiating smile Natalya Dmitryevna tossed off her little speech.

The tablecloth was spread on a bare spot in the forest. Leather pil-lows—the seats from the phaetons—were brought over. The plates were filled with sandwiches, sardines, cheese, hard-boiled eggs, sausages, slices of ham. And the inevitable bottles made their appearance.

"Where have the children gotten to?"

"Ko-o-lya! Tosya! Ta-a-nya! Halloo!" Ivan Antonych shouted with all his might.

From somewhere in the distance the children's answering voices could he heard: "Halloo! Halloo!" The children had already managed to escape, to go inspect and clamber over the neighboring trees and bushes: Kolya led the way and explained things, like a veritable Cicero; Tanya was behind him; and Tosya, with a serious face expressing the philosophical wonder of an Aristotle, listened—he was barely able to keep up and he was plainly embarrassed to be in the presence of a girl.

They came running back, out of breath. Kolya already had some booty in his hands.

"Papa Vanya! Look! I tell you, look! A hairy caterpillar! This one here. Do you see it?"

"It's an apollo."

"And not damaged. Give me some paper; I'll make an envelope. And we saw some grosbeaks. Really and truly!"

"Where?"

"On a wild cherry tree. Sitting there and pecking at the old berries. A whole flock. If you want, we can go take a look. It's just a couple of paces—"

Ivan Antonych hesitated. Then decided after all to stay where he was: it would have been awkward . . .

"Hand me the corkscrew, if you would."

Pop! Pop!

"Ivan Yegorych. Even hermit monks accept this stuff! And some for you, Anton Ivanych?"

"Thank you, but I don't drink."

"Now, Kolya! Run and fetch the drivers. Look lively! Hop to it!"

Kolya ran to the carriages.

The three strapping Jewish cabmen, in their gaberdines tied with sashes, wearing caps like yarmulkes, from which there jutted thick braids of red hair, looked at one another uncertainly and said something incomprehensible, but they came along anyway.

"What can we do for you, Your Honor?"

"Well, here, have a drink, please! Surely you do drink?"

"But how can this be?"

"Well, it just is. Will you drink?"

"We'll drink."

They each drank a glass of vodka, and wheezed, but resolutely refused hors d'oeuvres and could not keep the look of disgust from their faces at the sight of the ham, even the smell of which, it seemed, made them feel sick. Expressing their gratitude for "the treat," they moved off to the side, and pulled out of their large pockets identical red cloths, in which some sort of food was wrapped. Then breaking it into little bits and carefully gathering up the crumbs, they began to eat.

After the repast everyone went for a walk in the depths of the forest, which lured them with its breathing air of freshness. The handsome beech trees, with trunks it would take several people to reach around, trunks as smooth as the body of an immense caryatid, marked only here and there with blotches of dark brown moss, lifted their crowns up toward the sky, but those crowns were lost in the overall green chaos. The sprawling oaks with their wrinkled, wizened bark, like the skin of centenarians, spread their branches in all directions, like gnarled and knotty arms, and their carved and fretted leaves enframed their solid torsos with a scattering of green. Hiding in deep shadow were the tender little white bells of Solomon's seal, hanging in rows beneath the dark green leaves. Stubby little branches of wintergreen rose from the earth, giving off a gentle, barely perceptible aroma. Jutting up among the ferns were light green horsetails, remote descendants of colossal species long extinct. And stalks of willow herb, with their tender pink flowers, were sticking up high . . . The subtle aromas of fresh grass and rotting leaves were carried in the air, which was filled with primordial delights. Somewhere above, a woodpecker tapped. Titmice chirped. Onto the half rotten trunk of a large fallen tree there hopped, out of some thicket, a teensy little wren; it began to chatter, flicked its tail, and darted like a baby mouse into a heap of fallen branches.

"Papa! The wild pear tree! How big it is!"

"But where are your grosbeaks?"

"Over to the right. Let's hurry."

Ivan Antonych separated himself from the company and went off with the children. The grosbeaks weren't in the cherry tree any longer, but on the ground the remains of the feast were in evidence, bird droppings and pecked-over, dried-up cherries.

"See, see? They were just here. The bird shit's still fresh." Kolya shouted almost in an ecstasy: the convincing material proof was in his hands and he held it right up under his father's nose.

"Ugh, throw that stuff away. I can see."

Tosya was smiling slyly. Tanya got red in the face: she was not used to such plain talk or plain actions. Everything here was amazing to her: the first time in her life she had been in the forest.

"Halloo!" women's voices could be heard.

"Come on, kids, let's go back."

The rest of the company was moving slowly, taking baby steps to keep pace with the weakest link in the chain. Little remarks were flying back and forth; they were taking pleasure in the verdant growth, the flowers, the fresh air, the rays of sun. And at the same time each one was thinking to himself or herself in a vague flow of consciousness that seemed to dissolve into something large and tender and quiet. Yelizaveta Ivanovna was gathering a bouquet, and her shapely figure bent over frequently as she picked a flower here and there: one felt like singing and weeping aloud, not out of sadness, but just because, for no reason.

Ivan Yegorych was tapping his stick against the gigantic tree trunks; he'd like to bring home dozens of planks of wood like this! And how much brushwood, how many fallen trees—all going to waste here. A regular treasure!

Natalya Dmitryevna felt fear for her husband and child: my dear ones, weak and sickly as they are, won't this exhaust them?

Lyubov Ivanovna was tormented by one thought: was the nanny going to be able to feed baby Andryusha all right? What if the milk turns sour? It was so risky to leave them at home a whole day—but Lord, how beautiful it was here.

Anton Ivanych limped along behind everyone; although he found it pleasant, it wasn't really that pleasant: it was hard to walk, and when you got down to it, there was nothing very special . . . On the other hand, it wasn't so bad to be out in nature, not bad at all . . . And he attentively observed this nature he was thinking about, through his high-powered glasses, with his shortsighted eyes.

The time flew swiftly by, like an unseen arrow. The children hadn't had enough running and playing before the grown-ups were tossing words around enough to make you cry!

"Isn't it time to go back?"

"Yes, we should be going while it's still light."

"How far is it?"

"About twenty versts."

"The sun's still high."

"Yes, but we still have to pick up the hunters."

Kolya stood with trembling lips: he wanted so badly not to leave, but he could see that no pleading would do any good. Still, how wonderful it was in the forest! With all his heart the boy felt a kinship with nature's domain, its trembling, palpitating life, its play of images. He was like a living refutation of both the dry, rationalistic outlook that sees only firewood in a grove of trees and the romantic outlook that with unrestrained fantasy sees gnomes and trolls and all those other daydreams. The superstition that had taken root since the time of that great wit and fantasist, E.T.A. Hoffmann, with his magical fairy tales full of gold and diamond fountains, stated that the trembling rhythms of nature could be experienced only in the form of the consciously magical and supernatural, that is, by revealing behind nature some sort of different, secret, and mysterious world. Kolya rejected this prejudice with every fiber of his being. No less than the comical professor in one of Hoffmann's tales (*Klein Zaches*), Kolya loved to "do botany," to make herbariums and keep collections. But this did not prevent him one bit from hearing all the voices of nature—real, actual, genuine nature, with its starry sky, its scarlet dawns, the rustling of its leaves, the crash and rumble of its storms, and the gentle glow of moonlight. He bathed in the aromas of sweet-scented grasses, gloried in the tender gusts of warm air, melted into the colors and sounds . . . And now the boy stood there with imploring eyes: couldn't we stay just another hour among these trees, with the velvet of the mossy carpet, the gleam of golden rays through the emerald scales, the riot of verdure . . .

"Come on, come on. Let's get going. It's time."

Unwillingly the children helped pack up the cups and glasses. Waste paper was gathered in a heap and buried, so that picnic droppings would not spoil the primeval purity of Mother Nature. They took their seats in the phaetons again. The horses switched their tails. The little harness bells rang and whips snapped in the air as the carriages rolled jauntily from the forest. The sun had already begun to slip down against its blinding blue backdrop. The distances were indistinct in a pale blue haze, and above the corn fields you could see the hot air shimmering. It capriciously gusted and flowed back and forth in nearly visible streams. Up ahead fields of sunflowers blazed like gold coins. The river like a ribbon of molten silver wound its way nearby, overshadowed by the thick green velvet of reeds. From somewhere now and then muffled gunshots could be heard, like knocking on a distant door. The grasshoppers and field crickets kept up an unceasing chirring and chattering din. And then the carriages were descending from the hills into the valley, and the boys began to shout:

"There! There they are! See? Over there!"

Far up ahead the tiny figures of the hunters, spread out at irregular distances from one another, were striding along. Beside them, even tinier, like miniatures, ran the dogs. Now and then a hunter would aim his gun, you could see the smoke, then after some time—how strange that stretch of time was!—the muffled sound, as though fired from under a pillow, would reach the viewer. The people and the dogs were fussing around, running from place to place, bending down—apparently looking for things and picking them up—then pacing along in different directions again . . . The carriages were now coming close to the hunting grounds, and the hunters, who till then had paid no attention, started waving their arms and blowing into their gun barrels: this metallic sound, like that of a horn, so sweet to the hunter's ear, quavering in the air, now reached the ears of the entire company.

"Our people have shot something. I wonder what."

"Probably nothing much."

"Nothing? But they were shooting so much!"

"Shooting is one thing, but hitting is another," Tosya piped up in his thin, little voice.

The elder Stanevich shielded his shaggy-browed eyes with his hand, and said authoritatively:

"They're carrying something. That means they bagged some game. Mikhailov has something swinging at his side—and the others, too."

"I see it," cried Kolya. "I see it, too!" And he clapped his hands.

"Papa, don't you see? Take a good look! It's on Mikhailov's left side, and on the right of the other two. Isn't that right, Ivan Yegorych."

"That's right."

The orders were given, and the phaetons rushed, bumping, along the road, raising a vast cloud of dust behind them—and they thought nothing of it, but the ones to the rear had to pay! It was a good thing the summer had been rainy and only a moderate amount of dust filled the nose, eyes, and ears.

At last they arrived.

"Ivan Antonych! We're hellishly tired," Mikhailov's bass voice boomed, deliberately avoiding any mention of their booty. "It would also be good to have a drink. You'd have to wait for us here a little bit."

"Of course. Be my guests. Ladies! See after your gallant warriors: they've earned their reward. Lyubochka! Yelizaveta Ivanovna!"

"Don't trouble yourselves, we'll do it. There you see, my cavaliers have already gotten down to business without being asked."

And, indeed, the other two hunters had dealt with all the difficulties of unpacking in one second, dragging out all the food and bottles in short order; they popped the corks with gay abandon and set their jaws to working, baring their strong, white teeth, which gleamed brightly against their sunburned faces: just like a pair of Fenimore Cooper Indians.

The rest of the company looked over the game killed that day; Tanya was especially proud of her father. But Kolya was furious: in a hunter's net, he found a merlin, still alive but with a broken wing, and he carried it over to Mikhailov.

"Kolya, I winged that bird and brought it here for you," Mikhailov was barely able to say this, his mouth was stuffed so full of ham sandwich that knots of muscle stood out on the sides of both cheeks; only with effort was he able to move his jaws, and it was obvious that he would still have to perform some extraordinarily complicated moves with his tongue to make the food that was so diligently being processed go down. He was puffing and snorting, champing and grumbling, but his eyes were shining.

In fact how could they not be shining! Lying in a heap were two braces of partridges; about twelve in each. Their ash-colored, reddish-brown wings and brick-red tails were bunched together, forming an entire little hillock on the grass; next to them were two huge bustards, splendid birds, each weighing about a pood (thirty-six pounds), with opalescent, speckled wings, long necks, and bluish gray heads with whiskers on either side; they had limply laid out their proud necks on the ground, their dark eyes closed forever beneath a tender pale-blue film; the whole shoulder bone of one had been blown to bits and drops of blood had sprayed its entire body, sullying the lovely arabesques of the bustard's coat. On three handsome mallards the elegant "mirrors" were gleaming: that was the name for the shiny dark-green feathers on their wings. Next to them lay some quail: they had been crushed, poor things, under the weight of the other birds and could hardly be recognized—just some dirty, gray, bloody lumps . . .

While everyone was looking over the game that had been bagged, the hunters took their pleasure: they removed their boots and, with the ladies' permission, unwound their footcloths, drank, ate, and occasionally cast well-pleased glances at the noncombatants.

"And what is that?" piped up Tosya, dragging a strange-looking bird out from under the pile of bodies. It was about the size of a chicken, but had a long neck and a fairly long bill, and it was soft and fluffy all over, like a reddish-brown duster.

"Papa!" cried Kolya. "It's a bittern! Really and truly! A bittern! A bittern!"

"Ha, ha, ha!" Mikhailov rumbled. "Ask Pavel Vasilyevich if you want to know what kind of thing that is. Get him to tell you."

Pavel Vasilyevich, one of the hunters, was sitting there with mud all over him. It had already dried, but his clothes were smeared with it, and even his face, if one looked closely, was pockmarked with bits of it, as though he had suffered a severe case of smallpox. He shrank back, embarrassed, but his two friends kept poking him in the ribs, urging him to tell about something that apparently was not at all pleasant for him.

"Cut it out, for God's sake, or I'll let you have it."

"No, no, tell the story, Pavel Vasilyevich, don't be modest. What's there to be ashamed of, here in your native land!"

But Pavel Vasilyevich kept quiet. He preferred to give a thorough chewing to the fairly tough smoked sausage. *Tarde venientibus ossa* (or, "Those who arrive late get the bones"), as the Latin proverb goes. The better portions had already been taken, and what was left for Pavel Vasilyevich, who in the sphere of consumption had manifested less haste than his colleagues, was, if not the bones, then at any rate the somewhat tougher pieces. But does that really matter to a hunter?

"You don't want to? Then we'll tell the story for you."

"You'd do better, Mikhailov, to tell about how you shot at the rabbit and missed."

"Me? At a rabbit? You're out of your mind!"

"Yes, my friend, a rabbit. I had a perfect view of it."

"Nothing of the kind! I never shot at a rabbit."

"You didn't? That's good! What was that thing, then, that came running at you from my direction, behind that little hill, to the left? A lion? Or a tiger?"

"Hey, I shot at some partridges, two of them, with both barrels, and I got 'em."

"That partridge of yours was pretty funny looking: with four feet and long ears—"

"Hey, what are you trying to pull the wool over people's eyes for? The devil only knows what you're talking about. Who was it, according to you, that shot the two large bustards?"

"You did. That's not what I'm talking about. You shot the bustards. But you also missed the rabbit. Missed by a mile. From twenty paces. And that rabbit went galloping off, leaping sky-high, not just running—"

"You're imagining things, you know that? But here's some material evidence. Ladies and gentlemen! Take a look at this enlightened person. He's all pockmarked, don't you see? All splashed with mud from the swamp he got stuck in. He was yelling to us at the top of his head that he'd shot a small bustard. Do you get that? A small bustard. In a swamp yet! There you have a real hunter!"

It turned out that Pavel Vasilyevich, when he flushed a bittern out of the reeds, was convinced that he had shot a smaller bustard, although he couldn't understand how a steppe-dwelling bustard could have ended up in the swamp. Before he found his kill, however, and discovered it was a bittern, he had been incautious enough to shout out that he had killed a bustard. And in his haste he had slipped and fallen and taken a pretty good bath in the rust-colored mud of the swamp. These exploits of his, taken all together, came back to haunt him many times over: he was teased about it all the way home and poor Pavel Vasilyevich didn't know how to get out of it. Meanwhile, it was true that Mikhailov had shot at a rabbit and missed, but everyone believed his denials—except Pavel Vasilyevich, who had seen the whole thing in detail. Mikhailov's many partridges, which he had carried in on his back (that was the hump on Mikhailov's back that Ivan Yegorych's sharp eyes had detected), outweighed all the rest.

"Hunters, it's time to be going! Will you be ready soon?" Ivan Antonych addressed Mikhailov.

"Right away. We're pooped out, Ivan Antonych, dear friend. Don't get angry at us: you made a mistake by including us in your company—now you're paying for it."

"Oh no, it's nothing—" Ivan Antonych muttered somewhat confusedly. (And the thought flashed through his mind that he had said the wrong thing, that it sounded rude.)

"We'll be right with you. Forgive us," said Mikhailov.

At last they had all taken seats and began the final journey. Mikhailov again had his daughter on his lap, pressing her against his powerful, hairy chest, which showed through his unbuttoned, sweat-soaked shirt.

The sun was already sinking toward the horizon, and the entire east was in flames. The slopes of the hills were touched with gold. The sky was burning like a violent bonfire. It spread out wide like an immense, sparkling brocade of precious stones on which dark-blue patterns and shapes had been sewn with dazzlingly bright borders. The sun kept falling lower and lower with a speed that defied comprehension. Its gleaming rays like arrows pierced the clouds, which, turning blue, pressed modestly against each other, as though embarrassed by the magnificence of the giant heavenly body. The fiery red ball was sinking into a vast unruly element of purple ocean. From the fields the breeze bore perfumed, honeyed aromas, as well as the sharp and bitter smell of wormwood. An enormous flock of jackdaws all at once filled the sky, and the harsh, guttural sounds of a thousand birds—as though metallic diaphragms were breaking—came down from on high, in harmony surprisingly, with the quiet stealing over the evening.

Like a prolonged echo, in limitless space,
Blending in a chorus, harmonious, languid,
In distant mystery, inseparably fused,
All colors, sounds, and smells merge into one.

The sun was already touching the edges of the earth. It flattened and spread out, as if making a final desperate effort to hold on, not to go under, not to drown . . . But it kept sinking and sinking in an ocean of crimson purple, and there was nothing on the darkening edge of the earth it could hold onto.

Already a wave of coolness, arising out of nowhere, swept past, lavishing its fresh breath on everyone. Already the last small bright-red segment

on the horizon had submerged. Already the spreading fan of sun rays, pro-
jected from below the earth, was turning pale, as though fatally diseased.
The riot of purple-crimson color faded. The golden grandeur died away.
The orange tones grew pale. The tender shades of green, lit with gold,
retreated in silence before the imperceptible advance of elemental blue, a
light-blue, almost a pale violet. The stars came out and started up their
twinkling, and the immense, unbounded vault of the night sky began to
blossom with a miraculous scattering of silver. And far off in the distance,
amid the shades of night descending on the earth, already could be seen,
pouring themselves out, the lights of human habitation, the town . . .

Chapter 7

In Byeltsy a smallpox epidemic broke out. Not that it was a big epidemic, but several cases of genuine smallpox and several deaths were recorded by the doctors and the police on the appropriate forms and with the appropriate signatures—after that, could there be any doubt? And so Kolya's parents decided to have the full complement of the Petrov family, both large and small, vaccinated a second time for smallpox. Kolya became terribly frightened by the prospect of this operation. This was strange: when a large dog nearly chewed him to the bone after clamping down on his left shoulder, he didn't even cry out; only after it was all over, with his face white as a sheet, he moaned softly through his tears, while his wound was being bandaged: "She . . . she bit me." He was scarred forever. He was able to make the most hazardous journeys over rooftops and into the tallest trees without any fear. He would hang from the limbs of trees head down, and there was one time when he had to stay in bed for about two weeks, unable to move his head—he had nearly dislodged the vertebrae in his neck. Once he was shinnying up the bare trunk of a tree, grabbed the first branch with his hands, and letting his legs hang, found himself unable to climb down again. He hung by his hands until they brought a fireman's ladder and carried him down; only by great effort was he able to unclench his fists. In other words, his adventures had been quite diverse and, in all their variety, quite full of risk. But he had not held himself back. His fear of the smallpox vaccination, on the other hand, was extraordinary: either because the image of the doctor with his cold cutting instruments confounded him, or because the words "smallpox vaccination" had a horrifyingly incomprehensible ring—and whatever is incomprehensible or unfamiliar intensifies fear—or perhaps he was scared of the itching red bumps and didn't want to be simultaneously half-sick and half-well for several weeks; or perhaps it was all of those things together—at any rate, the youngster decided to evade this operation at all costs.

There arrived a doctor who had the grim visage of an augur and the serious demeanor suited to one conscious of himself as a savior of suffering humanity. Of course there was nothing he could take personal credit for: he had not discovered the smallpox microbe nor originated the theory of immunity nor invented serum; his role was limited to the performance of some hand movements technically as accessible to anyone as the flipping of an electrical switch to a person having no inkling about the nature of electricity. But he wore an expression as though he were holding in the pocket of his tussore jacket the keys to the greatest secrets of medicine, as though ordinary mortals should regard him with superstitious deference, as though matters of life and death depended on him, as though he were a sacred vessel of great wisdom. With comical superseriousness he laid out his coldly glittering instruments and pharmaceutical "preparations," called for alcohol, and with extraordinary self-importance began washing his hands, then boiled his instruments in water and rubbed them with alcohol—all this in mystery-shrouded silence, ritualistically, like some high priest.

He was supposed to start with Kolya. But Kolya was nowhere around. A search was organized. With a dissatisfied expression the doctor waited: just think of it, his precious time was being wasted! Ivan Antonych was infuriated; this was damn well embarrassing—in front of a doctor! He raced through the orchard, shouting, and finally caught a glimpse of his son's red shirt. He rushed after Kolya—who fled. At one point it seemed that his father would catch him, but Kolya in an instant cleared the fence into their neighbor's vineyard. A big surprise awaited him there. The neighbor's cow, notorious for her butting habits, was in that vineyard for some reason. She came to Kolya's father's aid, lowering her head and charging the boy. In terror he rushed for another fence, a high one that separated the vineyard from an open field, and managed to get over that one too just in time, escaping literally from under the cow's horns. He even felt the animal's hot breath on his back as he made his leap and came down on the other side. His heart was pounding like a captured bird's. He stopped to catch his breath. His body was bathed in cold sweat from top to toe. He had lost all his strength, and for the longest time was unable to get his bearings or grasp what had actually happened. It had all flashed by with such lightning speed.

Meanwhile at the house the sacred rites began. Ivan Antonych fell all over himself apologizing for the delay, roundly cursing his son, but they had to go ahead without him: the doctor gave everyone a smallpox shot, and they treated him to tea with cognac, with which he was abundantly satisfied. Then having received his due compensation, he went his way.

Toward evening Kolya presented himself, all covered with dust and looking as guilty as the prodigal son returning to his father's house. His parents decided to punish him anyway and locked him in the room where the bathtub was. Kolya looked around. The room was empty and boring. The punishment offended him to the depths of his soul. What was so awfully bad about what he had done? What gave them the right to order him, Kolya, around like that? If he didn't want a smallpox vaccination, why did they have to force it on him? He felt a bitter lump in his throat from the insult of it all and was overcome by spasms of dry sobbing. His lips trembled and tears rose to his eyes. On top of it all, he was hungry, but he chose not to ask for a single crumb, out of pride: since they had forgotten to feed him, even though he hadn't had anything to eat all day, there was no use talking to them . . .

Then suddenly a plan formed in his head. He tested the window, released the fastenings, and, quick as a monkey, slipped out into the front garden. After a moment's thought, he crawled into the thick bushes that grew right under the windows. There he made a little den for himself, flattened down the grass, and intertwined the branches above his head so that they wouldn't stick out in all directions or catch him in the eye. Then he settled down into his lair, giving himself over to bitter reflections. Let them hunt for him now! Let them learn what it means not to have him! They were the ones who had hurt and offended him—now let them weep.

"Kolya! Kolya!" muffled voices could be heard.

Silence.

"Kolya! Come here this instant!"

No answer.

Kolya waited expectantly. From the bushes he could see the door to the room he had fled being opened. Lyubov Ivanovna entered with a candle in her hand and froze in shock: Kolya wasn't there!

"Well and good. That'll show them," the boy thought to himself. He could see the flame of the candle guttering and the shadow swaying on the wall. Then his mother leaned over the bathtub—apparently to check— had he drowned there? The tub had been filled. There she stood stock still. Then she opened the window. The flame of the candle wavered in a current of air, and from his refuge Kolya could see the melted wax dripping from the candle. Holding his breath, he sat there, so close.

"Let them, let them" was what he thought. And he began to imagine that he had actually gotten lost, disappeared, even died. His mama and papa were gazing at his corpse, weeping and bitterly regretting that they had hurt his feelings. He wanted to think: it serves them right! But despite feeling sorry for himself and enjoying this vision of his parents' repentance, he began to feel sorry for them, too. He felt his tears already mingling with theirs. He couldn't restrain himself any longer, and sobbing he cried out:

"Mama, I'm here! I'm here!"

A mother is a mother. She had already forgotten her son's transgressions. Her heart knew only joy, and nothing else—gladness that Kolya had been found, that he was well and unharmed. As for all the rest—it was as though it hadn't happened, had simply never existed.

"How you frightened me, Kolya. For a moment I thought you had drowned in the tub. Where were you?"

"I . . . Mama . . . I was in the bushes."

"What in the world were you doing there?"

"I . . . I . . . I had . . . I felt—"

"What are you crying for—you silly fool. Vanya! Come here!"

And Kolya's mother told her husband the whole story.

"What did you do this for, Kolya? Aren't you ashamed? You frightened your mother so badly she could have fainted. Don't you know she just gave birth, that it's bad for her to get upset?"

"I didn't want—"

"And what did you run away from the doctor for like a flaming fool?"

"It hurts—"

"You're just a little old woman. That's what!"

"Papa, don't lie. You know I'm not a woman."

"How could you not be? You're afraid of a little scratch. What a hero! Wait till I tell Tosya what a scandal you created. A regular Uriel Acosta. And what's this in the back of your pants?"

It turned out that on top of everything Kolya, while jumping over the fence to escape the cow, in the grip of fear had soiled himself in the most unseemly manner and in the heat of the moment hadn't even noticed it. But the soiled pants put a humorous twist on everything that had happened, and the defect disclosed by Ivan Antonych simply served as an impetus to final reconciliation. To Kolya what had seemed tragic a moment earlier now seemed almost funny. And really, would Uriel Acosta have run from a doctor? And wasn't it foolish to have sat in the bushes and wept at what he imagined was his own corpse? Why, none of it was true; he had just made it all up.

Soon Kolya was greedily gulping down cold cutlets, thickly salted, followed by dumplings made from cherries. The cherries had been ripening on a plate in the cellar, were loaded with juice, and were amazingly tasty.

Kolya filled his little cheeks with these tasty dumplings, and life no longer seemed at all as bad as it had seemed just an hour before . . .

One lovely day Andryusha's elderly nanny took Kolya and Volodya with her into town. They went from store to store, buying all sorts of things: soap, candles, carrots, tooth powder, meat, grapes . . . The nanny contrived in an unimaginable way to squeeze it all into her basket, carefully separating one item from the next with paper wrappings—otherwise a terrible mess might result. Toward the end of their shopping they entered Popov's grocery store. It was filled with the smells of mint spice cakes, vanilla, caramel, and Dutchess pear (the same smell—pear essence—as the varnishes used nowadays on quality passenger cars). Along the walls there were shelves crowded with products; here, too, there were glass jars with candies of various sorts, all stuck to one another; and cone-shaped sugar loaves wrapped in heavy, dark-blue paper; and tin boxes with printed patterns containing the tea distributed by the Perlov company; and smoked whitefish; and sausages whose surfaces had already been touched by mold; and legs of lamb; and bottles of wine, vodka, and beverages of all sorts, to suit every taste, some thick and bubble-shaped, others slender with elongated necks.

The owner was a Russian, a precise and cleanly old man, in a tidy gray jacket, who exercised supervision over a number of fine young fellows standing behind the counter in white aprons and occasionally taking a pencil from behind the ear to tot up the customers' purchases. The proprietor was thin, seemed to be in good shape, and wore a neatly trimmed gray beard. And as he walked around the store he rubbed his hands together—not because he was cold but just so, for the fun of it. His job was to be the prototype of polite behavior; he even wore a soft collar with a tie—in short, the last word in good manners. While the nanny was picking out various items he came over to the boys.

"Whose boys would you be?"

"The Petrovs.'"

"The assessor of taxes?"

"Yes."

"Pleased to meet you. Do you like candy?" he asked Kolya.

"I like it."

Popov went to the jars, got candy, and held it out to Kolya and Volodya. But Kolya suddenly turned away and said sharply:

"We're not beggars."

The shopkeeper didn't know how to respond: there was no way he could have expected this kind of retort from a small boy. Volodya also puffed himself up. The nurse finished her shopping, and while the store owner was thinking over the situation, the three of them said good-bye and walked out. The boys had heard so much about bribes that to Kolya the candy that Popov was urging upon him in his capacity as an inspector's son appeared as a bribe of a certain kind; that's why he had flared up, as he always did in critical moments, big or small. By the next day the story of these children had gotten virtually all around town: well, well, look at what kind of kids these are? As for Popov, he adopted the pose of praising them, interpreting their behavior as the result of their parents' being painfully strict toward them—although, as he put it, they were only children, and there was no point in such strictness. He wanted to avoid any possible conflicts over this incident.

The Petrovs' usual existence was disrupted by the sudden and unexpected summoning of Ivan Antonych to Kishinyov, the provincial capital, where the higher officials lived and where the province's tax office was located. He quickly got his things together, taking various papers, documents, reports, statistical materials, and the most important current files, and set off for Kishinyov. There he was received with polite coolness, and several compliments were even addressed to him regarding his "irreproachable honesty." But in the course of this icy conversation with his superiors, when little digs began to be made on the subject of "catering to the Yids" (and this was done with exculpatory and supposedly understanding smiles), and when transparent hints began to be made to the effect that Ivan Antonych conducted himself in a way unlike the others, and that this "originality" went against the grain (we all need to walk in step, you see), Ivan Antonych understood that a mine had been placed underneath him and all that remained was for him to set it off. Actually, if the truth be known, during the course of the conversation he did not very clearly weigh all the pros and cons; he simply was overcome by an inner rage; he wanted to spit in the face of his well-groomed, finely chiseled supervisor in his brand new civil servant's uniform. He did not spit, but he did utter some cutting remarks that left no room for retreat: his bridges had been burned, and he announced there and then that he was submitting his resignation, gave a parting bow, and headed for Byeltsy.

As soon as he got back he discovered how far matters had progressed already. It turned out that while he was on his trip to Kishinyov, a new personage had arrived in Byeltsy, a certain Primerov, one of the young ones, a greenhorn really, whose function in Kishinyov was to serve as an official for "special assignments" and who was evidently connected with the highest police authorities. He had come to Byeltsy as a candidate for Ivan Antonych's post, and even hinted at that fact in a rather unambiguous way. In a small provincial town, word of any such thing would spread with the speed of a radiogram. The entire little world of the Byeltsy chinovniks was alert to the fact that Ivan Antonych's days were numbered; therefore immediately, as though by the wave of a magic wand, a readjustment of the entire front line of official relations took place and a rather substantial human chain turned, if not its back, then its side to Ivan Antonych. This circumstance, however, did not overly distress him: he was in the throes of indignation and was already spitting on everyone and everything from a high tree, describing many with cutting and pointed remarks, from which he had earlier refrained.

Primerov in the meantime was functioning very energetically, cobbling together a body of "public opinion." He was a young man, unimpeachably dressed in a jacket of most excellent English design, on the lapel of which there flashed his diamond-shaped enamel university pin. (The young man had graduated from the law school of one of the universities in southern Russia.) His hair was neatly parted at the side, and with the greatest care his forelock was graced with a wave. His shoes shone, and at his waistband he sported a thick gold watch chain. On his right hand he wore a ring with a "stone." His starched linen gleamed like newly fallen snow in bright sunshine. In speaking, he drew out his words, partly with a nasal ring, partly through his teeth, distinctly and with great self-importance, as befit a person enjoying the confidence of his superiors. He walked just as expressively as he talked and even moved his hands, it seemed, with a certain calculation: the young man's hands seemed to think for themselves! He had been quite fortunate in the matter of his physiognomy: he had a pimply and somewhat ruddy, unimpressive face, a nose like the gizzard of a bird, and a rather sorry-looking light-red mustaches, which he kept trimmed and clipped, although he virtually had to hunt with a magnifying glass for the object of his trimming and clipping; his crafty little pig's eyes attempted to be very expressive, sometimes nearly flying out of their orbits, although nothing ever came of all this effort. All these shortcomings were made up for by "style," and Primerov was a great specialist—one might even say, an old hand—at keeping up appearances.

He could play endlessly at such card games as vint and preference. And his capacity for cognac was amazing. He did not permit any "buddying up" toward himself. On the contrary, his entire conduct demonstratively expressed the "pathos of distance," that special social distance observed among bureaucrats on different rungs of the hierarchical ladder. Above all, Primerov knew how to instill fearful respect for his person. He had not yet assumed an official post, but people were already trembling in his presence: the Jews were trembling (they had their own, very accurate information about him), the Russian tradesmen were trembling—the former and the latter were already anxiously thinking about the "gifts" he would require—and the chinovniks themselves were trembling; what if he starts to shuffle people around like a deck of cards—reassigning one here, another there: the man carried a great deal of weight, he danced at the balls of the governor himself, and, it was said, he was even courting the daughter of His Esteemed Excellency, the governor. In a word, Primerov's credit in the world of the chinovniks was already very high, and those of the Molchalin type were already lined up and standing at attention, with all their deep reserves of servility, fear, hope, flattery, obsequiousness, and other outstanding bureaucratic virtues.

On the next day of Our Lord, Primerov appeared at church in his uniform, occupying the foremost place in the ranks of the local chinovniks, who deferentially made way for him. He took them all in with the tender glance of the benefactor addressing his protégés, as though recommending himself as the leading proponent of autocracy and Orthodoxy in the post he was to occupy. Then he assumed a grand pose, in keeping with his high status, and crossed himself from time to time with little gestures, slowly and lazily, as though he were giving the Lord his due only in keeping with the wishes of his superiors. Ivan Antonych was not at church; he only went there when it was absolutely necessary from the government service point of view, and when he was there he felt extremely foolish. Thus Primerov at church, it could be said, carried through an official bonding with the entire upper stratum of Byeltsy officialdom; it was as though he had been anointed with the joint unspoken blessing of all the chinovniks.

When the service ended and people had begun to leave, there were already respectful figures converging from all directions upon Primerov, with bows and handshakes of what is known as "the utmost sincerity." He accepted all these tokens of acknowledgment as his due. And then there unfolded one of those fast-paced conversations that go winging by but often prove to have a determining effect on a whole range of interpersonal relations.

"Well, how are things here among you?"

"Fair to middling, Aleksei Vasilyevich. Nothing special."

"Well, gentlemen, I'll speak frankly with you: I will be tightening things up."

"We will gladly try to also; it is our common duty."

"They say that the Jews have been given their way here completely: that everything reeks of garlic."

"There are such defects."

"How can this be? You are Orthodox people, after all, you serve the tsar and the fatherland—"

"There is permissiveness. What can we say? It exists. The Jews among us have gotten above themselves."

"Well, now, who's to blame for this? It surely isn't God's doing. Ha, ha, ha."

"Among us, Aleksei Vasilyevich, there is one—Ivan Antonych—who has been very weak in this regard."

"Yes, I've heard this before, in Kishinyov, that he's soft on—that he caters to the Jews."

"Yes, he does. To tell the truth, you know, he's Orthodox only in name. He seems to be a Russian, but in relation to those people—"

"And what does he get for this? Nothing?"

"Everyone says he gets nothing."

"Hmm, yes? Well, as for me, gentlemen, I myself don't very much believe he gets nothing. Favors are not done for such people for nothing. But of course that is your business—believing. Especially since—"

"Well, who really knows, Aleksei Vasilyevich; after all, we ourselves don't know for sure—it's just that everyone said so, and so we—"

"Well, enough of this. For my part, gentlemen, I declare that I will make things hot for Jews. I won't be an Ivan Antonych for them. This you should know in advance."

"Yes, sir."

"Our duty is to make this town a Russian town, do you understand?"

"We understand."

"Are there Russian traders here?"

"Yes, there are."

"And what about them? Are conditions the same for them as for the Jews?"

"Ivan Antonych didn't make any distinction. But everyone knows that the Jew—you know it yourself, Aleksei Vasilyevich—the Jew is pushy. He'll worm his way in everywhere and wrap people around his finger."

"And Ivan Antonych didn't . . . uh . . . help out our own people?"

"He's all the time talking about equal rights. About what's written in the law and what isn't."

"A seditious person! And you put up with this?"

"Well, after all, they're the higher-ups—Ivan Antonych that is."

"Did you at least write to Kishinyov about this?"

A pause. People thought to themselves: we so much wanted to, but it just wasn't the thing to do. Some of them secretly had sent written denunciations against Ivan Antonych, in spite of everything. But they couldn't bring themselves to mention it: what if it turned out he stayed in his post? Better to keep quiet for now; things will become clearer later on; there's always a time for everything.

"They say some people did write. But we don't know for sure."

"Hmm, good fellows, there's no denying that."

"But now you have come, Aleksei Vasilyevich, and your words will surely be listened to. At last we'll have a firm Russian hand in our town."

"Yes, indeed—under me, gentlemen, everyone will feel that hand—you can't play tricks on me—I'm strict, you know, but I am just—yes, gentlemen, exactly that: strict, but just."

"You can tell the falcon by the way he flies, as our fine Russian proverb says."

"And in Latin, gentlemen, there is something similar: *ex unque leonem*. That is—in Russian that is 'I know the lion by his claws.' "

"That's it, by his claws—heh, heh, heh—by his claws. Very well put. Hits the nail on the head."

"I thank you, gentlemen. I trust that by our common effort, in harmony, we shall . . . ah-h . . . fulfill our . . . our duty."

Primerov had been given an excellent light carriage. But within a few days he managed to avail himself of a heavy carriage as well, writing off the expense under the heading "for presentability to the public," and he went rolling off, escorted by the servile glances of a handful of officials, the rulers of fate in that small district.

Ivan Antonych found himself in the absurd position of someone who has been replaced de facto but not yet de jure: such a person lives a double life; he is a living human being, in the flesh, with all the attributes of a subject of the Russian Empire, that is, with a body, a soul, and a passport; on the other hand, he is nothing more than a shadow in a Chinese shadow play. The appearance remained, taking material shape in the uniform he wore, but the actual function was gone. The exact same words that he had spoken previously no longer meant what they had. He might speak, but nobody listened: his social being had altered, and with that everything else changed too. It was a good thing that Ivan Antonych cut off all his civil service ties, stopped receiving guests, and immediately began preparing to leave for Moscow: in this case his impulsiveness served him well; otherwise he would have been forced to drink from the bitter cup at every step.

Within the family his decision to leave was received with some ambivalence. On the one hand, everyone was angry and upset. On the other, they were glad that an end had come to their petty-provincial, backwater existence. Of course, for Lyubov Ivanovna, moving involved great difficulties and worries: she had three children on her hands, one of them a nursing infant, and they would be traveling for three days straight on the railroad, not to mention the additional travel by horse and carriage. And then, how were they going to live? As it was, they'd be making this trip just trusting to luck. Ivan Antonych did not have a job. What prospects did the future hold for them?

Nevertheless, even for Lyubov Ivanovna, leaving Bessarabia was a solution of sorts, however painful: for her, life in Byeltsy had become repulsive in the extreme. As for Ivan Antonych, whose personality was not at all inclined toward pessimism, he had become extremely excited and agitated and was already soaring in the clouds of rosy hopes and prospects: everything, it seemed to him, would go easily, much more easily than the way it turned out. He was already making plans, high-spiritedly reciting poetry, setting Kolya on his knee, and, together with him, getting lost in daydreams.

Kolya was eager to get to Moscow above all because his latest passion was to obtain some new Devrien publications. He had seen the prospectuses for them—with illustrations! These books, *Life of the Sea* and *Atlas of Butterflies of Europe and the Central Asian Possessions*, were the objects of his most cherished desires. Until the final hour came, the hour of departure, Moscow beamed out to him like a giant lighthouse; everything there was wonderful and enticing . . .

All the Staneviches, both the younger and the older, were very much aggrieved over the imminent departure. They had shared their lives with the Petrovs, become accustomed to them, and liked them not only as tenants but as people. The elder Staneviches, native Moldavians as they were, had for the first time met Russians who did not snort at their way of saying "please" (*poftim, poftim*)—no more than they would have at the German *bitte* or the Italian *prego*; they watched the Moldavians do their native dance (*dzhok*) with greater interest than they would watch the more familiar and universal waltzes and polkas. Between the Petrovs and the older Staneviches there was not the slightest strain or coolness or insincerity: on the contrary, everything was simple, clear, and humanly decent. The basis for this, to be sure, was the daily life in Byeltsy, narrow and limited by its very nature—there were no lofty ideas flying about there. But within the limits of that existence, better relations could not have been imagined. Yelizaveta Ivanovna Stanevich, who had an interest in both literature and music, felt bitter sorrow and nearly wept when she heard the news of the Petrovs' coming departure. She was not welcome in Byeltsy "society" and spent most of her free time with the Petrovs—here there was, for her, a hearthbed of culture and a source of diversion. And yet it all was coming to an end!

When Ivan Antonych sent a telegram about their departure to one of his brothers, a doctor, and to his sisters-in-law, the reality of that departure was suddenly borne in upon everyone with the force of reality, as though a steamboat had suddenly taken shape out of the fog: there it is, waiting for you, and you have to hurry and get up the gangplank.

Packing was under way full force; from somewhere, large wooden boxes, plus wrapping paper and nails, were obtained; things were folded, encircled, wound round with paper; there was the pounding of hammers, people got splinters in their fingers, made a great fuss, and turned the entire apartment into a state of such jumbled confusion that it seemed to be not of this world. Kolya was preoccupied with a problem: how to ship his precious collection of butterflies, which were immeasurably more fragile than the most fragile porcelain. He too made a fuss, demanding enormous quantities of wax in order to place his tiny boxes (holding butterflies) in the gentlest of cradles, till everyone was sick and tired of his pestering as he whirled about under their legs like a little demon. Volodya zealously helped him. The infant Andryusha, completely thrown off by this frantic Tower-of-Babel-building all around him, wailed frantically, and all attempts to calm him were in vain. Wet sheets, bottles of milk, pacifiers, medicines—all these were swept up in the most absurd way in the whirling hurricane of things torn from their accustomed places. They seemed to go crashing and spilling into one another. Only after several days did a new order emerge: sealed tight with large nails, the silent boxes stood there like coffins, smelling of tar and shavings.

Sadly Kolya wandered about the orchard, saying goodbye to all that was dear and familiar there. His heart ached and sobbed and seemed ready to break into pieces. Everything was filled with memories: there in that thuja tree he had caught a robin; it was down that walkway that Yelena Vladimirovna had chased him; here he had found a saturnia cocoon; those were the trees he had climbed in search of a shrike's nest . . .

Here in this orchard they had spent clear, sunny summer days and quiet evenings, when in the slanting rays of the sun thousands of midges had danced in swarms like living specks of dust. Here they had walked and breathed and gloried in the smells of spring, the sounds and colors, when the whole orchard was drowned in the gentle white snow, and the pink, of blossoms, when the apricots were flowering, and the apple trees, and the pear and cherry trees, and the bees had buzzed as they worked their way into those honey-bearing calyxes in search of their booty; here among the burdocks on the just-fallen virgin snow they had set out snares for goldfinches and greenfinches . . . and oh, how those wild, free birds had thrashed about in the nooses! And here was the place where Ivan Yegorych had killed the hamster with his shovel . . . It all came to life before little Kolya's eyes, and went filing past him: the games, the friends, the birds, the butterflies, the trees, the joy, the sorrow, the thrill of success, the tears,

Yelena Vladimirovna, Tosya . . . Living chunks of flesh were being torn from his body, and they quivered, dying but unable to die.

But to everything in this world there comes an end; there even comes an end to the torments suffered in those intermediate states of transition when the last secret tear of one's soul is bitterly swallowed, and the crisis passes, resolving itself into some sort of new phase, which even as it comes into existence is fated in turn to pass away, to disappear in the eternal changing of the times and seasons.

Time's bell had rung, and the Petrovs were already on their way back to their native haunts where they had their roots.

Chapter 8

Ivan Antonych had three brothers, two of them doctors: Georgy Antonych and Mikhail Antonych, or as the family called them, Zhorzh (for Georgy) and Mikhalushka, or Monkey (for Mikhail). Despite their close kinship, their similar education and training, and their work in the same profession, it is hard to imagine two more opposite human types.

Georgy Antonych was adroit and agile, with a dense mat of soft hair on his head and large, mirthful eyes; he was clever, witty, and a favorite of the ladies, by no means a platonic devotee of the fair sex; he was quick, confident, resourceful, and quite liberal, even radical in his views. For many long years he had worked as the town doctor in one of the districts of Smolensk Province and among the local intelligentsia was considered the "life of the party." He was an excellent doctor; his patients loved him dearly, and not just the women patients, although there was an obvious bias on their part. His knowledge of medicine was superb; he was considered a splendid practitioner and kept up with the specialized literature in his field. Yet to tell the truth, he took a deeply skeptical attitude toward the literature and when speaking candidly on the subject would advance two theses which, in his opinion, constituted the fundamental basis for good medical practice: first, do nothing to cause the patient harm; second, convince the patient that he or she is bound to get better. His view of medications was quite negative, and he prescribed only certain insignificant items. To do him justice, the results he achieved, for whatever reason, were always better than those of the other doctors. He did not in the least resemble Le Sage's "Doctor Sangredo."*

*Doctor Sangredo (also spelled "Sangrado" and implying "bloody-handed")—character in the novel *Adventures of Gil Blas of Santillane* by Alain René Le Sage (1668–1747).

Georgy Antonych was always cheerful and welcomed his patients warmly, turning on the charm especially with the women. When his patients took leave of him—in most cases, with the exception only of very severe illness—they somehow felt that their spirits had been lifted; they experienced a general "raising of the tone." Georgy Antonych was also a fanatic for neatness: he was always well-dressed, well-groomed, and wearing a fresh change of underwear.

Mikhalushka pursued his profession in the countryside, working at a zemstvo hospital. Short in stature, nearsighted, wearing a pince-nez, overgrown with a thicket of beard, and quite serious in demeanor, he was shy, not superintelligent, and slow in all things: in his thinking, his movements, his speech. His conscientiousness was extraordinary, but precisely because this quality was carried to the extreme it became in him a fundamental defect.

At one time when he was going to graduate from the *gimnaziya* and was supposed to take an exam for a certificate of competence, it suddenly seemed to him that he was not prepared, although he was perfectly ready to take the exam. And no matter how they tried to drive him out of the house, he stubbornly refused to move from the sofa, where he lay reading Herbert Spencer, and since he didn't take the exam, he had to repeat a year: once he got it into his head that he was "not prepared," no force on earth, it seemed, could move him from dead center.

He would put one leg over his head and let it rest against the back of his neck, like a monkey (whence his nickname), and meditate for hours.

Zhorzh loved to do a sardonic imitation of Mikhalushka confessing his devotion to some beloved lady: "You know, maybe, today I'll kiss you— no, maybe tomorrow—but then again, maybe I should today? Yes, maybe today—no, better tomorrow—"

He had studied seriously and attentively for his profession, but his learning did him no good at all. This was because he had the saintly naivete of reporting to his patients all his diagnostic doubts and hesitations: what you have may be such-and-such, but you have some symptoms that point in quite the opposite direction; in these situations such-and-such noted authority recommends doing thus and so, but this other authority says to avoid that like the plague; not everything is known as yet in the field of medicine; and so on.

And the patient would think to himself: what kind of doctor is this, the devil take him; he doesn't think out a damn thing for himself, apparently. And the next time, this patient would be only too quick to turn to some other Aesculapius. Of course in an out-of-the-way village this kind of excessive consideration had to be dispensed with; the workload was enormous; sick people came in from all over the district, so there was simply no time for all these theoretical hesitations, and besides you couldn't really get such conversation going with the peasants. Still, Mikhail Antonych never completely uprooted this tendency to play the medical Hamlet. In fact he didn't try to uproot it, but continued to assert the necessity in principle of discussing, considering, studying the problem from all sides. This rather slow-witted bumpkin was, on the other hand, a most remarkable chess player, and among the people he encountered, not a person was found who knew chess theory and practice as thoroughly—here he stood beyond competition. He lived like a landless peasant, pursued a solitary existence; didn't care how he dressed, so long as his body was covered; and in his free time, tired out, he would lie around and read.

He had no dealings with women, smoked no tobacco, drank vodka not at all, and never played cards. He liked his solitary, almost hermitlike existence. He raised chickens, ducks, and turkeys. From the entire lexicon of his speech, not a very expansive one, two words were most commonly selected: *govennik* and *milochka*, each of them meaning "dear one" and expressing a slightly different degree of endearment. His attitude toward people was a good one. He felt a certain respect toward the powers that be, and did not entirely deny the existence of God. On the contrary, he even found certain bases for believing, quoting Shakespeare's phrase about "more things in heaven and earth than are dreamt of in your philosophy." Here, too, he said, there was much that had not been studied . . . His temporizing character and way of thinking, his searchings for something solid, firm, and unshakable were characterized by a certain inner conservatism; there was no play of mind or will about him at all.

The village of Tesovo, where Uncle Misha's hospital was located, was no different from thousands of other villages in central Russia: dilapidated, sightless-seeming peasant huts with roofs of blackened straw were constructed there the same way as elsewhere; in front of them there grew, in the same way, scrawny, stunted rowan trees, their bark chewed by horses; the same kind of brick church with golden onion dome plus the same inevitable tavern were there; the peasants suffered in the same way from landlessness, taxes and fees, and rent payments; they starved, drank vodka, and got into brawls in the same way; they were eaten alive in the same way by kulaks, district police officers, village constables, police superintendents, priests, and zemstvo officials; and in the same way, the large landed estates hemmed in their tiny plots. The hospital reflected all the physiological by-products of this social existence: injuries from drunken brawls, exhaustion from undernourishment, congenital syphilis, blood poisoning in the case of mothers giving birth, the coughing of consumptives, rickets in children, bloody flux, herpes, plica polonica, scrofula. The waiting room of the hospital was always packed full with the suffering and the pregnant: peasant women nursing their infants and peasant men in their bast shoes—and everything was gray, miserable, filthy, and unhappy. In the reception area, where the smell of iodoform and carbolic acid pervaded, and where jars and bottles crowded the shelves, groans could be heard, and sometimes weeping. Often the peasants had to travel dozens of versts to reach the hospital, and sometimes a patient was brought in, in such bad condition that medical treatment was completely superfluous: for a child over here things had already gone too far—the child had turned blue; as for the man over there, because of the bumpy ride, almost all his insides had come out through a gaping wound; in the case of an expectant mother suffering from eclampsia, along the way to the hospital she had given up the ghost entirely.

In the ward lay the seriously ill patients: emaciated, nothing but skin and bones, they were like corpses under white sheets; their sunken eyes slowly took in the unaccustomedly large and well-lit room, and they longed to be in their own homes to die, in their stuffy, filthy huts, where their tortured souls would find more warmth. In the quarantine ward, typhus, diphtheria, and scarlet fever reigned. On stretchers to the mortuary, attendants carried the stiffened bodies covered with a piece of canvas—here all torments ended, all sorrows, joys, and hopes; here the only presence was *mors immortalis*, deathless death.

From Bessarabia the Petrovs descended upon the homes of both brothers: they had to find shelter somewhere, at least to begin with. Kolya's parents took refuge at Georgy Antonych's, along with the infant Andryushka; Kolya and Volodya were sent to Uncle Misha's in Tesovo. Visiting there at the time was the grandmother to whom Kolya had sent news of the death's-head moth. In addition, Uncle Misha had adopted an abandoned peasant lad, Fedya—so that some companionship for the Petrov boys was also assured. And here, after the orchard in Bessarabia with its flowers, rose bushes, apricot trees, Kolya and Volodya found themselves in the society of carbolic acid, iodoform, the dreadful mortuary, and scenes of severe illness, crippling poverty, weeping and groaning, and grisly deaths. For them this was something entirely new and unusual; it surprised and shocked them; in fact they were frightened by the starkness of life's everyday tragedy bearing down on them full force. Kolya knew that terrible illnesses and death and poverty existed. But all that, for him, had been more of an indefinite abstraction, shadowy ideas outside the realm of experience and feeling. But here the abstractions were made flesh, impinging directly and immediately on all the organs of perception and screaming aloud in their terrible voices . . .

No matter how glad Kolya was to see his grandmother and Uncle Misha, the hospital environment seemed so dark and gloomy that he felt as though a cold, heavy weight was weighing him down. For the first few days he went around quite subdued, looking in the hospital windows with fear and curiosity, staring at the attendants in their white coats carrying sick people and corpses around with professional indifference, as though they were pieces of firewood or calf carcasses. Timidly he came up to the porch where people were standing and sitting, waiting their turn, and he saw on their faces so much sorrow and mute despair that he felt guilty for living without sorrow of his own. He was even more surprised by a seemingly insignificant incident, a brief phrase, a comment tossed off by a big, clumsy, black-maned peasant who gave the boy a nasty look and said, for no apparent reason, "Agh, you fancy lords! Prob'ly eat meat every day."

Immediately Kolya imagined the meat—cooked with salt and horse radish, which he really did eat every day, when for others it was an unattainable luxury.

He did not feel offended at all by the peasant. On the contrary, he felt as though he were to blame for this meat cooked with horseradish and salt. This reproach was a reproach from that huge world, little known to Kolya, which sent its offspring, wounded, crippled, half dead, to the hospital. Kolya saw the peasant children, huddling fearfully around their parents: they cast mistrustful glances from under their brows and held tight to the skirts of their mother, whose ailment had brought them to the hospital; for the most part they had pale, earthen-colored faces, swollen bellies, skinny little knees, and the legs sticking out from under their ragged clothing were covered with scratches and sores—as though life had given them an early thrashing and scorned their soft, weak children's bodies. Sometimes Kolya wanted to go over to these wild, fair-haired, shy creatures. But he, too, felt shy and could not bring himself to say anything.

That's how the first few days went by. But people get used to everything in this world. And little by little Kolya learned to cope with the new situation and grew accustomed to the scenes in the hospital, but this world of misery, need, suffering, and death, which had newly been revealed to him, entered into his soul forever.

The little house where Mikhail Antonych lived with Kolya's grandmother was in the courtyard of that same hospital. Strutting around the courtyard were burly roosters and hens; fat ducks, quacking away, waddled about as well; turkeys, flaring their wattles and fanning out their tails, would puff themselves up and stamp down the earth around the scrawny-necked females, who acted as though all these masculine amusements had absolutely nothing to do with them. When a hawk or kite would suddenly descend from the heavens, its shadow gliding smoothly over the ground, the roosters would turn their heads sideways to the sky, sounding the alarm with the warning sound "waark," and the hens would rush into the barn.

Not far away, on the other side of the ocher-colored fence, stood posts with rails to which the arriving peasants tied their mournful-looking nags. Fastened to the rails were feeding boxes for hay. The horses, it seemed, shared all the misfortunes of their owners: oats they hardly ever saw, their ribs stuck out, their sides were caved in; their shabby hides were covered with scratches and bald patches; they stood gloomily with their heads lowered, their whole bodies twitching, chewing their hay in a melancholy way. And it seemed they fully shared the sentiment expressed in the peasants' saying: If only the Lord would take us sooner—that's how fed up they were with this life. On the other hand, just as in human existence, the hospital swine felt fine about things. They wallowed in the muck, got into the trough where feed was put out for the ducks, devoured everything that came their way, and were as optimistically disposed as Doctor Pangloss in Voltaire's *Candide*.

Volodya soon began to share Uncle Misha's love of raising poultry; he even learned to tell by feel whether a hen was about to lay an egg or not—and he was immediately awarded by Kolya with the semi-scornful nickname "hen feeler." As for Kolya, his passion was catching wild birds, and he felt no attachment to anything domesticated. Once he came close to suffering serious consequences from his disdain for the peaceful pursuits of poultry breeders. He needed a good float to fish with. He had already pulled enough hairs—for fishing lines—from the tails of the peaceable horses, who made no protest. Now he wanted to use a turkey's fat tail feather to make his float . . .

As he crept up ever so quietly, from behind, on a turkey lost in its own amorous preoccupations, in order to yank a decent-sized feather from its tail, Mikhail Antonych, looking out the window, noticed what was going on. He grabbed the dog whip hanging on the wall and rushed out toward Kolya with the intention of giving him a good beating. He was in such a rage it was no joke—that's how protective he felt about his birds. Kolya of course ran away, but for several hours he lived in fear of being soundly thrashed. And because in his whole life no one had ever thrashed him, or had even tried, it was understandable that the prospect of experiencing this kept him at a respectful distance from his uncle. He did not come home, and presented himself only after lengthy negotiations with his grandmother, who loved him very much and who wangled a full pardon from his uncle. The turkey remained unharmed, and Kolya's softer parts were spared an acquaintance with the whip. In the end he had to be content with making a float out of an old feather lying on the ground, but it turned out to be not a bad one at all.

Near Tesovo there flowed a small river with some deep pools. Near one of these a mill wheel was turning. And there was a dam. If you looked down from the dam, it was easy to see large, sleepy broad-backed chub hovering motionlessly next to the moss-covered pilings, and in the mysterious depths schools of large striped perch swam by. In the dark water bleakfish frolicked, doing their abruptly changing choral dance with flashes of silver, cheerful and light-hearted, just beneath the surface. All you had to do was drop your line, after just fastening a housefly on a bent pin—and instantly there would be something dark-blue and silvery quivering in midair. Now and then a water bug came scampering out on the surface of the water; it would stand still for a moment with its oar-feet outspread, produce some bubbles, then, rowing swiftly, would disappear into the watery recesses. All three boys were in the habit of coming here—Kolya, Volodya, and Fedya. They spent whole days by the pond, fishing poles in hand. The rest of the time was spent in making lures for roach: bread with cotton wool wadding and sunflower seed oil (the oil to give off a scent and the wadding to keep the bread from slipping off the hook); good red earthworms from the well-moistened soil were for the perch; for the chub they used grasshoppers; and for the bleak, flies or ant eggs. The boys' pockets were full of all kinds of trash: the little boxes that held these fish snacks would get worn away, and a powder of the most complex composition would result: bread crumbs and the sticky legs of grasshoppers, the eyes and wings of flies, remnants of worms and microscopic bits of soil—just the kind of aromatic tobacco mixture an old witch would like.

Each fish that was caught was put on a *snizka*, a loop or ring formed by running a stiff cord in under the fish's gills and out its mouth, then the fish was allowed to splash around in the water so that it wouldn't "fall asleep." Each boy had his *snizka* and afterward the luckiest and most skillful fisherman prided himself on his garland of strung-up fish. At night the boys dreamed of the smooth surface of the pool, an extraordinary bite, lures sinking deep into the water, and fish of unusual size . . .

When they got tired of sitting by the pool, they took the basket and, rolling up their pants legs as far as they would go, went running about in the shallows scooping up fish. There was everything here—movement, laughter, surprises, small adventures, arguments, squabbles, accidental successes and failures. On the sand bars they caught gudgeon; under the rocks, tadpoles and sprats; by the shore, among the algae, where the bottom was covered with slimy silt and one's foot would slip suddenly into a patch of icy spring water, they came across tench, fat ones that would swim listlessly back and forth in the basket amid clouds of scooped-up soil. From time to time, as they ran full speed they'd manage to knock a small pike into the basket, and then it would have to be thrown up on the bank for a while, or else the slippery fish would be sure to get away as it kept avidly flapping its tail . . .

Once in the middle of the night everyone in the house was awakened by church bells ringing in alarm. Gusts of wind, altering the sound, made it seem ominous and sobbing.

"Fire! Fire!"

In nothing but their nightshirts everyone ran to the windows. Even Grandma, with her gray hair down, barefoot, in a long nightgown, jumped from her bed and glued herself to the window. Beyond the river the sky was aglow. Like a great bonfire in the black velvet night, peasant huts were burning. Whole swarms of fiery insects were sweeping upward and disappearing into the bottomless heights of the sky. The flames at times would contract and seem to be dying down, and the glow would become paler— then it would blaze up again violently, in gigantic, bursting fountains of fire, and the sky would become coppery red, frightening and ominous.

Kolya stood by the window and shivered. His teeth were chattering. He had goose bumps. Suddenly he jumped back from the window, pulled on his clothes, and ran outside.

"Kolya! Where are you going!"

"The crazy imp!"

"To the fire!" could be heard through the door (which had banged shut) and already he could be seen running headlong toward the river.

After making his way across a little bridge over the river, in which specks of fire were madly dancing, twisting and twirling in darkness that seemed to have been exploded by satanic illumination, Kolya finally reached the scene of the fire. A thick crowd of people was standing about. They were all jabbering away, giving advice, shouting, cursing. The air was dry and hot; it breathed of fire. One hut had already burned almost to the ground, its black remnants, turned to coals, were smoldering, slowly going out; now and then the fire would suddenly find something new to feed on, something it seemed not to have noticed at first, and then it would viciously pounce on it and devour it with its blazing fiery maw. A second hut had recently caught fire, and it was spreading about a fearful spark-filled flame, thrashing red and gold tails in the air, whipped on by the wind. Cursing and shoving one another, peasants with gaff hooks were pulling down the flame-encircled timbers. With a crash the timbers would fall to the ground, throwing clouds of sparks around. Several brave men, including Stepan the village blacksmith, were rushing into the very heat of the flames with buckets of water, trying to drown this unleashed elemental force. They leaped back out with singed eyebrows; they smelled of smoke and courage, inspiring universal admiration.

"Look, Stepan has gone in again."

"Ai-yai-yai, it's gonna crash down. Stepan! Look out, that timber's about to fall!"

"What a wind! Boys, we've got to protect the other houses. The fire is whipping so!"

"Let's get going! Hey, what are you doing, you old sons of bitches, poking your hooks where they're not needed."

"What are you telling us for! We know what to do!"

"Good Orthodox people, fetch water, please! Why are you standing around, like in a trance, like a bunch of blockheads! Bring water! Vanka! Petka!"

The boys, too, ran for water. Kolya grabbed a bucket and with the others ran to the river. At that moment he was not thinking so much about the misfortune, the sorrow, the disaster that the fire meant for those burned out of their homes. No! He was entranced by this fiery whirlwind, the clouds of sparks, the droning of the crowd, the flames dancing against the sky and in the water, the reflections of the fire in people's eyes, the movement all around, the energy of the daring firefighters, the large numbers of people who had climbed down off their stoves, the unusual nature of all this collective activity, the storm of fire, shouts, gestures, the brilliant light in the darkness of night.

"Hey, lads, faster! What're you slackin' off for?"

Huffing and puffing, the boys brought up the water, then dashed off again, three buckets at a time, to the enlivened, sparkling river . . .

"What are you doing here, you little rascal? How dare you run off without permission?"

Kolya saw before him the figure of Uncle Misha. All rumpled, wearing a short jacket over his night shirt, no hat on his head. He was squinting at Kolya shortsightedly through his pince-nez, like an owl at the sun.

"But Uncle Misha, I'm bringing up water—"

"Bringing? I'll bring you up—by the hair! Your grandmother's over there, moaning. She thinks we've lost you. That you've been killed."

But Uncle Misha tempered his anger with mercy. His life, after all, was so one-dimensional, monotonous, and gray that the fire had become a spectacle breaking up this thrice-accursed dreariness. In a moment he had slipped away into the crowd and was offering advice that was just as useless as most advice is in such cases.

With a crash the roof caved in, and columns of fire swept up, dancing, into the air, writhing like serpents against the black skies. It smelled of smoke and heat and flame, and the fiery seed sprayed forth and broke into its mindless, elemental dance. The crowd drew back, retreating under the pressure of the wave of flame that seemed to leap out of the fiery furnace.

"Look lively! Bring it up! Fetch it here! Okay, boys. Give it a strong pull, once. All together, once. Right on target. That's how we do it."

Swaying back and forth the peasants chanted, working their long gaff hooks in tandem. There was a fairly substantial wind, but fortunately the neighboring huts were surrounded by large linden trees, and their leaves, trembling, curling up, and dying, bore the brunt of the assault from the spray of fiery seed.

"And what are *you* here fer, dokhtur? Ya could of been gittin yer sleep?"

"I came to get my nephew."

"Which one is he?"

"The one over there bringing water with your boys."

"That little feller? What a live wire. But what's this nephew of yers doing this fer?"

"He heard the alarm and ran out of the house."

"Well, now isn't that somethin'—"

"So how'd the fire get started?"

"Who the heck knows? Either someone dropped a cigar in the hay or a match got dropped or maybe a spark from the stove. Who the heck knows? It's a good thing only two households got burned out. Just the other day in Timokhino a fire swallowed up a dozen and a half households, just like that, like a hungry pike. All the folks that got burned out were left with nothing, God help us. What a shame."

"How did that one get started?"

"Oh, that was a different story. They were having their patron saint's day. You know, they all drank their fill. Once they had gotten good and drunk, do you think it was long before they had a disaster? Now they can cry, but they'll never cry enough."

The fire, it seemed, was breathing its last. Its death agony was at hand. The frame of the burning house was already half collapsed or dismantled.

"Once again, boys. Get a hold! Have you got your hooks in?"

"We've got a hold. Start the chant."

"One strong pull—now!"

The blackened timber crashed to the ground. Angry little golden tongues of flame still licked over it, but that was all. The still burning embers, red as pomegranate seeds, erupted now and then into momentary bright flames. But the glow in the sky was shrinking and growing pale. The fire was dying.

Little by little the crowd began to disperse. Kolya and Uncle Misha, too, headed for home. The fires were going out; only some charred black mounds were still smoldering, and in places they, too, were covered with ash. The black night became still blacker, and even the stars seemed barely visible, like a rash that had not yet broken out on the sky's vast breast. The feelings aroused in Kolya from everything he had seen had not yet subsided; his eyes still saw the fire; the crash and din and hubbub still resounded in his ears.

"Where in the world did you get to, God forgive us," his grandmother squawked, clasping her hands. "I was going to send Fyodor after you. Have you no fear of God! And Misha, you're a fine one. You run after the boy and then you yourself disappear."

"It's nothing, Mama," Mikhail Antonych muttered, suddenly having become Kolya's accomplice in crime. "After all . . . it was a fire . . . well, look here . . . we're all right . . . everything's all right. We need a little tea, Mama. You can't go right back to sleep after something like this."

"I've already started heating the samovar. It's probably boiling already. Come on and bring him along; I'll brew the tea now."

And now they all sat down to this out-of-the-ordinary, middle-of-the-night tea, which seemed unusually tasty and somehow very special. Blowing on the tea in the saucer after burning his lips, Kolya sipped the hot liquid, breaking all the rules of etiquette and propriety. But no one noticed at a time like this; you could have eaten a piece of fish with a knife and nothing would have been said.

Outside, through the windows, it was dark, not a glimmer of light. Where the bright flames had recently blazed there was a solid black abyss in which you could make out nothing. The table, the lamp, the tablecloth, the ring-shaped rolls, the gooseberry jam, the samovar—it all seemed so small and insignificant compared to the wild violence of the fire and the turbulence of the crowd, as though a leap had been made into another world, a tiny little one in which you could barely turn around . . .

The next day Kolya headed for the ash heap, the remains of the fire. It was a lovely summer evening. From the fields drifted the smell of ripening rye. Corncrakes were calling in the water meadows along the river's edge. Light, sweet-smelling breezes, warm and tender, barely touched your face and seemed to embrace you. An opal mist was spreading along the horizon. The dome of the church was gleaming like molten gold, and the cross at its peak was burning brightly against the sky of cobalt blue. Kolya made his way up the steep slope of the river bank to the scene of the fire.

All that remained of the thick timbers were fragments chewed through by the teeth of flame, black chunks of burned timber amid piles of light gray ash. The skulls of earthenware pots and clay bowls, fragments of dishes, nails, and bones in the heaps of ashes—that was all that survived from this place where people had lived. And, Lord, how the beautiful, centuries-old linden trees had been mangled! On one side they had been badly burned and disfigured: all their leaves had turned brown and curled up, their branches twisted out of shape; the dry, deathly rustle of the leaves was pitiful and sad . . . Barefoot boys were digging through the ashes in search of some unknown treasure. But everything here was dead; nothing was even smoldering.

Still, life goes on in its own way. Young men were already strolling along the street, with a chip on the shoulder, with their caps pushed back and their forelocks recklessly allowed to fall any old way beneath the visors of those caps. They walked along arm in arm with an accordion player in the middle, his big accordion on a leather strap. With gay abandon he would squeeze out his chords, sending the latest melodies bubbling down the length of the street. On the outskirts of town, by the barns where large logs were lying, maidens' voices were responding in their thin, liquid, almost shrill tones.

> A wondrous moon's aflo-oat abo-ove the river.
> The still of night ho-olds a-all in its embrace.

Suddenly they rose to a higher register:

> There's nothing in the world that I be nee-eeding,
> Nothing but to see you, o-oh my-y dear.

The "wondrous moon" was succeeded by a doleful song about an unfortunate peasant girl:

> Every birdie has its nest.
> The she-wolf has her chi-ild.
> But I an orphan, what have I?
> No-othing in the wo-orld.

The peasant lads with their raucous voices belted out a tune whose words were naughty, but the feeling was not. The song was about a prostitute:

> Her sad fate brought her to the bordellos,
> And she slept with the officer fellows.

Full of melancholy were these Russian folk songs. They sang of "evil fate," oppression, parting, sorrow, orphanhood, unlucky love, and poverty, as the autumn winds sing sadly in the trees. Nowhere are the typical features of our life registered so expressively as in our folk songs; that's where you'll find the truly solid sedimentary deposits of our life.

Even the imitations that have gone into general circulation, such as the songs of Delvig, Neledinsky-Meletsky, and Tyupin, involuntarily follow the same basic outlines, speaking of a cheerless life whose few joys are so fleeting and changeable that they are inevitably followed by sorrow and unhappiness, like dark shadows. The motifs of sadness and longing flow on and on across the entire country: "I lost my ring," "Burn down, my torch, I burn down with you . . ."

The village, eaten up by the power of money, was already exchanging cries of grief and desperation with the city: "Parting, oh sad parting, a stranger's land I'm in" and "Marusya, she took poison" were being sung across the length and breadth of the vast empire of the tsars. And from the underground depths, from the bottom of this giant fermenting vat, there were rising and merging together little streams of protest, of bitter dissatisfaction with life as it was, a search for ways of forgetting, of escaping into the fantasy of primitive romanticism, recollections of the great rebel heroes of the people, prison songs, and the mischievous songs of the factory folk who here and there were starting to raise their heads . . .

The down-and-outs and the prison inmates spread these songs everywhere, and already with a certain touch of anger, lines were being sung like these from "Sasha, angel, pure and chaste."

Where the sun does not shine
Where the dawn does not show fair
I'm condemned to end my life there
By o-o-order of the ts-a-ar!

And Kolya listened with surprise to a song whose words were not yet entirely clear to him:

That, my lord, is a government building,
The Aleksandrovsky Tsentrál.*

Evening was coming. In the outskirts, where the barns were, the peasant girls were doing a round dance; the old men and women were sitting on the logs, chewing seeds and talking quietly; and the peasant lads were going all out with the accordion and dancing the squat-and-kick Russian dance. Later they went off in pairs through the dark corners beyond the barns into the fields of rye where there were hiding places.

*Central prison.

Make way, whisp'ring rye, grown so high,
Keep a precious secret, I beg you . . .

From somewhere in the distance a self-assured young man's voice rang out:

Oh, the midnight hour has come
And I've taken a pretty girl,
Took her by her fair white hand,
By her fa-air white hand!

Eventually a patron saint's day came to Tesovo, too—that is, the holiday of the saint in whose honor the local church was built. There was a grand and solemn service at the church, with a choir. Later the same day a fair opened. The tavern was filled almost from the first hour of the morning. Outside the village on the meadows stood tents with various goods for sale, primitive sweets for the most part: walnuts and ordinary nuts; brown pods from Tsaregrad; round, white spice cakes; stamped gingerbread from Tula; cheap, sticky, colored caramel; little homemade toffee bonbons; chocolate in the shape of a shoe sole, "mon pensier"; and halvah. The village children, dressed in brightly embroidered shirts and dresses, were already dashing from tent to tent, spending their precious kopecks; they smeared their mouths handsomely with chocolate and colored candy and gazed with envy at the ice-cream vendor and the different kinds of kvas, lemonade, and fruit soda. Here, too, was the temptation of all temptations—a merry-go-round with a canopy, with wooden horses you could climb up on, with the ringing of harness bells, the noise of the organ grinder, and other kinds of wonders. The crowds of people strolled in close-knit rows—people from other villages had also come to Tesovo for the festival and fair. The music played, the merry-go-round revolved, creaking and groaning, the girls uttered their piercingly shrill cries, more for show than from real fright, and the boys yelled, too. Next door a Petrushka doll was, from within a tall booth, being pounded with sticks, and in the end, with strange throaty cries, he perished under a rain of blows; varicolored balloons hung in the air like enormous clusters of grapes; the children were being tempted on all sides—by "denizens of the sea" (little glass devils in tubes filled with water), by sweets, by balls, by toys.

"Hey, buy our wares, good Christian people! They're on sale. On sale. A denizen of the sea, full of respect for the village ladies. He chased after the girls, and found himself in a glass bubble."

"Hey, we've got good balloons and balls. Get 'em, kiddies, while you can!"

"Hey, we've got bliny! Bliny! Piping hot, right out of the oven, two for five!"

"Ice cream, the finest. Made from the best cream!"

"Get your halvah. Halvah! The whole world's talking about it. Buy it up, good peasant folk, lay your coins down, just five kopecks."

"Good Orthodox Christian people," the owner of the "denizens" was pouring it on. "I caught this little devil with a lasso. I stuck him in a bottle so he wouldn't catch the girls."

"Dolls, dolls! Big ones, like the real thing, big as life! Won't you buy, your worthiness, for your children?" The sprightly seller of dolls was addressing a local wealthy peasant, a kulak, who was pompously approaching the tents in his dark-blue *poddyovka*,* boots gleaming like glass, a brand-new cap on his head.

From a distance with greedy eyes gazing at all this magnificence—the spice cakes and gingerbread, the merry-go-round, the dappled toy horses with bobbed tails, and the freakish-looking dolls—were the barefoot children of the poor: there was nothing to dress them up in for the festival; they didn't even have a quarter-kopeck piece. They couldn't bring themselves to plunge into the very thick of the fair; instead they shyly watched from afar, feeling themselves on the outside of life, including this part of it.

Alongside the tents, next to the Petrushka, sat a blind beggar, his legs folded. He was rolling the blue-tinted whites of his eyes to the heavens, and in a piercing nasal voice, trying to drown out all other sounds, was intoning:

Learn the truth: what is five?
The five wounds of Christ,
The four Gospels,
The three persons of God,
The two natures of God,
The one son of Mary,
Jesus Christ,
Who rules over the priests,
Mightier than the tsars . . .

"Good Orthodox people, give, in the name of Jesus, give a little kopeck to a blind man, give out of your generosity. I will pray to God for you, always, now and forever, world without end."

*poddyovka—light, tight-fitting coat typically worn by old-fashioned Russian gentry.

A pregnant woman, pale-faced and hollow-cheeked, with arms that were desperately thin and a belly that was monstrously swollen, tossed a kopeck in his hat.

"Christ save you."

"Hey, you Sashkas, good little kanashkas, won't you change my folding money," someone's rollicking voice rang out from the merry-go-round. From the tavern people were coming, already seriously under the influence. Near the merry-go-round a crowd was pushing and shoving. Noise and commotion, songs, occasional curses. Girls were being hugged and fondled; out of habit they squealed and shrieked to demonstrate their purity.

"Whad'ya think you're doin', you cross-eyed devil?"

"Uh, I'm just here. What are you doing, Marukha, going away?" the "cross-eyed devil" replied, unceremoniously squeezing the breasts of another hefty woman. "Hee, hee, what have you got here?"

"I'll tell you what *you've* got, but the hell with you," she laughed. "Better look out, or I'll let you have it, and how—"

At that moment a magnificent landau approached along the highway; a pair of beautiful horses, an imposing coachman, mounds of pale pink and white lace, umbrellas, and a bouquet of hothouse flowers. It was the local landlady Sotova taking the liberty of coming to observe the people. With her, in the capacity of escort, was a county police superintendent in uniform, two daughters, and two governesses—one French, the other German.

All the noise of the fair subsided. Many took off their hats and caps and bowed to the gentlefolk. The grande dame viewed the plebeian scene from the carriage through her lorgnette. The little girls got out, with their governesses. They wanted to come a little closer, but immediately a call rang out:

"Nicht weiter, bitte, Mariechen. Bleiben sie hier."

"Ah! Le peuple russe! Il est bon! Cette scene est tres pittoresque, madame!"

The madame, smiling condescendingly, agreed. The police superintendent was making some explanations.

"Schon genug!" (All right, that's enough!)

"Can't we watch another minute?" the girls complained.

"No, children, a little at a time is best. There are drunken people there. We're going home!"

And the carriage disappeared. The landlady had had her fill of gazing at *le peuple russe*; in general, all this was of little interest to her.

"That lady's got a fine rear end on her," a peasant lad who'd had a few was grinning. "Ah'd like to take a ride on a merry-go-round like that! With harness bells already—"

"You better look out. For talking like that, you know what they'll do to you—"

"Hey, ah didn't mean nuthin.'"

"Yeah, you better watch it."

In the tavern there was a great Babel going on—shouting, singing, the sound of dishes breaking, a genuine Sodom and Gomorrah. The smoke from the low-grade tobacco was pouring out the windows.

"Oh, joyful days there were," roared a voice satanically, drowning out everything else. It was the blacksmith Stepan, who had behaved so heroically at the fire, a tower of strength and a real desperado. He was squandering his last pennies on drink.

"Styopa, my friend, that's enough." Ivan Kolesnikov, his neighbor and friend who had had quite a few himself, was trying to reason with him.

"Get out of the way."

"But Styopa—"

"Out of the way, I say. Or I'll give you such a wallop you won't be able to count your bones."

Stepan was no longer responsible for his actions. He was completely soused.

"Stepan, let's go home." His wife had suddenly appeared, a thin little woman, flat-chested, with a plain hair-do. "And where in the world is your jacket?"

"Get out of here!"

"Where's your jacket? Styopa! Do you hear me?"

"Go away! I'll kill you! Get the hell out of here!"

"You drank that away, too? You blood sucker!" she was screaming now at the tavern keeper, who was patting himself on the belly behind the bar. "Tyrants, you eat people alive! There's no justice good enough for you, you vipers. You fleece the people! Robbers!"

She was screaming in a voice no longer her own. She thrashed about hysterically, weeping and sobbing, helplessly grabbing onto people, now one, now another. Stepan rolled his eyes senselessly. A kind of vague, heavy anger was growing inside of him, at whom or at what he didn't know. He had the urge to pounce on his wife, this weeping, sobbing thing, and take out his anger on her, but instead he broke away and ran from the place . . .

In the evening the next day Mikhail Antonych came in tired, barely on his feet. He had had an extremely hard day; he had to sew up a serious knife wound in the blacksmith Stepan's side; Kolesnikov's skull had nearly been staved in by a wooden stake and he was in the hospital, with a concussion; one fellow from a neighboring village had had a rib broken; the right arm of another had been severely dislocated; about five others had less serious injuries; he had had to make a house call on the priest, Father Vasily, who had gotten so drunk they thought he was going to die; one peasant woman was in danger of having a miscarriage from a blow to the abdomen—in a word, the usual results of a patron saint's festival among good Orthodox Christians.

As it turned out, late at night a bloody battle had developed. Some fellow from a neighboring village, also drunk, had made a pass at a Tesovo girl. Her boyfriend flattened him with a punch. His buddies interceded in his behalf. And then the cry of the Tesovo crowd went up: "They're beating our people!"—and the whole county got into the fray. They turned to the tried-and-true weapons of their grandfathers—wooden staves—and a full-scale armed encounter began, whose results had now been recorded in the hospital log.

In silence and with eyes unmoving Kolya listened to Mikhail Antonych's account of these events. The samovar on the table kept purring idyllically, but Kolya pictured to himself the knife wounds, the cuts, the broken ribs, the fractured skulls . . .

"It's all because they've begun to forget God. That's His way of punishing them. They're just like animals, real animals—without God, man is worse than a dog," Kolya's grandmother voiced her opinions.

"That's not the problem, Mama. We have no schools, but we do have vodka. That's the problem," muttered Mikhail Antonych.

"Well, even your schools won't help without God. They've forgotten Jesus Christ Our Savior. Lord, what sinfulness!"

"Grandma?"

"What do you want, Kolya?"

"How about the priest there? Uncle Misha says he nearly drank himself to death. Was that with God or without?"

"Bad Kolya! Be quiet! Who taught you such things?"

"Gee, don't get angry, Grandma."

"It's my son Ivanushka who has corrupted you. You, too, going down the road to ruin, just a baby, still drinking milk." The grandmother flew into a rage. "So this is the punishment that God has sent."

"There is no God." It suddenly burst from Kolya's lips after a long pause, as though he were drawing some sort of mental balance sheet on the preceding conversation.

"I curse you! Antichrist! Evil One!" The old woman had become completely unbalanced. "God will punish your father, too. Oh, Lord, what have I done to deserve this? That I should live to see this day! What kind of children are these, little ones who raise their hand against God!"

"Calm down, Mama. What are you getting so worked up for? Calm down, dear heart."

But Grandma couldn't calm down after this. She roared and sobbed. She paced up and down the room like an ancient tigress enraged by the theft of her beloved cubs. It seemed she was about to take her grandson by the hair and bite his head off for the glory of her kind, forgiving God.

"Mama, enough." Mikhail Antonych kept trying to calm her, making signs to Kolya that he should keep his mouth shut. But Kolya, too, had gotten a burr under his tail; his heart was seething and beating so hard that he could feel it thumping and could hear the blood rushing to his head.

"Grandma, you ought to be saying shame on your priest and his God."

Grandma screamed and ran into her bedroom, where she remained, sobbing. By now Mikhail Antonych had gotten angry at Kolya; he was at wit's end and didn't know what to do. Besides, he was deathly tired; in the course of the day he had done several operations, aside from the usual visits with patients, examinations, and bandaging of wounds. Silently he pointed out to Kolya the place where the dog whip was hanging, and said he was going to his mother's room to give her some Valerian drops but would be back. To the depths of his soul, Kolya felt hurt and offended. Outraged at the threat of a whipping he, too, began to sob, burying his face in one of the pillows on the sofa. Volodya, who had been sitting there in silence the whole time, with his kind and naive eyes wide open, also began to whimper; he rushed over to his brother, embraced him, kissed him, pleading with him through his tears: "Kolyechka, dear, don't."

Now Mikhail Antonych was completely flustered.

"Kolya! Dear boy! I was just joking—"

The boy continued to sob soundlessly, his whole body wracked with emotion. Mikhail Antonych just stood there, spreading out his arms nonsensically. Then he made a gesture of hopelessness and went off to his own room (whatever will be, will be!), locked himself in, and undressed: sufficient unto the day, for him, was the evil thereof. Such, at Doctor Petrov's residence, was the balance sheet of the patron saint's day at Tesovo.

The next morning Grandma announced she was going to Moscow, and no matter how they pleaded with her, she remained intransigent. Kolya threw himself on her neck—he felt so sorry for Grandma; after all, she loved him very much and had always interceded for him; their friendship went a long way back. But it was all to no avail, and Mikhail Antonych was obliged to tell the hospital coachman to harness up a horse. Grandma went away, half apologetic, half embittered.

The servant Stepanida took over Grandma's rights and obligations in the realm of housekeeping. She was a plump, pockmarked, good-natured woman who, it seemed, had never gotten angry at anyone in her life, never was offended by anything, and never cried. She was healthy, strong, always very composed, and honest as the day is long. She looked on Mikhail Antonych as somewhere between a helpless child and a holy saint, and felt no shame about walking right into his room when all he was wearing was a shirt and no drawers. She didn't regard him as an adult male. For Mikhail Antonych she was a genuine treasure, and from the point of view of the housekeeping, he suffered no loss whatsoever by the departure of his mother, Agniya Ivanovna.

Chapter 9

While the blacksmith Stepan was a patient in the hospital ward, Kolya began visiting him. Stepan was a great nature lover, a hunter and fisher, and the boy would talk with him for hours, listening to his stories and telling him about his own Bessarabian adventures. Stepan's wife would come to visit her husband in the ward, bringing along their son Vasya, who was a whole year younger than Kolya. Thus began Kolya's acquaintance with Vasya. They soon became fast friends, and Kolya started visiting him at their home in the village.

Stepan's home, a traditional Russian peasant hut, or *izba*, stood next to the smithy, on the outskirts, at the very edge of town. It was like almost any other *izba*: with a framework of old timbers, a straw roof, a low clay wall shored up with brushwood around the outside, and small windows made of pieces of glass stuck together. Inside the hut there was only one room, with nearly half its space taken up by the huge Russian stove. Diagonally across from the stove, two walls extended from the "corner of honor" where the icons and other holy images, blackened with age, were hanging; against the walls stood two rickety benches. The holy pictures—cheap popular prints, old and torn—were so soiled and flyblown that one could only guess what was being depicted. On the wall hung a clock worked by weights. Attached to the weights were a large nail, a rusty lock, and even an empty vodka bottle; otherwise the clock wouldn't run. The air in the hut was stale, musty, and sour, smelling of sweat and steamed felt boots, and it was hot. For some reason the windows were never opened, even in summertime. Fastened to the ceiling in the middle of the room was a tub-shaped cradle in which a nursing infant would scream and sob violently the minute someone stopped rocking the cradle or overfeeding it with poppyseeds. On the wide, flat surface on top of the stove, in a pile of filthy rags and blankets, which had turned from red to greasy black and which stank of muck and urine, three other children were stirring about. The oldest of them was Vasya; the two others—a girl and a boy—preferred not to climb down off the stove. But Vasya was already helping out with the housework, tending the cattle, watching the baby, taking lunch to his dad at the smithy, helping to clean the hut and the cattle shed, and rinsing the wash in the river.

On the stove and walls, rust-colored "Prussians" (cockroaches) skittered about, waving their whiskers; the females carried their little eggs with them on their sides, like tiny lacquered suitcases. The roaches were so numerous that at night, when the smelly little tinplate lamp was put out, the rustle of hundreds of insects could be heard, pouncing on leftover crumbs of bread or bits of porridge. Bedbugs, fleas, and lice tormented the children by night, and they scratched desperately, moaning in their sleep, scratched till they bled; they had so many scratch marks their bodies reminded you of geographical charts or tattoos in red ink.

In the courtyard, half of which was roofed over and strewn with straw, a cow and a skinny nag stood in a dark corner. The smelly, sucking mire did not prevent the pigs from enjoying the pleasures of life. On the wall you could make out an old plow and the teeth of a harrow. The loft was packed full of hay nearly to the ceiling.

Stepan's family was barely able to make ends meet. Like many peasants, Stepan rented some land from the landlady Sotova—or as they called her, Sotikha—the same one who had stopped to observe the fair; this fine lady lived mainly off the rental payments of the starving peasants. Her superintendent, a swindler and a scoundrel, displayed great skill in reaping a harvest off his brothers in Christ.

Stepan earned a little at the smithy. But there weren't enough hands to work the land: the children were a constant weight around his neck, while his wife, in spite of everything, managed to plow and to reap and to cart manure together with her husband. On top of that, they had to go into debt to the tavern keeper, who had no scruples about taking even Stepan's jacket. Of course the family never saw meat: bread, potatoes, porridge, cabbage—that was it. Mashka the cow saved the day; there was milk for the children in spite of everything.

Kolya quickly got used to this way of life and little by little came to know the peasants' worries and concerns: his new friend Vasya sometimes reasoned like a grown-up peasant. In his spare time Vasya taught Kolya to play knucklebones and skittles. Knucklebones became his passion: he chalked up good hits, and learned to play so well that soon he was beating the grown-up fellows, even at *shtrafy*, an especially competitive form of the game. Kolya's uncle, Mikhail Antonych, was amazed one day to find an entire collection of knucklebones under the sofa—that was where Kolya's new treasures were kept.

When Vasya came to the hospital to see his father, Kolya would persuade him to come to Uncle Misha's house. At first the boy was shy and didn't want on any account to enter the fancy quarters of the "dokhtur." It was Stepanida who broke down his stubborn reluctance; this kind woman established such a rapport with the boy that an extraordinary feeling of trust came over him and, despite himself, he stepped across the enchanted threshold.

Mikhail Antonych's modest quarters were a surprise: to Vasya they seemed on the scale of a palace. He had never seen a place with several rooms; he had never seen a sofa, a desk, a rug, shelves with books on them; this all seemed to him like riches of the grandest sort, and he even winced as though blinded by all these objects completely new to him. He could not bring himself to sit on a chair, because all he knew was the bench that everyone shared. He had never held a newspaper in his hands. A guitar seemed like a marvel to him. He goggled at the splayed leaves of the philodendron, with its roots in the air. Kolya patiently explained to his friend the significance of all these objects, and in his heart there resounded the reproach:

"Agh, you fancy lords! Prob'ly eat meat every day."

The social world now became clearly differentiated in Kolya's mind. Previously people had been divided into two large categories: grown-ups and children, with the grown-ups usually deceiving the children, keeping them in the dark. Later, grown-ups had been divided into good and bad, kind and mean. Now another duality had surfaced, the division of the world into rich and poor. When Kolya remembered Heine's poem "The Slave Ship" or William Ratcliffe's monologues at night in the Scottish tavern, he saw them in a new light. He began to be ashamed of the meat he ate "every day," of his clean underwear, and the whole semi-gentlemanly round of their daily life, and as for the landlady's fancy lace, umbrellas, hats, and lorgnettes, he began to nourish something akin to hatred and contempt toward them. The closer he came to the life of the poor and the firmer his friendship became with Vasya and his family and friends, the more burdensome for him became those outward symbols, from clothing to so-called good manners, which expressed his belonging, even incidentally, to the world of the rich and their accomplices. What kept him from falling into some child's form of asceticism, however, was his precociously developed disbelief in God and the healthy appetite he had developed as a result of living continually in nature's lap. Nevertheless, he developed a love for the people of the "lower orders" of society as well as a kind of nihilism regarding all the conventions of the life of the upper echelons. By no means did he shuffle his feet—Kolya, shuffle his feet?!—but pulling himself back, he would maintain a gloomy silence when he chanced to meet some fine "lady" and he scoffed at their whole way of life just as he did at his grandmother's God.

At times some detail etched itself in his consciousness and became a major symbol for him. Once he saw the emaciated breast of Vasya's mother, from which she could not squeeze a single drop of milk for her wailing infant. The pathetic, wrinkled, sagging breast of this half-starved woman was imprinted on his brain with surprising vividness.

On one occasion he had the urge to kiss the skinny scratched knees of Vasya's younger brother, although he did not then know that repentant medieval ladies out of love for Our Savior would, all in tears, kiss with their refined lips the suppurating sores of the poor and downtrodden. But Kolya was not feeling ardent devotion to the Lord who gave his life for us. He was not condescending to "those beneath him," but simply saw them as the same kind of people he was, with whom he felt life was no worse and in many ways freer and more interesting than with the well-schooled boys and girls from that other world, who couldn't tell a birch tree from an aspen and who probably thought that bread grew on trees or that you could sow groats. He simply began to look at the world from the bottom up instead of from the top down, and the interests, concerns, and worries, the sorrows and afflictions, the hopes and joys of the "lower orders" became nearer and dearer to him, because more and more his life became one with theirs.

Soon, however, there occurred an event that nearly cost the boy his life. It happened this way. Mikhail Antonych took all three boys with him one day, plus Vasya, who was playing with them in the yard (with his father discharged from the hospital, he had more free time now), and went down to the river for a swim. It was a Sunday and all of nature seemed to be celebrating the resurrection.* The sun was shining in all its magnificence, generously pouring an abundance of luminous blessings upon the earth. The brilliantly shining sky was turned upside down in the river. An undisturbed stillness hung over everything, except for an occasional sound from the village—a dog barking, someone singing, the chopping of an ax. They all undressed on the riverbank, which was overgrown with low, thick grass. Beyond the grass, and sharply distinguished from it, was a strip of the large-grained kind of sand that a river deposits. It extended out into the

*The Russian word for Sunday (*voskresenye*) means "resurrection."

stream to form a sand bar. Along the edge it wasn't deep, and the boys could frolic and play in the water as much as they wished. Warmed by the sun, they all happily went in deeper, began wallowing around, splashing one another, cupping their hands and sloshing them through the water to produce a fountain of spray; then they decided to play leap frog and with much whooping and hollering began to jump over one another's backs, falling into the water, laughing and sputtering, grabbing one another by the legs, dunking one another, and taking pleasure in the comical snorting of the one being dunked.

It was a glorious mass of confusion, and even the staccato voice of Mikhail Antonych, who was not very cheerful by nature, could be heard laughing. During the free-for-all Kolya had caught sight of a beautiful white water lily and without saying anything started to go get it. Suddenly he felt the bottom give way beneath him and he went under. All he could remember before he lost consciousness were the times he had wrongly upset his mother and made her cry. The others did not notice right away that he had disappeared.

"Where the heck is Kolya!" Mikhail Antonych suddenly shouted in alarm. Everyone froze: there was no sign of Kolya; he had sunk out of sight. The water had grown still. Everything was quiet. Everything was terrifyingly quiet.

Mikhail Antonych, who was a fairly good swimmer, dove down and immediately bumped against the drowning victim. With no great difficulty he dragged him to shore. They stretched Kolya out and began doing artificial respiration. The boys watched with mortal fear in their eyes as Mikhail Antonych went through the procedure. But now the water was pouring out of Kolya's mouth and ears . . . And now he began to breathe . . . And now he opened his eyes . . .

"Well, how are you, foolish boy?" he could hear Mikhail Antonych's voice rumbling worriedly right next to him, affectionate and grumbling at the same time.

"I—it's nothing—the water—," the boy burbled and suddenly threw up an entire bucketful of water . . . and exhaustedly closed his eyes again.

"Never mind, never mind. It will pass," said Mikhail Antonych, and he began using the rough fabric of his own trousers to give Kolya a rubdown.

In a little while Kolya was sitting up with everyone else and laughing. He no longer believed that he had nearly drowned. It seemed to him that it hadn't happened, or if it had, it was not serious, that he had done it "on purpose," or perhaps it wasn't him at all that this had happened to. At one point reality and unreality became so confused in his mind that he couldn't sort them out. But these strange feelings and his strange remarks and comments were completely incomprehensible to the others. They thought maybe Kolya had gone off his rocker a little from fear, but the fact was, he hadn't had time to feel fear—the whole semi-catastrophe had been played out with such lightning speed. After a while he got up and began jumping, now on one leg, now on the other, tilting his head to the side, and everyone was amazed at the ever new quantities of water that kept pouring out of his ears.

"Hey, you've had enough to drink for all next week!"

"Look out you don't make a puddle in the sheets during the night!"

"On the other hand, that'll teach you to go chasing after water lilies—"

"Well, I'm just gonna learn how to swim; that'll show you," was Kolya's answer to his friends' jibes. And sure enough, he later became an excellent swimmer. But that was much later.

Fall was coming. The leaves on the trees were turning yellow. It began to get cold at night. Kolya and Volodya continued to live at their Uncle Misha's. Their father's search for a position produced no results. Lyubov Ivanovna and Andryusha were still guests at Georgy Antonych's. Their father traveled many times to Moscow, darkened many a doorway, sent out letters, appeals, announcements, and turned to several people from whom he expected assistance—but still matters failed to move from dead center. Some refused him outright, others did so indirectly, still others promised him everything but did nothing. There was hardly any money; they were in fact living at the expense of his brothers. As winter approached they decided they had to move to Moscow, to stay with Ivan Antonych's third brother, Yevgeny: Kolya had to be placed in a school, and Ivan Antonych ought to be in Moscow to continue his pursuit of a job; besides, in the order of things, it was now necessary, *volens nolens*, to turn for help to the third brother.

Ivan Antonych set off for Tesovo to get the boys and bring them back to his older brother Georgy's home; then, all together, the whole family would head for Moscow.

"Papa! Papa's come!" Kolya shouted, catching sight of his father drawing up in a carriage and rushing to greet him. Ivan Antonych got out and hugged the boy.

"Well, how are things, Kolya my dear. Is Misha home?"

"Yes. Things are fine. Are they bad for you?"

"Yes. I came to bring you to Uncle Georgy's for a week. And then we'll go to Moscow. Hello, Monkey." Mikhail Antonych had already come down off the porch. The brothers hugged and kissed.

"How are you getting along with Kolya and Volodya? Are you thoroughly sick of them? Grandma stopped on her way through; she complained a lot about Kolya to Lyubochka. Please forgive us, Misha."

"Come now—dear Ivan—it's nothing. Everything's fine. The boys are wonderful. The thing with Mama was over believing in God . . . It's foolishness. Oh, but the other day Kolya nearly drowned."

"Drowned?" Ivan Antonych had turned pale.

"You probably haven't eaten anything. Let's have supper. Stepanida! Set the table, my dear; we'll have supper right away. Vanya's hungry as a wolf, it looks like . . . Yes, your scamp nearly drowned."

"Papa! How about some knucklebones—" And Kolya brought forth his treasures, bragging about his winnings at the game.

"Don't start talking to me with your teeth sticking out. You'll have to get rid of those knucklebones—give them to whoever you want; we can't be taking knucklebones with us. You'll have time enough for that later in life, dear boy, ha ha ha. Better that you tell me how on earth you nearly drowned."

"Uncle Misha pulled me out! And you should have seen how the water poured out of me! It was really something," Kolya began telling the story, almost inspired.

"Hmm, really? You had a close call. Thank you, Monkey. It's a good thing Lyubochka didn't know anything about it—"

"Let's go eat, Vanya, supper's on the table. I don't have any vodka."

"Hey, I'm alone and I'm not drinking . . . But you know, Mama really got seriously angry. She told Lyuba I was corrupting my own son, that God would punish me, and she even prophesied, you know, that I wouldn't find a job because God was angry with me. Our little Mama has really gone wild! And Volodya, how are you? You didn't drown, did you?"

"I didn't drown, Papa. But Kolya cried."

"When was that?"

"When Grandma was cursing him."

"And you didn't cry?"

"Oh, I cried too."

"What were you crying for?"

"I felt sorry for Kolya—"

"Ye-es? You're a good son of mine." Their father pulled Volodya over to him and tenderly kissed the little fellow who always seemed to feel other people's suffering intensely.

They had an omelet with ham and drank several glasses of tea.

"When are you planning to leave."

"I'll stay overnight, then off we go."

"Stay and visit a little."

"No thank you, Misha. I told Lyubochka that I'd be back tomorrow. Well, now what? We've eaten, we've drunk. What next? Want to have a battle of chess? I haven't played for so long. And your fame as a chess player precedes you—"

They sat down to play. It was terribly boring for the boys to watch the still figures on the board. Every move was thought over for nearly half an hour. Everything was forgotten, especially time. The boys eyelids were starting to stick together, and soon they fell asleep at the table; tomorrow they had to go. But the adult brothers kept sitting like stone idols, their eyes glued to the chessboard, and only now and then could be heard a whisper:

"If I do that, then he'll do that; then I that, then he that, I that, he that."

"What are you kids doing hanging around here?" Ivan Antonych suddenly came to. "Go to bed!"

And he buried himself again in his calculations.

"Whose move is it?"

"Yours, Ivanushka."

"Aha. So if I go there, you there—then I go there!"

"You'll lose your rook for nothing, and your queen will be in danger."

"Oh, sorry, I didn't notice."

Ivan Antonych was not a bad chess player. But Monkey had a special skill with combinations, an extraordinary memory, and a superb knowledge of outstanding chess matches and problems of all sorts. As a result he was able to checkmate his brother in the most refined and elaborate ways, and Ivan, despite his mathematical bent, invariably lost.

"But time's up. We've sat here too long."

"Listen, Vanya!" Mikhail Antonych said in a somewhat embarrassed tone. "Won't you take a little money. I'm all alone here, you know, except for Fedya."

It was Ivan Antonych's turn to be embarrassed. He turned red: in truth he didn't have even half a kopeck; in Moscow he would need to sell some of his things. It was really a scandal! On the other hand, it was awkward . . .

"The trouble is, Monkey, my dear, I don't know how I could repay you. Not one damn thing is working out!"

"I'll lend it to you without interest, and without a repayment date. Please take it. I have it all ready—"

He slipped a roll of bills into his brother's pocket. Ivan Antonych was deeply moved. He became serious and stopped talking; he squeezed his brother's hand, thanking him wordlessly.

Early in the morning Kolya got up and went out ever so quietly. It was a clear day. The gentle purity of autumn was in the air. Everything seemed to be made of cold, multicolored crystal. The grass was wet, and Kolya's shoes were immediately covered with large drops. Sharply etched against the sky, light-blue with barely noticeable shades of green, were the outlines of trees, the black patterns of branches, the roofs of houses. For Kolya, as always before a departure, there was a duality about everything: he was eager to get on to new places, but he painfully regretted the loss of the past. In his thoughts he relived everything that had happened in Tesovo, and felt he was leaving it forever.

Then suddenly, as though he had snapped out of a reverie, he swept off like a whirlwind toward the village: he hadn't said good-bye to Stepan and Vasya . . .

Just as suddenly he turned back again, tiptoed into the house, gathered all his knucklebones in a sack—there were twenty complete sets—and every one had an individual meaning for him. Again he ran toward the outskirts of the village.

Stepan was splitting wood outside his house and, like every good woodsman, expelling his breath with a sharp "Ha!" at each blow. He was driving a wedge into the thick body of the log; lifting the sledgehammer over his head, he brought down one more solid, mighty blow and the log split in two down its whole length, revealing the bright yellowish pallor of the heartwood.

"Uncle Stepan. I came to say good-bye. Is Vasya at home?"

"He's home. You're leaving already? What for?"

"Papa came. We're all going now."

"Vasya's gonna howl something awful. What's the bag for?"

"I brought him my knucklebones."

"Go on in the house. He's prob'ly still snoozin' up over the stove."

Kolya opened the door. The hot, stuffy smell of the *izba*, so familiar to him, poured out. Vasilisa, Stepan's wife, was feeding the infant. Vasya was already sitting at the bench, with sleepy, swollen, slightly runny eyes.

"Kolya! What are you here for?"

"I'm going away now, Vasyenok. I came to say good-bye. I brought you the knucklebones."

"You're really going away?" Vasilisa blurted out, pulling her dirty cotton-print jacket over her breast.

"This very minute. I just had time to run over to see you at the very last moment."

A rush of bitter pain kept Kolya from saying anything more. Vasya's lips were quivering.

"Good-bye, Vasya."

Kolya kissed his friend, and forgetting even to shake Vasilisa's hand, ran out with tears in his eyes: he couldn't stand long good-byes. He ran over to Stepan, not even looking him in the eye, took hold of his enormous paw, and ran on, hearing only what Stepan called after him.

"May all good things come your way, dear lad—"

He ran without looking back: farewell, farewell . . .

At home everyone was up. Sitting and drinking tea. The windows had steamed up and were weeping. The samovar was singing in its high, thin, plaintive voice. Stepanida had baked rolls and cottage cheese tarts and made them hard-boiled eggs for the road. She stood there saying nothing, just looking at the departing boys, and her kind face displayed a mother's sad longing . . .

The final moment of parting had arrived. Everyone took his seat in the carriage. The coachman waved his whip.

"Giddyap!"

Already the springless carriage was bumping and bouncing over the road. On the porch they were waving their hands, their handkerchiefs, shouting something, but you couldn't hear it; all you could see was their mouths moving . . .

It was about twenty versts over back country roads to the nearest railroad station. There were no woods in the area. The road wound between fields and meadows, flat and joyless. It was lovely out, a clear, fine autumn day. The fields had already been harvested, the grain taken in, and the stubble of straw lent a dimmed-down golden color to the strips of farmland. The rooks hadn't flown south yet, but they were already gathering in large flocks and, with their blue-black feathers flashing in the sun, strutted freely and portentously about the empty fields. The winter wheat spread out like green velvet. A caravan of ducks passed over the river. Somewhere high in the heavens cranes were calling.

The little villages were all hunched over. In the front yards clusters of red showed from the rowan trees, their bitter berries filling up with juice. There was a smell of freshness, of damp earth, of autumn. Visible far off in the distance were scraps of fields, a ribbon of a river, snaking roads, and villages scattered among the fields with the domes of their churches and gleaming crosses.

Occasionally they encountered people on foot, wearing bast slippers, with knapsacks over their shoulders—beggars, pilgrims, both men and women. You could see that pieces of black bread were all they had in their canvas pouches. They moved along with slow, measured steps, lost in their thoughts, sunk in their cares and worries. There is something elemental in those monotonous movements, that steady step. As though they weren't walking but were being drawn along, the way birds are drawn by some powerful ancient instincts, the secret call of nature, to fly across continents and oceans, taking their great long routes, and no one can hold them back . . .

From time to time a birch or linden alley would branch off from the road: these were the driveways to the luxurious estates of the gentry. Their massive homes were visible in the distance, with their balconies and shapely columns—regular palaces surrounded by the green of parks and grounds with artificial ponds like mirrors. The porticos and colonnades, the summerhouses, and the marble statues frozen in stony magnificence were hidden behind hundred-year-old lindens, pyramid-shaped poplars, and silvery blue spruce trees from foreign lands. Sometimes there was a flash of glass from a greenhouse, where at tropical temperatures, peaches, oranges, and pineapples were ripening. Flagstaffs rose triumphantly over the surrounding fields, demonstrating the power and authority represented by these estates of the titled nobility. In these grand old nests of the gentry, the splendor of the times of Empress Catherine and Tsar Alexander I was still reflected, maintained through pitiless robbery, and with the steady influx of value, thanks to the peasants' blood and sweat, life went on in its old familiar way. The ancient portraits of illustrious ancestors wearing their stars and ribbons continued to look down from the walls. Parquet floors gleamed. The ring of silver and crystal could be heard, along with refined French conversation. Yearning looks were exchanged. And snow-white tablecloths graced the dining room tables. Nor was it evident to the eye that they were soaked through with blood and tears. Blood and tears.

But now the carriage had come to the station. Ivan Antonych and the boys got out, brushing off the straw that had stuck to their clothing; they were stiff from sitting, and it felt good to stretch their legs—their feet had fallen asleep and felt like pins and needles. Ivan Petrov paid the driver. A gendarme could be made out, standing on the platform. The pimply-faced cashier informed them that a train was due in half an hour. They had made it! Much more and they would have been late. On the station platform, other than the gendarme, there wasn't a soul. They had to take a seat on the bench. Having nothing to do, Kolya began to read the inscriptions scratched or carved with penknives or nails on the back of the bench and even on the seat. They were not notable for wit or imagination: "Manka's a dummy," "Varka's going with Semyon," "I love pretty ones," and other messages—unprintable of course.

"Papa, look at your watch. How much time is left?"

"Five more minutes."

Soon the clickety-clack of the approaching train could be heard. It grew larger, becoming more and more distinct, and soon, like a giant dragon thunderously lashing the length of its scaly metallic body, with a moan of its whistle, puffing and thumping, the combination freight and passenger train came rolling up along the rails. The Petrovs got into a third-class car and took seats by the window. The car was dirty and smelled of cheap tobacco, but it wasn't crowded. Next to them sat an old peasant in bast shoes, brown homespun clothes, and an ancient cloth hat; he had watery eyes and a long gray beard that had yellowed. On one of his eyes was a cataract. He had a young man with him, about twenty-five, silent and with a beaten-down look, wearing a torn, dark-gray *katsaveika*, a loose, open jacket usually worn by peasant women. In neighboring compartments were tradesmen, peasants carrying sacks filled with carrots, potatoes, apples; dairy women with chunks of butter wrapped in rags; and a team of carpenters with their saws, axes, and other tools hidden in large gray bags of thickly woven hemp. They were smoking homemade cigars, rolled from newspaper, and from moment to moment, after each puff, would spit, skillfully expelling tobacco juice between their teeth.

The third bell rang. The locomotive produced a peculiar hoarse sound, not quite a groan, not quite a whistle. It gave a convulsive jerk. The whole train shuddered as though its mechanically fitted parts were clashing against one another, and after a few moments, trembling and with great strain, it moved off dead center. The station buildings, the guardhouse, and two trees with grackle nests swayed and swam backward. Several passengers took off their hats and devoutly crossed themselves.

The locomotive was wheezing, sending out clouds of steam, and as it built up power, overcoming inertia, it picked up speed. Already the telegraph poles, bushes, and trees were sweeping back, blending in with the multicolored strips of farmland. Beyond them, at a slower speed, the more distant prospects were receding, as though the entire scene were rotating on a very large axis. A crow, flapping its wings exhaustedly, tried to keep up with the train—but it fell behind more and more and finally disappeared. The telegraph wires kept dipping down, then rising up, as though they were tossing on the waves. Harvested fields, meadows, bushes, occasional trees flashed by—it was as though the train devoured them all without a trace as it sped through space, clanking and roaring.

"Petrukh, you start, okay?"

"Wait a bit."

"Come on! Let's cheer up this place—"

One of the carpenters brought out an accordion from somewhere, and to the rhythmic beat of the train and of the instrument the carpenters began to sing their ditties, with no letup in their smoking, spitting, and chewing of seeds.

Tram tam tiri ri ri tam tam
Tram tam tiri ri ri tam tam

We're from Vladimir Province
We're from Pokrovo district
Tram tam tiri ri ri tam tam
Tram tam tiri ri ri tam tam
My plane's dull, it won't plane the wood
My saw—well, it just will not saw . . .

Gradually the voices grew louder, enlivened additionally by a glass of vodka that began to pass from hand to hand.

"Tickets. Tickets please, gentlemen!" The chief conductor and two assistants were checking on all the passengers.

The passengers began looking for their tickets, some digging in their pockets, others into large sweat-stained leather pouches, some into a kind of red kerchief tied in a bundle, in which the ticket was wrapped like a baby in swaddling clothes.

"Was that you singing?" the chief conductor asked, approaching the carpenters.

"That was us."

"No singing allowed in the railroad cars."

"What the heck! Why not?"

"It's not allowed. That's all. It's the law. One that was needed, seems like."

The carpenters weren't very happy with the explanation. They sighed regretfully, as though submitting to the dictates of fate. But before the conductor and his assistants had gotten through the next car, they had already struck up a new melody.

Into the open fields I go
In sorrow and sit beneath a birch . . .

At last the train arrived at the little station in the district capital.

"We're here!"

The Petrovs disembarked. They had hardly any luggage. Stepanida's supplies had been eaten up. Ivan Antonych took Kolya by one hand, Volodya by the other, and that's how they proceeded, as a threesome, to Uncle Georgy's. The houses were one-storied, mostly of wood, occasionally brick, surrounded by gardens with many fruit trees. Broken fences, with holes in them, leaned crazily. The lampposts had lighting fixtures fastened to them, in which the kerosene lanterns were not always in one piece; the wooden pavements had rotten boards, some of which had already crumbled into a reddish-brown powder, so that gaping holes looked out onto the world like black spots. There were brick office buildings painted the color of egg yolk, next to which a village policeman stood, looking sleepy. There was a mournful-looking town square with the inevitable cathedral and with traces of attempts to pave this elegant plaza, where fat red-footed pigeons strutted pompously over remnants of horse dung, displaying the rainbows of their neck feathers to the sun. These were the sights our travelers saw as they made their way to the residence of Georgy Antonych.

Georgy Antonych occupied an entire house, a small wooden one, but well built, with four rooms and an orchard. His office was not badly furnished, with bookcases in which a substantial collection of medical literature and specialized periodicals were concentrated; he also had the most indispensable physician's instruments, and on the walls were portraits of medical luminaries, both Western European and Russian: Pasteur, Charcot, Oppenheim, Zakharin, Botkin. Among them, too, was one of the founders of Russian chemistry, Zinin, who happened to be a distant relation of Georgy Antonych's and was therefore especially revered. In the hallway, which also served as a reception room for clients, on tables in front of a large leather couch, various magazines were laid out: *Russkaya Mysl* (Russian Thought), *Russkoye Bogatstvo* (Russia's Wealth), *Niva* (Cornfield), *Vestnik Inostrannoi Literatury* (Bulletin of Foreign Literature), *Vestnik Yevropy* (European Messenger). There were also the latest issues of the newspaper *Russkiye Vedomosti* (Russian News), organ of the liberal professors of Moscow, notable for its rather boring solidity and excellent information on foreign affairs. Large windows made the room bright and attractive. Ficus trees, club palms, and philodendron, encased in heavy wooden pots bound with iron hoops, grew almost to the ceiling. In the back room lived Ivan Antonych with his wife and baby.

Lyubov Ivanovna ran out to greet the boys. They rushed over to her.

"Mama!"

And they clung to her.

From the office emerged "Uncle Zhorzh," cheerful, impeccably dressed, holding a cigarette between his teeth.

"Ah, our Voltairean has arrived! Well, come on over here."

(Georgy Antonych had of course heard grandmother's complaints about Kolya's godlessness, but had apparently forgotten for the moment the distinction between Voltaire's deism and actual atheism, although he seemed never to forget the lessons in applied physiology given by Kunigunde.)

A flood of stories poured forth with much ooh-ing and aah-ing, exclaiming and sighing. Lyubov Ivanovna listened horrified to the story of how her firstborn had nearly drowned, and in her thoughts she punished herself for agreeing to let her boys be separated from her. (As if that could change matters one bit!)

"What's happened is over and done with, Lyubov Ivanovna. All's well that ends well," Georgy Antonych laughed. "Kolya, want to go for a walk with me? Or do you want to eat?"

"No thank you, Uncle Zhorzh, we've been eating the whole way. Stepanida packed us—"

"Who's Stepanida?"

"Uncle Misha's housekeeper. She supplied us with everything."

"Well then, shall we go? Lyubov Ivanovna, will you allow us? I guarantee you he won't drown—not in the watery ocean or the ocean of life."

"Are you going for long, Yegor* Antonych?"

"Of course not. Maybe an hour and a half."

"All right. Only please don't let him out of your sight."

Georgy Antonych went for a walk twice a day for his health: once early in the morning before he settled down to work and again in the evening before supper. Taking Kolya by the hand, he went outside and headed down the road leading to the river. People they met recognized him and bowed politely. He would respond with unusual liveliness.

"Georgy Antonych, where is it that you're going?" a pleasant female contralto suddenly rang out. Some lady was heading toward them, and Georgy Antonych became livelier than ever and began to beam.

"Ah, sweet Antonina Nikitichna. Some mysterious force must have brought me out here to see you—"

"Naturally, naturally. And what addition to your family is this?"

"This is my nephew, Kolya. Allow me to introduce you to this young Voltairean who was recently saved from perdition."

"Your nephew? But I heard that your nephew was a nursing infant?" She said this ironically as she gave Kolya her hand.

In his surprise Kolya said nothing. He had been watching their interaction carefully. She was an elegant lady, shapely, wearing a beautiful black silk dress (visible from beneath her overcoat), with a black silk rose on her breast. But her hair, which was precisely styled in long, wavy locks, was white as snow. It contrasted in a most original way with the black of her brilliant, intelligent eyes, in which sparks of humor played.

While Georgy Antonych was answering her, she looked now at him and now at the boy, as though assessing the situation and considering something.

"You know what? You should come to my house and have some supper."

"I thank you, but we can't."

*Yegor is a variant of Georgy.

"There'll be no 'can'ts'! For heaven's sake, Georgy Antonych, what's the matter with you? Here a lady is making you an offer and you—you're rejecting it? Can this really be you?"

"I give up. I surrender."

Georgy Antonych gallantly kissed the hand of his interlocutor and turned to Kolya.

"I'll show you something of the world. You don't object, do you?"

Kolya said nothing.

Antonina Nikitichna Vyazigina was considered an extreme liberal among the local landowners. Her estate was organized and operated in model fashion, with machinery, a greenhouse, and a manager who was a trained agronomist. She aided the zemstvo schools, expressed discontent in regard to the local authorities, openly circulated cutting remarks about them, and made a brave show of her liberalism, not without enjoying a certain chic. This did not prevent her from taking in an exceptionally large income from her dairy facilities and charging her peasants fines for damage to her crops. (After all, order must be maintained, for heaven's sake!)

She grew rich off the backs of farm laborers and seasonal workers, but she attributed her good fortune not to their labor, but to the progressive force of the capital she employed in rational and enlightened manner. If the true mechanism and actual source of her income had been revealed to her, she would have considered that a travesty. If local workers, peasants, and farm laborers had encroached seriously upon her possessions, she would have seen that as a very great injustice and in the name of civilization and culture would not have thought twice about calling on the governor to send armed forces to subdue the "unenlightened mob." But since the "mob" at that time had not yet begun to move, she indulged herself in Frondeurism and the luxury of liberal phrases and concerns about enlightenment.

In a word, she was a typical landowner of bourgeois-progressive persuasion. Hers was a strikingly independent and authoritative personality; she read rather widely, subscribed to progressive magazines, admired the dispatches from London sent to *Russkiye Vedomosti* by "Dioneo," and was a devotee of English mares and the English constitution. Toward the landowners of obscurantist bent who let their estates run into the ground while disporting themselves in the capitals* or at foreign gambling dens, who rented land to the peasants at ungodly prices, who ran their properties in the ways of their ancestors, who clamored for subsidies, and who were the main support of the absolute monarchy, the autocracy—toward

_____
*Moscow and St. Petersburg.

them she took a scornful attitude, regarding them as political opponents and hopeless idiots who were destined for the scrap heap together with the autocracy, which she considered an "anticultural force." She viewed socialism from the same standpoint as did *Russkiye Vedomosti*, that is, as utopian nonsense, if you were talking about real socialism and not margarine reformism decked out with socialist phraseology, to which she had no special objections. Among the Russian hereditary nobility, however, the tone was set by the "died-in-the-wool patriots," and therefore she stuck out in these circles rather like a white crow. They even condemned her for using the polite form of *you* (instead of the condescending *ty*) in addressing her coachman; in fact, she wouldn't use *ty* with any of her servants, or other people's either. The "dyed-in-the-wool patriots" hated everything new with a blind hostility, because it was undermining all "the sacred foundations"; they were afraid of seeding machines, schools, hospitals, literacy, newspapers, and they saw "corruption" everywhere: even if a chance piece of sugar should fall into a peasant's mouth that was considered a decline of moral standards, an expression of the way the masses were becoming corrupted. They were still—these alcohol-soaked Catos of the Russian aristocracy—the dominant power, though their power was being eroded on every side. They made fun of Vyazigina as a *femme émancipée*. But they also feared her somewhat, especially because her views found support, and she had her imitators.

It was toward this person's home, then, that Georgy Antonych and Kolya were directing their steps.

Antonina Nikitichna owned her own house in town—a one-storied house on its own grounds, built of brick, with large plate-glass windows, but with no pretensions to any particular architectural style. The door was opened by a very pretty housemaid, who looked more like a last-year *gimnaziya* student or a refined young lady doing volunteer work as a social obligation. Antonina Nikitichna led the uncle and nephew into the living room, having given instructions for dinner, and Kolya didn't even have a chance to look around before they were called into the dining room and seated at the table. The room was brightly lighted by a lamp fastened to the ceiling. Against the wall opposite the windows stood an enormous, splendid-looking walnut sideboard, exquisitely carved, obviously the work of a master craftsman. Around the table were heavy chairs, also of walnut, and in the same style as the sideboard. The walls were paneled in a fine veneer. On the snow-white, perfectly ironed tablecloth was a serving dish with cold partridge, as well as salads and small silver salt shakers at each person's place, napkins folded in a pyramid, a crystal bowl holding tender, aromatic pears, large olive-and-carmine-colored peaches, king-sized apples, and tangerines. (For some reason Kolya's attention was drawn to the *salt*: even the *salt* "they" had was somehow extra special—not grainy and gray but a perfect white, and all ground up into a fine, uniform powder.) A cluster of bottles containing red wines and white wines awaited the diners' pleasure.

"Please, gentlemen, help yourselves. Don't stand on ceremony."

The guests fell to.

"Georgy Antonych, despite everything, your manners are not *comme il faut.*"

"In what way have I failed to please you, Antonina Nikitichna?"

"It is not nice to forget your old friends the way you have."

"Meaning?"

"How long has it been since you last looked in on me? Truly? I might have thought you had ended your earthly existence if I hadn't heard from others that you were flourishing as ever."

Georgy Antonych waved his arms as though repelling an attack: "If you were not a representative of the fair sex, I would say that this smacked of defamation of character, if not of outright slander against the innocent."

"How's this? You still have the nerve to try and justify yourself? Ah, my friend, that isn't very noble of you."

Antonina Nikitichna pressed the servant's bell: the partridge had already been finished, and it was time to move on to the next course.

The maid brought in, under a silver cover, a steaming dish of trout. Georgy Antonych shot an appraising sidelong glance through his pince-nez and immediately encountered the burning eyes of his hostess. The silent cross-examination lasted for just a moment.

"Well then, what do you have to say to justify yourself, kind sir?"

Georgy Antonych began citing the most varied reasons why he had not been to see her: for a certain time he had been very busy; then he hadn't been well; finally, he *had* visited her the previous Sunday—didn't she remember?

"The elephants of patience and the donkeys of reflection have run away. Oh, do not drive the owls of wisdom out into this night."

"Where is that from?"

"Just so. A parody of Solovyov. Let's change the subject. Doubtless t'would be better."

"Have I really not given you satisfactory explanations?"

"Not a bit. Now, you say your young nephew is a Voltairean? . . . Oh, what are we sitting here for? . . . Let's go in the living room. Masha!" She addressed the maidservant. "Please be good enough to bring coffee and Benedictine to the living room."

They went there. A squat black bottle with the inscription *liquoris monastorum benedictinorum* appeared, together with slim elegant liqueur glasses and small cups of black coffee.

"Would you like me to play something for you?" the hostess turned to Georgy Antonych, forgetting for the moment about the "Voltairean," who the whole time had not been feeling quite himself—although he had eaten the partridge, the trout, and some peaches with pleasure. In the living room stood a handsome concert piano, a Beckstein.

Georgy Antonych knew absolutely nothing about music. His reply, though, was that he felt ecstatic about hearing her play. Their hostess sat down and gave a masterful rendition of one of Chopin's nocturnes. It was obvious she was playing for her own satisfaction; she knew perfectly well that the doctor was musically a dunce, but she wanted somehow to work out her own reactions, overcome her pent-up feelings, pour them out—if necessary, spit them out, "objectify" them—and thus, if only for a time, to distance herself from her surging inner emotions and lack of serenity.

"Excellent."

"Really? I'm very happy."

The conversation turned to local matters, the town, the zemstvo, medicine, and en passant they chewed over the bones of some good friends who were not present.

At last Georgy Antonych made a sudden start: "Excuse us, Antonina Nikitichna, but it's time for us to go. Lyubov Ivanovna will be—"

"And who is that?" the hostess inquired sharply.

"His mother." Georgy Antonych pointed at Kolya. "I promised her I'd bring him back in an hour and a half maximum and here we have been sitting with you for two and a half at least."

"Is it such a sacrifice?"

"Don't be harsh, Antonina Nikitichna. You know—"

"I know. I know. I know all too well—Well then, until next Sunday. I'll be expecting you. Good-bye. And good-bye, my little Voltairean—"

It was already quite dark outside when the Petrovs left Vyazigina's house. Stars were shining in the sky, and a crescent moon sailed like a silver boat on a dark-blue ocean. Stumbling over the damp ground, they went along past fence after fence, trying with difficulty to make out what was in front of them.

"What was wrong with you, Kolya. You said nothing the whole time, as though you were mute."

"Hmm."

"You didn't like the lady?"

"No, it's nothing."

"They say you're a desperate character. And not particularly quiet. So what's wrong?"

"Nothing."

His uncle couldn't get any sense out of Kolya, only this "Nothing."

At home his parents were worn out from waiting.

"Where in the world did you disappear to?"

"We stopped to visit a charming lady. Kolya needs to be introduced into society!"

Kolya said nothing.

It was time to go to bed. Andryusha, surrounded by pillows, was smacking his lips in his sleep as though sucking on a pacifier. Volodya was lying on a couch; you could hear his measured breathing. Kolya was supposed to lie down next to him, on a bed made of chairs pushed together with a small mattress laid over them. He undressed and lay down; whirling in his head were knucklebones, Stepan, Uncle Misha, Vasya, the *izba*, peaches, Antonina Nikitichna with her snow-white hair . . . Almost through his sleep he heard a conversation:

"What's to be done? I've already sold my bracelet and my watch."

"But what about Misha's hundred rubles?"

"They have to be paid back, Vanya. And then a lot has to be spent on moving if you count all the costs. We have to sell some things. But the sooner we move, the better."

"You really think so?"

"What else? No one's going to go out of their way on your behalf, believe me. You've already seen how naive you can be. If it wasn't for the children—you simply have no idea about that side of things."

"We'll get by somehow, Lyuba."

"I hope so. But things are going to be very tight—I have no doubt about that. Soon there's going to be nothing left to sell. And we won't get by without arguments and unpleasantness. People are people! It's going to be terribly painful living at someone else's expense, Vanyechka."

"Come on now, things'll look better in the morning."

"That's a poor consolation. What about later?"

"What *about* later?"

"Vanya, I'm pregnant again—"

Kolya fell asleep.

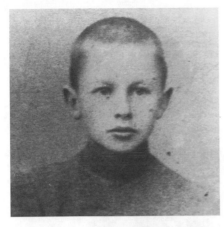

Nikolai ("Kolya") Bukharin as a schoolboy. (ANNA LARINA COLLECTION)

Bukharin (*right, standing*) with his brother Vladimir ("Volodya"), their father, Ivan Gavrilovich (*left*), and a relative. (ANNA LARINA COLLECTION)

Bukharin's mother, Lyubov Ivanovna, around the turn of the century. (ANNA LARINA COLLECTION)

Nadezhda Lukina ("Manya Yablochkin"),
Bukharin's cousin and first wife.

(ANNA LARINA COLLECTION)

Nikolai Bukharin, 1925, at the height of his political influence.

Ivan Gavrilovich Bukharin with his two sons, Vladimir (*center*) and Nikolai, mid-1920s.   (ANNA LARINA COLLECTION)

Bukharin, 1929, the year he was ousted from the leadership.

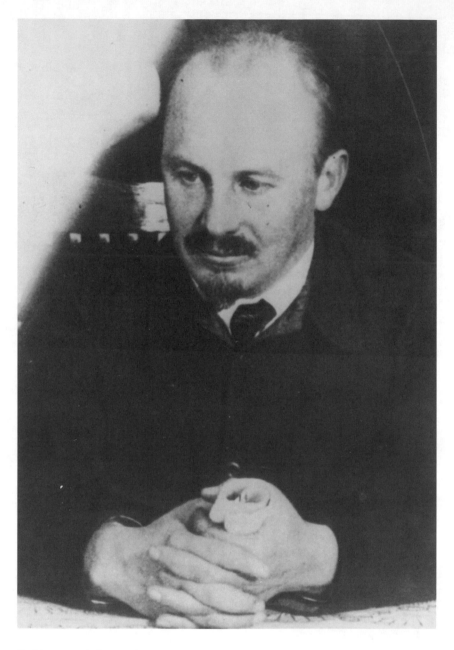

Bukharin in defeat, early 1930s.   (COURTESY STEPHEN F. COHEN)

Bukharin, the "little monkey," still climbing trees, in the Crimea, 1930.

Chapter 10

After lengthy torments the whole Petrov family ended up at the apartment of Ivan Antonych's younger brother, Yevgeny, on the second floor of an old building in the Babyi Gorodok district of Moscow, in a very low-lying area, not far from the Church of St. John the Militant. The building was dank, oozing with moisture, and full of cracks, as though an earthquake had struck. The plaster was coming down in whole strips, baring the crisscrossed, worn wooden laths and pieces of dirty wadding. Leaky spots and patches of mold gave the building an especially unclean and unhealthy appearance. Its roof hadn't been painted for many years, it was eaten with rust, and the paint was peeling, covering the roof with a kind of indeterminately colored mange. The stairways inside were rotted; here and there a step was completely missing. The doors, whose dented brass handles looked as though pieces had been bitten out of them, creaked mournfully. The ceilings leaked and were decorated with greenish patterns and designs. In the corners of the ceilings so much putrid dampness built up that even the spiders, called Vanya-Cut-the-Hay, avoided them. (This kind of spider was so named because if you pulled off its long, thin back leg, it would make movements like a reaper with a scythe.)

To make up for the spiders, those damp spots became the nesting places for repulsive, fat, lavender-gray wood lice; cold and slippery to the touch, they would fall from the ceiling onto the table, the bed, or on your head. Even the glass in the windows seemed to have formed bubbles because of the dampness, drabness, and cheerlessness of this house.

On the first floor was a laundry and a shop where boxes were made. The laundry of course was always damp; hot clouds of steam swirled in the dim air, through which bent human figures with bare arms could scarcely be made out. Piles of multicolored laundry—undershirts, underpants, napkins, handkerchiefs, sheets—were lying about in wet, twisted strands or had been tossed in the corners in disorderly fashion. Steam rose from the troughs foaming with soap. On the floor there were pools of dirty water, and little rivulets of blueing snaked along. The door to the courtyard was open summer and winter. Every minute someone was running out of the laundry with tubs of dirty water and tipping them over right there to empty them out, painting the earth or the snow in blue-gray tones. Criss-crossing the little courtyard was a maze of clotheslines on which the washed laundry was hung to dry. In the summer the wind would fill the clothes like sails, and sometimes a gust of wind would tear a poorly pinned shirt or sheet off the line. In the winter the drying clothes would turn into cold, crunching crusts.

The denizens of the laundry lived and worked in the same soaking wet, rotting quarters—that is, in three little rooms packed full of people, laundry, washtubs, soap, diseases, coughing, and curses. The prematurely aged laundry women, all tattered and torn, were as one in being emaciated creatures with sagging breasts, wrinkled faces, hands as scraggly as dry, gnarled sticks, fingers corroded by soap and alkali. Because of their hopeless life and heavy, joyless, accursed labor, all of them, almost without exception, drank vodka, argued, and fought and as a result were always covered with bruises and scratches. Their husbands or lovers engaged them in mortal combat, beating them regularly. And all this was crowded into the tiny space of a few square meters, where people and things were thrown together as in the witches' cauldron of Gogol's *Night on Bald Mountain.*

In the box-making shop, from early in the morning till late at night, people glued boxes together out of cardboard. There was the smell of paste and glue, of human sweat and cheap tobacco. People sat there from dawn to dusk, almost never standing up. The owner worked right alongside his employees. Before lunch he would treat them to tea so that their swollen bellies would require less cabbage soup and porridge and he could save on the cost of food. The workmen were young, tow-headed fellows, with pale, drawn faces scarred by too much labor and vodka and not enough food. Sitting at their tables, they sang melancholy songs, and on Sundays would get drunk and act rowdy or else crash on their bunks, completely wiped out—only to rise the next day with yellowed, swollen faces, unbearably painful headaches, and the irresistible desire to get drunk again no matter what.

Adjacent to the courtyard was a tiny little garden with several acacia bushes, shabby and dilapidated. Hanging on these bushes there always seemed to be some threads, old rags, and scraps of clothing. The ground was covered with broken glass, corks, remnants of torn shoes, and dog excrement. It was rare that a green blade of grass would sprout here, and if it did, it would quickly wither in the barren soil. This little garden was the favorite hangout of a number of dogs and cats. But these concomitants of human life were mangy and skinny, with broken legs, stuff coming out of their eyes, hungry, homeless tramps who would sit under some bush, gnawing in vain on an old bone on which there had been nothing of nutritional value for a long time, either on the outside or within. During their nuptial exercises they would tear at one another without mercy, ripping out the last clump of fur. One of the amusements of the residents of the house was to harass the animals or throw stones at the hapless, cringing mutts, while whistling, whooping, and hollering.

Huddling all about among winding, crooked alleys were other houses of the same kind, or else, one-storied wooden buildings with leaning walls and a piece of wire hanging by the gate that you could pull to ring the doorbell. A narrow wooden sidewalk bordered the cobblestone pavement, between whose stones, in especially out-of-the-way places, grass grew here and there. The houses were filled to overflowing with people verging on beggary and surrounded by heaps of junk that had been deposited over the course of years, as though in a giant garbage can. For good reason, secondhand dealers, ragmen, and dog men looked in here frequently. The dog men would catch stray dogs or buy them for kopecks, then sell them to a knacker. Tatar junk dealers would wander through all these back alleys, looking around with their narrow little eyes and crying out in a high, thin patter: "Shurum-burum. Good stuff. Sell or trade." Staid Russian traders would look in the windows, asking in their deep bass voices, in a singsong way but stolidly: "Haven't you got some old things or old boots to sell?" Bottle men with large hempen sacks would dart in and out of the backyards, repeating monotonously, also in a singsong fashion: "Bottles and bones, bottles and bones!" The Tatars carried the most enormous bales on their backs, full of clothing of various sorts, from bald fur coats to handkerchiefs and lace, from brand-new items to those that were completely worn out. All these goods were sold or exchanged and a balance sheet was kept. One and the same item frequently passed through several life cycles, and to each such cycle there corresponded a particular social set of consumers: the new item would be worn by so-called respectable people; the worn item would be sold to some impoverished person who still had some standing in society; when it was completely frayed it passed down to the poorest of the poor, the beggars and those who "lived by their wits," the lumpens. The variations in these metamorphoses were quite substantial; there were as many combinations as you could wish, and these rags followed their own laws of commodity circulation, with the secondhand dealers, those peddlers to the poor, serving as agents and intermediaries in the process.

Yevgeny Antonych had moved to Babyi Gorodok not long before, with his brother's needs in mind. All his calculations led him to conclude that there could be enough money to rent a four-room apartment and, if necessary, to support Ivanushka's family only in the event that they wouldn't have to pay too much for the apartment itself, and they couldn't think about the quality of the place. Grandmother came to stay with them, too, and by mail she summoned Fedya as well. Yevgeny Antonych was a bachelor himself, but an ancient lady, an aunt or cousin once removed, by the name of Ufochka, who could barely shuffle her legs, ended up in his care as well. They were all obliged to fit themselves into four rooms. One was a dining room and common room. Ivan's family was squeezed into another. The third was occupied by Grandma, Ufochka, and Fedya. And Yevgeny himself found shelter in the tiny fourth room. That was what fell to his lot. This was a real sacrifice for him. But he was a man of fine character and rare generosity. He was the only one of the brothers who had not graduated from a university; instead, he felt obliged to go to work as soon as he left high school. For a long time he had worked at the editorial offices of *Russkaya Mysl,* but now he was an accountant at a cloth merchant's firm, the Andreyevs', and all day long he sweated in a "barn" located in the Sredniye Traders' Rows (or Middle Commercial District), near Varvarka. He was taller than his brothers, and balding, with very kind eyes in a round face and the most genial-looking nose, like a potato, on which sat a substantial pince-nez. He was always humming something or singing or he would declaim with great feeling, but in a droning, monotonous fashion, melodramatically raising his voice at the end of each line.

At eight o'clock in the morning everyone had gathered to have tea in the dining room. Yevgeny Antonych was hurrying on his way to work. He had just washed and sprinkled vegetalis on his balding pate, then taking his seat, he recited some lines, voice rising at the end:

"An artist-barbarian, with his sleepy brush . . ."

The ancient Ufochka for the hundredth time, smacking her lips, repeated her only story—about how, despite Georgy Antonych's advice, she had failed to have a set of false teeth made for her.

"Now, Yegor Antonych told me. He said, 'Ufochka! Have a set of false teeth made for you!' "

In relating this, her wrinkled hundred-year-old face was lit up by a tender smile.

On the table were rolls, buns, and butter, and in the sugar bowl, crumpled bits of sugar. But these goodies were not there simply to be consumed—take whatever you like and eat it! Ah no, each person had to measure carefully how much he or she could take, so as not to eat up someone else's portion: some held back more than others, but each had his or her sights lined up. Want made itself felt at every step, and every scrap of sugar was weighed on invisible scales. A kind of inner tension resulted from all this, expressed now in a sharp look, now in an abrupt gesture or comment.

Over tea in the morning the whole situation was eased by the inexhaustible kind-heartedness and gentleness of Yevgeny Antonych. Jokingly he would toss the children a roll or sugar or butter, doing it skillfully and with tact. At lunch, when he wasn't there, things became more complicated: every trifle grew into a problem. Who would get the marrow from the big soup bone? How to divide it up? How should the scraps of fried meat be divided? How much butter could you put in the buckwheat porridge? The duties of leadership in this regard fell, by patriarchal custom, to the grandmother. But there was an antagonism involved here. Like many mothers-in-law, in the depths of her soul she did not care much for her son's wife, for Lyubov Ivanovna, who had "stolen" her beloved Ivanushka. The grandmother considered Lyuba the source of all the freethinking, the "corruption of morals," the improper raising of the children, and Kolya's lack of faith. She assumed that Ivanushka, too, had fallen victim to Lyuba's "corrupting influence." When they lived apart, all this passed unnoticed. But now it began to leak out. Grandmother showed obvious favoritism toward Fedya, simply to spite Lyubov Ivanovna: Fedya received rewards for his virtue, so to speak, in the form of all sorts of pieces of butter, meat, or sugar. Lyubov Ivanovna was ashamed to get into arguments over such matters—but she loved her own children. When there was obvious unfairness she restrained herself, kept a stiff upper lip, but later would hail one of the secondhand goods dealers and sell one more dress or kerchief or shawl in order to buy some buns surreptitiously and slip them to her boys when she had the chance.

Meanwhile, Ivan Antonych simply could not find a position anywhere. Soon almost everything had been sold that could be: Ivan Antonych's uniforms and frock coats, Lyubov Ivanovna's ballroom dresses from their Byeltsy days, and her fur coats.

It all evaporated somehow with extraordinary speed: before you could turn around it was gone. Ivan Antonych saw this and understood but helplessly spread his hands. At first he met with indignation the humiliations and insults he experienced in searching for a job; later he grew accustomed to them. He felt especially oppressed by the petty and more than petty domestic conflicts. The most demeaning thing in life is when it becomes petty.

Occasionally Kolya would be sent to the store to sell old newspapers by their weight, and old books. He himself secretly scoured around in the backyards, gathering up bones and bottles and selling them. He even discovered by digging in the little garden that there were entire mounds of old bones and all kinds of rags in the ground there. Busying himself this way, his hands grew coarse and became covered with a kind of crust. The kopecks he earned were spent on pieces of toffee—he had quite a sweet tooth, and there wasn't much sugar at home—and he would share these treats with his dearly beloved Volodya. He kept a secret store of junk, and as soon as the "bones and bottles" bell rang he would sell the goods he had ready and run to the store for candy or a cookie with sugar on it.

He was sent to school, late in the season, when it was already the middle of the school year. It was the same school where he had spent his early childhood. He was placed there thanks to Mikhail Vasilyevich Yablochkin, who continued to be the headmaster there. Thus he found himself again in those old familiar places. He was given a hearty welcome at the Yablochkins' home. During early morning recess, when Kolya would come to eat breakfast at the Yablochkins', Manya would take pains to serve him especially juicy cutlets, bubbling with sauce and gravy. How extraordinarily tasty those cutlets were! Manya had seen how poor the Petrovs had become and understood that the boys weren't getting enough to eat. It would have been hard not to notice: their shirts hung loosely from their shoulders, they had holes and patches in their socks, and their clothes weren't ironed. Hungry longing was evident in the stealthy glances they threw at the sugar, the tea with lemon, the eggs. She felt sorry for the boys, especially Kolya, with whom she had been such close friends earlier. But the friendship was not renewed in the way it had been—their paths in life had diverged too much, and to his own surprise, Kolya didn't even tell Manya about the wonders of Bessarabia. Only once did the past seem to be remembered and repeated: Kolya brought her his pride and joy, the dry, preserved "death's-head." Manya seriously and attentively examined it. And this unknown type of moth brought to her from a far land gave her a picture of a kind of life that was entirely different.

The children carefully moistened this treasure over the samovar, where the steam came out of the little hole in the top. The dried-up ligaments became soft and soon the legs and antennae could be bent, then Kolya pinned the moth to a good cork mounting.

Early in the morning, after barely managing to swallow down a cup of hot tea, Kolya would grab his knapsack and run to school, going from all the way down in Babyi Gorodok, up onto Yakimanka Street, then onto the Polyanka, and finally to the old familiar Ordynka. There was the house where he had been born. The schoolboys and schoolgirls were sitting on the steps, waiting for the caretaker to open the doors. And when those doors opened, they charged into the building in a noisy crowd, shoving and pushing their neighbors from behind, pounding on the knapsacks on their backs, and ran to the coat racks: each had his or her own number. Like a flood of jackdaws they spread out on the main staircase, beneath which the school clinic was located; then forming a line like a long snake, they went through a cursory medical examination: the medical attendant, Yelizaveta Alekseyevna, daughter of the school chaplain, Father Voskresensky, would press each one's tongue down with a little flat piece of wood and look at his or her throat to check for tonsillitis, diphtheria, or other calamities. After each use the little wooden stick was dropped in a basket, to be sterilized with steam later on, for use again the next day.

After medical inspection, when the bell rang, they formed up in the large assembly hall for prayers. The singing teacher, who also taught handwriting, was Ivan Alekseyevich Zolotov, a frail consumptive with a huge adam's apple that protruded unhealthily from his long, thin neck. He would take up the tuning fork, set the tone, and, conducting with his hands, give the signal to begin.

"Heavenly Father, our comforter, the Spirit verily," the chanting began.

"Who art in all things and fulfillest all things," the well-proportioned and harmonious chorus continued.

"Giver of life and preserver of the worthy," the thin, pure descant rose up.

"Come to us and be among us," the altos prayed in convincingly low voices.

"And cleanse us of all evil, and dear Lord, save our so-ouls," the chorus ended the prayer, and the voices died away.

The children ran to their classrooms, and the lessons began. Kolya immediately went to the head of the class in all subjects. His handwriting was so good, like calligraphy, that it excelled the teacher's own. This the teacher readily admitted, with pleasure assigning Kolya the grade of A-plus. Two others competed with Kolya for first place: Nartsissov, a very neat and tidy boy, son of a low-ranking civil servant, had smoothly combed and parted black hair and a crystal-clear voice in the higher registers; he always excelled in the school choir; then there was Yakovlev, son of a laundry woman, whose shirt barely fit him. This extremely capable boy suffered from a terrible inherited disease. His nostrils were eaten away, and his nose gave off such an intolerable stench that he always sat alone. No one could bear to sit next to him or share his desk. Yet he had a remarkable mind for mathematics, and was quicker than anyone in the class in solving problems the teacher presented orally.

Kolya became close friends with two other classmates: Khruslovsky, who shared Kolya's love for drawing, and Mozgalev, son of the cleaning woman at the school. Khruslovsky was thin as a reed, with a lean face, flattened from the sides, a long nose, and slender hands. Mozgalev was the opposite: he looked puffy, chubby, even fat. At school they called him Mizgir (Spider). He constantly suffered from large boils or abscesses in the underarm area. He lived in the school basement, where Kolya went to visit him when "Mizgir" was sick and didn't come to class. For the first time Kolya made proper acquaintance with those stone corridors into which a dim light descended from above, where one's footsteps on the asphalt floor produced a hollow echo, and where a stale and oppressive dampness prevailed, causing the faces of the basement dwellers to grow pale and making their bones ache.

In Moscow Kolya plunged again into the world of books, continuing to read in as disorderly a way as before: he spent time with Spanish novels, Molière, Korsh's history of ancient literatures, and the Apocalypse—all this was swallowed whole with unusual avidity. In this reading, the Apocalypse took on a special importance. At school, in classes on the Law of God, Kolya referred to the fact that he knew about this book. The priest was shocked and began to question him, to see if it was really true. Kolya answered the questions but complained about the book's incomprehensibility. Then the fat priest, who was not at all inclined toward philosophizing, declared that reading the Apocalypse was forbidden to ordinary laymen by a special church decree, and he demanded that the boy abide by this rule. But since forbidden fruit is the sweetest, the honorable servant of the Lord in this way actually spurred Kolya on to read the book from cover to cover, and much more attentively. Its triumphal but incomprehensible pathos, cosmological cataclysms, the trumpeting of Archangels, the rising of the dead, the Beast, the last days, the Whore (*Bludnitsa*) of Babylon—the entire high-flown, ceremonious eschatology of this mystic document and its symbolic imagery made an impression on Kolya, despite his precocious atheism. He began to imagine that he himself was the Antichrist. By pure chance, at that very time there came into his hands the "Lecture on the Antichrist" by Vladimir Solovyov. As Kolya was reading it, when he got to the place where the Antichrist wished to leap into the abyss and "something like an electric current" stopped him in mid-air, shivers ran up and down Kolya's spine. He approached his mother and cautiously tried to sound her out on whether she herself was a *bludnitsa* (not knowing what this word meant), since the Antichrist was supposed to have been born to a *bludnitsa*. His mother was completely dismayed as to the meaning of all this. But Kolya had his own ideas and kept them to himself; he had no intention of explaining what exactly had caused him to ask this strange question.

He was going through a special kind of spiritual crisis—or, more exactly, was passing through its last phase—the impetus for which had come from his grandmother's curse. The boy soon overcame this final assault from ancient notions and conceptions that were hiding out somewhere in the lower reaches of his soul. He was especially tormented by dreams. He dreamed that he went to see Mozgalev in the cellar of the school building. He was walking on an asphalt floor. It was dark. His steps echoed hollowly in the corridor. But he could not find the door to Mozgalev's room no matter how he tried. He walked and walked, but still there was no door. Suddenly he felt as though he was hopelessly lost, as in the Labyrinth of Crete. Already he was hurrying just to get back to the light of day—but the exit wasn't there! The corridors stretched out and disappeared into infinity. He was running, couldn't get his breath. The floor was getting hotter and hotter. Finally, it got so hot that Kolya could barely stand it. He was in hell. Huge vats, like the ones they make asphalt in, were standing in rows, and big, hairy demons with three-pronged pitchforks in their hands were boiling sinners in them. The heat became unbearable and Kolya awoke, gasping for breath.

Or he dreamed that late on a dark night he was lying on the floor. It was a warm night; the sky was bestrewn with myriads of stars. They were twinkling, giving off blue, green, reddish, and golden rays. Suddenly the stars moved from their positions, and a starry dance began. Their numbers multiplied, they circled around in a silvery swirl, and they kept growing larger and larger, flashing with pale red fire. The patterns they formed were of indescribable beauty. The hosts of dancing heavenly bodies came closer. And suddenly from among them there burst a gigantic, blindingly bright raspberry-colored sun. "A comet! A comet is coming at the earth!" Kolya thought as he woke up bathed in sweat.

Or he dreamed he was sitting by a window. The weather was beautiful; the sun was shining gaily and cheerfully. There was fresh foliage everywhere and the trees were in bloom. Kolya noticed that the sun's rays seemed to be passing through a three-sided prism: rainbows were dancing everywhere. These were no ordinary colors; the usual patches of sunlight were not there. Everything was filled with the seven shades of the spectrum. Suddenly—ker-chunk! An enormous icicle had fallen from the sky. Then another, and another! "That's the reason for the rainbows: the water vapor in the air has turned to ice; destruction is inevitable." One after another, more and more frequently, the icicles were falling. They were knocking down trees, crushing houses, covering the ground with mountains of ice that shone with the seven colors of the rainbow. And suddenly a deafening crash buried everything with it.

These nightmares, in which apocalyptic catastrophes were mixed in and alternated in bizarre fashion with concepts from natural science, soon passed, and Kolya arrived at complete peace of mind, breaking free from religious fantasies forever. Still, the most varied and contradictory ideas were knocking about and clashing in his head. As the unforgettable Kozma Prutkov said: "Many people are like sausages: what they are started with, they carry around in them." Children are particularly trusting when it comes to books, and to printed matter in general. They haven't yet tasted life; they think everything written or printed is true. Talleyrand's aphorism about language is also unknown to them. It is not surprising, then, that books had such a decisive influence on Kolya. When he was reading, he entered the world of books entirely, forgetting everything else. After reading novels about Spain, he was filled with respect for the noble qualities of its knights; in fact, so much did the Spanish hidalgos win his sympathies that during the Spanish-American war he was wholeheartedly on the side of the Spaniards and was deeply indignant when the predatory trans-Atlantic republic managed without any difficulty to smash the fleet of the venerable but rotted-out Catholic monarchy.

After reading Korsh's thick folios Kolya began to live in the world of Greco-Roman mythology and heroics, among youths with golden curls, those born out of the foam, in the Agora, in atriums, under porticos, among statues, lares, penates, and urns, in the crowd of Plutarch's heroes, to whom he eagerly fled from the world of "bones and bottles," "shurum burum," and the petty concerns and quarrels of everyday life.

On the other hand, he devoured many volumes of Molière and paraded before the grown-ups his familiarity with the world of cuckolds, lovers, pushy servants, Mascarilles, Sganarelles, Tartuffes, the ridiculously affected creatures and virtuous philistine raisonneurs of Molière's world. "An old man!" his grandmother said. "Why, look at him! He's an old man. Knows everything he's not supposed to." His grandmother never guessed that these very reproaches gave Kolya the most genuine satisfaction.

On Sundays Kolya loved to go to the Tretyakov Gallery. Here he would roam for hours on end, going from room to room and pausing for long stretches in front of his favorite paintings. He couldn't tear himself away from Repin's *Ivan the Terrible*, with his desperate, mindless, insane eyes, the mild eyes of the dying son, and the ghastly pool of blood on the floor. Surikov's *Execution of the Streltsy* made him shudder. The *Boyar Lady Morozova*—her eyes burning with the stern magnificence of heroism, the chains, the beggars, the officious priest, with the vicious look on his foxy face, the running boy, the boyar's daughters. All this was so alive to him that when he left the gallery he felt the impact of these paintings as though he had seen it all in reality. The Russo-Byzantine art of Viktor Vaznetsov astounded him, the awesome flaming eyes of the angels, the large, mild eyes of the black-browed Virgin Mothers, the two fantastic birds with human faces, Sirin and Alkonost,* the three bogatyrs and the field of battle, where under a dim early evening moon the carrion crows of the steppe tear at the corpses of the fallen. He stood transfixed before Ge's canvas *What Is Truth?*—in a hallway whose floor is suffused with light, the well-fed skeptic and Roman official, Pontius Pilate, is questioning a hounded and exhausted Christ, who looks so human! Kolya would feast his eyes on the brilliant portraits by Serov, only dimly aware of the artist's refined and elegant style and the deep, penetrating power of this exceptional master. In love with nature, Kolya also fell in love with the lyrical paintings of Levitan, a Jew with sad and thoughtful eyes, who more than anyone was able to convey the feeling of the Russian countryside. His *Golden Autumn, By the Pond, Eternal Peace*, his spring landscapes with dark-blue shadows on snow—all these enveloped the boy with that feeling of tender sadness in which the human sense of ego dissolves entirely. Of the earlier painters Kuindzhi pleased Kolya more than the rather dry Shishkin, and he was willing to stand endlessly, drinking in the shining sun of *Birch Grove*. Thus he would make his way from room to room, then return to his favorite paintings and gaze at them longingly, his old familiar friends.

Eagerly Kolya began to take up drawing—both pencil and charcoal— at school. He drew pyramids and cubes; from plaster models, he drew masks and figures, an arm, a torso, other parts of the body. At home he would sometimes plant himself in the dining room, when it wasn't occupied (the Petrovs' room was so crowded you couldn't turn around in it), spread out sheets of ivory paper, place his finely sharpened pencils on the table, along with charcoal, an eraser, a photo, and a stump for softening pencil marks. Then he would painstakingly draw portraits or copy pictures he especially liked from some old magazines, or he would draw something "from memory." Once he found an excellent old reproduction of Leonardo's *Last Supper* and for several evenings in a row sat working on that. He was especially struck by the movement of the hands and fingers of the apostles: these hands seemed engaged in lively conversation, taking the place of the mouths which were closed. And Kolya's copy "came off well"—at least that's what everyone around him said.

Meanwhile, in his family the semi-starvation existence went on as before: Ivan Antonych continued to search in vain for a position; just as

*On Sirin and Alkonost, see glossary.

before, nothing worked out for him; as before, they shared bits and fragments of food; just as before, petty, unpleasant arguments broke out and
Lyubov Ivanovna, worn out by the whole situation, shed silent tears; as
before, it was necessary to sell more and more things to the secondhand
dealers, the only difference being that now even the most essential items
were being sold; as before, the infant Andryusha would be crying in his
wet sheets and his father would carry him in his arms, soothing him and
singing him verses by Fet to improvised, off-key melodies in which there
was indeed no melody whatsoever. In the backyard the same old cursing
and quarreling went on. As joylessly as ever, day after day, work proceeded
in the laundry and box-making shop, and the same old voices of the junk
dealers of various types and specialties cried out as before.

The winter had already passed, and the sun was beginning to shine
more brightly and cheerfully. Rivulets of dirty water ran through the yard,
flowed into the street, and gurgled in swift, foaming streams along the
edges of the sidewalks. The buds on the sorry acacia bushes began to swell.
In the workshop the windows were opened wide and, in the evening,
Kolya would take a seat on the window sill and listen to the shop hands
singing songs as they worked. Sometimes the songs were senseless to a rare
degree. From the window there came singing:

> Spinning and twirling a blu-ue balloon
> Spinning and twirling abo-ove my head
> Spinning and twirling it's going to fall
> The cavalier's going to steal the lady

Suddenly they switched to a devil-may-care motif:

> If you so wish it
> Of Malanya we'll sing.
> Malanya, my pop-eyed beloved!
> She ought to go home barefoot—
> And soak her head!

But this genre got to be boring, and then there rang out an extremely
popular song about the Boers: "Transvaal, my country, you're burning, all
aflame." And in its closing lines there sounded a note of vague longing for
justice, a hope for something better:

> It's come, it's come, the bitter hour
> For my native land.
> Oh, women, women, pray for us
> And also for our sons.

In general, the Boers were extremely popular. The names of President Kruger, of Botha, Delarey, and other Boer generals were widely known. The tsarist politicians, who were stripping the hides off the lesser nationalities of the Russian Empire, professional organizers of pogroms against the Jews, ideologues of obscurantism, and devotees of the Orthodox Church, in order to spite "perfidious Albion," with which they had old scores to settle, not only placed no obstacles in the way of the glorification of the Boers' heroic efforts, which actually were quite amazing, but suddenly themselves were smitten with a tender love for liberty. Sure! Even that highly placed personage who sported a set of world-famous whiskers, the loquacious emperor of Germany, Kaiser Wilhelm, sent a telegram of greetings to President Paul Kruger when the Boers successfully repelled a bandit-style assault by a British unit, guided by the ever so mighty hand of that uncrowned king of the English landowners, rich men, conquerors, and pirates in Africa—Cecil Rhodes.

Into the glorification of the heroic struggle of the Boers, the Russian people, however, inserted their own content, something far removed from the calculations of the crafty tsarist diplomats or the motives of the German Kaiser, who later, while preparing for the World War, wrote to his chancellor: "First, shoot the socialists, behead them, and render them harmless—if necessary by means of a bloodbath—and only then, an external war. But not before." The voice of the people sized up the Boers as being their own kind, farming people, "the little guy" who had successfully beaten back the well-armed troops of the all-powerful rich folk. When the workmen, the factory hands, and the peasants looked at pictures of the Boer War, they saw the Boer generals wearing ordinary jackets with wide-brimmed hats on their heads, in ordinary high boots, with rifles slung with leather straps. In and of itself, the civilian appearance of the defenders of Transvaal inspired daring thoughts. And among the masses, the seeds of dim hopes and aspirations which had been drowsing deep in their unconscious and subconscious minds, began to sprout with ardent sympathy for the glorious exploits of the Boer fighters.

> Nine sons in all is what I have.
> Three of them—no more alive.
> But fighting for freedom like men possessed
> Are a-all the o-other six.

In these words about freedom, for which the young sons of an elderly Boer were fighting, could already be heard a distant suggestion that a different kind of life was possible. But the time had not yet come.

Sometimes, on holidays, if the shop hands were still on their feet, Kolya would play knucklebones with them. They even played for money, sticking copper kopecks in the ground next to the bones—three strikes to win one kopeck. The kopecks that were won, worn and damaged, with shiny edges, and scratched by many blows, were considered a special treasure, like the medals of an old soldier.

Once when Kolya was sitting on a window sill in the box-making shop, one of the shop hands, while fidgeting with his nose, asked him a question:

"Hey Kolya, know how to put together a giant kite for us?"

"Out of what?"

"Couldn't you get an old torn sheet from your mother? We could darn it and sew it and glue it, put it together in a minute—it wouldn't take long. We could make such a kite that everyone would go 'Aah.' "

"But what would we fly it with? A big one would break the string."

"We'll get some special English twine. You just get the sheet and leave the rest to us. Agreed?"

"All right."

Searching around in a box full of dirty laundry, Kolya found a small, torn sheet. "It's only good for rags anyway," he consoled himself in committing this theft. "Besides, I can return it. And meanwhile, what a kite we'll have!" These were Kolya's thoughts as he tasted in advance the pleasure of seeing a toy of unheard-of size fluttering high above Babyi Gorodok.

All Sunday morning was devoted to the kite. They stitched up the sheet, attached varicolored patches, and glued six pieces of lath to give it shape—strong, thick ones that had been well trimmed. Two of them crisscrossed diagonally and four were on the edges. They were sewed with extra strong thread to fasten them down. Now the basic kite was ready. Next a tail had to be fashioned for it. In flight, the weight of the tail had to balance the main part of the kite. They got some bast and made a kind of harness where the very long tail attached, then tied on the twine, which Petrukha had gotten from somewhere, and proudly took the kite outdoors. It was no easy thing to get this mechanism into the air. They had to go high up the hill with it, almost to Yakimanka Street. There Mitya held the kite up high, like a priest with a miracle-working icon, while Petrukha, down below, held the loose end of the "tow rope."

"Here we go!"

Mitya released the kite as Petrukha ran. The kite rose smoothly upward.

"Petrukha, let it out more, unwind!"

The roll of twine began to spin with unbelievable speed. The kite was heading off into the heavens . . .

"Ouch, dammit, it's pulling so hard! It's cut all my fingers. Kolya! Want a try?"

"Sure."

Kolya was barely able to hold the string: the kite was straining higher and higher, pulling so hard that the string really did cut your fingers. To make up for it, the effect on the neighborhood kids of Babyi Gorodok was electrifying: they were staring at the kite from every yard. Pigeon fanciers were staring out their attic windows, shaking their heads and going "Ah!" The greatest enthusiasts begged and pleaded for a chance to hold the cord for a moment, to feel how it "pulled." The giant kite was triumphantly sailing high in the sky—and the other ordinary kites looked so pathetic, hanging low in the air like little kids, impotent and insignificant.

It was a total victory. Both Kolya and the shop hands were exultant. Suddenly, quite unexpectedly, the connecting piece at the end of the tail flew off. The kite jerked upward, swung around, then plunged headlong, describing a swift circle in the air, then another, and then, going head over heels and making one more giant circle, it rushed toward the earth and was lost from view behind the roofs of the houses. The cord hung limply . . .

"Agh, that mothering so-and-so thing. It crashed, goddammit. Let's go find it. Follow the string."

But their search took them nowhere. Someone, somewhere, no one knew who or where, had quickly cut the cord. The boys recovered only part of it. They never found the rest. "Thus their feast ended in sorrow."

Chapter 11

In the spring Kolya passed his exams and, with an award, moved up to the final grade of elementary school. On the other hand, the summer was unhappy to a rare degree. The Petrovs couldn't dream of going to the country; they were barely staying alive as it was. It was stifling hot. The paving stones were on fire. The asphalt sidewalks got so soft that the tracks of shoes could be seen in them, and even the heels and toes of barefoot kids and beggars left their imprint. The mud in the yard turned to dust, then back to mud again when they poured out the dark-blue wash water from the laundry. Cracks formed in the ground. In the Petrovs' room there reigned a heavy smell of wet diapers, sour milk, urine, spit-up, drool, and dirty underwear. The boys found refuge in the churchyard: there they came across patches of soil covered with green grass, and now and then a golden dandelion. In three big birch trees, rooks had woven their nests and, flapping their wings, would caw furiously.

Sometimes, before vespers or the evening service, the boys would climb up the steep, winding stone stairway of the tower and ask the bell ringer to let them ring the bell. The bells were hung in strict order: there were tiny little bells that rang out with clear, clean little silver voices; then there were larger bells, whose voices sounded manly and confident; finally, there was a great big bell, whose mighty bronze bass would boom out and whose giant clapper would bang against its sides like a battering ram—it was frightening even to stand under it. The bell ringer was considered a great master of his craft. The ropes from all the bells were concentrated in his hands or attached to his feet, and by operating his four extremities, dancing and tapping his feet and moving his hands with extraordinary quickness, he would play out entire symphonies. The sounds would flow back and forth, play about, stand out separately at one moment or blend into a perfect chord the next, and their metallic chatter would be drowned out suddenly by the crash and roar of the great bell, sending its thick, powerful waves into space.

From the bell tower the whole of Moscow was visible, in all its multicolored expanse, like a Persian rug. The huge golden dome of the Cathedral of Christ the Savior burned brightly where the sun's rays struck it and were reflected in a fiery radiance. The Moscow River wound along like a ribbon. The Kremlin's ancient cathedrals formed a compact little group, their cupolas and crosses gleaming. The tsar's palace and the towers at the corners of the Kremlin's crenelated walls rose high, with the two-headed eagle on a cupola. Among the houses large and small, and the shacks and hovels, there snaked the streets and narrow winding lanes of Moscow, and sprouting up among them were countless churches with their steeples. Far off in the distance hovered the Sukharyov tower. Visible in the other direction was the light blue of the Sparrow Hills, bounded by the river and the hazy green of suburban gardens.

Pigeons and swifts made their nests in the bell tower; its floor was covered with bird droppings. With piercing cries the swifts, with their sharp black wings, would cut through the clear, bright air as they darted to their nests and flew off again in whole flocks. The height, the wide view, the expanse was breathtaking—but only for half an hour.

Other than going to the churchyard and the bell tower, flying kites and catching butterflies, the boys had nothing fun to do. Only once did Ivan Antonych manage to take them to the Sparrow Hills. They went across Kaluga Square, where the squat white Kazan Cathedral of the Mother of God was located, past the Meshchanskoye Academy, to the Neskuchny Gardens. It was a long way, with no horse-drawn streetcars in that direction. They had to drag their way through the heat for quite a few miles. From moment to moment, gazing at the houses they passed, Ivan Antonych would shout: "Over there, that's Sidorov's house. Where Ivan Petrovich used to live."

"What Ivan Petrovich?"

"Krutikov, of course!"

"What Krutikov?"

"How could you not know Krutikov? I gave him lessons . . . wait a minute . . . yes, it was in 1887."

"Papa, I wasn't even born then."

"Phooey, damn it, I completely forgot . . . Oh, and over there Ivanov used to live—and over there on the right—see it?—Mama and I used to live there."

Ivan Antonych, a veteran Muscovite, not only knew all the streets and alleys but also a countless number of houses linked with one memory or another. But he mixed up years, dates, and seasons in the most ungodly manner.

The boys' fatigue left them as soon as they found themselves amidst foliage, grass, woodlands. The steep Sparrow Hills were cut with deep ravines and gullies and thickly overgrown with birch, alder, and walnut trees. Their reddish-brown clay slopes descended to the Moscow River, which made a big bend in that location. The water flowed calmly, and the woods were reflected as though in a quiet backwater. Where the downward slope of the wooded ravines ended, at the very foot of the hills, ancient black poplars with big, gnarled trunks were solidly ensconced in the earth, their slender leaves trembling in the sunshine with a silvery sheen when the wind blew them "the wrong way"; they seemed to bristle against the wind's misplaced caresses. Between these great trunks, washing over the roots of the poplars, little black streams trickled, disappearing at one point in the vivid green grass, resurfacing the next as they bubbled and gurgled over blue-gray stones. The water was fresh and icy cold, straight from the spring. A smooth green clearing extended from there to the Moscow River itself, where rowboats were waiting and a ferry man took his earnings in copper coin.

From the hills a vast panorama revealed itself. In the distance, wavering in a light-blue haze, was "the capital built of white stone."* It was all done in the gentle tones of a water color, as though woven out of air, like a mirage. Closest of all, across the river and beyond the gardens planted with cabbages, the Novodevichy Monastery, with its steeples and towers, stood like a watchman. Farther away, everything was lost in a nacreous mist, a veil of atmospheric currents the color of mother of pearl.

The sun was setting. A freshness stirred in the woods. A shadow fell across the river and slowly crept farther. Moscow turned pink, with the subtlest rose and opal tones through which the golden domes of the "forty times forty"† burned with blinding fire.

Exhausted, the Petrovs returned late in the evening to their home in Babyi Gorodok. There was a buzzing in the boys' feet, worn out by so much tramping. They wanted to sleep. They had had their fill of fresh air and were slipping away, their eyes no longer seeing, their heads slumping onto their chests. Sleep came, closing over and washing away all impressions . . .

With the autumn, school life began again. It wasn't a burden for Kolya at all; on the contrary, at school he was given tasty cookies the likes of

---

*Epithet for Moscow.
†The number of churches said to be in Moscow.

which they didn't have at home; for breakfast he would go to the Yablochkins, hungry saliva forming in his mouth as he pictured in advance the way his fork would press into the pink center of the tasty cutlet. His studies came easily to him. At school he could "draw from nature." He got used to regarding any school "nonsense," like Bible study, as a necessary formality—you give the right answers, and that was the end of it. He coped with Old Church Slavonic without any difficulty; everything seemed to go along of its own accord, as though it were a game. During prayers he sang in the school chapel choir and sometimes read the lesson for the day, but in doing so he didn't experience the slightest religious sentiment; rather, he felt at these moments as though he were reciting for an audience.

One fine day it was announced at school that the pupils would be taken on an excursion to the Zoological Garden to see some Negroes from Dahomey who had just arrived. The children lined up in pairs, and went shuffling off down the sidewalk. At the bestiary, not far from the monkey cages, where marmosets and baboons were clambering, the unfortunate Dahomeyans, men and women with infants, had been placed in a circle surrounded by guards. It was still warm, and the Negroes were only half dressed where they stood or sat. Their black skin had an oily shine to it, gleaming almost dark-blue in some places. Their strong white teeth glistened from behind thick, sensual lips. Their eyes—large, bulging, and vividly white—had a sad and surprised look. A crowd of Russian people stood staring at them like animals: poking them, making crude jokes, laughing.

A man in a knee-length cloth jacket made fun of them: "Ugh, look at these un-Christian devils. It's like they've been smeared with soot. Damned heathens."

"Everyone knows: if you're mug is black, your soul's black, too."

"You think they've got a soul?"

"Who the heck knows."

"Aren't they cannibals? They say there are cannibals who gobble up human ham steaks."

"Is that so?"

"Really. It's the truth."

"Probably they are cannibals. Heck, it's a good thing they're behind bars."

"They're not cannibals, and you're a bunch of idiots!" Kolya put in his two cent's worth, then ran away while the "idiots" were considering how to react to his interjection. His outburst had happened without his intending it. This was the first time he had seen live Negroes, and their appear-

ance surprised him. But he had read "Uncle Tom's Cabin," and his beloved
Huck Finn had his dear friend, Negro Jim; he remembered Heine's "Slave
Ship"; and all the blood had rushed to his head when he heard this
exchange of opinions among traders and corn chandlers, making jokes at
the expense of the black-skinned people.

"Petrov, where are you going?" This was said in surprise by Nikolai
Palych, the teacher accompanying the children: he had seen Kolya run
away from the railings around which the people staring at the Dahomeyans were crowded.

"I don't want to look at the Dahomeyans anymore. They're not animals.
Give me permission, Nikolai Palych, to go look at something else."

The teacher's eyes turned upward. He seemed to be weighing something.

"All right. But just don't get lost. Later on we'll all go for a walk in the
garden."

Kolya went wandering around the menagerie. He was drawn to the elephant. The enormous Indian elephant stood in one spot, virtually immo-
bile. When he raised his pillar of a leg, he made his heavy iron chain clank,
like a forced-labor convict of old. His skin was all wrinkled and hung in
folds, like ancient bark. Now and then he seemed to test the air with his
trunk in a lazy way and immediately sank back into forgetfulness. If someone tossed him a French roll or a kalach, he would catch the food skillfully
and, bending his trunk, direct it toward his mouth. Then his keeper would
say:

"Bow down, Zemba, say 'thank you!' "

And this enormous creature, son of the jungles, would go down on his
knees, his chain clanking.

Nearby in a small pool with filthy black water, providing barely enough
room for his bulk, a clumsy hippopotamus was snorting. In a neighboring
pavilion, behind thick iron bars, the large predators were kept. A handsome tiger was furiously pacing back and forth in his cage, lashing his tail.
The lion was lying with both front paws under his head, eyes closed,
drowsing. The elegant leopards and pumas, their graceful bodies all sinewy
and shapely, opened their maws ever so wide, as though in evil laughter or
getting their jaws set for a meal. The bears were stamping around, pigeon-
toed, by the edge of their cage, rumbling and licking their paws. Their
emerald eyes held something mysterious and enigmatic.

Kolya went on to the bird pavilion. Here there was a deafening uproar:
all kinds of birds were singing, whistling, chirping, chattering, jabbering,
and twittering in different ways and different voices. The harsh, screeching cries of the parrots could be heard clearly through all this unbelievable

cacophony. Red and blue macaws with their long tails; cockatoos, faintly pink and white, with mobile crests bobbing on their heads; intelligent gray parrots; and all sorts of little birds, virtually indistinguishable from one another, holding onto the wire of their cages with their feet and beaks, all were scrabbling from place to place and were wildly, hoarsely, piercingly screeching, like hundreds of cartwheels needing grease.

In large aviaries there fluttered Australian finches, shiny starlings, and thrushes of all varieties; the monstrous noses of toucans peeped out of holes in hollow trees; and the malicious cackle of a laughing gull came pouring forth. The curlews and sandpipers bustled about importantly—there was plenty of everything here. Kolya could breathe easy: he had something to look at as long as he wanted.

Then he went to visit the birds of prey, the largest and mightiest of the birds. There was a cage with vultures, kings of vast icy spaces, carrion eaters with naked necks—huge birds that drop down for their meal from immeasurable heights. There they sat, with heads lowered gloomily, downcast, with their wings drooping and eyes grown dull, and from their once mighty wings, torn and tattered feathers dropped to the floor. Lifting their tails, they scolded one another. The American condor, like a beggar, propped himself against the wall, looking all twisted and dull. White-tailed eagles, golden eagles, mountain eagles, the mighty inhabitants of harsh landscapes, were transformed here into listless, unhappy, unhealthy creatures. Only the eagle owls seemed not to feel so bad, staring about with their mystical bright-orange eyes. Kolya was reminded of some lines from Pushkin:

> I sit behind bars in a dungeon so dank
> Young eagle, brought up as a captive . . .

He went past almost all the cages and pavilions, returning at last to the monkeys. Monkeys of all sorts—marmosets, baboons, hamadryads—sat or lay in various poses, climbed about, jumped from limb to limb on a dead tree, or swung on the trapezes hung from the ceiling. A small marmoset, like a little old man with a wrinkly, pink face, was dexterously sorting Chinese nuts, picking through them with his fingers and casting sorrowful glances at the public. He examined each nut carefully before putting it in his mouth, just like a human being, then cracked the shell, jaws working rapidly as he scratched himself behind the ear. Another, making his way on all fours with his tail in the shape of a question mark, came down along the cage wire and, making a sidelong jump at the first monkey, began stealing his food. They both began to squeal, rolling on the floor, locked in a tussle, and then, suddenly jumping away from each other, went ambling among the tree limbs, their tails switching. The boy could stand and watch the monkeys forever. He knew that "man descended from the apes," and he was all eyes as he gazed at these four-legged relatives of his, trying intently to penetrate the secret of their existence. What were they thinking? What were they feeling? What strange beings!

"Petrov! There you are! We've been hunting all over the zoo for you." Nikolai Palych came up, with a train of kids behind him, leaping and laughing at one another, like a gang following its leader. "Line up two by two, children. That's right. Now let's go home!"

And the squad of youngsters went marching back to school.

At school that year they were getting ready for an unusual holiday. Celebrations of Pushkin's centenary were coming up. So great was the aura surrounding the dead poet that even the tsarist government, one of whose most illustrious representatives, Nicholas I, "Nicholas the Bludgeon," had harassed Pushkin, sent him into exile and, after the poet's death, ordered his corpse secretly removed, hidden under some matting and escorted by gendarmes—even this tsarist government was pounding all the kettle-drums in honor of the poet. A redoubled propaganda campaign was under way, including through the schools, promoting a false and rather ignoble version of Pushkin, one inspired by the poet Zhukovsky, who had been a courtier and sycophant of the tsars, author of sentimental ballads, and "singer" of the autocracy's armed might—this version alleged that Pushkin had had a reconciliation with the tsar and the church on his bloody deathbed. They published booklets for children in which this difficult and defiant genius, a mischief maker and a rake, a man of quick intelligence and great wit, a biting critic and mocker of authority, and a friend of the Decembrists, who had dashed off these memorable lines:

> We'll entertain the Russian people
> By hanging from the highest pillar,
> With the intestines of the last priest,
> The very last tsar.

This real Pushkin had been reworked to portray a "good little boy," a loyal and virtuous servant of the powers that be, a Derzhavin of Nicholas I's regime. This soothing balm was officially distributed around the country in very large doses. Persecuted during his lifetime, passed over in silence after his death (it was no accident that even the moderate liberal Ivan Sergeyevich Turgenev had to serve a prison term because of a simple obituary he wrote about the great poet)—Pushkin had now become an object of hypocritical concern as *nôtre célèbre poete russe*. Now the autocracy wished to walk hand in hand with the poet—or at least with his shade, which had grown to such gigantic proportions in the consciousness of a widespread and numerous public, thanks especially to the writings of Belinsky.*

All sorts of busts, statues, cantatas, speeches, and eulogies were being prepared. To be sure, this was not the same kind of triumph (in falsifying Pushkin while honoring him) as the one achieved, with his own special mastery, by that inspired reactionary, Fyodor Dostoyevsky, who had proclaimed in hysterical tones to all of Russia: "Submit thyself, proud mortal!" As for Turgenev, he was no longer among the living. Everything had grown more petty in official and semiofficial circles. They made up for this, however, with the greater breadth and range of this centennial propaganda campaign, and even the public schools received circulars on how to commemorate the poet.

And so, at the Aleksandro-Mariinsky Academy preparations were also being made for the celebration. In this regard, assignments fell to the lot of Khruslovsky and Kolya Petrov: they were to draw two large portraits of Pushkin that would be displayed in the assembly hall during the ceremonies.

Kolya set about this task with awe and trembling. Even before this, for his own pleasure, he had sweated over a drawing of "Pushkin's Fatal Duel," in which figures had stood out black against the snow, the trees were covered with frost, and the wounded Pushkin, lying on his side, took aim at his opponent, Dantes. But that drawing had been simply "what it was," created just for himself. Now he would have to work with everyone else in mind.

The project was overseen by the drawing teacher Zaikin, a kind and amazingly gentle person, with a meek look in his eye. He was married to the daughter of Krasavin, a wealthy merchant, had some means of his own, and lived in well-appointed quarters in the home of his mother-in-law. Zaikin had decided that the boys would work on this project at his home.

Kolya loved Pushkin with a passion, as he did Lermontov and Heine. He knew by heart long passages from *Yevgeny Onegin*, as well as almost all of Pushkin's fairy tales and a great many of his shorter poems. Secretly, by himself, he had wept over the prose tale *Dubrovsky*. He got the shivers from reading *Songs of the Western Slavs*, Pushkin's brilliant translations of the brilliant fabrications by Prosper Mérimée. He mourned as he read Pushkin's remarkable elegies. The complex simplicity of this genius, the preciseness of his wording, the aptness of his imagery, the great simplicity,

*On Belinsky, see glossary.

in which there was absolutely nothing superfluous, where everything was in its place, where expressiveness reached its ultimate form—all this made Kolya feel so close and intimate with Pushkin, it was as though he were a living part of life. True culture has that kind of power. And Kolya kept racking his brains about how not to end up with mud on his face in carrying out this assignment. It troubled him and he could find no peace. His hands grew numb with cold. Sometimes he felt he would have to refuse the assignment, that it was beyond his power, that he was sure to cover himself with shame. And over what? Over Pushkin! But then he would be entranced by the prospect of "doing the best drawing," and it seemed shameful to refuse.

At last the two boys found themselves at Zaikin's place. Khruslovsky was the son of a poor woman who earned a livelihood by doing odd jobs, taking in laundry, cleaning, and so on; he lived in a house that was jammed full with the poor and the indigent. As for Kolya, he had already seen a thing or two in life, and his existence at the time was by no means "full-bellied." So when the two of them, before anything else, were seated at a table and given some ever so tasty hot chocolate with cream, they suddenly felt as though they had entered Paradise—so far removed was their material existence from such simple amenities of life.

Zaikin had prepared two excellent drawing boards, to which first-rate "ivory" paper had been tacked. Also, there were shading pencils, "mossy stumps" (for softening pencil marks to enhance shading), erasers, photos, and other accessories, including portraits of Pushkin that it was their assignment to "enlarge." The room was quite spacious, the sun shone in through a large window, and Zaikin arranged himself at the same table, to be close to his pupils while doing his own work (some sort of vignettes done in water colors, used in advertising and produced in response to orders from various customers). And so the work began.

The boys went to Zaikin's every other day, or every third day, and for them these visits were a festive occasion: it was great to work there; it was quiet, cozy, and cheerful; and they were given hot chocolate with cookies every time—that was really something just by itself. Meanwhile, at school another kind of preparation for the festivities was under way: they were memorizing poems, putting on "living scenes" (dramatizations from Pushkin's life and work), and arranging dress rehearsals. Kolya was supposed to recite the tale of the fisherman and the golden fish, as well as the poem "To the Slanderers of Russia." (The latter poem had of course been chosen for political reasons—to show how "patriotic" the poet was—in keeping with the patriotic spirit of the occasion.) Kolya was thoroughly familiar with the tale of the fisherman and the fish and already knew it by heart, but when it came to "The Slanderers," he didn't fully understand what it was about. Still, reciting it seemed more interesting to him than reading such Bible lessons as, "Whither shall I turn away from Thy Spirit and whither shall I run to escape Thy Countenance?"—which he had had to do at school more than once.

At last the portraits were ready. Of course they were the work of school-children, but during preliminary inspection the teachers praised them. First-rate passe-partouts were made for them: Kolya's was placed in an oval frame; Khruslovsky's, in a rectangular one.

On the day of the actual celebration the schoolchildren were taken else-where to an official ceremony, where a monument was unveiled. There were thick crowds of people and many policemen. But none of the children, dwarfed by the crowd, could see or hear anything. They saw only the backs and heads of those standing next to them, heard the confused babble of speeches and applause, heard music playing and something being sung, then after being tortured by long, weary hours of standing around, they returned to the school, exhausted and dispirited.

In the evening the school ceremony was held. The assembly hall, brightly lit, was hung with evergreen garlands; by the walls, in heavy tubs, laurel trees and palms had been placed. The portraits of Pushkin were drowned in flowers fresh from the greenhouse. All the teachers, pupils, and parents had gathered. Even the school supervisor had come, a pompous gentleman in a pince-nez, wearing a black frock coat with medals on the lapels. Out of the corner of his eye Kolya looked at the portrait he had done: How is it? All right? Seems to be all right. But which is better, mine or Khruslovsky's? In Khruslovsky's the hands came out better; in mine they look kind of wooden. But in mine the eyes are better, if I do say so—on the other hand, his background is really good . . . So went Kolya's thoughts.

Meanwhile, in the assembly hall a chorus had already sung a cantata, then both teachers and pupils came forward to recite Pushkin's poetry. And now it was Kolya's turn: first he was supposed to recite the fairy tale and later, as the last item in the literary part of the program, "The Slanderers." He walked up to the speaker's platform and immediately froze in fear. For a moment it seemed to him he had forgotten everything in the world. He saw flashes of faces in the audience, the glow of the lights, the candles in the candelabras, the entire hall filled with people. He had lost it all: there was nothing, absolutely nothing, total emptiness. Cold sweat stood out on his forehead, and his hands trembled. This lasted only a moment, chronologically a tiny point in time but one that stretched far out in his mind.

Just as suddenly as everything had disappeared it came back again. And as Kolya recited the first lines, his complete self-confidence returned; he entered into the spirit of the tale and felt himself to be now the old man, now the persnickety old woman; he could hear the roar of the sea, and see the golden fish, in all its wisdom, flashing through the waves.

Kolya could see that his teacher, Nikolai Palych, was beaming; that Aunt Manya was whispering something to the school supervisor, who was listening and nodding his head approvingly; that his parents' faces were all aglow—as were those of women in kerchiefs, plain-visaged men in shirts and jackets; and that the schoolkids were staring at him, open-mouthed, not daring to utter even one word.

Kolya finished. The entire hall began to clap. He was rooted to the spot—had never experienced anything like it. Aunt Marya beckoned to him, crooking her finger. But out of embarrassment, and overwhelmed by emotion, he ran over to his classmates and stood against the wall, breathing heavily, back in a corner. He was no longer aware of anything. All his perceptions dimmed, and he came to only when a voice began saying: the third-grade pupil of class "B" Petrov will now read "To the Slanderers of Russia."

This time Kolya didn't lose his head. He started right away in lofty tones, and it was not without exhilaration that he recited the poem. Its success with the public, however, was much less than the previous one: terms like *anathema* and *bards* did not get through to the mothers and fathers, to whom all this phraseology and subject matter were quite alien. To make up for it, the school supervisor came up to him when the reading was over, patted him on the head, and pronounced, in a low, rumbling voice:

"Excellent. Well done—"

"He also does drawings, Mr. Supervisor," Nikolai Palych began boasting after "The Slanderers."

"Really?"

"If you would wish to take a look. That portrait there is his work."

"Not bad. Not bad at all. Something will come of you, my boy. Keep it up. Keep it up!"

Kolya didn't know what to say, and muttered something incoherent. The supervisor slapped him on the back. The school doctor, Aleksandr Nikitich, with his mane of gray hair, closely shaved face, and enormous nose with a wart on it, tapped Kolya indulgently with his cane—that was a sign of the highest level of his enlightened appreciation. Father Voznesensky, the priest, came up, dragging his heavy body along in a silk cassock, and with one hand holding the large cross on a heavy silver chain that hung at his breast, rasped out: "Splendid work, dear boy, excellent recitation, especially of 'The Slanderers.' Truly magnificent." And he held Kolya by the chin for several seconds.

After the literary portion of the proceedings, there were instrumental and vocal numbers and "living dramatizations." The sets for the latter had been painted by Alyabyev, another art teacher. Even though during his work on them he had demanded strong drink, claiming he needed it to do the job, and had gotten very drunk, the sets were really fine, and Kolya had been quite astonished—I would like to be able to paint that way!

But now that the sets were already being put to use, Kolya, physically tired and drained by all the emotions he had experienced, was hardly aware of anything more. His head began to throb, and he sat there, face pale, with his eyes half-closed.

"Kolyechka, what's wrong?" asked Marya Ivanovna, seeing her nephew's pallid face.

"I've got a headache—"

Marya Ivanovna was immediately concerned.

"Come over here, Manya!" she called to her daughter. "Take Kolya to our place and give him some phenacetin. Take it from my little table, the right-hand drawer. You know the one? Let him lie down a while, then he should go home—"

Thus ended the Pushkin celebration for Kolya.

For the next few days Kolya lived on memories of his moment of glory. He took the Pushkin portrait home. Later the memories grew dim and diffused. The Pushkin portrait was moved from the dining room to the commode. Flowing from the future into the present there came a succession of new, petty preoccupations.

At home everything went on as before. Ivan Antonych continued to make his painful rounds looking for work, without results. Lyubov Ivanovna was getting ready to give birth once again and thought fearfully of what lay ahead. At school they were going through decimal fractions, and at recess played tag and cops and robbers. Lent was approaching. One was supposed to fast in preparation for Communion.

Ordinarily in the Petrov family the practice of fasting had not been observed. But now that Grandma held the reins, she promoted these customs and rituals persistently and without deviation. To be sure, in the extended family living in Yevgeny Antonych's flat there was already a kind of "Lent" under way—their diet did not include much fat. But sometimes they had a chance to gnaw on a bone or smear a bit of butter on part of a roll or have a sip of milk. Now, however, there was nothing but potatoes with Lenten butter, and Lenten sugar instead of the real thing, and not one scrap of meat. Before dinner Grandma would pray demonstratively, whispering and sighing loudly and casting menacing glances in all directions. Fedya would pray with her, imitating her gestures. The rest tried not to meet her gaze and to wait her out, until she had finished her visitations with God Almighty.

"Vanya, are you going to confession?" she addressed Ivan Antonych, her large eyes giving him a searching and severe look.

"What are you bringing that up for, Mama?"

"What do you mean 'What for'? You're such a sinner! How many years since you fasted?"

"Since high school, I guess," Ivan Antonych answered with a slight smile.

"Ach! Christ and the Saints! Don't provoke God's wrath! Repent before it's too late." Her voice shaking with indignation, Grandma nearly screamed these words.

"Let it be, Mama. You know very well I'm not going to any confession."

"Antichrists! God will punish you one of these days. You'll see. You'll die of hunger. At least have pity on the children—Lyubov Ivanovna, you at least should speak to him, since he won't listen to me."

"I can't force him, Agniya Ivanovna," her daughter-in-law responded softly.

"Well, you just wait, Vanya. God will punish you with His righteous wrath. And don't be complaining. You yourself are to blame." (Grandmother used *vinovati*, the Church Slavonic pronunciation for "to blame," instead of the modern one, *vinovaty*.) "You never cross yourself—and what about you, Zhenya?" she turned to her youngest son.

"Me, Mama? Why, what for?" he said, looking at her with his kind eyes.

"What do you mean 'what for'? Are you an Orthodox Christian, or aren't you?" Agniya Ivanovna's temper flared.

"Never mind, Mama. Let's at least eat our meal in peace. What's the point? If you're a believer, fine, be a believer—no one's preventing you. But you shouldn't interfere with others," he bit off these words impatiently.

"Lord of Righteousness! Why have you punished me with such children? Accursed sinners, Lord forgive them!" For a long time Grandma was unable to calm down; she kept muttering and sighing, exclaiming from time to time. But since it was necessary to eat, the technical requirements and logic of the eating process eventually got the better of her indignation and things went by without a violent domestic scene of the kind that sometimes broke out in that old house in Babyi Gorodok.

Kolya couldn't get away from fasting in preparation for Communion after all, because at school it was necessary to submit a church certificate stating that the indicated servant of God "had been at confession and partook of the sacred Christian mysteries." His mother doled out a twenty-kopeck piece for this purpose. Of this sum, Kolya decided to give the priest only five kopecks.

Inside the church it was solemn and still. People stood in a line stretching toward the screened-off area where the priest was hearing confession from the parishioners, granting them remission for their "trespasses," whether committed intentionally or not. They moved about like so many shades, all silent, with pale, serious faces, preparing for repentance. Several were on their knees, bowing their heads to the ground, just short of knocking their foreheads on the stone slabs of the church floor. Others were crossing themselves, with deep sighs, as though in the next few minutes they would have to mount the scaffold. There was a smell of rose oil, incense, and wax. In the semi-darkness lamps of different colors were burning in front of the icons, along with slender wax candles. Their reflections played in tremulous flecks of light on the silver and gilt vestments and halos of the icons and on the metal candle holders, and they sparkled and trembled in the precious stones and cut glass of the icon lamps. The blackened faces of the saints, worn down by the thousands upon thousands of reverent kisses by supplicants, gazed out sternly with their Byzantine eyes. In this silence, this gloom, this stony chill, there was something deadening, something that spoke of the grave.

From behind the screened-off area into which the penitents disappeared, mysterious whispering and muttering could be heard. Those exiting from the area after confession hurriedly crossed themselves and left the church. And now it was Kolya's turn. Not without trepidation he went behind the screen. "How will I answer if he asks me about God, faith, the Church? Should I lie through my teeth? But if I don't lie, they'll kick me out of school. And no Aunt Marya will be able to save me!" Without having resolved this problem (whatever will be, will be), he went in.

But the priest didn't ask him about any such lofty matters. He covered Kolya with a stole, and in a tired and indifferent whisper, exuding a stale smell of tobacco from his mouth, enunciated:

"What's your name?"

"Nikolai, Father."

"Do you use swear words?"

"I am guilty, Father."

"Disobey your parents?"

"Guilty."

"Do you do well at school?"

"Yes, I do."

"You don't steal sugar from your mother, do you?"

"No."

"Nikolai, servant of God, is granted remission of his sins—" The priest began to mutter and pushed the cross at Kolya (who was supposed to kiss it) with such force that he almost hit him in the nose. The latter put a five-kopeck piece in the dish and left in a hurry, as though escaping from a crypt. Outdoors it was bright and smelled of spring. The skies were light-blue, and all curly with soft, puffy spring clouds.

In the yard Kolya told about not being scared one bit at confession, about the priest asking him nonsense and almost bumping him in the nose with the cross, getting only five kopecks instead of twenty for his trouble. The story was accompanied by as much blasphemy as Kolya could muster, the kind that would probably have given Grandma a fit. But the shop hands were big boys now, with mustaches, and they could take it, although they still had religion in their heads in the form of certain fears concerning God and the Devil. Kolya went so far—boasting a little in the process—that the fellows, the shop hands and the neighborhood kids, began to besiege him.

"Kolya, don't show off too much! There was one guy who showed off like that, and during Communion his arm got paralyzed."

"Go tell that to your grandmother."

"No, really, Kolya. Fooling with priests is something else. And at Communion, you know—God's there."

"Hey, do we really eat the Body of Christ, the ham hocks of the Lord, and lap up His Blood? Real flesh, human and divine? That means we're worse than cannibals. God-eaters, some kind of carrion crows. Why, I'd throw up if I believed such fairy tales."

"Kolya! Hush, hush!"

"But really—" Kolya wouldn't stop. "All there is, is Communion bread and church wine. The kind they call *kagor*, the kind they sing about in the song."

> The monks of the cathedral,
> Having sipped of the *kagor*,
> Were standing by the fencepost
> Heavily leaning o'er.

And forgetting about the argument, the others joined in, in unison, in an inspired chorus:

> Were standing by the fencepost
> Heavily leaning o'er.

"You know what?" Kolya continued the conversation. "Let's make a bet.

I'll bring you back your Body of Christ from Communion. And here we can take a look at it from all sides."

"Hey, come on, Kolya, you better drop it."

"I'm not dropping anything. What's the matter? Scared?"

"Yeah, well, how are you going to bring it?"

"Simple. Under my tongue. When the priest sticks it in my mouth on the little spoon, zip! I'll swish it under my tongue. Then I'll lay it out right here on this bench for you to see."

Kolya pointed at the dirty little bench in the garden.

"Well, what do you say? Who's against it?"

Everyone was silent, shifting from one foot to the other.

"Still, Kolya, you ought to be more careful. Maybe the fellow's arm really did shrivel up."

"Don't worry. No arm of mine's going to shrivel. And I'll bring you the Body of Christ."

On the day of Communion Kolya went to church, to attend mass. It was an impressive ceremony. The church gleamed with gold and silver. The bright rays of the sun, coming in the high windows, by the very cupola, were transformed down below into light-blue columns by the fumes of the incense holders. The choir sang with clear and joyful voices. The bells rang triumphantly. The crowds of the faithful were waiting for the Christian's greatest mystery, when the bread and wine turns into the Body and Blood of Christ. They had already relieved their souls of the burden of sin, been cleansed of evil, and joyfully awaited their Communion with God, the Savior of humanity, risen from the dead. The girls in white and pink dresses, with flowers in their hair, rapturous and deeply moved; those taking Communion for the first time, wearing little ribbons tied in bows, their faces shining; the old ladies with their wrinkled brows and wrinkled hearts, feeling deeply stirred as they waited hopefully for the joyous blessing; the men, all dressed up in bright silk shirts, frock coats, and uniforms—depending on their rank or order as mortals—all were preparing themselves for the great mystery. The liturgy was reaching its highest point.

"We lift up our hearts," the clergyman-prophet, dressed in bright gold vestments, sang out to the believers.

"We lift them up unto the Lord," the many-voiced choir responded harmoniously; the high, thin sounds of the descant rose up, higher and higher, till they were echoing under the very dome of the cathedral, while somewhere down below the basses subsided, sonorously holding a low note.

"Come, eat, this is my Body—" the priest intoned, addressing the faith-

ful in the name of Christ, the Lamb, who suffered for their sins, was crucified, and rose again.

But what if my arm really does shrivel up?—agh, what nonsense!—and
yet— Kolya was thinking to himself, giving in ever so slightly to the collective intoxication of the ceremony.

"Take, drink, for this is my Blood which was shed for thee for the
redemption of sins—"

Foolishness! The thing is just not to swallow it, not to lose my head—
or maybe I could take it out with my finger without being noticed—but
they'd see me!

"And now receiving Communion is Fyodor, servant of God—"

Dammit! You have to take the Body from the spoon with your
mouth—then he wipes your mouth with the cloth—then they give you
"the warm stuff" to drink—then you have to kiss the cross—how'm I
gonna keep from swallowing it?

"Now receiving Communion is Mariya, servant of God—"

The main thing is to hold my tongue firm and not move it until everything's done—

"Now receiving Communion is Dmitry, servant of God . . . Barbara,
servant of God . . ."

"Your name?" he heard the priest whisper.

"Nikolai—"

"Now receiving Communion is Nikolai, servant of God."

Kolya held the Body of Christ firmly under his tongue—no, baby,
you're not getting away—the wine came within an ace of washing it out
from under. But he didn't let go!

Then he ran home from the church. Firmly held beneath his tongue
was a little piece of Communion bread. Now I'll show 'em! "You'll lose
your arm." Ha! What fools! . . . Such thoughts were running through his
head.

Like a whirlwind he sped and soon reached the windowsill of the workshop. Making a mooing sound, he pointed at his mouth, as if to say: "All
done! The promised prize is right here under my tongue."

The shop hands ran out into the yard and called to their neighbors.
Kolya, with his eyes cheerfully flashing, waited till everyone had assembled—he was not about to show them one by one!

Finally everyone was there. Kolya spat out onto his palm the piece of
Communion bread and put it on the bench. Everyone jumped back, as
though it were a bomb that might explode.

"Look out, it's gonna make fools of you . . . Well, what do you say? Did
it get eaten? Did it get chewed up? I said I'd bring it and I did. There's

nothing to be afraid of! You see, I still have both arms, and my tongue didn't even shrivel up. There, see, just a little piece of Communion bread; it's pink from the wine. You can sniff it—it smells like wine, not blood. See?"

"But how'd you do it?"

"Like I said: under my tongue. Hey, you know what? Let's give Communion to the turkey in the churchyard."

"What a thing to think of!"

"Really, it'll be fun!"

And the boys ran to watch the unheard-of spectacle.

Thus, in the summer of the nineteen hundredth year after the Birth of Christ, in the original capital of the Russian Empire, instead of the servant of God Nikolai there partook of the Body of Christ a turkey without a name in the yard of the Church of John the Militant, in the district of Babyi Gorodok.

Chapter 12

At the turn of the century, Russia was a huge historical fermenting vat, where the great juices of social life, all in ferment, were rapidly changing the time-honored lifestyles, the relations of social forces, the existing habits, norms, ideas, and worldviews. It was still not that long since the eloquent ideologist of Russian barbarism and autocratic Byzantine despotism, Constantine Leontiev, had expressed the hope that he would succeed in "freezing Russia," protecting her from the paths along which the decayed West was developing, heading inevitably and unavoidably toward a great social catastrophe. This fine gentleman-aristocrat, who loved ceremonial mass at home, refined cigars, purebred borzoi hounds, and charming Oriental women, who served for a long time as a diplomat in Constantinople, and who died of syphilis as a monk in the celebrated Optinaya Monastery among ascetic "elders," saw in sly and crafty Byzantium and Orthodoxy "the pillar and affirmation of truth."

It was still not that long since Slavophile landowners, wearing bobbed hair and truly Russian *poddyovkas*,* had carried on bitter battles with the Westernizers, the advocates of European civilization, and frightened so-called society with the "ulcer of proletarianism," in all ways demonstrating the advantages of a guardianship by noble landowners over "our good Russian people."

It was still not that long since the Narodniks (Populists) of various persuasions had expatiated on the impossibility of capitalist development in Russia, arguing that through cooperatives and the *mir*,† the country would turn to "production by the people."

---

*For *poddyovka*, see footnote, page 125.
†*mir*—a form of communal land ownership among Russian peasants since ancient times.

It was still not that long since Fyodor Mikhailovich Dostoyevsky, the brilliant epileptic who had faced execution for participating in a socialist discussion circle and then defected to the side of "Orthodoxy, autocracy, and the national principle," had preached the idea of a Chosen People, who, under the supreme leadership of an Orthodox tsar, would accomplish the Kingdom of God on earth, having captured holy Constantinople, the cradle of the true religion.

But now the factory whistles and industrial smokestacks had put an end to those utopian dreams. The "ulcer of proletarianism" grew with irrepressible force, along with the power of money, along with the "parvenu" Russian bourgeois. The old high-born and titled aristocracy still remembered the days of Empress Catherine I, the brilliant balls, the Homeric banquets, the splendor of gentry life, the gold and silver dishes, the incomparably outfitted carriages. They held in their hands the entire enormous machinery of the state. They supplied the officer corps, from His Majesty's Life-Guards to the blue uniforms of the gendarmes. They provided the personnel who served in the tsar's well-trained, cunning, expert diplomatic corps. They sat in the Cabinet of Ministers and filled the ranks of the higher official bureaucracy, occupying positions in the Governing Senate and the Holy Synod. As metropolitans and bishops they stood at the head of the Russian clergy and monkhood, with its innumerable churches and extremely rich monasteries. They controlled the vast majority of the land of this immense state, which had extended its bloody hands not only "from the cold Finnish cliffs to fiery Colchis"* but also into the colossal expanses of Asia.

Yet these aristocrats, embroidered with gold, wearing ribbons and stars, with epaulets and without epaulets, with swords and without swords, had already begun to outlive themselves. They drank, ate, made merry, and pillaged as before. As before, they boozed, squandered their rural incomes on oysters and champagne, expensive French and Italian courtesans, English horses, the playing of roulette and cards, and pleasure trips abroad. As before, they amazed foreigners with their unbridled luxury and unbridled extravagance. As before, the *prince russe* was in this respect beyond comparison, and his reputation among foreign actresses and proprietors of gaming houses and gambling dens never dimmed.

However, the results of this extravagance among those with titles and "expansive Russian natures" were rather telling, with all sorts of social implications. From all directions an outcry was raised about the impoverishment of the nobility. The heraldic aristocracy had become frayed. It was becoming

*A phrase from Pushkin's poem "To the Slanderers of Russia."

necessary to mortgage and to mortgage again the ancestral estates, or even to auction them off. It was becoming necessary to fell the ancient "cherry orchards," paying for the sins of whole generations of gentry—the ax of history was remorseless: it did not take proud tradition into account. Estates passed into other hands, as did homes in St. Petersburg and Moscow, where "the lions on the gates and the flocks of jackdaws on the crosses" increasingly became the property of the Russian merchants and factory owners.

These new people operated methodically and quietly. But they had already grown into a great social force that had to be reckoned with: they carried a heavy purse, and not only for the sake of genteel politeness did the nobility have to bow and scrape before the might of capital at this point. And behind the owners of capital, like a dark shadow, stood the black masses of factory workers, among whom there were already emerging ideas that set even the most hardened, even the most unconcerned representatives of the landlords and the autocracy to thinking: "sedition" could take forms much more dangerous for the supposedly eternal structure than all the kinds of riots and revolts that had so far taken place, for here the potential force of the revolution was concentrated at the very heart of public life—these were not some kind of Yaik River Cossacks at the remote edge of the world.

The bourgeoisie had already advanced their people, the prominent captains of industry, who strove to make up for the time that had been lost historically. They wanted to come to power and, for this purpose, were even willing to make use of the workers, who might pull their chestnuts out of the fire for them. Some of these wealthy men had come from the lower classes, Savva Morozov being a striking example of this sort. Stubborn, strong-willed, bright, a person of wide scope and considerable prospects, he hated the imperial authority and considered it doomed despite all its outward prosperity. In his factories the workers sang a song in which they taunted him sardonically:

Hey, our little Savva, what a swine is he,
It takes three arms to reach around his be-elly.
He eats three good square meals, boys, every day
Evil sorrow's never come his way.
He's fixed himself up—with three mistresses,
Dark-skinned Italian governesses.
And with the pennies from our sweat and toil
He's had silk dresses sewed up for them all.
They stroll around, each one a lovely peahen
Giving our dear Savva satisfaction.

Such things, however, did not prevent the energetic Morozov from contributing money for the revolution or from associating with representatives of the most extreme political trends: in his eyes they were simply the best, most truly reliable historical broom, which, like the French Montagnards, would fearlessly in their plebeian way make short work of the noble aristocracy, chop off the arrogant and foolish heads of the aristocrats, and then, having done their business, would give way, by the will of the unalterable laws of history, to the enlightened bourgeoisie, who would transform Russia into a great, civilized, enlightened, bourgeois country.

The tall, corpulent, elephantine Mamontov, a businessman, organizer, stockbroker, outstanding entrepreneur, participant in numerous joint-stock companies, which had begun to grow like mushrooms in manure, was recognized as a patron of the Muses and Graces: theater, literature, painting—everything fell within the sphere of his interests. The most famous luminaries of these worlds were his friends. The frail, graying, methodical Sergei Shchukin, in his gray two-storied house with bright plateglass windows on Znamensky Lane, created a remarkable museum on the basis of the latest foreign paintings—such a collection of golden Gauguins and most tender blue Claude Monets was not to be found anywhere in Europe. Almost all the fashionable French impressionists, and after them Cézanne, Van Gogh, Degas, stood out beautifully here with their most luxuriant creations: Shchukin wanted to imitate in foreign painting the reputation of Pavel Tretyakov.* Konstantin Sergeyevich Alekseyev, offspring of the proprietors of the gold-thread factory "Alekseyev and Shamshin," became, under the name Stanislavsky, the organizer and soul of the world-shaking Moscow Arts Theater. Sytin, who, like Morozov, came from the lower classes, turned into the most prominent publisher in Russia and owner of the country's best printing houses, which became huge printing factories, with English machines and thousands of workers. The foremost Russian bourgeois understood very well the complete necessity of taking up the most important ideological positions for themselves.

But the more these foremost bourgeois abandoned the Russian provincial horizons and the more they came into contact with world culture, which was already beginning to give off the smell of the rotten lily, the clearer it became that they had gone past ripeness and were unable to ripen again. They strove to pluck more quickly the most valuable flowers of European culture, but the latter, imbued with all the poison of social contradictions, were already giving off the mortuary aroma of sweet decay.

*Founder of the famous Tretyakov Gallery.

In Russia itself social conflicts were becoming more frequent, and forebodings of a storm that would be devastating to the bourgeoisie shook the depths of their social consciousness: the flood would come; it was inevitable. Russia, drawn into the orbit of world culture, was already dancing to the insidious tune of its historical fate and, with the speed not of Gogol's troika but rather of an electrical spark, was flying toward great historical cataclysms.

The stricken younger generation of this bourgeois class and its intelligentsia soared into an ethereal realm of symbols. Reality for them was too crude, base, and vulgar. They thirsted for a different world, unearthly, immaterial, a world of most delicate daydreams, a world of mysterious music, a world of allusions. Everything natural seemed to them a lower form of existence. They were already singing of terrible sins, carrying Baudelaire's *Flowers of Evil* a step further. They broke sharply from all the traditions of Russian art: to speak of some Nekrasov or Repin became among them a sign of barbarity, of unbearably poor taste. *De la musique avant toute chose*—Music above all!—they made this poetic slogan of tender Paul Verlaine their own. Arthur Rimbaud, the talented poet, dandy, adventurer, and homosexual friend of Verlaine, became their idol. The mad talent of Edgar Poe served them as a model. They ran from life into clouds of illusion.

Valery Bryusov, the son of a trader in cork, held in his strong hands the corporal's baton in literature. Tall, thin, with an angular face and prominent cheekbones, black hair, thick eyebrows, and a burning stare, imperious, cold and passionate at the same time, exceptionally hard-working and talented, Bryusov determined the direction and stood at the helm. Beside him an entire pleiad of new poets produced their creations. Andrei Bely, the son of an eccentric professor of mathematics named Bugayev, who had transformed the real world into the abstractions of the most abstract mathematical disciplines, was one of the most typical representatives of the school. Thin as a match, with a delicate girlish face, bright china-blue eyes, a small head with fluffy, thin, golden hair, he reminded one of a sleepwalker, an astral, incorporeal body that had found itself by chance in an alien world of living people and material things. He moved like a sleepwalker, like someone bewitched forever—it seemed as though he saw nothing, that he was constantly about to fall over something. Close to him stood his friend and comrade Aleksandr Blok, also the son of a professor. Blok was tall, stately, handsome, with curly hair and the head of an Apollo, except for his overly large nose. His purebred figure and elegance of manners were striking. More than anyone else he was linked with the philosophical admirers of Vladimir Solovyov, that strange religious dreamer with the eyes of an angel and the mouth of a depraved devil. Lopatin, the Princes Trubetskoy—Sergei and Yevgeny—were the expositors of this idealist religious philosophy, which rather smelled of Lenten oil, an erotic cult of the Madonna, and the mysticism of Platonov. In music this psychology was expressed in the work of Scriabin, remarkable in its own way; in painting, above all in the sick genius of the insane Mikhail Vrubel.

This ideology of the new, bourgeois aristocracy was, however, an ideology of the elite. For the broadest social circles it was both too ethereal and too refined and lifeless. The average educated bourgeois and intellectual lived for Chekhov, Repin, Mikhailovsky. But Maxim Gorky had already appeared on the scene in the ragged shoes of the lumpen-proletariat, to replace them later with high proletarian boots and set off on the path to his future glory. And at his estate of Yasnaya Polyana, like an old recluse elephant, a global colossus, sat Leo Tolstoy, whose great artistic genius was being undermined by religious moralism and tragic conflicts with the narrow-minded mother of his numerous children.

In politics, literature, science, philosophy, a general demarcation of trends, ideas, and people was occurring. The factory gave rise to Russian Marxism along with the proletariat. There appeared new people who, making use of everything necessary from the legacy of Belinsky, Chernyshevsky, and Dobrolyubov, looked with cold eyes upon the sentimental utopias of the Narodniks, and in brilliant—for the time being, literary—battles gained victory after victory. The radical intelligentsia was split. The old authorities collapsed. While the spiritual aristocracy of the bourgeoisie was taking in the aromas of exotic orchids and chrysanthemums from the conservatories of Western European decadence, the new ideologists of the proletariat were mastering the gleaming weapons of Marxism, that highest product of the revolutionary side of Western European development. Everything here was in motion, everything was in a state of struggle, everything was vital, real. The fetishes and idols of feudalism and the new idols of the bourgeoisie were smashed to dust. The respectable, bearded, Narodnik elders—Lavrov, Mikhailovsky, Vorontsov—were confronted at bayonet point. The elders looked with amazement upon the new, noisy, cocky, energetic young people who made no claim to any sort of uniqueness or exceptionality (*samobytnost*). They openly regarded themselves as followers of a German, Karl Marx, and brought a certain discord and dissension with them everywhere. Where everyone spoke of the people, they spoke about classes; where others preached tolerance, they uncovered contradictions with sharp relentlessness and obstinacy; they looked at everything with cheerful, mocking eyes and scoffed at respectable people: merits, they say, are merits, and you won't get far with the past—indeed, for them nothing was sacred. They busied themselves with Smith, Ricardo, Kant, Hegel, Feuerbach, the French materialists. Their Marx they knew by heart. They delved into the figures of land statistics, into the reports of factory inspectors, into piles of raw data. Their energy and obstinacy were amazing. True, among them there were those who were more compliant: the red-bearded Peter Struve; the good-natured, nearsighted, overweight Tugan-Baranovsky; Berdyaev, who, with black curls, looked like a Spanish monk who had overindulged himself and was now afflicted by a tic that made his tongue stick out; the quiet Sergei Bulgakov . . . These were the "Legal Marxists," who stood aside from the fire, smoke, and flame of the struggle.

But among the Marxists there were also people of another sort. Especially Ulyanov. His friends called him Old Man because of his wisdom, although he was still young. He had a bald skull, the huge dome of which indicated an outstanding intelligence. His eyes were sharp: they seemed to drill right through his collocutor. His character was iron. His energy colossal. A man of incomparable erudition, he kept up with all the facts, even the smallest. In his hands the merest statistical detail became grounds for wrath and hatred against the whole social system, a sentence of condemnation, and a sword. His mind was like a sharpened revolutionary guillotine. His arm was authoritative, short, strong. And he himself was short, rather small, with a small, reddish beard, a native Russian from Simbirsk. He had an excellent command of languages and kept abreast of world literature. But it was not a chair at the university that he aspired to. No! He was leading workers' circles. He was an underground activist. He wrote inflammatory leaflets, illegal pamphlets. He brought together reliable cohorts, out of whom later an invincible army would develop. His brother had been hanged—but he was following his own path. His scholarly articles, signed with the pseudonym "V. Ilyin," were an unbroken phalanx of arguments that invariably destroyed his opponent completely. But he was also a brilliant strategist, tactician, organizer, practical worker. He strove to fan every spark into a flame. *Ecce homo!*

The Populists had not encountered such an opponent before. Except perhaps Plekhanov, whose book on monism in history had inflicted serious wounds on subjective exceptionalist (*samobytny*) sociology as a whole. However, even Plekhanov did not have such an iron death grip. The liberals took a closer look: why, this was a dangerous wild animal, a true revolutionary tiger. He would have to be dealt with! But Ilyich only grinned his sly grin.

He loved to infuriate his adversary; conflict was his element. But he could not endure playing at conflict. He regarded everything very seriously: it was his life's work, the work of the class that would lead all the masses, that would overthrow the autocracy, and that would go still further, to a victorious communist revolution. Was this a dream? Yes, a dream, but of the type that relies on knowledge, on force, a dream that ought to become a reality, and that would.

The old Narodnik movement fell apart under the blows of the Marxists. Some turned into ordinary liberals of a "labor" variety, respectable *Kulturträger*, "promoters of culture," developing paunches and becoming content in the bosom of the zemstvo. They sputtered against Marxism, continued to put the words "proletariat" and "capitalism" in ironic quotation marks, and stubbornly denied a class struggle. Others adopted certain features of Marx's teaching, were no longer afraid to speak of the proletariat, but cooked up such an ideological jumble of the most contradictory ingredients that it reeked of nauseating eclecticism from miles away. The orthodox Marxists, on the other hand, with great consistency defended the harmony, the magnificent integrity of their worldview and immediately sounded the alarm and displayed a furious intolerance, which was regarded by spineless people as a doctrinaire attitude and dogmatism, as soon as they noticed any deviation. They advanced in a tightly closed phalanx and attacked all dissenters, for behind this "dissent" hid active classes, groups, tendencies. The discussions of the most abstract theoretical issues—markets, crises, the differentiation of the peasantry—anticipated the coming armed discussions. The great issues of life were resolved in advance as theoretical problems. And this real life trembled in every formula and every statistic.

Marxism conquered one position after another. In the revolutionary underground it recruited strong supporters among the workers. In the legal press it clearly scored more and more new victories. The government closed down some journals—others sprang up. The government made arrests—they studied in the prisons. The government sent people to internal exile—in exile they read German booklets, studied foreign languages, wrote scholarly works. The government released them—and they returned to their posts; tirelessly, systematically, with a confidence of iron, they continued their work. The regular police and secret police had already discovered more than once that in the workers' strikes that were flaring up the "roots and threads" led to the Social Democratic troublemakers. These "roots and threads" were becoming more and more numerous. The working class was revealing its nature and was already stirring, testing its shoulder muscles, now here, now there.

The Fronde opposition faction was growing in the countryside in the liberal zemstvo movement, among those landowners who were switching over to the capitalist way and among the "third force"—doctors, teachers, statisticians. Traditional rural Rus was eroding and becoming stratified. The kulaks, cattle dealers, moneylenders, innkeepers, and middle men contributed their part to the destruction of the old rural way of life, helping the landowner and the landowner's government. In this hard life, lovers of truth emerged, sects grew—the Stunde, Dukhobors, Malakans, Tolstoyans, who sought to avoid military service and here and there refused to pay their taxes. But also emerging from time to time were people who made do without sacred texts, who were thinking about driving the landowner from the land. Strikers from the cities and industrial settlements, exiled back to their homes, sowed the seeds of rebellion, and sometimes these seeds sprouted well.

In Poland, Georgia, the Baltic region, the possessions in Central Asia, the northern Caucasus, Finland, and Ukraine, oppressed peoples were groaning and the gunpowder of discontent and protest against the heavy shackles of autocracy was accumulating. Nicholas Romanov himself, autocrat of all the Russias, King of Poland, Prince of Finland, and so on, a short man, with his reddish-brown hair parted on the side, was one of the most limited tsars of the Romanov line, having neither intellect nor will nor striking individuality—in general, an all-round mediocrity. The Russian diplomat Count Osten-Saken talked about him boldly to the German Prince von Bülow: *L'empereur Nicolas a une indifférénce qui frise l'heroisme* (Emperor Nicholas possesses an indifference that borders on heroism).

Most of all Nicholas feared revolution and, after that, his wife, an imperious German woman who was very much taken with her position as all-powerful empress of this gigantic state. But Nicholas loved his wife sincerely, not only out of fear. The empress was not averse to giving orders and placed matters of monarchical prestige before all others. Weak-willed and at the same time crafty, Nicholas, like all people of this type, was ready to go on adventures, the entire sense of which he was unable to grasp owing to his limited nature. Pretending at times to be all but a pacifist (not by accident was it he who called the Hague Peace Conference in 1899), at the same time he would sign death sentences without batting an eye, and in foreign policy dreamed about Constantinople and the straits, about new conquests in the Far East, about the glorification of his reign through victories of the Christian army of the Russian state.

Bismarck, evaluating the international situation, as early as the 1880s made a characteristic observation. "In the Russian barrel," he said, "fermentation is taking place and a rumbling can be heard that causes alarm. One fine day this may lead to an explosion. For international peace it would be best if the explosion were not in Europe, but in Asia. Then it would be enough for us not to stand directly in front of the plug, so that it does not hit us in the belly." The old wolfhound of German imperialism, however, had an ulterior motive here: for his purposes it would be extremely helpful to weaken Russia by means of a fairly large bloodletting in the East, drawing her forces away from her western borders. He had resolved, after the Paris Commune experience, not to enter into a European war at this time, saying that for such a war three dynasties would have to pay with their existence. But the court circles, the idle great princes, those in shady financial operations, businessmen who hovered about the court—all of them sang with golden voices about the traditions of Peter the Great, about a secure footing on the Pacific Ocean, about Russia's worldwide historical mission, about how "the Japs wouldn't dare," about the future eternal glory of the Russian military. Nicholas dreamed about these military exploits, shutting his eyes to the machinations of the adventurers, titled and untitled, civilian and military, on the eastern borders of his kingdom. He cherished the idea of history presenting him, Nicholas Romanov, with a laurel wreath, as the supreme leader of the victorious Orthodox armies. The feeble-minded tsar did not understand that he resembled, more than anything, a mouse crawling into a skillfully contrived mousetrap.

Chapter 13

Regarding politics Kolya Petrov was as innocent as a clean sheet of white paper. Political problems, because of his young age, were not something he was capable of thinking about. When he chanced to read in *Russkiye Vedomosti* reports on debates in some foreign parliament and saw in parentheses in italic type: "commotion on the benches of the extreme Left" (and he came across references to such "commotion" quite often), he would get angry: Why were these people always interfering? When, in the same respected journal, he came across a reference to the supporters of *Capital* he sincerely supposed, in his innocence of heart, that they were talking about capitalists.

The energetic public life of the time and the currents stirred up by it came to him mainly through so-called belles lettres. From the Yablochkins he would purloin little books by the Symbolists—the Petrov family followed poetry very closely; that was a long-standing tradition of Ivan Antonych's, which passed down as an inheritance to his son. The only thing was, there was no way to buy books anymore. Nevertheless they gained access by borrowing them from friends, and one of Ivan Antonych's old associates even arranged a gift membership for him in the Bessonov private library.

One of the books Kolya came across, and which he devoured with his usual voraciousness, was Max Nordau's novel *Degeneration*. It was not one of the subtlest books ever written. But it made a powerful impression on Kolya precisely because of the sharpness of its tone, its scorn for the "decadents," its examples of senseless passages, which stood out with special vividness in Russian translation, where the music of the poetic speech in the original was lost in arid prose.

Kolya had an excellent memory, and he learned by heart and would recite examples that especially impressed him, such as: "O colors. And how heavy is the burden of old taxes. Hourglasses at which dogs bark in May. And the astonishing envelope of a Negro who has not slept for a long time. Grandmother, who would like to eat oranges and could not sleep. Over on the bridge there is a crocodile, and a policeman with a swollen cheek is waving silently. Two soldiers in a cattle shed, and a razor blade with notches in it. But they had not won the largest pot. While on the lamp there were black spots." This abracadabra reminded him of a children's song he had heard the village boys singing in Tesovo. All in unison they would sing: "One, two, three, four, five, / The hare went for a walk, all alive." Followed by a nonsense refrain made up of meaningless "words":

Enta penta likadei
Fuksy kendra gramotei
Ashimbrot ashimbrot,
Grali srali drugish tot.

He was even more astounded by Baudelaire's *Une charoque*, in a translation by "P. Ya." (Yakubovich-Melshin), in which decomposing corpses spread their legs "like dissolute women" and "there crawled, like a thick porridge, millions of worms." To be sure, not everything in Nordau's book was comprehensible to Kolya, but he absorbed the main idea—decadence—and this assessment settled solidly into his consciousness. It was under the influence of this idea that he took a negative attitude toward the modernists, childishly making fun of them in a defiant, naughty, exaggerated way.

He graduated from elementary school with flying colors and was the first to answer all the questions in the final exams; true, during dictation he had written *pod uztsy* (by the bridle), whereas several of the teachers thought *pod uzdtsy* was the correct spelling, but during the oral part of the Russian test he began to argue with his teachers, contending that the *d* could be dropped, as in the words *uzy* (ties that bind) and *uznik* (prisoner), not to mention such words of related derivation as *vyazat* (bind; knit) and *venzel* (monogram). The teachers looked at one another and decided to leave the question open; thus the assertion that he had made one error was withdrawn. Kolya even overheard one of the teachers whispering to another, during the argument over *uztsy*, "A ripe one, eh?"—and the other teacher nodded. The student received a certificate of merit and was awarded several volumes of Pushkin's works bound in bright blue covers imprinted with gold designs.

His parents decided to send him to a *gimnaziya*, directly into the second year. But to do this, he had to be prepared in Latin. Lyubov Ivanovna had an acquaintance, an elderly teacher, with a son who had just graduated from the *gimnaziya* at the top of his class and who agreed for a trifling sum to prepare Kolya quickly. Natalya Andreyevna (that was the elderly teacher's name) was retired and living on a pension. She suffered terribly from dropsy, was barely able to move her heavy, swollen body around, and sat most of the time in an armchair, with her legs wrapped in a plaid blanket, reading through steel-framed glasses. Warm-hearted and outgoing, she greeted Kolya as a younger son and before all else treated him to tea with sugar and lemon. Together with her son, Gorenka, a tall, thin, long-legged youth with a cataract on one eye, she occupied a small room in a house on Zubovsky Boulevard.

Gorenka, shy, delicate, and retiring, retrieved his tattered books from a trunk—a Latin grammar by Nikiforov and a reader by Semyonovich—and instruction began. For Kolya Latin was by no means a dead language or a dry and boring subject, as it was for many, in fact most boys his age. To be sure, he did not resemble the whining little boy in Heine who didn't want anything more to do with his friend, because his friend didn't know the genitive case of *mensa*. Having read Korsh, Kolya's mind was filled with images of Greco-Roman life, and the language of the Romans, the grand and glorious Romans, interested him intensely. With the memory he had, he was able to absorb the Latin vocabulary and rules of grammar without any effort: he was never a "grind" or a rote learner; but he always had a grasp of what he was supposed to know and even what he was not supposed to. He learned all the intricacies of Latin so quickly, all these *ut finale, ut consecutivum,* and *accusativus*'s, *cum infinitivo,* and so on, that Gorenka decided to jump ahead a bit and start having Kolya read Caesar's memoirs of the Gallic wars: *C. J. Caesaris commentarii De bello gallico.* Kolya was in rapture when he began to hear the actual words of the actual memoirs of the famous leader of the Roman legions: *Gallia est omnis divisa in partes tres, quarum unam incolunt belgi, aliam—aquitani, tertium—qui iprosum lingua celti, nostra galli appellantur* (All Gaul was divided into three parts, one of which was inhabited by the Belgians, the other by the Acquitanians, and the third by those who in their own language call themselves Celts, but in our language are called Gauls). That was how the memoirs started. And Kolya felt the breath of history blowing on him from a long bygone era.

But he really went wild when the modest Gorenka, snuffling, wheezing, sweating, and turning red, told him about Caesar's adventures along other lines, citing verses that Caesar's soldiers sang about their leader when they occupied an enemy city.

Urbani servate uxores,
Moechum calvum addicimus.

City dwellers, guard your wives.
We're bringing a bald-headed libertine in.

In the fall Kolya passed all his exams without any difficulty and was accepted into the second year at the *gimnaziya*. In the process his parents managed to plead successfully that he be given a scholarship as the son of a teacher.

The First Moscow Boys *Gimnaziya* was located across from the Cathedral of Christ the Savior. The facade of this large gray government building did not open directly onto the street. In front of it was a little garden through which you had to walk to reach the front porch. The schoolboys went in the back way, by a side alley. They came into a "detachable unit" with a stone floor; it was dusty and hard to breathe in there; galoshes lined the walls and uniform coats and service caps hung on the coat racks. In the four-storied building itself there was a school chapel and a huge assembly hall, which consisted of "two worlds," or two stories in one—that is, it was two stories high. On the walls hung portraits of tsars, and famous people who had graduated from the school, and there were large marble plaques with the names of pupils or alumni who had received gold medals. On the bottom floor was a gloomy dining room, surprisingly reminiscent of the refectory in some impoverished monastery: the sunlight could barely make its way through the tiny windows; the low vaulted ceilings bore down on you with their weight; the long tables and benches stood in rows, as in a barracks—all in all, a miserable scene! The rest of the premises were occupied by classrooms, bedrooms for the boarders (as opposed to the day students), and a gym; also, a physics laboratory—or rather, a poor excuse for one, shabby and pathetically furnished with old junk instead of real equipment; a kitchen; and living quarters for the teachers and servants.

It was a time when some cracks were appearing in the rigid system of classical education, which for years had inspired terror and awe—a system of thick-headed rote learning of dead languages, not one that made a living link with the history and culture of the Greco-Roman world, a system of complete disregard for the natural sciences, not to mention modern technology or political economy. The needs of social development were already creating a demand for people of a different kind. "Normal schools" (*realnye shkoly*, nonclassical secondary schools) with completely modern curricula were starting to sprout. The diehards of "classicism," usually extreme reactionaries, were unable to maintain their positions, and in the very heart of the *gimnaziya* the Greeks and Latinists were somehow losing their hold—the ground was slipping from under their feet; they yearned nostalgically for the good old days and taught their subjects in an ever more slipshod manner; their former intimidating hauteur had completely evaporated. They were like little old ladies who would grumblingly repeat an endless number of times the old refrain about the golden age that reigned when they were young: everything was cheaper then; people were taller and healthier, real heroes, not the weaklings that you have today; the weather had been much better; men were more handsome; manners were more virtuous; goods were made better; and everything in general had been so much more attractive. Their day was obviously coming to an end.

The principal of the school, a man of Czech origin, Iosif Osvaldovich Gobza, was a Latinist himself. Tall, portly, with bulging eyes, as in Basedow's disease, with a crimson face, covered with bluish spots and veins, with a fleshy nose and amazingly bright red lips, he reminded one of a turkey when it steps forth in all its glory. He spoke with a most comical accent and, while doing so, would roll the whites of his eyes so dreadfully that the students were barely able to keep from choking with laughter.

"Ya . . . vill . . . bee arrestit . . . for two hours!" he would shout dreadfully at some guilty pupil, who would cover his mouth with his hand so as not to laugh right in the principal's face.

And yet he had no desire to be terribly strict; in fact he did not fully utilize the powers and prerogatives of his office.

The school inspector, Fyodor Semyonovich Korobkin, was notable for his short stature and enormous bald spot; his closely cropped hair lay like a fringe around his ears and the back of his neck. He was very well educated and knew what he was talking about not only in his field of mathematics but in a whole number of other subjects, including philosophy. He was a remarkable teacher and had the ability to present even the dryest mathematical propositions in such a lively and vivid way that even the lazybones paid attention. This did not prevent the schoolboys, however, from making up an ironic song about him, sung to a popular tune, "We're the Fellows from the Factory." Fairly often, when this rather strict mathematics teacher, who was nevertheless respected by the pupils, was walking down the hallway, he would hear rollicking voices belting out a tune:

Fedya, our cu-urly he-eaded boy
Fe-edya, our cu-urly he-eaded boy
Fedya, our curly headed boy,
A uniform full of ho-o-oles
Has he!

He had such tact, however, that he would walk right by and pay no attention, even though the song was aimed directly at him.

The teacher of Russian language and literature, Vladimir Aleksandrovich Sokolov, wished to appear as an "original." He was by no means a stupid man and knew his subject well, but he was a great cynic and indulged in highly frivolous conversations with the students. His distinguishing feature was an enormous nose deeply divided at the end, as though there were two separate noses hidden within, each trying to go in a different direction.

"I have a nose, gentlemen, in the Byzantine style," was his lofty way of referring to his own physiognomy.

"What's that bright red button, red and spreading, that has popped out on your face?" he would address some pimply youngster. "It's early in life for you, it's early . . . nyaa, nyaa, nyaa," he would intone, and meanwhile, beneath the rostrum where he stood, his leg would be jumping.

Or he would ask:

"What are you doing there, my angel full of marsh gas, fidgeting in your seat? Do you have a needle up your — ? Maybe your farting muscle popped? Ha, ha, ha! Nyaa-nyaa-nyaa."

He often used nonsense words—made-up words like *rakaliya*, *kanalstvo*, *sikambry*—and was exceptionally keen on telling jokes. The students loved to "get him talking": when someone didn't know his lessons and was afraid he'd be called on, he would tell Sokolov a new joke; the whole class would neigh like a bunch of stallions and Sokolov would weep from laughter, tears running down his Byzantine nose and dripping on his threadbare uniform; every minute he was wiping his pince-nez with a handkerchief. And thus a whole hour would go by to everyone's satisfaction.

History was taught by Vitaly Osipovich Einhorn, a short, fat man, who would go waddling along on his short, crooked, but well-developed legs, swaying from side to side. He had been blessed with a large not quite Armenian, not quite Jewish nose and thinning black hair that was carefully slicked down and parted on the side. He was called Vitasha or cuttlefish.*
He was a strict teacher, who was also an active researcher and had a number of published works to his name (on officially approved topics of course); he kept up with the latest in historical science and delved into the archives himself. Often with no rhyme or reason he would use the term *seemingly*, inserting it in practically every sentence and pronouncing it "seeingly." The students' malice took the following form: when they wanted to give Vitashka trouble, they would start talking, with serious looks on their faces, like this:

*The Russian for "cuttlefish" (*karakátitsa*) was used jokingly to mean a short-legged, clumsy person.

"Vitaly Osipovich, aren't we, seeingly, going to get through, seeingly, the Merovingians this year, seeingly?"

Cuttlefish would feel obliged to pretend he didn't notice. He would just shoot sidelong glances at the students, who sometimes couldn't hold back from a snort or a chuckle.

The Latin teacher—also a Czech, like the principal—was Ivan Fyodorovich Zbraslavsky. He had an excellent knowledge of Latin, but didn't know Russian very well. There is a Latin grammatical form known as the "Greek accusative" (*accusativus graecus*) which expresses relationship, and he would translate it into Russian by always including the word *relationship*: for example, "The Bacchantes were hairy in relationship to the chest—" It was at his expense that a joke went around the school: the poor man had supposedly translated the Latin proverb *Ars longa, vita breva* (Life is short; art is long) into Russian words meaning "The belly is short, but the thing is long."*

The school chaplain, Father Stefan, was honored with the nickname "Sikerdon, the red-coated stallion." Indeed he had a red beard, but the stallion part was tacked on, not because it fit him, but because it was so incongruous: he was extremely mild-mannered and devout, reading not only books of theology but also books of secular philosophy, and he loved to talk, while raising his eyes toward the heavens, about beauty and high-mindedness as being manifestations of the divine. Just as Einhorn constantly used the word *seeingly*, with Father Stefan every third word was "well, sir." The students would take bets among themselves on how many times "Sikerdon" would use the phrase "well, sir" during the hour. Moreover, the count was kept rather loudly, and from a corner or the back of the room (which was called "Kamchatka") you could clearly hear the numbers "twenty-three," "twenty-four"—and the honorable clergyman would fidget awkwardly at the rostrum.

The modern languages studied were German and French. The energetic German teacher, Artur Ludwigovich Plesterer, was nicknamed "Klistir" ("Enema") because it echoed his last name. It was not an appropriate nickname, because actually he was an excellent teacher. In class he spoke only German, forcing the students to answer him in German. The results he obtained were outstanding. On the other hand, Monsieur Cordet, the French teacher, a kind, sweet man, with large eyes and black hair, was so meek and mild and treated his students so leniently that they got completely out of hand.

*In Czech the word *zhivot* means "life," but the same word in Russian means "belly"; in Czech *shtuka* means "art," but in Russian it means "thing" or "piece."

Occupying a special place among the teachers was Dmitry Dmitryevich Galanin, an educator well known in Moscow, whom the students called "Cheech Meech," or just plain "Cheech," or "Isn't That Something!" He taught physics. He often wrote for educational magazines or specialized physics and mathematics journals, was the author of many books, and was considered one of the most advanced and knowledgeable educators. But in regard to philosophy he was an extreme idealist and sympathized with the followers of Solovyov, who professed an amalgamation of Christianity, liberalism, and socialism. The students loved him. He was very humane, and nothing officious or bureaucratic was discernible in his manner. Unfortunately, his students never learned any physics; they goofed off, and he was by nature incapable of making them straighten up or, in defiance of all expectations, of punishing them. Often during an experiment some piece of equipment would break in his hands. Then extreme surprise would register on his face and he would proclaim, while touching his index finger to his turned-up nose, "Now isn't that something!"

He was very tall, heavily bearded, and wore glasses. His son, who studied at the *gimnaziya*, was even taller than he. His wife was notable for similar dimensions. A riddle made the rounds among the students: "Two Cheeches, two Meeches, and in between a hole." This was supposed to denote the Galanin family.

The *gimnaziya* students had their own social world, with traditions passing down from generation to generation. A state of permanent war existed between them and the "normal school" students. The *gimnaziya* students called the others "omelet with onion," the latter responding with "blue ham," a reference to the color of the stripes and piping on the *gimnaziya* uniform. In the upper grades these traditions followed both a serious line of descent—that is, that the best and most talented students would take up science and politics—and a less serious line, having to do with adventures and feats of debauchery. This was the sphere of the students from wealthy families, the dandies who, when they got to the university, formed the core of the so-called *byelopodkladochniki*—those with white linings under their coats, university students of aristocratic appearance and reactionary views.

In the lower grades there flourished a constantly enriched body of folklore and apocryphal writing whose content was anything but decent. There was Barkov,* and there were reworked versions of Pushkin's *Yevgeny Onegin*, Lermontov's *Demon*, a poem called "Ferdinand and Isabella," and similar works; above all, there was the famous "Golden Alphabet," where

*On Barkov, see glossary.

the first line in each verse was perfectly decent, while the second one was absolutely unprintable.

Life at the *gimnaziya* provided a breeding ground for a unique type of creativity. There were very comical translations of popular songs into Greek and Latin: the third-year students sang in the language of the ancient Hellenes about "three young maidens" who "went a-walking" ("treis parthenoi"); those in their second year would drum the Ukrainian song *I shume i gude / driben didzhdik ide* (It rumbles and thunders / and the rain comes down) into an ungodly mangling of the language of Ovid and Vergil:

> Et tonat
> Et bromat
> Coelum pluvium dat.
> Quis me, quis me, iuvenalam,
> Usque domum reducat?

They also made up indecent verse. Geometry gave rise to the rather famous "Pythagoras's Pants," which was sung with fervor during recess by a whole chorus of boys:

> Oh, the pants of Pythagoras
> Are equal in all directions
> And his buttons are a known quantity.
> Why is *x*, then, feeling squeezed?
> Because *x*, you know, is very large—
> That's how the pupil answered.

The German language gave life not only to very ancient nonsense like this:

> Némets-Pérets-Kolbasá
> Kupíl lóshad bez khvostá.
> (Pepper-Sausage the German man
> Bought a horse that had no can.)

There were also school songs that parodied the rules of conjugation and declension. The custom was to memorize these rules in verse form: the Latin grammar books and the grammars of modern languages often abounded in such "poetry." The students sitting in boredom at their desks cut loose and really outdid themselves.

> Ich bin (I am)
> Dubina (a play on "Du bist"; Russian for "a piece of oak," a "club,"
>   but also "blockhead")

Poleno (Russian for "log")
Brevno (Russian for "log"; also, "dullard")
Ich war (I was)
Varvar (a barbarian)
Sobachyo (and dog doo)

Nonsense translations were extraordinarily popular, and here the boys' imaginations came up with immense riches: if genuinely Russian proverbs (such as "A peasant's house is known not by what's in its corners, but by what's in its pies") were translated literally into French or German the result would provoke Homeric laughter. Most popular were sentences like this: *J'aime de baiser les éponges de ma cousine.* In Russian, the sentence said, "I love to kiss my cousin's *gubki*"—*gubki* literally meaning "lips" but also "sponges." The Russian sentence "Sreda ego zayela" (He was devoured, or oppressed, by his surroundings) came out in French as *Mercredi l'a mangé* (Wednesday has eaten him)—because the Russian word *sreda*, whose root meaning is "the middle" can be translated as "the surroundings," i.e, that in the middle of which one is, or as "Wednesday," the middle day of the week. Any German would laugh like one possessed to hear: *Ach, du, meine Seele, rote Mamselle.* This was the literal rendering of "Akh dusha moya, krasna devitsa" (Oh, my dear, you beautiful girl). Instead of "beautiful girl" it came out *rote Mamselle* because in Russian *krasna* means both "red" and "beautiful."

The students contrived to translate the Russian phrase *Daite nozhik, daite vilku, ya zarezhu svoyu milku* (Give me a knife, give me a fork; I will cut up my meal) into German in this way: *Gib mir Gabel, gib mir Messer, ich werde meine Liebste fressen* (Give me a fork, give me a knife; I will devour my beloved). At the *gimnaziya* the word *milka* could mean one's "meal," but it is also Russian for one's "beloved."

They would pose clever riddles to one another, for example: *trinum et unum, sed non Deus; initium mundi et finis saeculorum.* Literally, this meant "Having three parts and being one, but not God; beginning of world and end of ages." The answer to the riddle turned out to be the Latin letter *m* (the beginning of *mundus* and the end of *saeculorum*).

Or they would offer a meaningless set of Latin words to be translated: *secundum servi vos bibere.* The corresponding Russian words were *po, raby, vy,* and *pit.* Put together, this gave the Russian sentence: *Pora by vypit* (High time for a drink).

Well-known love songs and other popular songs were reworked. The students' version of one song came out like this:

One inclement autumn evening
A maiden sat at a sausage stand
Holding a dreadful piece of sausage
In her trembling hand.

In short, they came up with every kind of clever and fanciful construction. There were a great many of these jokes, riddles, fables, songs, bits of verse, and even long narrative poems in Russian, German, French, Latin, and Greek, in a barbaric verbal mishmash in which all the different languages were deliberately mixed together into a single viscous mass by the special stirring stick of the students' inventiveness. A new arrival would be completely dumbfounded by all this super cleverness pouring down on him during his first days, because all the older students would try to share with him their experience in this special field of knowledge and to outshine their friends in this type of erudition.

Kolya Petrov suddenly found himself in completely new surroundings: in grade school the children had been from urban, lower-middle-class families, poorly dressed and not very well washed, and they brought their families' habits and way of life into the school. At the *gimnaziya*, however, were the sons of large landowners, wealthy merchants, prominent bureaucrats, and courtiers—all well-washed and well-dressed, with pink complexions, their hair neatly combed and slicked down, and Kolya stood out among them in his wretched little jacket, purchased from a used-clothing dealer, and his poorly sewed overcoat, put together by his mother from scraps of material from officers' uniforms obtained from the same source. Because of his height he was immediately given two nicknames: Lilliput and Little One.

But no one tried to initiate him into his new social world with kicks and punches, as was often done to newcomers. Either the other boys were impressed by his brilliant test scores or by his biting tongue, or perhaps it was his physical dexterity or the various interesting stories he knew how to tell. At any rate, no one tried to pick on him as an outsider; instead he was quickly accepted—lock, stock, and barrel—as "one of the boys." Some of the hard-working but not very successful students burned with envy and spread rumors that he was a terrible grind, who spent all his time studying. But in fact Kolya never even had dictionaries, and before the lesson he would hastily copy the "vocabulary" from someone and instantly memorize it. He listened to the teachers attentively, and since almost all of them gave advance notice of the lesson for the day, he would know it in good time. It happened once that the Latin teacher called him to the front of the room when he had barely had time to copy the day's "vocabulary" from his neighbor into his own notebook. The ink was not yet dry when he found himself walking to the front.

"Petrov is in for it today," he heard the whisper from the row of desks where the real grinds sat.

"All right, Petrov. Well, sir. Let's hear what you have to tell us," Zbraslavsky started in, his glasses glittering and his fingers tugging at his patchy red beard and sideburns.

"First, vocabulary. What is the Latin for 'frog'?"

"Rana."

"Stork?"

"Ciconia."

"To devour?"

"Devorare."

"Third person plural?"

"Devorant."

It was the same story with the strict German teacher. After Kolya had related a short and simple story in German, Plesterer clapped the work-book shut in a satisfied way and asked the class, with a look of pride in his pupil, "Was fehlt ihm doch?" (What did he get wrong?) And answered himself pompously, "Gar nichts!" (Absolutely nothing!).

"Listen, Lilliput, what do they feed you to make you do so well in every-thing?" Kolya was being confronted by the German teacher's son, Fritz. There was a song about him going the rounds.

Fritz, Fritz,
Willst du grütz?
Nein, Mama,
Ich will kaka.
Fritz, Fritz,
Want some kasha?
No, Mama,
I want kaka.

"Nothing special," Kolya answered. "Just some of that kasha that you won't take."

And everyone began teasing Fritz good-naturedly.

Two students competed with Kolya for the honor of being first in the class: Matveyev and Sokolovsky. Matveyev was the son of a peasant who lived on the charity of a wealthy Moscow family, the Fedotovs, who were merchants and owners of real estate. Their son was a student in the same class. Matveyev was a peaceful, obedient sort who had been schooled in the strict traditions of the merchant families' favorite book, the *Domostroi*. He lived under the constant threat that his "benefactors" might withdraw their philanthropic aid. At home he shoveled snow in the yard and was always on call, like some errand boy in a shop. At school he tried with all his might to master his lessons, so that his grade book would always show good marks and so that old man Fedotov wouldn't get his back up. He had black hair and a dark complexion. Physically he was quite strong and had a lot of endurance. He came to school together with the merchant's son, who was a flabby, pink-cheeked fellow, a fair-haired boy with facial coloring in the softest tones, a sparkling clean, light-gray uniform made from the best officers' fabric, and a collar that was always white as snow. Everything he wore was first class, of the finest quality, and this impressive attire stood in sharp contrast to the rough fabric and brass belt buckle that Matveyev wore.

Sokolovsky came from a family of the Polish gentry; his mother had her own two-storied brick house in Moscow, on Lower Lesnoi Lane, near the Cathedral of Christ the Savior; her sister was married to an elderly professor at Moscow University and was a fairly well-known figure in the liberal women's movement. Sokolovsky's father did not live in Moscow; he worked as the manager of some large estate near Warsaw, was acquainted with Polish radical circles, and knew the Polish "legal Marxist" Ludwig Krzywicki.*

The Sokolovsky family was a typical liberal bourgeois family with traditions from the court nobility. In it there reigned a spirit of culture and liberalism comme il faut that disliked any kind of "excesses" and looked down on the "common people," but at the same time condemned the crude barbarity and Asiatic despotism of the autocracy. Here parliamentarism, science, liberal reforms, clean tablecloths and napkins, shampooed hair, *Russkiye Vedomosti*, the waters at Carlsbad, and refined French pronunciation were all woven together into a single whole. Mechik (the Sokolovskys' son) spoke French and German extremely well, read a great deal, and had exceptional talents, learned his lessons easily and fluently, and showed no sign of injury or bitterness when Lilliput took the lead— whereas Matveyev acted envious, as though the latecomer had stolen something from him. Of course this was entirely understandable, since Matveyev feared losing what he had: the merchant Fedotov might in fact stop paying his way if Matveyev lost his position at the top of his class. Indeed he lost his position—but no catastrophe resulted.

Among the three aspirants to first place in the class, Kolya was the liveli-

*Ludwig Krzywicki (1859–1941), Polish scholar and essayist, an early supporter of scientific socialist ideas, and the main translator into Polish of Marx's *Capital, vol. 1.*

est and most outgoing, and he quickly established good relations with everyone in the class. Of course their attitude wasn't always based on the purest or most unselfish of motives: they liked Kolya for slipping them the answers when there were written assignments, for knowing how to prompt them in a whisper and let them copy from him, and for displaying an extraordinary virtuosity in all these things. For this reason he soon found protectors, large and oxlike, who placed him unreservedly under their sponsorship and were ready to make mincemeat of anyone who dared lay a hand on Lilliput.

At one point stamp collecting became a fad throughout the class, and Kolya got swept up in it too for a while, but soon, during that same year, it began to bore him: it was a dry and lifeless activity! He decided that it made as much sense to save buttons from old trousers. After all, there were so many buttons, Russian and foreign, European and American—and all different! Having found such a marvelous general formula to justify a negative attitude toward stamps, he could not give it up but used it every way he could to tease and irritate the most avid philatelists, who so proudly spread out their albums with Bolivian or Chilean stamps; they were so taken with their stamps, it seemed, they must have imagined the countries from which these stamps came in the form of one huge canceled postage stamp.

And all the while, Kolya's grade book glittered with nothing but A's.

Chapter 14

After lengthy torments Ivan Antonych finally landed a job—as a "monitor" at the Komissarovskoye Technical Academy, nicknamed "the Komissarovka." Volodya was sent to that school as well, starting with first grade. During this time Lyubov Ivanovna managed to give birth to one more son, who was called Pyotr. At home it was as though they were really trying to build the Tower of Babel: their little room had gotten so crowded you couldn't fit another person in. You could hardly breathe for the foul-smelling sheets, the diapers, and the roaring of infants. During the childbirth process Kolya and Volodya were parceled out to live with friends temporarily—otherwise it would have been impossible to provide the mother in childbirth with even the minimum conditions animals require. Ivan Antonych ran around the apartment, holding his head; he would stop and listen to Lyubochka's groans, then start running again. But everything turned out all right.

Fortunately, it was not long after his wife gave birth that Ivan Antonych was given his lowly position—but even that meant bread on the table after the many hard years of joblessness, of living off the charity of others, of semi-starvation, of distress, feuding, and hurt feelings over a crust of bread.

The Petrovs decided to separate from their "extended family," to free Yevgeny Antonych from the heavy burden: a small apartment was rented in a building owned by a certain Mokhov, on Valovaya Street, near the Serpukhov Gates. Here there was neither yard nor garden. Properly speaking, there was a yard, but this small, paved area could have no meaning for the children. Also housed in the building was a print shop, which smelled of inks and asphyxiating gasses. Next door was a small chemical plant, from which came the odor of chlorine. Still, one could at least sit and walk around in the apartment, and, most important, one didn't feel constantly under siege. You could sit and read in the living room. The door to the bedroom, whence came the shrieks of infants, could be closed. In a word, it was much more comfortable there than in the communal apartment in Babyi Gorodok.

The first thing was to get the boys some clothing. Ivan Antonych bought two suits, one for Kolya, one for Volodya, from the steward at the Komissarovka—they were worn-out "boarding house" suits that were going to be sold to the secondhand clothing dealers. The boys spent an entire evening using benzene to remove the greasy patches of sweat and oil from the lapels of the jacket and the flies of the trousers. There was no use being squeamish about all this—what was the alternative? Finally the suits were ready, and the boys were able to disport themselves in something "new."

In the spring, as summer vacation for pupils and teachers drew near, Ivan Antonych came to an agreement with the art teacher at the Komissarovka, one Mikhail Samoilovich Kellat, to take the boys with him to the country, where he usually rented a simple peasant's cottage and went strolling about with his sketchpad and paints among the meadows, fields, and woods of the region. The boys were in seventh heaven, especially Kolya, for whom a beloved but unfamiliar world now opened up, the world of true art, the world of paints and colors. Palettes, brushes, canvases, posterboard, lacquers and varnishes—all this he knew only by hearsay. But now he would see it all firsthand and—who knows?—maybe he'd have a chance to take up an artist's brush with his own hand.

Mikhal Samoilych (as he was known more familiarly) was in the highest degree a bizarre and original figure. His outward appearance alone was striking enough. His very long head, with a crease down the middle of the skull, gave the impression that two heads had grown together, and both of them were bald; in the back, at his neckline, surprisingly, there hung long locks of dark hair, as was only fitting for an artist; his face was pale, as though patted with flour, and he had little, swollen, yellowed bags under his eyes. He wore a large, wide-brimmed hat and a raincoat, and in his hands he always seemed to have a walking stick he had fashioned for himself from a tree branch; he was hardly ever without it.

There had apparently been some tragic event in his past, after which he had fallen into a morbid religiosity, just like Gogol near the end of his life. He fasted regularly, prayed often, and his dry, bloodless lips, at work in a secret, mysterious way beneath his whiskers, were forever mumbling something. He spoke in a soft voice that came from the chest, in short sentences only, and seemed to be not at all of this world, an eccentric, one touched by God, almost a holy fool, but a surprisingly kind, meek, and gentle person. He chain-smoked, making his own cigarettes out of some repulsive kind of cheap tobacco. As he wandered through the woods he would sing to himself in a low voice, psalms and songs no one else knew. He was afraid of women and hid from them, apparently considering them emanations from Hell, vessels of sin and temptation. At one time he had graduated from the celebrated Moscow Academy of Painting, Sculpture, and Architecture and had even won a gold medal for his graduation project. After graduating, however, he had withdrawn from the world, and although he worked to earn a living, he kept company with no one and lived like a true hermit monk.

In recent times the son of one of his cousins, a boy named Sasha, had moved in with him in order to study at the Industrial Academy on Miusskaya Square. He was a lively and intelligent fellow, with a harelip, who was not averse to sometimes teasing his uncle. Mikhal Samoilych also loved to fish and could sit evening after evening by a still backwater, watching his fishing line's motionless float and listening to the voices of nature subsiding.

At last the longed-for moment came, and the Petrov boys found themselves at the country cottage. They spread out on the floor two mattresses filled with hay. The three of them (Kolya, Volodya, and Sasha) slept side by side, in a row, covered by one large red blanket that Mikhal Samoilych had inherited and that smelled of brass and naphthalene. You could feel bits of hay sticking into your body—but that was nothing; such things were mere trifles in comparison with the river, the woods, the sun, and—painting! In the small storeroom, where Mikhal Samoilych took up his residence (he never undressed in front of the others, as though ashamed of his own body) there was a portable easel, a large sketchpad, and a box filled with paints. This was the first time Kolya had seen these little tubes of paint. Brand new and bursting full, they had a cheerful metallic gleam about them. Old, used tubes lay about in disorder, half squeezed, twisted, smeared with paint, soiled and discolored, often lacking caps or split along their sides so that a thick solidifying mass was oozing out. Brushes lay in the box as well, round ones and flat ones, columnar and brush-shaped; some of them had been trimmed or clipped in a special way by Mikhal Samoilych to suit his own tastes. The palette bespoke its owner's slovenliness: it had obviously not been cleaned for years, although Mikhal Samoilych loved to "paint with kerosene."

Yet how many different colors of paint there were! With the artist's permission, Kolya began to study them carefully. Even their names seemed to him the expression of something very special and extremely fascinating:

carmine, rose dorée, cinnabar, or vermilion, cobalt blue, Prussian blue, indigo, sky blue, ultramarine, chrome, lemon yellow, cadmium yellow, ocher, terra sienna, asphalt, Paolo Veronese (veronese green), emerald green, terre verte, and on and on—what colors didn't Mikhal Samoilych have. Last of all, there were the large, thick tubes of lead white, or ceruse. All this filled Kolya with an extraordinary feeling of respect. What richness! What complexity! No longer was it just a matter of a child's set of water colors, little tablets with four basic colors with which one could paint the wretched little pictures children paint. This was the real thing, the genuine article. And he, Kolya, was there, right next to it. He wasn't just dreaming; this was real life, and he was touching all this multiplicity and variety with his own hands!

One fine day Mikhal Samoilych gathered the boys together, picked up some loaded cartons (which he had packed himself to take along), and they all headed into the woods to do some sketching from nature. A lovely place right next to a brook was chosen. Hanging down all around were the branches of spruce trees, their trunks huge and covered with moss, their branches all bearded silvery and gray. Down below, among the ferns at the bottom of a shallow ravine, ran a little stream—you could see its sandy bottom and the stones over which little watery flecks of light flashed and wavered. Sunlight played through the thick green foliage of spruces and alders. Chaffinches, moving along the branches in staid and measured manner, would now and then break into their brief but lovely trill. You could smell the aromas of flowers and grasses. The thick vegetation was in some places overgrown with hop vines, which made their way through the branches, ever upward, extending their palmate leaves, seeking the light. A cool freshness pervaded, allowing one to relax and enjoy, to think and work.

Mikhal Samoilych distributed the boxes and brushes.

"Try painting something."

Kolya was so surprised he could barely keep his wits together. But Mikhal Samoilych gave them simple, basic instructions. And they all set to work, even Volodya.

At first, for Kolya, nothing would come out right: he would make an outline in charcoal, but when it came to applying the colors, everything turned out dull and drab, there was no perspective, everything was drowned in the monotony of a uniform, deadening green. He was in a quandary and had no idea what to do. Mikhal Samoilych came over, smiled, took the paint brush, and with what seemed to Kolya extraordinary audacity began mixing up colors that seemed completely out of place. A few strokes of the paint brush—and the sketch suddenly came to life.

"Be bolder, Kolyushka. Don't be afraid. Make the shadows deeper, a darker blue. Don't you see there, in nature, how dark the patches are?"

Kolya became bolder. And things began to come out better.

"And what about you, Sasha?"

Sasha had a lot of courage. He dashed off big, thick strokes "just any old way," but his painting also suffered from a uniformity of tone. Mikhal Samoilych made the necessary improvements.

"Hey, Volodyushka, what are you doing?"

Volodya had gotten his colors completely mixed up.

Mikhal Samoilych came over to Kolya again. He fixed the trunk of the spruce tree, adding a little lilac color to it, put two or three strokes of shadow under the boughs—and suddenly the trunk stood out distinctly.

"Look at the diversity and variety of color. See how the leaves on that bush are rounded? But you have them flat. There on the left is a bright green, but to the right—look carefully—there are two dark patches. You have it looking almost all the same. No matter how many twigs you put in a single painting, without variety of color you'll get nowhere. Do you understand?"

"I understand, Mikhal Samoilych—only nothing will come out right for me."

"Today it won't come out right—tomorrow it will. Just look closely. And don't get upset, don't try to rush. Sit for a while. Think. Step back and compare your sketch to your subject in nature. That's the way things will move along."

For a long time more the boys sat there, working away. They got covered with paint but were totally happy.

"Not bad for a first round. Now it's time to eat. Take kerosene and a rag, clean your palettes and brushes—and let's go home!"

On the way home Mikhal Samoilych was mumbling to himself, lines like: "Out of youthfulness, therefore, many passions bestir me." He strode along in front wearing his wide-brimmed hat and swinging his staff.

That was how their first painting lesson went—out in the open, just like they used to do at Barbizon.

Mikhal Samoilych was notable for his extreme impracticality in everyday life, although he considered himself a very practical person. Once a week he went off to Moscow to buy provisions. Usually they ate scantily: mainly porridge with milk, plus a baked potato with butter. But after the long walks in the fresh air it all tasted delicious. Agafya (the housekeeper attached to the cottage) would bring two earthenware pots up out of the cellar; they would be "sweating," with droplets of water on their outsides, and she would pour thick, sweet milk into bowls; and they would sprinkle big grains of salt on the porridge. Each potato was a regular meal unto itself! The boys lived well at Mikhal Samoilych's.

Once he brought from the city a well-filled bag made of bast.

"I've bought some sturgeon meat here—it's marvelous sturgeon—and some ham."

The sturgeon turned out to have gone completely bad, and the smell that came from it was quite overpowering. But Mikhal Samoilych considered it just wonderful. They boiled it, made some stewed cabbage, and as they ate, they would nearly die from laughter whenever Mikhal Samoilych said: "Eat up, the sturgeon is excellent—"

Mikhal Samoilych had no understanding about food. On Sunday he brought out the ham bone, with the skin still on it, which he had brought from Moscow.

"Kolyushka, don't you want some pork rind?"

The "pork rind" was covered with mold, and Kolya, who first sterilized it under boiling water from the samovar, then summoned up all his reserves, took a bite of the rind so as not to offend his host.

Later, when the boys were alone, they cursed for an entire hour, and from then on they teased one another with the memory: "Kolyushka, don't you want some pork rind."

When Mikhal Samoilych would go off to Moscow for a day or two the boys were left entirely to themselves. The first thing they did was rush off with the local village boys to where the horses were pastured overnight. They brought their famous big red blanket, the housekeeper gave them a half-length fur coat, and they spent a wonderful night out on the meadow, next to the stream. The stars shone brightly in the night sky. The horses could be heard snuffling and snorting nearby, and once in a while there was the stamping of their hobbled feet. Then everything grew quiet again. The boys made a campfire and sat around it, huddling together, the red flecks of light playing on their faces.

"Better put some juniper branches on it, or else it'll go out—"

They all ran in a happy bunch to the nearby clump of trees to get juniper branches. The shepherd boy had a big knife—for protection against wolves. They used his knife to cut the bushes with their prickly needles and dark-blue berries, then dragged their booty back to the fire. It blazed up immediately, giving off thick, tarry, strong-smelling smoke, crackling, whistling, and singing as the fire with its tongues of flame licked up the fresh greenery from the thickset juniper bushes.

"Hoo boy, the mosquitoes sure don't like that thick smoke," said a freckle-faced lad with light blond hair.

"We always burn juniper at our house to keep away mosquitoes," answered another.

"The black grouse like to eat the juniper berries," the shepherd boy observed impressively, making himself a walking stick from the sturdy branch of a stripped juniper bush. He carved some intricate twisting patterns and insignia on the stick.

"Also, you can make good poles from it to fish for bottom fish," the first boy continued. "At one end it's real thick, but at the other it's as thin as a hair, but it won't break, no way, only bend. Makes a real good fishing pole."

"Uh, what can you catch on the creek bottom here?" Kolya asked, interested in this new information.

"Whatever you like. At night we catch burbot here, but over at the lake—you know, on the other side of the woods—you can get really good tench with worms for bait. The tench over there are really 'normous, real wide, good as gold—"

In the grove an owl began to call, hooting, moaning.

"The other day Filka caught a baby owl."

"Where? Who has it now?" Kolya was all ears immediately.

"Caught it in the grove over there. Pulled it out of a hole in the tree. All furry. Strange. Like an animal, not a bird. It couldn't fly, but scramble!— boy, it could scramble. It was a riot!"

"What did you do with it?"

"Well, Petrukha got it, but good, with my whip. Did it in."

"What did you do that for? Are you guys crazy?"

"Hey, what do we need it for? You know they eat up the baby rabbits, owls do."

"You have baby rabbits?"

"Not right nee-ow. But las' year a baby rabbit grew up over at Uncle Filipp's—a big red one—it would drum on the ground with its paws, real smart like."

"What happened to it?"

"You know what happened. They cut it up and ate it. Plenty of fat on that rabbit."

Hanging like a brass bowl in the sky was the moon.

"Kolya, is it true what they say, that Cain is sitting up there on the moon?"

"Baloney."

"Then what're those dark spots up there?"

"Mountains."

"You say there's mountains on the moon? You're makin' that up—"

Kolya went into an explanation. And Sasha backed him up. The village boys listened with eyes wide . . . The fire was burning down.

"Kolya, let's go to sleep. Or tomorrow afternoon we'll feel as though we'd gotten an enema with broken glass and vinegar," said Sasha.

"All right. Spread out the sheepskin coat."

The boys began to drowse off with their faces turned to the sky. Volodya curled up into a little ball. And the rest fell asleep. Only the shepherd boy stayed up: he sat by the dying fire, weaving himself a new pair of bast slippers. The old ones were worn out; it was time to toss them out, to dump them in some shah's or hermit monk's Lenten cabbage soup.

When Mikhal Samoilych wasn't there the boys loved to run down and take the horses for a bath. One day they took off to go to the river. It was a hot summer day. Both people and animals were languishing from the unbearable heat of the sun, which seemed to burn the skin with its piercing rays. Horseflies and gadflies were tormenting the horses, hovering around them in swarms and biting mercilessly. The boys would catch the larger horseflies and rip their heads off, then watch as the headless horsefly would start to fly up, then collapse and grab onto itself with its little legs or even use its back legs to straighten out its wings, smoothing them over from the topside down. Or they would stick a spear of grass in a horsefly's rear end, and the tormenter of horses would disappear, grass and all, into the wild blue yonder. The river flowed past, blindingly bright, like shiny metal. The water was so tempting . . .

The boys took off their clothes, jumped on the horses, and with whooping and hollering, whistling and singing, charged into the water. There was laughter, spray, and splashing.

"Out we go! Volodya, Sasha, back to shore!"

Kolya spurred the mare he was riding with his bare heels, driving her toward shore. When she quickly ran up the bank, though, he felt himself slipping off her wet rump and a moment later he lost consciousness: he hit his head on something, lightning flashed before his eyes, then total, absolute darkness covered everything . . .

When he came to he saw he was lying on the ground. Volodya was standing next to him, tears pouring from his eyes. He was begging and pleading: "Kolyechka! Kolyechka! You're alive, aren't you? You mustn't die!"

Kolya's head was all bloody, and where it dried, got stuck in clumps in his hair. It turned out that when he was sliding off the mare's rump, she—trying either to shake off the horseflies or to free herself from her rider's control—had kicked him in the head with her well-shod hoof and bloodied it good and proper. A huge lump swelled up with a big cut in the middle. In the hot sun the blood got baked together with Kolya's hair, and there developed a hairy, matted lump of the kind called plica polonica.

When the first minutes of confusion had passed the boys began to discuss the question of how to hide this matted lump from Mikhal Samoilych, who was due back from Moscow that evening. There was no question it had to be hidden: otherwise they would lose all their freedom, which they had been enjoying to the fullest. They decided that Kolya should start wearing a cap, and at dinner he should sit with the wounded side away from Mikhal Samoilych. They gave one another a solemn vow not to say anything about what happened. Sasha began to express concern about showing the wound to a doctor, but Kolya protested so strongly that the matter was dropped.

They all firmly agreed to keep their lips sealed. And they stuck to their mutual vows. The only thing was that dear, kind Mikhal Samoilych couldn't understand why Kolya categorically refused to have a haircut. Still, when all was said and done, he wasn't all that concerned about the haircut.

Mikhal Samoilych loved nature deeply, in his own way, and he understood it well. He would wander through the forest, making his way into the worst thicket there might be and sloshing through bogs and marshes in search of beautiful, varicolored mosses, queerly gnarled branches, or huge clumps of tinder fungus. He would cut disfigured, oddly patterned, lumpy growths from birch trees, break lovely garlands of cones from spruce trees, gather flowers, ferns, the dying crimson leaves of aspens, and clusters of berries from rowan trees and guelder rose—all this material he would drag back to the cottage, arranging remarkable decorations out of it. The boys strongly supported him in these efforts: it was a case of complete mutual understanding. But they didn't have enough living things that would move about instead of sitting or lying in one place. So little by little they came to the idea that they needed to obtain some kind of animal. They decided to catch a squirrel.

From Moscow Mikhal Samoilych brought some fine metal screening that was used to cover food to keep flies off, and he placed an order with the village carpenter to make two large cages according to his, Mikhal Samoilych's, own design. The cages were soon ready. But how they dressed them up! Mikhal Samoilych and the boys put birch bark on the solid wood of the closed side of the cage and on all other wooden parts. Inside they fastened the prettiest pieces of fungus, gnarled limbs with holes in them, and knotty boughs of oak. They glued brightly colored leaves and bits of moss to the birch bark. In a word, they produced such artful cages that any decorator who specialized in making such items for zoos would have been envious. But actually, they didn't succeed in catching any squirrels. Kolya made the rounds of every squirrel's nest he could find in his tree climbing, but they all turned out to be empty.

Once he climbed a very high spruce tree, in which a large, round squirrel's nest could be seen, right next to the trunk, way up high. With much effort he made his way up through the branches, little bits of bark, dry needles, and other detritus dribbling all over his head and getting in his eyes. He poked into the open hole in the side of the nest with his right hand, then pulled it back in horror: the empty squirrel's nest had been taken over by bumble bees!

On another occasion a squirrel was chased out of a tree, and Kolya ran after it. The squirrel was high-tailing it across open ground toward a tall pine tree. Kolya grabbed it by the back, but it instantly sank its teeth into his finger, and he let go . . .

How ashamed of himself he felt! The squirrel escaped up the tree and, looking down from above, mockingly chattered and scolded, switching its tail. It looked and looked and then rushed off, like one possessed, and disappeared from view.

There was no help for it; the opportunity had been missed. Mikhal Samoilych was obliged to buy some squirrels at the Truba. He bought a "full set," a male and a female. When they were released into the large cage—and such a well-furnished one, at that—after sitting for so long in the tiny cage of the peddler at the Truba, they went half mad with joy; they began to chatter, flicking their tails, climbed the branches, and soon set to the nuts and sunflower seeds with great appetite, hiding half of them in the moss, carefully burying them and covering them over with their dexterous front paws.

Sometimes they were let out of the cage and they'd scamper around the log walls, slipping and falling, then clambering up again with surprising speed, taking hold of the slightest indentations or irregularities in the logs. Soon they became quite tame and would get up on the table, hopping about freely and picking up crumbs, tasting or rejecting leftover bits of food; they got up on people's shoulders, crawled into their pockets, allowed themselves to be petted, narrowing or closing their eyes and making gurgling-groaning noises . . .

Later the village boys brought a baby rabbit, and that was how the second cage became inhabited. At first the rabbit was terribly shy, but after a while he adjusted. It's true that the air in the room was none the better from all this, but that wasn't a huge problem because during the day the windows were kept open all the time: they were closed only when the squirrels were let out of their cage.

Several times Kolya went to do studies from nature with Mikhal

Samoilych, who assured him that progress was being made. But Kolya had a passionate desire to paint some special subject: a purple sunset with clouds that had glowing edges, a fire at night, a tree by the light of the moon. He didn't yet know how to cope with the most elementary aspects of painting and was already in a hurry to undertake the most complex. He was striving to achieve certain subtle effects with light and shadow and of course was failing every time.

Autumn came. The leaves of the birch trees turned yellow, and amidst their gold the aspens blazed with fiery crimson. Mikhal Samoilych was getting ready to make a trip to Senezhskoye Lake and decided to take Kolya with him. They took along paints and fishing rods, just in case: Mikhal Samoilych told stories about the unusually good fishing one could find there in the autumn. He had once lived in a cottage not far from the lake and knew all its surroundings quite well. And so they set off.

This was the first time Kolya had seen such a large body of water. The lake was a wide expanse of blue with real waves on its surface. It didn't look anything like the quiet little creeks with ponds and backwaters where the trees and bushes were reflected, as in a mirror. It stretched out far into the distance, and the woods on the opposite shore appeared as a light-blue mist. Entire thickets of high reeds extended along the shore, their leaves rustling dryly—as though an indistinct whisper were flowing along in a wave. The travelers' goal was to reach a little village where Mikhal Samoilych had lived previously, to ensure themselves a place to stay. At first the road went along a lakeside marsh, over fallen reeds, from which water trickled with a squelching sound, then over firm meadowland, beyond which there began an oak forest. The oaks were neither very old nor very young; they had about half a century to their credit and, with their roots firmly planted in the damp, dark soil, they lifted their crowns, jagged, spreading, and not entirely green, to the sky.

"Oh my goodness, saints preserve us. Where did you come from, dear one, to show up at our place like this?" the old peasant woman greeted Mikhal Samoilovich. "I never expected you, had no idea you were coming. It's like you fell right out of the sky."

"Kolya and I have come to spend some time at the lake, Fedosya Stepanovna. We'd like to stay at your place."

"Do us the honor, father. But who's this boy, a relative of yours?"

"No, a friend."

"Oh, so that's the way it is. Would you be staying long?"

"Two days or so."

"Why so short a stay? Give yourself a treat and stay longer. But what am

I doing, old fool that I am, chattering away, when I have things to do. Let me run and start the samovar, and I'll boil you an egg."

The old woman went hobbling off to the other side of the cottage.

Soon she had spread out on the table a decorative table cloth with fringe around the edges, a purring samovar, flat cakes of rye, a pail with pink, heated milk in it, and hard-boiled eggs.

"Eat to your heart's content! It's been so long since you've visited us, Mikhal Samoilych, dear father. Probably you haven't had time. But I often think of you here. Are you living in Moscow this summer?"

"No, in the country—"

"Why not with us? Did you forget? Or was it bad here?"

"I always like to tramp around in new places, Fedosya Stepanovna."

"So you're being an artist. Well, sure enough, that's your business, not mine. But come, have something to eat. Please. Let me pour you some tea. Only we don't have much sugar—don't judge us too harshly for that."

"Thanks very much. And don't worry, everything's fine. Kolyushka, eat some flat cakes. Grandma Fedosya bakes the best flat cakes."

"What riches we have we're happy with."

Having fortified themselves with Fedosya Stepanovna's hospitality, Mikhal Samoilych and Kolya went down to the lake again. The western sky was ablaze in robes of purple. Towers of pink clouds piled up to colossal heights with patterns of tender light shading off into tones of blue and violet. Kolya was already thinking in terms of colors: here there was rose doree and India yellow; over there was carmine and cobalt; and in the forest glades there was veronese green and a touch of sky blue.

Kolya chose colors from among the old tubes of paint Mikhal Samoilych had brought along in a box.

They'd have to hurry to capture the beauty of this moment . . .

"Mikhal Samoilych, let's stop here. What a study this would make!"

"All right. Only we'll have to paint fast. It's getting dark, and it's hard to catch it in time: it all changes from second to second."

They sat down. The lake was alive with reflections of twilight between darkening shores. Kolya hurried, barely taking the time to squeeze the paints out. Mikhal Samoilych worked calmly and with assurance; he didn't bustle about but still managed to have enough time. While Kolya was going through torments trying to pick out the shades he wanted, the experienced artist unerringly found the right nuance. He didn't have to make so many trial runs, sampling various colors—everything seemed to come out as it should, of its own accord; past experience had developed into a sure instinct; both hand and eye took hold of what was needed, almost automatically. Not without envy Kolya watched his teacher: how smoothly and easily everything flowed for him! It was as if he were merely playing with the brushes and paints. Sometimes it seemed to Kolya that Mikhal Samoilych was dabbing out a blotch of color that was totally wrong. But then it was surrounded by other colors and itself took on a different hue, as part of the whole, and the grandeur of the luxurious purple festival in the sky was already being reflected on the artist's canvas.

Mikhal Samoilych softly sang a passage in Old Church Slavonic under his breath: "Oh soft light, holy glories of our heavenly father, blessed and holy—" He would glance up at the sky. And the lights of the sunset would sparkle in his eyes.

Kolya didn't even want to look at his own sketch. He was in utter despair—what greensickness! A pallid effort! All the enthusiasm that at first had seized him now evaporated. The wings of his soul hung limp: It's not coming out right . . . I can't . . . I don't know how! he thought. And he didn't want to work on the painting anymore. On the other hand, there it was, staring him in the face, this fool's effort, this sorry testimony to his own incompetence. A vague thought crossed Kolya's mind: It shouldn't even exist. And with one swipe of a rag he erased everything he had done.

"Kolyushka, what are you doing?"

"Mikhal Samoilych, it was such garbage. It made me sick to even look at it," Kolya responded almost in tears.

"Don't worry. It's a good thing you take all this so much to heart. You'll learn quicker. You just have to keep starting over, starting over. Don't give up. Don't fall into despair. What was it you wanted? To have everything come out just right without any experience? You know you couldn't start talking Greek right away. It's the same thing here," Mikhal Samoilych comforted Kolya, stepping back from his own study and continuing to look, now at it, now at his subject in nature. "All you have to do is make a little bit of an error, and the whole thing is wrong; then you fix it up a little bit, and it all comes alive. Karl Bryullov said that that's where art begins, with that 'little bit.' Bryullov was—"

"Yes, I know, Mikhal Samoilych: *Last Day of Pompeii*."

"The very same. But he was a terrible drunk, you know, and a degenerate, Lord forgive him—"

"He used to get drunk with Glinka and Kukolnik."

"Where do you know that from?" Mikhal Samoilych was surprised.

"I read it."

"Ah, you're such a smarty-pants! But it's time to call it a day: you can't see any more anyhow."

Mikhal Samoilych cleaned the brushes and clapped the easel shut. It was already quite dark when they got back to the cottage.

"So now what have you been doing out in this Egyptian darkness," Fedosya Stepanovna waved her hands. "Come quick: I've already fixed you supper. I cleaned a herring, and there's potatoes; also, porridge with milk. But you'll have to sleep on the straw—I don't have any other bedding."

"Please, don't worry, for heaven's sake."

"What worry. I'm glad to have guests. Otherwise I'm always alone, like an owl in a hole in a tree. That's just the word for it. A regular owl."

The next morning Mikhal Samoilych woke Kolya, who had been sleeping like a log.

"Kolyushka, Kolya. Time to get up."

Washing up quickly at the outdoor washstand of clay and swallowing down some hot tea, Kolya went with his artist friend back to the lake again, but this time in a different direction. When they arrived and began hunting for a more comfortable spot on the shore, a morning fog had spread over the lake. The pale white masses of fog, twisting and swirling, would at one moment bunch together into a solid wall, at another would break into wisps through which the mirror surface of the lake could be seen. There was a calm on the water, and not a single wave rippled its wide, smooth expanse. The sun had already climbed high, and through the fog it looked like a red ball hanging in the sky. Its light glistened in millions of diamond sparkles on the cold, dew-covered grass.

"My, but it's brisk," said Mikhal Samoilych as he laid out his paints and sketchpad.

"Yeah, sorta cold."

"It'll be a nice day anyway. Kolyushka, don't sit right on the wet grass like that; you'll catch cold or get sciatica. Bring that wheelbarrow over. See it? That old wheelbarrow over there that someone forgot. No, you're not looking in the right direction. Over to the right more, by that bush—"

Kolya brought over the fairly heavy wheelbarrow, with which stonemasons had apparently kept themselves busy when repairing a dike along the shore.

"Now we're all set. Get the fishing poles ready while I dig for worms. There's swarms of them here. I brought a jar along."

Mikhal Samoilych dug up a whole jarful of worms, which curled and twisted about, sticking their red, ringed tails up along the side of the jar. The paints were brought out, and the brushes. The fishing lines were cast, and they started to paint . . .

But Mikhal Samoilych had barely made two strokes with his brush before his float suddenly sank as though someone had hit it over the head.

"Aha, my dear, you've taken the bait! Ooh, what a fish!" said Mikhal Samoilych with emotion, trying to take the hook out of a big perch that was thrashing and writhing, goggling its eyes, and opening wide the bright red insides of its gills.

"Kolya, look lively!"

Kolya's pole was bent over. He reeled in his catch. A green pike weighing about half a pound hung on the hook.

"So, the fish are biting well—say, my perch must have swallowed the hook—can't get it out. I'll have to use a knife." Mikhal Samoilych's hands were already bloody.

"Mikhal Samoilych, welcome!" someone's voice suddenly rang out. "I recognized you by that hat of yours."

Out of the bushes an old watchman with a fishnet was coming toward them.

"Been here long?"

"We arrived last night."

"Good timing."

"Why's that?"

"The fishing right now is rich as all get-out. Wasn't like that maybe ten years ago. You using worms? Try using small fry instead. There's millions of 'em here. I'll scoop some up for you right now with my net and dump 'em in the wheelbarrow. The fish here'll bite right away, even on somethin' dry. By noon, with two poles workin', you'll catch about a pood."*

"Really?"

"I'm tellin' you the truth."

The old man, wheezing, went down to the bank and after a few sweeps poured hundreds of silvery, quivering little fish into the wheelbarrow. They flipped about, fell on the grass, kept moving, but then grew still.

"Don't matter if they dry out. The perch and pike will gobble up anything, right in midair. That's how greedy they are. Hey, but where are your sacks?"

"What sacks?"

"Why, for fish."

"We were going to put them on a string."

"That won't do. I'm telling you, you'll catch a whole pood. You go ahead and cast your lines using fry for bait, and I'll bring you a couple of sacks later on. S'long, then, for now."

No sooner had the fishermen cast their lines than they both had bites immediately—huge old pikes splashed and trembled in the water and landed heavily on the ground when brought to shore. The fishing was extraordinary. It wasn't even like fishing any more. It was more like a

---

*More than twenty pounds.

turkey shoot. They had to keep pulling fish out of the water, over and over, and tearing the hooks free. Their hands got covered with blood, slime, and sticky fish scales. You didn't have to wait: the fish would take the bait on the fly the minute it dropped in the water. Soon the watchman showed up again with some sacks over his shoulder.

"Well? Did the old man tell you the truth or not?"

"The truth, old man."

"Well, there you have it. You must have spent the night at Fedosya's, right?"

"Yes, why?"

"I was thinking about the sacks."

"We're going to pay you not only for the sacks but for your advice, too. That's all there is to it."

"I humbly thank you. But as for the sacks, that's nothin.' I've got plenty of them. And I can always get more at the mill."

"That's all right . . . Hey, Kolya, you asleep at the switch?"

Kolya's fishing pole had bent more than double. He started reeling in. The pull was strong. Must be a big pike on the line, he thought.

Kolya let the line out, then reeled in again, "torturing" the fish to wear it out until he could bring it in close to shore and scoop it up in the net. Sure enough, it was a hefty black lake pike, not really very long, but thick, like a log; it had swallowed not the bait fish but a perch that had previously taken the bait, and even the perch was still showing signs of life.

"Hey, that's really something!" the watchman shouted. "What a hungry pike, I mean! But how come it didn't spit out the perch? Must have gotten caught in his teeth, looks like. You've got yourself more than a pound of raisins there, no lie. Darn thing, how it's clashin' its teeth. Keep hold of it! Or it'll get away."

The pike, flapping on the grass, kept working its way closer and closer to the lake.

"You'd better get it into a sack and be done with it. That's the way."

Kolya "packed up" the pike and, together with the watchman and Mikhal Samoilych, began gathering up their catch. There was half a sackful already.

"What time have you got, Granddad?"

"It's after nine o'clock."

"Is that all?"

"I told you: if you sit here till noon, you'll have a whole pood. Me, though, I've got to get over to the mill. So, about the sacks—"

Mikhal Samoilych quickly pulled out some money and settled accounts with his old acquaintance.

"Many thanks. You've got to come here more often. We've got really good fishing here. On Sunday there's such a crowd you can't move. And even weekday evenings they come here from Moscow. God help us!"

"Thanks, old man."

The fish kept biting with no letup. Painting had been forgotten; not a word was said about it. Now and then they put fresh bait on the hooks, cast their lines, reeled them in, took their catch off the hooks, cast out again. It began to seem abnormal if many minutes went by without a bite.

Around noon Mikhal Samoilych, leaving Kolya at the lake, walked back to Fedosya Stepanovna's place to get a horse—for bringing home the catch.

That same day the fishermen went back whence they had come, taking their booty with them, although they left half of it with their kindly old hostess.

"Sturgeon?" Sasha asked his uncle sardonically.

"No, no, perch and pike."

"No pork rind?"

But Mikhal Samoilych didn't get the joke.

Chapter 15

At the Yablochkins', life went on in its own way. The older son, Nikolai Mikhailych Yablochkin (also nicknamed Kolya), was already passing through his fifteenth year and would soon be entering his sixth year at the *gimnaziya*. Another son had been born, Vasya, a charming child with huge blue eyes, shadowed by long, dark lashes. He was the universal favorite, and even the sickly Mikhail Vasilyevich, irritable as ever, sometimes picked him up in his hands (which looked like those of the evil wizard Kashchei in Russian fairy tales), and Mikhail Vasilyevich would smile, something he hardly ever did. Kolya Yablochkin had grown up like a wild thing, locked in constant battle with his father, introverted, closed off, and embittered. He could not boast of great health: gaunt, lean, and scrofulous, he too was always fussing with jars and bottles, ointments, pills, and mixtures. All day long he would stay in his room, hardly ever going out for a walk and never seeing much of nature. Instead he gave himself over entirely to his books and the defense of his independence. He was an outstanding student, industrious to an extreme, and he loved unconditional order among his notebooks and books: everything about him was always orderly and clean, without even an ink spot—the *gimnaziya* teachers considered him a model pupil. His assiduousness evoked astonishment, and Marya Ivanovna often worriedly asked her son:

"Kolya, shouldn't you go for a walk? You never see the sun."

"No desire to."

"You'll have time to do your schoolwork."

"It's more interesting here."

"At least go out in the garden!"

"What? Haven't I seen it before?"

And his mother would give up. Kolya Yablochkin would continue to grind away at his lessons, reading bent over at his desk like an old man. He was at the top of his class, and his comportment was exemplary: the fighting and fussing and mischief of schoolboys did not tempt him in the slightest; he steered clear of them, with contempt in his heart, but in fact he was simply incapable of taking part because of his physical constitution and cheerless personality. He could not tolerate the bawdy language used at the *gimnaziya*, the jokes and vulgar versifying; his attitude toward them was one of scorn and revulsion. He grew tall and his face took on the appearance of an emaciated Jewish youth from the provinces: a long nose, black eyes, with slightly pink eyelids, shoulder blades that stuck out from a back that was somewhat hunched, hair black as coal, with a slight curl to it, and slender hands with the long fingers of a violin player. He loved music passionately, but hardly ever talked about it, preferring to enjoy it in solitude, within himself. The perennial battles with his father, the insults and humiliations imposed on him from early childhood, fostered a certain dryness and crustiness of character: many of his friends called him Rusk* and this nickname reflected part of his true essence.

He could not stand his father; nor could he regard the school environment, with its petty squabbles and intrigues, hypocrisy and narrow horizons, as in any way ideal. He got in the habit early in life of taking note of all instances and phenomena of a negative nature—counting them over, like beads on a string—and the life that went on at that time seemed to him more and more akin to bedlam. His intensified reading only reinforced this universally critical outlook, which had begun with his family but extended wider and deeper. Among Kolya Yablochkin's friends there were older ones who had already undertaken a serious study of social life, read thick books, and sometimes also acquired illegal literature, printed on onionskin paper. These little sheets were read and reread until they were nothing but filthy sweat-stained scraps.

Among the university students and some *gimnaziya* students in the upper grades, hot arguments were already going on between Marxists and Narodniks, and passions blazed; young men and women, their cheeks aflame, discussed the latest controversies; and some of them were already living a life the others could only guess at. In Kolya Yablochkin's class at the *gimnaziya* independent student circles had been formed, fairly innocent though they were: they read Pisarev, Chernyshevsky, and Dobrolyubov, wrote essays on "the meaning of life," on classical education, on "the woman question," on materialism. The green shoots of a fundamental critique of the tsarist system kept growing. And all of Russ-

*In Russian, *Sukhar*—the term for a dry crust of bread.

ian literature suddenly took on a special meaning and a special significance.

Kolya Yablochkin pored over Henry Thomas Buckle and John William
Draper, and read Pisarev with rapture: he was terribly pleased with Pisarev's idea of "rational egoism," his crushing condemnation of Pushkin for
excessive chumminess, his defense of Bazarov,* his furious advocacy of
Ludwig Büchner's materialism, and for the harsh and brilliant scorn, the
arrogant youthful pride, with which Pisarev attacked all supporters of the
powers that be, the do-nothings, the philistines, the lords and masters.

This was a highly specialized world, and Nikolai Yablochkin submerged
himself in it with the same caustic obstinacy that had helped him master
Titus Livius, Sallust, and Homer. He proceeded with extreme thorough-
ness, step by step, going farther and farther, chewing his way through page
after page of ever new volumes. Lightweight oppositional literature also
circulated hand to hand. One such item he brought home was *A History
from the Gostomysl to the Present Day*. He and Manya learned it by heart,
and Kolya fully understood its closing lines:

> It's slippery to go walking
> On other people's stones.
> But of things quite close to us
> We'd rather hold our tongues.

They got engrossed in reading Saltykov-Shchedrin, and for Kolya
Yablochkin, that author's *History of a Certain City*, together with Aleksei
Tolstoy's *History*, came to represent the fundamental backdrop to the
whole "Imperial State of Russia," a picture completely different from the
raptures of Karamzin, the sober rationalistic apologetics of Sergei
Solovyov, or the semi-official historians Zabelin and Kostomarov. In general Kolya Yablochkin was fascinated by history, and he already understood clearly how far removed real history was from the official doctrines
promoted in every way, including the works of Vasily Klyuchevsky, a
highly talented professor who had the face and figure of a crafty Muscovite
official of olden times.

On one occasion Kolya Yablochkin brought home a manuscript copy
of Leo Tolstoy's *Gospel*. Bending over by the lamp with the green glass
shade, Kolya and Manya read out loud:
"And Mary became big-bellied . . . As for Joseph, he was a good man—"
"Kolya, what does that mean, 'big-bellied'?"
"Pregnant."

*On Bazarov, see glossary.

"But why?" (Manya, although she was fourteen, had not yet been properly educated in such matters.)

"That's something you'll learn for yourself later on."

"But why can't you tell me now?"

"You're too young to know."

"I resent that—"

"Don't get angry, little sister . . . Come on, let's read some more—"

And they read on. Kolya Yablochkin had long since taken leave of religion, and under his influence, Manya had too. But the amazing simplicity of Tolstoy's writing, the artlessness of his language, his recounting of the whole story of the Gospels in terms of everyday life and customs, in contrast with the official version of the Church, made everything extremely interesting from beginning to end, and it was with great enthusiasm that the children went through these notebooks which had been copied out painstakingly by someone in lovely calligraphic handwriting.

Kolya Yablochkin was advised to read Chernyshevsky's *What Is to Be Done?* He chose to enjoy this celebrated novel by "the great Russian scholar and critic" all by himself, considering Manya too young for this also. He locked himself up in his room, turned on the light, and in two or three sessions had finished the book, which opened up a whole new world to him. Things went on in this vein: the further you go in the forest, the more wood you find. Kolya Yablochkin had some concept of socialism already, and knew the names of Plekhanov and Lenin by hearsay. The Marxists, the Narodniks, the various parties, the illegal literature—they all swam indistinctly before his eyes, as though seen through murky water. Yet he was drawn to the sharpness and decisiveness of ruthless revolutionary criticism, and to the seriousness, secrecy, and risk.

Kolya Yablochkin also brought home stories of student gatherings and workers circles—and student songs, which circulated widely and were very popular among young people. Sitting on the sofa, Kolya and Manya would sing together under their breath:

How our Klegels, the ge-ne-ral,
Did gather all the ge-en-darmes:
Hey, you dark-blue u-ni-forms,
Search all the apa-art-ments!
They went through every apa-art-ment
But never found "The Sici-li-an."

They sang other songs: "There is in Moscow, the capital, a certain noisy neighborhood"; and "Aristotle, Greece's wise philosopher"; and Yazykov's "From a far-off, distant land . . . ," plus dozens of others, cheerful songs, mocking and challenging ones, and painfully sad ones—songs that student youth sang at parties as their young hearts burned with rebellious joy and, yearning for battle, they felt up to their knees already in the ocean of life.

Thus in the apartment of Mikhail Vasilyevich, a loyal servant of the tsar and the fatherland, a devotee of the church and its saints, sedition had crept in—the extirpation of which was the chief concern of the imperial government. The nest of sedition was Kolya Yablochkin's room, where a separate world had its dominion. The girls, Manya and Sasha, slept in the "children's room"; Kolya Yablochkin had his own room, with a wide sofa instead of a bed; a bookcase where, behind glass doors, stood many wise books with only their spines sticking out; a bedside table in which the little medicine jars and vials were kept. Between two large windows with brown Holland shutters stood a desk that had seen better days. It had a lamp on it, an inkstand, and neatly piled stacks of books. Kolya Yablochkin kept this room of his locked—the key he used was a large, long one, uncomfortable to carry in his pocket. No one but Manya dared go in there; even Mikhail Vasilyevich, passing by in the hallway, would do no more than cast menacingly gloomy glances from under his brows at the locked door of his son's room.

It seemed that even the air in Kolya Yablochkin's room was somehow special: Marya Ivanovna's room smelled of perfume; her husband's study smelled of Valerian drops; the "children's room," of clean white woven blankets; and the hallway, of naphthalene from the large trunk where fur coats and old dresses were kept. In the toilet, which was always well heated, was the smell of kerosene and roaches—huge, black ones, scuttling on the walls, their whiskers waving; the maid said the roaches were a sign of either good luck or the danger of fire.

In Kolya Yablochkin's room, however, there was a complex, mixed odor of boots, leather book bindings, and dusty old paper, as in archival storage rooms. Kolya always stayed locked in his room, as though in a fortress, appearing only at the dinner table, where he ate quickly and silently with a gloomy expression. Because of the constant tension, the wall of mutual hatred that could be felt between father and son, the others also remained silent. Then he would disappear just as quickly and settle back down to his books. Ever so rarely—when his father wasn't home—he would come out into the living room to play with his sisters. They would play skittles, setting them up under the dressing table with the mirror, or they would play tiddley-winks, with little round multicolored discs of bone that you pressed on with a larger disc to try to make them fly into a little wooden cup.

When the brass bell at the front entrance would ring, the children would run to the top of the stairs and look down through the railing to see who was at the door. There were two personages who had earned the children's special attention. One was a distant female relative, a small, dark, exceptionally talkative woman who loved to say spiteful things—Aunt Lipa. If she appeared at the door, the children would rush away from the stairs with shouts of "Lipa, Lipa, the Dwarf Lady!" That was how they expressed their dislike of her. When the local parish priest would arrive to visit their younger sister, Sanya, who was possessed of a certain dreamy religiosity—the priest was fond of this spiritual prodigy, young though she was—Kolya and Manya would shout at the top of their voices: "The priest, the priest!" So that the honorable cassock-wearer, hearing these salutes, would cast his gaze on high and, with his silk robes rustling, make his way to the "children's room" like a thief in the night, with a pretty well rendered mournful expression on his big, slightly cross-eyed face. They really hated this priest, and tried every way they could to make his visits unbearable. But the priest kept stubbornly coming back and simply tried to pass through the danger zone as quickly as possible.

Occasionally two friends from the *gimnaziya* would stop by to visit Kolya Yablochkin; these were the Kunitsa brothers, Vladimir and Lev, two tow-headed lads from Byelorussia. For a while they were getting sustenance at the Yablochkins' because they themselves had nothing to eat. Their father, the manager of a landlord's estate, had been killed on the highway one night either by peasants or by highway robbers; their mother went mad and drowned herself in a pond; and the children were brought to Moscow by relatives, who, through pleading, obtained scholarships for them to the *gimnaziya*. The boys, having passed through fire, water, and the trumpeting of the brass, knew all too well the dark and seamy side of life, and yet they were remarkable for their cheerful and derisive cynicism. They believed in neither God nor the Devil and loved to apply sandpaper to everything in the world, whatever they didn't like or whatever came within range of their sharp tongues.

They were not very handsome, being so pale: they had no eyebrows, and even their eyelashes were yellow. The older boy, Vladimir (nicknamed Volodya), was taller and fairly well built and had a crowded mass of freckles scattered all over his face—just like a sparrow's egg; the younger one, Lev (nicknamed Lyova or Lyovka), was short and hunched over, with narrow, slanted eyes, as though he were Chinese, and his lower lip stuck out, especially when he was displeased with something. The sharp-tongued Kunitsa brothers were not in the habit of expressing themselves modestly; on the contrary, they paraded their verbal naughtiness defiantly.

Having reached adolescence, they resolved all questions in a straightforward, unilinear, radical way, at the same time oversimplifying every-thing to an extreme degree: they viewed oversimplification as a sign of superconsistency. They brought the piercing air of street life into the Yablochkins' home. Marya Ivanovna was a bit fearful of them. Manya was amazed by them, and a lot of what they said, especially when they were laughing and making fun of things, she didn't understand. Kolya Yablochkin had befriended them, but he watched them guardedly lest they blurt out some indecency in his sister's presence.

All in all, the Kunitsa boys were a cheerful pair, and it was strange to hear their laughter in the Yablochkins' apartment, with its pervasive air of depressed spirits, medications, ailments, silence, and family disorder.

"So, Nikolai! You're wearing out the seat of your chair with your rump, eh? Ha, ha, ha." It was Volodya Kunitsa talking. "Come on, let's go out! Let's go for a boat ride, just a little spin—"

"I still have to read twenty more pages for today."

"You 'have to'? You 'have to'!" Volodya teased. "Who ordained this 'have to' for you, the Lord God? Are you carrying out the Lord's com-mandment?"

"I decided myself."

"If you decided, you can change your mind. Are you a man or a machine?" Volodya began shaking Kolya Yablochkin by his skinny shoul-ders. "You confounded Rusk! Dry Crust! You know, really, Nikolai, you shouldn't be thinking about socialism but about going to a monastery: you could spend all your time sitting and reading the *Chetyi Minei.** You could mortify the flesh with the chains monks wear—a good hermit elder could be made out of you, such a dry one, all steam-dried and scrawny, with no meat on the bone. You would acquire exceptional powers—so what if you were rotting and stinking . . . What do you say, huh? Haven't you made a mistake, dear friend, old cove, roach-behind-the-stove. Maybe you really are knocking at the wrong door—"

"That's enough talking nonsense, Vladimir—"

"I'm not talking nonsense. I look at you: you eat well, but your guts aren't strong. You wear clean clothes. You have all the books you want. What brings you to working-class socialism? What's it got to do with you? You don't really know life—you're an old man at an early age, a book mite. Do you really think the workers need such scrawny capabilities?"

"You know what, Vladimir, you better stop running on at the mouth.

---

*Chetyi Minei ("Monthly Readings," or menologia), a collection of biblical sto-ries, saints' lives, and other religous writings, dating from the sixteenth century and organized in twelve volumes, one for each month.

You're not capable now of discussing the question seriously, and I don't like to, nor am I able to, waste my time on mockery. I prefer more productive pursuits."

"Oh, you got me—you got me—you've frightened me. You'll be the death of me. You're so 'su-serious,' so 'cle-ever'—but *can* it, Kolya. Are we going to the Sparrow Hills or not? I ask you: yes or no? And please, drop all the dialectical higgledy-piggledy. Or else Lyovka and I will go find other company to keep: the world's not lacking in fun people. Meanwhile, you sit here and keep your tail end busy; only look out you don't develop hemorrhoids."

The older Kunitsa brother was already reaching for his cap. He shoved it onto the back of his head in a way that immediately gave him a reckless, devil-may-care appearance.

"All right, then, let it be so—," said Kolya Yablochkin, reluctantly separating himself from his chair.

"Please, don't imagine that you're doing us a favor or making a sacrifice for us—if you don't want to go, don't go. But if you go and then start whining, that won't do—Lyovka and I don't sing in a funeral choir and we don't like burial services." Vladimir began imitating a funeral dirge: "I am the lamb that has perished—"

"Call Manya. Why should she rot at home all the time?" said Lyova, who until then had said nothing.

"All right."

Their boots clumping, the three of them exited from Kolya's room.

"Manya, how about going with us for a ride in a rowboat, to the Sparrow Hills?"

"Be right with you. Just let me find a shawl."

Marya Ivanovna came out to find out what the clumping and talking was about. When she heard their plans, she turned to the older Kunitsa brother.

"Vladimir Sergeyich, don't you go drowning my children! I have such fear—"

"Ha, ha, ha! Marya Ivanovna! Lyovka and I were sailing rafts in Byelorussia ever since we were little; we'd get hold of timber on the rivers and go riding the logs. Don't worry, we'll return your precious ones to you completely intact."

"Don't play around on the water, please," Marya Ivanovna continued.

"Stop whimpering, Mama, we're going for a boat ride, not a bloody battle," Kolya Yablochkin said through clenched teeth. He always found it unpleasant in front of his friends to appear in the role of overprotected child, like a greenhorn or a softie.

The four of them went along Polyanka Street, then Yakimanka and the riverside embankment, to the Crimean Bridge. They descended a steep flight of steps to where the boats were. Kolya and Manya felt extremely awkward; they were really ill-adapted to the water, and every time the boat lurched they thought it was about to turn over. The Kunitsas moved around, completely at home, using their legs to balance off any abrupt movements, crawling past each other, putting in the oar locks, trying out the oars, and from the moment they cast off they began splashing around and playing the fool.

"Put the helm to starboard."

"Yes sir, helm to starboard."

And to the powerful strokes of the oars the rowboat sped upriver. On the left was the Bromley plant, on the right the Butikov factory; also, vacant lots and suburban gardens; the white columns of a summerhouse in the Neskuchny Gardens rose up amidst dark foliage, and the Sparrow Hills, covered with woods, showed blue in the distance. Gleaming little water beetles danced around. There was the smell of fish and river mud. A muffled splashing and gurgling was heard against the sides of the boat as it parted the waters with its bow. At the stern the water separated in two shining, clear-cut lines, flowing and playing, and for a long way behind the rowboat the trail of rough water snaked out, leaving its mark on the otherwise unruffled, mirrorlike expanse of the Moscow River as evening approached.

"What are you silent for, as though you were deaf and dumb?" Vladimir shouted, making a wide sweep with his oars and bending his whole body back. "Lyovka, join in!"

Heading down the Vo-olga Ri-iver
Down from Nizhny-y No-ovgo-rod
A we-ell ou-out-fit-ted ve-e-essel
Like an a-ar-row fli-ies along

And like a tuning fork trembling at a high pitch the song's refrain rose into the turquoise sky:

Like an a-ar-row fli-ies along

It was well done. Sung softly. A little sadly. But for that reason to the Kunitsas it wasn't good—or rather, it was good; not bad at all—but they needed to make it clear that, after all, this wasn't their genre. And abruptly breaking off the ancient song about the Volga, Volodya Kunitsa began to sing, tapping his boot on the bottom of the boat:

Prince Oransky went riding
Across the River Po
O, o-o, o-o,
Across the River Po.
To an Astrakhan lady
He uttered a bon mot
O, o-o, o-o,
He uttered a bon mot.

And after going through all the couplets about Aristotle, the Pope in Rome, Julius Caesar, the prophet Elijah, and so on, he belted out some final couplets of recent composition:

The government of Russia
Issued an ukase
Ase, ase-ase, ase-ase
Issued an ukase
That we should be exiled
To our own dwelling place.
Ace, ace-ace, ace-ace
Our own dwelling place.
With this kind of ukase
Us you can't surprise
Ise, ise-ise, ise-ise
Us you can't surprise
To the government of Russia
We will show our fist
Ist, ist-ist, ist-ist
We'll show our fist

The sounds died away. The boat moved forward, with the water softly lapping and slapping underneath.

"So what do you think, Nikolai. Will we have the revolution soon?"

"I don't know. But I do know we'll have it."

"Who's going to make it, do you think? The students, maybe?"

"The workers and peasants, and the students, too, those that are not from the gentry."

"The peasant is someone you don't know. He'll square off your head with a blunt instrument for the tsar's sake. He'll prescribe you a kind of socialism where you won't be able to carry your own shit away—sorry, Manya, I forgot—your hind end away in one piece. You're making judgments based on gentlemen's slobbered-over little books. You go 'Oh!' and

'Ah!' 'Oh, the beloved people! Ah, so long suffering!' But the peasant is greedy. He's a property owner, a beast, and a drunkard. He worships God and the tsar like a dog who licks the whip. And he's the majority in our country. I bust my head over this question all the time. That the Narodnik worshipers of 'the people' are sentimental fools is as plain as two times two is four. Repentant nobles lighting a votive candle before the long-suffering people. You can't get very far with that. Now, the workers—they're made of different stuff. But there's too few of them—that's the problem."

"You're wrong to hand all the peasants over to the tsar. What about the French Revolution? Were all the peasants supporters of the Vendée, eh? You say they're 'devoted to the tsar.' What about Stenka Razin? And Pugachov?* And the peasant rebellions before 1861?† The peasant will rise up. But he needs to be led. And the working class will lead him—that, it seems to me, is the way the Marxists present the problem. I've done some reading on this, but to tell the truth, I don't understand it all. In their literature there are so many references to illegal publications and to tendencies in Western Europe that it's not all clear to me."

"And will you join the revolution yourself?"

"I will when I've learned more."

"Soon?"

"I'll join when I've defined my stand. Sometimes when I read there's nothing but a mass of words; I have to sort it all out, thoroughly."

"Which way you leaning?"

"Well, certainly not toward the liberals. Nekrasov already summed them up perfectly:

But take a look—our Mirabeau
Is thrashing drunken Gavrila
About the face and whiskers
Because of a rumpled jabot.

"I have no tolerance for those gentlemen. As for the Narodniks, they seem to me some kind of Old Believers. They have more feeling than sense. You're partly right in what you say about them: sentimental fools. They also have a certain hidden Slavophilism about them, and I can't stand that kind of Lenten butter. The Marxists are a consistent, educated, revolutionary bunch. Although some sort of disagreements have now begun among them . . . But here, too, I haven't really gotten even a good whiff of what it's all about—what I don't know, I just don't know."

*Leaders of peasant rebellions in the seventeenth and eighteenth centuries.
†Year of the emancipation of the serfs.

"Over at the Molodtsovs' place, Margo told me, they've gotten ahold of Ilyin's pamphlet 'Who the Friends of the People Are' . . . They say it's a rare prize. Haven't you heard about it?"

"No, this is the first I've heard. What's in it?"

"Margo passed along what her brothers had to say, that it's a really brilliant crushing of the Narodniks. It dots all the *i*'s, they say, unlike what's in the legal press."

"You ought to get hold of it."

"Too late. The only way they got it was to give their word they'd only keep it for a day."

"Damn, how annoying! So it's already gone?"

"Apparently."

"Well, we'll have to wait and see. *Qui vivra—verra.*"

"See, Lyovka! Nikolai's talking French already. What are you trying to do, impress us?"

"It's just a saying that fits."

"Now you look here! There are these clowns whose every other phrase is something like *ceteris paribus, mutatis mutandis, sit venia verbo, feci quod potui, errare humanum est,* and so on. I wanta let them have it right in the mug."

"What for?"

"I'll tell you what for. Talk like a human being! We'll make a democrat of you yet—"

"Kolya," said Manya, "You know, sometimes I've listened to you and understood almost nothing you've said. Like Tolstoy's 'big-bellied.' "

"What's that all about?" the two Kunitsa boys pricked up their ears and drilled Manya with their eyes.

"Kolya refused to tell me where pregnancy comes from."

The Kunitsas looked at each other wide-eyed and suddenly began to roar.

"You mean you still don't know where children come from?" Vladimir laughed. "Hey, Lyova! Our sister Marusya has known about it for five years, hasn't she? And what are you—fourteen? Fifteen? Never mind! We'll explain it to you if you want—"

"Drop the subject, Vladimir," said Kolya Yablochkin severely, with an angry look at Kunitsa. "And I would ask you once and for all to abandon the idea of trying to 'enlighten' Manya along these lines. I'm telling you this in all seriousness. More than just seriousness."

An awkward silence followed. Manya's mild eyes looked with perplexity first at her brother, then at his friends; she saw clearly that there was some sort of secret here that would have to be solved without their help.

"Anyhow," said Vladimir, "it's getting dark. Time to turn around. You have to take the good things—a little at a time."

And he began to sing:

Holy God was sailing on the river
Whistling Hallelujah all the way

He leaned on the oars with all his might, and the rowboat shot downstream like an arrow; the water lapped against the hull ever so rapidly and the riverbanks began to move, sliding backward and disappearing behind them . . .

"I could go for something to eat, if the truth were told."

"Come to our house."

"Actually we're obligated to do that: I promised Marya Ivanovna I'd bring you back, almost had to sign a receipt—"

"That's not the point."

"But for me that is the point. And don't go swelling up like a turkey. I'm just joking. And you're getting all serious."

They arrived at the Yablochkins' hungry and tired. The springtime outing had been intoxicating and had sharpened their appetites. But then, the Kunitsa boys were always ready to dig in, and it seemed their starving stomachs knew no bounds.

"Did you all get back safely?" Marya Ivanovna greeted them.

"All well and unharmed. Nothing lost, nothing broken, all arms and legs accounted for," Vladimir saluted as he gave his report.

"Well, then, go have supper."

"That we'll be glad to do, Marya Ivanovna. Without hypocrisy and speaking in vulgar fashion: we're brutally hungry, like wolves; feel like we could eat a cow—tail, horns, and all."

"Enough, enough of your slandering yourselves. Go and eat. But wash your hands! Have a moment's patience to do that!"

The young teeth and jaws worked quickly. "The feeding of the beasts" Marya Ivanovna jokingly called it, glad that Kolya and Manya were eating and not sitting glumly at the table.

"We are grateful to you, Marya Ivanovna, that you have satiated us with your worldly goods."

"Don't be blasphemous."

"Never. In neither word nor thought. But could I ask for some tea? With lemon?"

"Please. Want it stronger?"

"How'd you guess?"

"Take some cookies. There's cherry jam. Don't be bashful."

"No one has ever accused us of that sin, Marya Ivanovna. Ha, ha, ha," Vladimir rumbled, emptying glass after glass.

"Manya, will you play something with me?" Lyova turned to her. "If so, I'll run home and get my violin. Or are you awfully tired?"

"With pleasure, Lyova. In the meantime I'll lie down and rest a bit."

Lyova ran headlong home for his violin, and Manya lay down to take a rest.

"Tired, daughter?" Marya Ivanovna came over to her. "It's impossible to wear you out though. Even when you can barely crawl, just like me."

In those days Marya Ivanovna was suffering from angina and from agoraphobia; she was afraid to be out on the streets, in city squares, in large open spaces, or on high stairways; her head would spin, and she might faint in the middle of a crowd. If she had to go even a few paces on foot, she would hold onto a wall, as blind people do. And she transferred her fears to her children: she fancied that for them to cross an open square was the same kind of torture as for her. For that reason she was always worried about the children: she constantly imagined all sorts of accidents, and she never knew a moment's peace when the children were out. To be sure, the children worried about their mother as well: once when she went to the Crimea for the summer at the doctor's insistence, they anxiously waited through each long day for news of her and were beside themselves with joy when she returned, alive, healthy, tan, and greatly improved by her time under the southern sun. For the girls, the seashells she brought them were considered virtually sacred objects, veritable fetishes, so greatly did they love their mama.

Lyova came running back quickly. Under his arm was his violin and a round black cardboard tube with sheet music. He was fussing about in the front hallway for a long time, taking his violin out of its case, rearranging himself, glancing sidelong at himself in the mirror; then he appeared in the living room (it was also the dining room, where the piano was), wiping the sweat from his brow—where a lock of straight reddish-gold hair was hanging down.

"Well, I'm ready, Manya. What shall we play. Want to do some Brahms?"

"What exactly? I don't know him very well."

"The Hungarian dances?"

"All right."

Lyova stood by the piano like a little gnome. But as soon as the first sounds rang out his face was transformed: his cheeks blazed, his eyes took on a kind of inspired expression, and tiny beads of sweat stood out on his brow. He became a very special person, who knew something the others didn't know, who felt something the others didn't feel, who saw and heard something the others didn't see or hear. His fingers and hand moved with devilish speed. His whole body was taut, as though an unknown force had taken possession of him, and he found himself entirely at the mercy of its unbridled power as it molded him with its fingers, shook him, and played with him. One moment he turned deathly pale; the next, bright red. Then his face was covered with blotches. You could see that he was trembling from head to toe. At the same time his arm was moving all in a fury, and a whirlwind of dancing, passionate sound flew out from under his violin bow, with the speed of lightning.

Manya watched him with amazement. The music took hold of her as well and twisted her about, and Lyova's emotion was imparted to her. Her eyes grew wider and darker than ever. She felt exhausted, as though a vampire was draining her of all her blood; but she didn't feel pain, she felt blissful, and she was willing to expire in the moment, to be transformed into nothingness, to dissolve and float away on the ocean of sound. She wanted to kiss that reddish-gold forelock on Lyova's not so pretty forehead—so plain to her was his elevation of spirit.

The sounds broke off.

"I can't anymore, Lyova. I'm deathly tired. Thank you, Lyovochka."

And she ardently pressed his hand.

Nikolai Yablochkin went away for the summer to work as a tutor in Voronezh Province. Vladimir Kunitsa also went away to study. Lyova remained in Moscow; only for economy's sake, he moved to another, still more miserable little room in a building densely populated by the poor. The Yablochkin family, according to their custom, went to stay with Grandfather for the summer vacation. The dressing room of the bathhouse there smelled, as it always had, of mint and birch leaves. The prickly raspberry vines grew as thick as ever, their aromatic berries—red and amber yellow—were easy to remove from the soft, white stamens, and they melted in the mouth. One day, when Manya had worked her way into a raspberry patch and was picking these ripe, sweet-smelling berries with her slender little hands, selecting the biggest and best, her name was called.

"A letter for you, Miss."

The letter addressed to her in clean, neat writing contained a mathematically exact description of the new room where Lyova had taken up residence, the number of pages he had read, and his plans for the future. Every week from then on Manya received just as clean, neat, exact, and outwardly dry-seeming letters.

Then, toward autumn, news came from Lyova that Vladimir had been arrested somewhere in Poltava Province.

Chapter 16

When Kolya Petrov and his brother returned from their summer with Mikhal Samoilych, having said good-bye to paints and painting, to Sasha, to the squirrels, the rabbit, the cages, and country life in general, Kolya found himself in his third year at the *gimnaziya* and, at home, in the midst of the chirping and squalling of children and generally crowded conditions. At school that year a crack visible to all appeared in the system of "classical" education and grew into a veritable abyss: compulsory instruction in classical Greek was canceled. Nevertheless Kolya signed up for Greek, just as he did for drawing.

For the first year the teaching of Greek as an optional course was assigned to Vladimir Aleksandrovich Sokolov, the Russian language and literature teacher. In order to whet the appetites of the students for the "divine speech of the Hellenes," Sokolov started right in, as soon as the necessary information in basic grammar had been provided, having the students read Lucian's *Dialogues of the Gods* and *Dialogues of the Dead*, in which, as is generally known, quite a few passages contain double entendre and outright indecencies, although they are often quite witty and clever. In general, this was Vladimir Aleksandrovich's favorite method: when he made an excursion into Western European literature, he invariably quoted from Goethe's *Roman Elegies*, especially the priapic elegy; when he gave lessons in Russian literature he would read Bogdanovich's poem "Dushenka"* off the blackboard with appropriate commentaries and would soon have the whole class rolling in the aisles. Still, it must be said that, together with this hot sauce, Sokolov pursued a systematic course of instruction, and did so fairly well.

*For Bogdanovich and his poem, see glossary.

It's true that the readers he used were full of the most boring, quasi-"Hellenic" exhortations about "virtue," "training for citizenship," "love of wisdom," and similar matters, but this had to be accepted as an unalterable fact of school life. The lessons proceeded in an atmosphere free of constraint. And in this connection, Kolya dredged up from the storerooms of his memory the *Aeneid* by Kotlyarevsky (while in Bessarabia he had found, in an attic, several small volumes of works by this Ukrainian author), and with Sokolov's encouragement, Kolya quoted some verses he knew by heart:

> Aeneas, the *magnus panus*
> And glorious king of the *Trojanorum*,
> Sailing the seas, like a Gypsy,
> Sent us to you, o worthy Czech.
> *Rogamus, Domine latine:* (We ask, o Latin lord,)
> Let not our *caput* (chief) perish.
> *Dimitte* (Dismiss us) from your land,
> Whether for *pecuniae* (money) or gratis.
> The students especially enjoyed such lines as these:
> But Juno, a real bitch's daughter,
> Started to cackle like a setting hen.

The whole class was in raptures over the "bringing down to earth" of an illustrious mythological figure.

One of Sokolov's good qualities was that, in passing, he provided a wide range of information from the history of the Greco-Roman world, and his colorful stories often contributed more toward an understanding of that world than the official part of the lesson. In general, while Sokolov to a certain extent corrupted the students with his frivolities, at the same time he tore some rents in the uniform of officialdom and, without even realizing it, undermined the system of decorous bureaucratic formalism, although to do so by no means entered into his calculations.

Kolya developed a great liking at this time for his drawing lessons, which were given at the school by the artist Kravkov, brother of the wife of a well-known "legal Marxist" and man of letters, V. M. Shulyatikov, who later won rather sorry fame with his *Justification of Capitalism in Western European Philosophy*. Kolya dreamed of having a set of paints, and suddenly they came into his life: his uncle Yevgeny Antonych gave him a wonderful present—five whole rubles—and he resolved right then and there to acquire the basic capital necessary to an artist.

In Moscow, located on Tverskaya Street, next to the famous English Club, with its massive pillars and magnificent, courtly lions guarding the gates, a structure celebrated by so many poets, stood the art store of A. Mo. A bell had been attached to the door so that when it opened a kind of sorry, broken-down jangle was given off down below. To reach the store from the street, one had to climb a narrow flight of wooden stairs between walls completely covered with paintings hanging in massive frames: there were landscapes, portraits, and genre studies—and all of them had been hanging there for many years, waiting in vain for a buyer.

In general, some sort of sad, maybe even grisly, secret hovered over this store—it was as though it had stepped right out of the pages of E.T.A. Hoffmann's fairy tales: everything was deathly still, as though under a spell. Sitting behind the counter on a low stool was the owner, a partially paralyzed invalid, apparently an Italian, with long hair, large protuberant eyes, and a big, greasy nose; he was short in stature and spoke in low, mumbling incoherent sounds; his whole body, even when he was sitting erect on his stool, was always in motion, the long, thin fingers on his spider-hands shook, and his face twitched; in short, he was always dancing the painful dance of St. Vitus. Working as salesman on the floor was another Italian, tall, bald, with a graying beard, clear eyes, and the softest voice imaginable; his manner was characterized by a uniquely stilted refinement, as though he were a visitor from some other world and was politely carrying out functions here that in fact were completely alien to him: there was nothing pushy, nothing loud—he would move along deliberately, take out paints, brushes, and boxes, and lay them on the counter—and he would do all this like some woeful shade, with a sad soft voice coming from beyond the grave.

Kolya had been directed to this store by Mikhal Samoilych, and it occurred to the boy immediately and came clear to him instinctively that there was a subtle, indefinable tie between the soft-spoken artist who sang psalms softly to himself and the quiet store of Mr. Mo—a connection quite far removed from the hustle and bustle of everyday life. Kolya himself, by his entire makeup, was far removed from this kind of pallid deathliness. But he liked the delicate atmosphere and the absence of any commercialism: the paints were shown to him in such a courteous way, he was advised on which were the better kind to choose, and their qualities and characteristics were explained precisely, with consideration given to the amount he was able to pay. As a result, for a number of years he became a regular visitor to this peculiar store.

There were other art stores in Moscow: one on the Arbat whose sign read "City of Nizza: Vendors of Paintings and Frames." (Kolya had the habit of reading signs backward and was overjoyed to discover that two of the large words on this sign—the Russian for "city" [*gorod*] and the Russian for "of frames" [*ramok*]—when spelled backward produced *komar dorog*, or "Mosquito of the Roads"), but you couldn't always find what you wanted in that store; then, on Kuznetsky Most, there were the famous stores of Avanzo and Daziaro, with their luxurious show windows, in front of which there was always a dapper, foppish crowd ogling the merchandise, but those stores were so expensive that Kolya couldn't bring himself to even cross their thresholds. Thus he remained loyal to the odd little store on Tverskaya.

Winter came. The meager pay of a school guard did not suffice for the Petrovs: theirs was a large family, and there were debts to repay, besides; Ivan Antonych was in fact up to his ears in debt. And so Kolya's parents decided, following the example of others, to offer tutoring for children wishing to take the entrance examinations for the *gimnaziya* and for the Komissarovka; they would bring their prospective clients into their own home. It was at his workplace that Ivan Antonych was first advised to do this—not only because he was an excellent teacher and his wife had teaching experience, too, but also because at his job he was obliged to do nothing more than watch over the behavior of the pupils and serve as chief monitor for the maintenance of order. The director of the school himself recommended several pupils. Thus it was done. They borrowed money and rented a large apartment on Protochny Lane, near the Smolensk market, a shabby, rather cold and depressing place. They moved there with all their belongings and took in three children, including one nearly full-grown boy, Vanya Vasenko, a former seminarian whom Ivan Antonych undertook to tutor in mathematics in preparation for the junior year at the Komissarovka.

Vasenko had sniffed at all the flowers of seminarian "culture"—fully in the spirit of Pomyalovsky's book *The Seminarians* (*Bursy*). He had been smoking for quite a while and his jagged teeth were yellowed with nicotine. Sometimes he also drank a little vodka, purchasing the small bottles called "little scoundrels," and he knew how to pop the corks out of them skillfully by slapping his palm against the bottom full force. He usually did this after a trip to the bathhouse, and when he arrived home, as he carefully combed his still-wet hair in front of the mirror, the smell of alcohol exuded from him. He quickly filled Kolya in on several intricate aspects of life. He told about Peter the Great introducing public houses, the so-called *bardaki*, into Russia; about the seminarians visiting these institutions; about anointing oils and unguents, the "dark" kind and the "ecumenical"; about a notorious seminarians' song of a priest's daughter, the only printable lines of which were these:

I sat with the priest's daughter under the stairs

And fed the priest's daughter—my hairs.

At first Kolya listened with eyes popping, but later he added this to his list of life's tricks and deceptions that grown-ups like to engage in, in this world.

On holidays he got in the habit of running over to use the library at the Rukavishnikovsky Shelter for Juvenile Delinquents. On Haymarket Square, near the Smolensk Market, there was located a dark brick building where these "delinquents" were held, and sometimes they were brought out for walks, lined up two by two. Their heads shaven and wearing greatcoats of coarse dark-blue material and absurdly large visored caps coming down over their ears, their faces pale with a greenish tinge and rapidly darting, puffy eyes, they would march down the sidewalk—like a dark-blue snake crawling along—looking around as though they expected to be pinched or punched at any moment from any direction.

In this shelter there was a library open to the public, and since it was only a five-minute walk from the Petrovs' apartment, Kolya took a great liking to it. In the silence of its reading rooms he devoured the dog-eared and sweat-stained pages of books by Gustave Aimard and James Fenimore Cooper. He discovered this library—and learned that anyone could go in and use it—from a sign on the door, which he had had occasion to run past many times.

The Petrovs did not live on Protochny Lane for long: the apartment turned out to be so damp and cold that the walls dripped and everything was covered with a wet, repulsive mildew and green slime; there was a danger that both they and their boarders might get sick. In the spring, after searching, examining, and appraising a number of other places, they moved to a building owned by a man named Blokhin off Georgiyevskaya Square in the Bolshiye Gruziny district. The merchant Blokhin's property consisted of a large plaster building, fairly ancient and cracking, and three wooden outbuildings scattered about the lot. It was into one of these that the Petrovs moved with their boarders, the tutoring students. The lot had a slope to it, and the little wooden outbuilding, painted an ocher color, had one story in the front, but in the back, nearly two: for under the first floor was a semi-basement. In the backyard stood barns and cattle sheds, long in need of repair.

Blokhin's property was inhabited by quite a varied assortment of types. In the main building lived the enormous family of the engineer Nemtsov, who had so many children that it seemed he was running a boarding house. The largest outbuilding was inhabited by some sort of government officials, who left for work early every morning and were never seen about the grounds. In the smallest outbuilding, which was built against a fence and consisted of only one room and a kitchen, lived an elderly clerk of the town governor's office, Ivan Flegontych, who was always busying himself in his little garden, where for almost two decades he had been cultivating wild grapes with skillfully clipped and neatly tied and arranged clusters; this microscopic garden was filled out with beds of roses, asters, stocks, and all sorts of other flowers, which for Ivan Flegontych, aside from his government office, were all the world he knew. The old man wore steel-rimmed glasses and had a pop-eyed, gray-haired wife; she wore the same kind of glasses he did, and would run around the yard, fat, dumpy woman that she was, hanging wet laundry on the line. What was particularly noteworthy about her was her unusually high, thin, squeaky voice.

The year the Petrovs moved into Blokhin's she surprised the inhabitants by unexpectedly, in light of her advanced age, giving birth to a child. For a long time this was the subject of passionate discussion, gossip, hypotheses, guesses, and old wives' definitive observations of the type: "It's God's will in everything."

The semi-basement was rented by a milkman, a crooked little old man with a turned-up button that was the only thing left of his nose, large gray eyes, above which great bushes were hanging for eyebrows, and a patchy beard; in all respects he was broken, twisted, deformed; one shoulder was higher than the other, one leg shorter than the other; one eye was looking at us, the other at Arzamas. He spoke through his nose, while quietly moving his wrinkled, work-calloused hands. The expression on his face was sad and kind: it was as though he were carrying life's heavy cross and knew he was doomed for eternity. He looked like an old worm-eaten root of a tree or a gnome pulled out of the ground who hasn't had a chance to shake himself off. For whole days he would busy himself with straw, manure, and hay; it seemed that the pitchfork never left his hand. He kept a cow in a shed, and it was the breadwinner for the whole family. He lived by selling its milk, as well as its manure for fertilizer, and he rented part of the basement to a master shoemaker. The milkman was a widower, who had two daughters: one was still a little girl, but the other—a snub-nosed, big-eyed, big-breasted young woman named Arisha—had the reputation around the courtyard of "going with boys" and "having a weakness for the front of the carriage."

The custodian's wife, the maids, and the wives of the government officials kept up a greedy surveillance over Arisha; they were constantly tormented by the question of whether she was "going with" someone.

"Ugh! That big-breasted thing has gone and powdered her nose again—"

"Disgusting!"

"Why doesn't her father get hold of her by the braids?"

"Where's he gonna get the strength for that? He's barely alive as it is. As for her—she's just busting out all over."

"Arishka! Cover up your breasts, you shameless thing!"

"What business is it of yours? You'd better just sit there and pick at your fleas."

"Ooh, you brazen hussy!"

"That's what I'm hearing from . . . Go on, keep yelping away . . . The wind blows and the dogs howl."

Vasily the shoemaker, who had rented part of the cellar from the milkman, sat with his awl, his last, and his waxed thread in front of the window, which was kept open in the summer, and cut leather for heels and soles with his shoe knife, sharp as a razor, bending his curly blond head to the side. His skinny, sunken, tubercular chest would emit a hoarse, prolonged cough and he would clear his throat and spit with desperation, holding his sides, as though trying to keep in place his ailing lungs that were about to burst. He had one journeyman and one boy "on apprenticeship." The apprenticeship consisted in the boy's being awarded blows, manhandled, and knocked around; he was regularly sent for vodka, and on any occasion was roundly denounced with the foulest language. Sometimes when the older ones were drunk, they would trounce him so thoroughly that it took a long time for the black-and-blue marks to fade away.

"What did they beat you so badly for?" he was asked by the milkman's girlfriend, Marfusha, a pockmarked woman well on in years who washed floors. She lisped so badly that she seemed to be talking bird language or Mexican; all her words had extra *tl*s in them, as in such Mexican names as Popocatepetl and Quetzl-Coatl—so from the very first the Petrov boys called her "Tlevo-Tle-Tlya."

"No reason. Just because," the lop-eared Vanya answered gloomily; he was blamed for everything that happened in life.

"Real-tly?"

"What do you think? I'm just talking air?"

"They're like King Herod, the way they mutilate that boy," the milkman would mutter, but he never protested openly: after all, the shoemaker was a paying tenant.

Vasily the shoemaker, however, felt crushed; he was amazed that he could have given the boy such bad bruises. When he was sober he was a kind and conscientious man, but when he was drunk he completely forgot himself and brawled like a madman. "Our Vaska gets awful wild when he's had a few," his friends said about him, but that didn't prevent them from egging him on to spend his last kopeck on drink.

Next to Blokhin's property was a house with a grand old park of linden trees, the home of Lady Makhova, a colonel's widow. The leaves of the hundred-year-old linden trees rustled softly, and around their roots was a thick growth of thorny dogrose. Where flower beds had once been, mounds remained, overgrown with nettles and burdock. The fences were full of yawning holes, and the few full-length boards still surviving stuck out here and there, pierced by old rusty nails. The house itself opened onto the street and constituted a bizarre spectacle. It was completely dilapidated, gloomy, and half in ruins, with a blackened iron roof and windows that hadn't been washed for decades, reflecting all the colors of the rainbow. Behind one of these windows there sat—all dressed up and covered with rouge, with cheeks of carmine red, a blue nose, and bright red lips, wearing a lace cap—an ancient, wrinkled, repulsive woman, like a caricature of a mannequin, like Pushkin's *Princesse Moustache*, risen from the grave and covered with dirt. This was Lady Makhova, the colonel's widow herself. She never went out of the house, and what went on inside no one knew. Also living there were an elderly caretaker and a vicious dog, huge and half-starved, that would rush, barking furiously, at boys who climbed over the fence into Makhova's park.

On the other side of Blokhin's property was a small Armenian church, behind which a large garden stretched, with a gully in which there grew ancient and spreading white willows, as well as a whole grove of young aspens with their quaking leaves. Along the edge of the Armenian garden, on the side away from the street, a brick fence had been built, and beyond it was a huge vacant lot, the property of wealthy merchants, the Medyntsevs, and the lot was simply called "the Medynka." Sprouting up on one side of it were shacks where beggars and thieves lived: pickpockets, burglars, and representatives of other specialties. Adjoining on the other side of the "Medynka" were the small alleys and cul-de-sacs of Vladimir Dolgoruky Street, known colloquially as the "Zhivodyorka" (One who skins creatures alive). There was only one street in Moscow that could compete with the Zhivodyorka, and that was the notorious "Drachyovka," which was solidly populated by prostitutes.

On the Zhivodyorka were many small shops; their owners were often highly experienced fences, secondhand clothing dealers and ragmen, prostitutes, and burglars. There were suspicious "family bathhouses with separate rooms," used clothing stores, soap peddlers, taverns for peasants bringing hay into the city, and tea shops, open at night, where they served tea kettles full of vodka—all this made up a flashy, multicolored heap. Here, especially at night, not only could you get the skin of a live dog but also of—a live human being. Not for nothing was this street called Zhivodyorka.

In the evenings, onto the pavements, there came from out of their rotting dens the most miserable, ancient, worn down, and ailing prostitutes, in their cups, wearing bruises, with their hair all tangled and instead of human voices, just rasping and hissing. These mounds of half-rotten female flesh found customers for themselves among the drunken horsecab drivers, the beggars who had drunk up their day's take, or peasants from the countryside who had lost consciousness after being worked over in the foulest haunts and dens of Moscow's lower depths. Here there was constant cursing, someone being thrown out of a tavern, someone roaring in a drunken voice, songs being sung in guttural abandon. Only a dim light came from the street lamps, and there was the smell of sour beer, throwup, and strawberry soap.

Such was the *Hinterland* of the Bolshaya Gruzinskaya district. On Georgiyevskaya Square itself a large church rose up. In front of it a public garden had been laid out. Nursing mothers with infants sat there, and nannies looked after their charges in red, blue, and yellow clothing, digging in the sand box, making mud pies and little gardens by sticking green branches in the dirt, quite unconcerned with the big problems of existence.

When Kolya and Volodya looked around the new place they were overjoyed: all the preconditions for bird trapping were there. In Makhovka's park and in the Armenian garden various species of titmouse were hopping about, on the burdock the prickly heads of goldfinches and greenfinches were pecking at shells, and the redpolls were hanging on old birch catkins—in a word, the opportunity here was undeniable. There was also an attic: they could raise pigeons there. (Ivan Antonych himself had been a great pigeon fancier in his youth.) They enticed him into the project. And soon from the market at the Truba they brought back a bird trap, some birds in cages, and a whole basketful of racing pigeons of various kinds. Work in the attic proceeded apace: a dovecote was built, and nesting places, and also a spring trap with a net for catching "interlopers." Kolya immediately mastered the technique of getting onto the roof and was soon crawling right alongside the gutters, bringing Marya Ivanovna to tears: it always seemed to her that he was about to fall and hurt himself.

"Well, Kolyun, are you satisfied?" Ivan Antonych asked him, looking up from below at the completed dovecote.

"Yes, you know I am."

"And you've already forgotten Kholodkovsky and his 'Living Things of the Sea'?"

"I haven't forgotten anything. Only it's much nicer here than it was on Protochny Lane. No comparison."

"Of course. But we don't have a chasing pole."

"I'll get one."

"Where?"

"From the Armenian watchman. I saw he had one lying around in his barn not being used. So give me a twenty-kopeck piece, and that'll be all we need."

Kolya got the twenty kopecks and soon ran back all puffed up with a large pole. Now the dovecote was equipped with all the accoutrements.

"Kolya!" Volodya shouted, sticking his head out the attic window. "Come here!"

Kolya climbed up to the attic. It was dry and dusty there. You had to bend your head so as not to hit it against the rafters, which had nails sticking out here and there. The pigeons were milling about in the dovecote, making their mincing little steps. They hadn't yet settled down in their new place, but were diligently filling their craws with birdseed, fluttering among the rafters, and greedily drinking the clean water in the saucer.

"Kolya, look at this purebred—"

Volodya had fished out one pigeon from among the rest and was holding it in the manner of a true pigeon fancier, so that its feet stuck down through his fingers. He turned it in all directions.

"Do you see its beak? And neck? And feathers?"

"Yeah. It's just a pigeon, nothing special."

"Are we gonna start adding to them soon? Look, what a flock—over there, to the left."

In the sky, flashing like little white stars, spreading out one moment, bunching up the next, a flock of "interlopers" was flapping about.

"No hurry—they're going back to their old haunts. Better that we wait a while. We'll start later, all right?"

"All right."

The people and the pigeons were making themselves at home in their new place.

Chapter 17

Neo-Malthusianism was not the way of the Petrov family, and as summer approached, another child arrived—a girl this time, who "in a christening of sorts" was given the name Yekaterina, or Katya for short.

And so it was that with a horde of children, plus several pupils who were being tutored—quite a wagon train!—the Petrovs moved to the village of Legchishchevo for summer vacation. Actually for the older generation there was no vacation: both Lyubov Ivanovna, nursing her newborn, and Ivan Antonych worked all the time now, knowing nothing of summer breaks or holidays of any kind: it was precisely on days off or during the summer that they had to put special effort into the job of preparing their charges; thus they were forever busy with spelling, dictation, math problems, German, and all sorts of other subjects.

Legchishchevo, a village near the rail station Lopasnya, had been recommended to them by one of the teachers at the Aleksandro-Mariyinsky Academy, a great drunkard and a burnt-out case, a mediocre individual, on the level of a village psalm reader, whose entire arsenal of wit was exhausted when at school, for example, he would recite some lines of verse:

> Our colonel was a born success,
> A loyal servant to the tsar
> And a father to his soldiers.

But he would alter the last line to say:

> A *chamberpot* for his soldiers

In reciting this he would titter and giggle in a hoarse and jarring voice, blinking his bleary, clouded little eyes. (He saw this as an act of great dar-

ing, and he did it as a way of showing up another teacher who, when reading a passage from Nikitin's *Coachman*—"he wasn't afraid of the Devil
himself, and when he flew along in his coach even the clouds were
amazed"—would change "the Devil himself" to the more prim and proper
"anyone.") In Legchishchevo, the teacher who recommended the place
had a relative, the village priest—and it was from him that the Petrovs
rented a cottage for themselves, along with a second one, where their
pupils were housed.

For the Petrovs, the summer turned out to be a foul and unhappy one.
Not that the weather was bad. No, the sun shone brightly and warmed
everything up. The green of the forests beckoned, as it always had. Playful
flecks of sunlight danced on the river. Birds sang. Berries grew in abundance. And there were plenty of mushrooms. But from the very beginning
of summer, whooping cough appeared among the Petrov children. They
had to be quarantined from the tutoring students. The unfortunate Petrov
boys were tormented by prolonged, wracking bouts of coughing: Kolya
and Andryusha or Volodya would go off into the woods and start filling
themselves up with wild strawberries: you'd look around and a moment
later someone would start whooping and groaning, standing there with
eyes bulging, filled with tears, and he would be heaving, barely able to
catch his breath from the torture of coughing.

The illness took hold of all the Petrov children, but Katya suffered especially—tiny, red-faced doll that she was—she cried, grimaced, tossed
about, and then one day, not a fine day by any means, she fell silent. Forever.

They buried her in the village cemetery, under some currant bushes, by
a low blue-gray fence. Lyubov Ivanovna wept bitterly at night. But she got
a grip on herself and stoically continued to work with her pupils. The boys
looked about in dismay and didn't know what to think. They continued
to cough, choke, and gasp, holding onto their chests for dear life. Sometimes they became totally indifferent to the world: it didn't matter if the
sun was shining or a cold rain falling and the wind ripping the heavy gray
clouds to shreds. What difference did it make when the world was so
unkind to you and you were being turned inside out, all your innards coming out through your eyes and mouth? The world seemed to have gone
murky and twisted, become agonizing and absurd; the boys perceived it
through tears and heaving spells that were endless and unendurable. Kolya
remembered, once in Bessarabia, seeing a rabbit being skinned. It had
been nailed to a door and its skin was removed the way a stocking comes
off your foot, leaving a bloody, blue and red body hanging there with terrible bulging eyes. It seemed to Kolya, when a fit of coughing would turn

him inside out, that he was that rabbit. Worst of all, you only had to think about coughing and a fit would start. When would it ever end? Maybe never?

Toward autumn one of the tutoring students was visited unexpectedly by his grown-up brother, a drunkard and debaucher whose face bore an amazing likeness to that of the poet Aleksei Konstantinovich Tolstoy—but gone to seed and turned insolent. He quickly established a rapport with the teacher and priest, and began to drink like a fish and get into brawls. Once he came across several coils of telegraph wire and unwound them all over the village. He would fire at the songbirds with a shotgun and make passes at the village girls—and there was no way to make him stop. All this only intensified the impression of the absurdity of life, and it seemed to Kolya, as he was convulsed with spasms, that the whole world had fallen sick along with him.

The summer passed like a bad dream: there one moment, gone the next. Katya's death was forgotten. After all, there hadn't been time to get to know her, any more than she had been able to know herself. The whooping cough also went its way.

They all found themselves once again on Bolshaya Gruzinskaya Street, and normal life resumed: school, pigeons, books, birds, Latin, math, the school desk and school bag—everything began to move in the traditional orbits. The only unusual thing was that one day Kolya was given two marmots as a gift, which he housed "for the time being" in his father's office, despite his father's protests. Just by chance the next day Mikhal Samoilych spent the night in there on the sofa, and in the morning his socks were missing. The search for them went under the sofa—the marmots had stolen them. The socks were floating in a small green-and-black puddle with a not very tantalizing aroma. There arose a hue and cry. One of the marmots slipped out—with Kolya right after it. The marmot ran across the yard and plunged into the Medyntsevs' property. Kolya went over the fence, caught up with the marmot, grabbed it by its fat back and carried it home. At the very last moment the marmot twisted around and took a healthy bite out of Kolya's thumb—leaving a piece of flesh dangling. Kolya howled in pain and rushed to his father. His father waved his hands helplessly—he couldn't stand the sight of blood—and giving Kolya a silver ruble, told him to run to the doctor. Kolya ran next door, leaving a bloody trail as he went, but the doctor wasn't in. Then, after binding his thumb in a handkerchief, he ran to the Zoological Garden, near which, by the police station, was a clinic, and he burst in there. The doctor put a bandage on his wound and made the following entry in his records: "Profession: high school student, First Boys School. Ailment: marmot bite."

Suddenly the reign of winter had come again. Out on the streets the kids would hitch rides on the wide, low sledges called *rozvalni* that passed by, sometimes getting as far as the Zoological Garden, or even Kudrino Street, before the drivers would catch on and chase them away. Tying a skate with rope to one foot and pushing and hopping with the other, they would slide over the ice-covered snow or, after a running jump, go speeding down the icy paths on the sidewalk cleared of snow by the passage of many felt boots. In the public garden they would build huge snow figures, rolling big lumps of soft snow, and it felt good to mash it together in freezing hands, warming them up later inside one's sleeves or in torn mittens from which red fingers protruded.

For eyes they stuck coals in the snow figure's "head," sometimes adding a carrot for a nose, and the little children, all bundled up and accompanied by their nannies, would come awkwardly crowding around, their eyes wide open with surprise, putting out their hands to touch the snowy giant.

"Nanny, Nanny! What're those?"

"Eyes."

"Real ones?"

"No, pieces of coal."

"Why?"

"To make it look more alive."

"Could you make a thing like that yourself?"

"Yeah, I could."

"Then why haven't you made one for us?"

"No time."

"But I want one."

"You don't want much, do you? How about some bird's milk?"

"Bird's?"

"Yeah, bird's."

"I want some. I want some bird's milk."

"Well, there isn't any such thing. Whaddya think, have you ever seen a chicken givin' milk?"

"No."

"Well, there you are. But you wanted some. It doesn't exist—and that's all there is to it."

"But why?"

"Why, why, why—you'll know plenty once you grow up. Let's go walk somewhere else now. I'm freezing, you know, from standing still in one place—"

"Hey, Nanny," the boys who made the snowman shouted. "What were you saying? About chickens being milked and cows laying eggs?"

"Enough out of you, bad boys! Come on, Fedya, let's go. Don't you have to pee-pee?"

"Hey, gang! Let's hop on the sledges!"

And this horde of holy terrors would rush over to the passing sledges, jumping onto them, chest first, right into the hay.

"Awa-ay we go!"

In the small front yard the Petrov boys made a high hill of snow and poured water over it to turn it to ice. In the evenings they would slide down it on toboggans and skates, speeding across the yard and around the side of the house, which connected with the backyard, their momentum carrying them all the way to the Medyntsevs' vacant lot. The only problem was that you had to be careful, at that high speed, not to bang your head on the fence or on something jutting out from the house. The whole crowd of them—Kolya, Volodya, Andryusha, and the tutoring students— would go clamoring outside and play till dark, skating, falling, squealing, laughing, and then, all red in the face, sweaty, torn, and covered with snow, come bursting back into the house, take off their coats, have some tea, then study and go to sleep.

On holidays they undertook great bird-catching expeditions. In the corner of the Armenian garden was a patch of burdock, and there, too, was a gate in the stone fence, a closed wooden gate full of holes: if you climbed over the fence and made a place for yourself next to this gate on the other side, the burdock thicket would be just two steps away and you could watch all the birds: goldfinches, greenfinches, redpolls, bullfinches, titmice, blue tits. Suspecting nothing, the birds would be pecking at seeds, hopping and clambering among the branches of the burdock bush. This is where the boys set their traps and snares, and then, barely breathing, lest the steam of their breath show through the gate, with hearts pounding, poking and prodding one another to be quiet, they would watch through the holes in the gate.

A titmouse had landed by the door of the trap. It looked craftily at the hemp seed bait. Now it's going to fall for it. No! What a clever bird—it stuck its blue and black little head under the triggering device, pulled out a seed, and fluttered away—now it was sitting on a bough, with the seed tightly held in its feet, drilling away at it with its beak. It flew back. Clap! It was in the trap. Now it wouldn't escape: it was thrashing about, scattering hemp seed, and chattering hoarsely at the stuff. The boys made not a sound. There would always be time to go get the titmouse: but right now a beautiful, fat, red-breasted bullfinch was hopping about next to a noose, occasionally pecking seeds and making inviting little peeps. It made a quick upward flutter. Was it going to fly away? How annoying! It would alarm the whole flock. Then it flew down onto the snow again. It was pecking at something. What a clean, fresh-looking bird—all its little feathers well-matched, not like the worn, frayed birds you'd buy at the Truba.

"Look, Kolya, it keeps getting closer," Volodya whispered.

"Quiet, blast you! You'll scare it away!" Kolya answered with great irritation, making expressive signs with his hands as if to say: Keep making noise, and I'll twist your head off.

The bullfinch was already sitting on the noose. Pecking at the hemp seeds, pecking them open, you could see, from the hulls falling about. Then apparently it sensed something wrong; it lifted one foot. Taking fright suddenly, it made a burst for freedom. But too late! With wings spread wide, it was making great exertions, in vain: the horsehair loop firmly held its leg.

"Quick! Hurry! Before he dislocates his leg."

The boys ran, like half mad creatures, scrambling over the fence and rushing back along it by a path that local dogs and they themselves had battered down. Then triumphantly they carried home their catch.

One day, arriving home from work, Ivan Antonych called Kolya into his office: "The Slavyanskys have come. They telephoned me at the Komissarovka."

"Is that true, Papa? You're not lying?"

"Why would I lie? How foolish you can be! Here's their address."

Out of his side pocket Ivan Antonych pulled a crumpled piece of paper on which there was written in pencil an address: Number such-and-such, Arbat Street, Apartment 7.

"Did Tosya come too?"

"Yes, Tosya too."

"Oh, that's great! That's super! Listen, Papa dear, let's go right over and see them! Why put it off? Huh, dear Papa? Well, what do you think?"

Kolya began to pester his father without letup.

"Well, actually, you know, they didn't really invite us—"

"Then what did they give you their address for, so you could pass it on—to Pushkin or someone? How formal you've gotten, Papa—that's because you work as a school monitor, isn't it? Foolishness, foolishness. You know it yourself. 'Nothing but fool's stuff,' as they say at the Sokolovskys. Come on now, Papa,

Arise and saddle your horse.
O'er fields and through trees,
Speed thou more quickly
To King Duncan's palace."

The passage Kolya recited was from one of Ivan Antonych's favorite poems by Heine.

"Let me think—"

"What's there to think about? Who are you, Uncle Misha? 'Come, let me kiss you—no, tomorrow would be better—no, today—no, perhaps tomorrow—' "

"What's that you're saying? Where did that come from?"

"Don't you know? That's how Uncle Zhorzh imitates your brother Monkey confessing his love to someone—but all this is nonsense—*ein Moment*—be right back—" And Kolya ran off.

"*This* is not nonsense!" he said, returning with Ivan Antonych's coat and hat and pulling the hat down over his father's eyes.

"Papa Vanya, for heaven's sake, get dressed more quickly."

"You little devil, you're sticking to me tighter than a birch leaf in a bathhouse."

"If I'm a leaf, ergo—what does that make you? In the Bible it says: Abraham gave birth to Isaac, Isaac gave birth to Jacob. But where does it say: so-and-so gave birth to a bathhouse leaf? You've gotten your genealogy all mixed up, Father, and you don't know how to get your coat on. Do you order me to dress you, sir?"

"Well, there's nothing else to be done. Let's go—Lyubochka! Kolya and I are going to the Slavyanskys."

Lyubov Ivanovna was busy tutoring. She came out for a minute: "Just don't dawdle around until midnight, please. And don't forget to give them my greetings. Maybe they can come visit us?"

They went out the gates.

"Cabby!"

"Where to?"

"The Arbat."

"Fifty kopecks if you please."

"Twenty."

"It's a long way, sir. Say, forty kopecks."

"Thirty, and not one bit more."

"Get in," the cabman unfastened the traveler's rug.

And then they were skimming along in the sleigh, on their way to the Slavyanskys. There are wonders everywhere, that's all there is to it!

In his joy Kolya started singing a song the high school boys had made up:

Toreador
Don't pee on the floor

Use the ba-ack door
Toreador . . .

"Stop being a fool, Nikolai! Aren't you ashamed?"

"What about you? Don't you sing things like that? Who sang this one—"

"Quiet, please. Or I swear we'll turn around and go back."

"All right, Papendras, I'm just joking. And you can't joke around with Mr. School Monitor. If you keep this up, I'm going to pick myself another father—ha, ha, ha," Kolya teased his beloved "little father." He felt light at heart: he was going to see Tosya, his bosom buddy. He thought to himself: What won't he have read during all this time? It'll be interesting! Interesting as all get out! We're going to live it up now . . . He could hardly wait till they got there. They passed Kudrino, Smolensk Boulevard, the Covered Market. And there was the Arbat, with Sevastyanov's bakery on the corner. Kolya had popped in there many a time to have a stuffed pastry. "What kind would you like? We have them with rice or with egg, with meat or jam." Memories flashed through his head in bits and pieces . . . And now Tosya had come . . . "Whoa! We're here. The first gate on the right."

The doorbell was answered by Natalya Dmitryevna.

"Oh my goodness, Ivan Antonych! Kolya! How good that you've come—"

"It's all Kolya's doing. He stuck to me, you know, like glue, till I'd no strength left—"

"And he did well. Superbly. Take off your coats. The coat rack's over here. You know, we're staying with my brother. My goodness, Kolya, how you've grown—well now, come on in—"

Natalya Dmitryevna led her guests into a room where, seated on a sofa, was a small, thin, delicate boy with porcelain eyes and glasses on his nose.

"Tosya!" Kolya rushed over to him.

"I am not Tosya. You are mistaken, Kolya," the boy announced, extending a weak hand.

"Don't talk nonsense, please."

"I assure you. I am Tosya's brother."

"Brother? Tosya didn't have any brothers," said Kolya, but already with a certain doubt. "He never told me about any brother—"

"From that you cannot conclude that he had no brother. I was in Moscow living with my uncle at that time, in this very apartment, and I don't know anything at all about that Bessarabia of yours. Tosya will be terrible sorry that you missed him: he has told me a few things about you."

Kolya said "You" in the polite form, then in the familiar form: "You're making a fool of me, Tosya. Stop playing this game."

"Mama!" the boy turned to Natalya Dmitryevna, smiling, his eyes gleaming. "Please tell Kolya that Tosya and I are two different beings, although we look very much alike, which of course is not surprising if you take into account the origins that we unquestionably have in common."

Natalya Dmitryevna smiled but did not reply: she simply gave a tender look, first at her son, then at Kolya.

Kolya was overcome with doubts: in actual fact, who was this? It seemed that Tosya was conniving—but his size really wasn't right and his eyes didn't seem exactly like Tosya's—what kind of devilish delusion?—well, maybe it wasn't Tosya after all.

"Um, will Tosya be coming soon?" Kolya asked uncertainly.

"You've gotten a little stupid in Moscow—ha, ha, ha! Ah, ha, ha ha!" Tosya burst out in a flood of laughter.

God, what a fool I am, no doubt about it. I'm so ashamed! What an insult! This thought flashed like lightning through Kolya's head, and he felt beads of perspiration on his scalp: How well he played his part, the scoundrel.

It seemed to Kolya now that he must have been a complete dunce to have wavered . . . How could there have been any doubt?

"Well, now, how clever Kolya is! How skillfully he pretended not to recognize me. He played the part so well!" Tosya was full of admiration for his friend.

Natalya Dmitryevna broke in: "That will be enough fooling around—Ivan Antonych, will you help me get tea? The children can sit here and visit in the meantime—on the other hand, expecting help from you in such matters—"

"Oh no, I'll do it with pleasure, Natalya Dmitryevna."

"What fun you had making a fool of me, eh? What got into your head to do that? Huh?" Kolya pounced on his friend, who was flushed with emotion.

"Well, but what were you trying to mystify me for?"

"Me? Trying to mystify *you*? You're out of your mind!"

"You're still putting on, even now! You knew me perfectly well the minute you saw me. But you put on such a face—you ought to go on stage."

"That's enough, Tosya. Drop it. In actual fact I really did . . . But tell me, what are you doing for fun these days?"

"I've been reading a lot of Stendhal. He loved mystification, too. Have you read the *Charterhouse of Parma*?"

"No."

"An entertaining piece . . . You're in your fourth year in high school now, right?"

"Yeah. And what about you? Are you going to a *gimnaziya*?"

"No, I study at home. Mama and I decided that I'll take a high school equivalency test. I've gone through five years already, in terms of the normal curriculum."

"Good work."

"And how about you? What have you been doing? And reading? You haven't given up on keeping birds, have you?"

"What's new with me? I still have birds. Come see them. I've begun painting. I'm going to the *gimnaziya*."

"What about books?"

"I've read *Degeneration*. Know it? By Nordau."

"I've heard of it but haven't read it."

"Tolstoy, Gorky, Chekhov, Andreyev. Timiryazev's polemic against Danilevsky—from the scientific sphere. Earlier I read books about the literature of the ancients—but not anymore. Molière. Skabichevsky's *History of Russian Literature*. I like Tolstoy a lot: *The Kreutzer Sonata* and *Resurrection*. I can't remember all the things I've read, Tosya."

"Well, in Tolstoy, you know, it's always God this and God that, although according to his own interpretation—"

"I put an end to any dealings with the gods, as you know, a long time ago. Here in Moscow I even brought the 'Body of Christ' from the church for the neighborhood kids to see—under my tongue. You should have seen them scatter in all directions."

Kolya told about his exploits in detail. They both began to laugh, egging each other on.

"Still, in Tolstoy there's always the same old Christian rubbish—wait a minute, listen to what I have to read to you."

Tosya jumped up from the sofa and began digging hastily among some fat notebooks with oilcloth covers: he opened one and began to read, in a whisper: "The social principles of Christianity promote cowardice, contempt for oneself, self-abasement, submissiveness, resignation— in a word, all the characteristics of riffraff, but the proletariat—" He paused: "That's the workers," then continued: "the proletariat, which does not wish to allow itself to be treated as riffraff, needs courage, consciousness of its own worth, pride, and independence, far more than it needs bread. The social principles of Christianity are characterized by sly, sneaky underhandedness, but the proletariat is characterized by revolutionary qualities."

"Where is that from?"

"Good, isn't it? Like a sharp spear in the very heart of Christianity. A shish kebab of priests."

"It's excellent. But where's it from?"

"That's Marx. Not the one who puts out *Niva* of course."

"The one that wrote *Capital?* You know I used to think the supporters of *Capital* were capitalists—ha, ha, ha!—what a fool! But where'd you read this? In *Capital?*"

"No. I was only able to read it in secret. You know, in Kishinyov a friend of Papa's brought him a secret revolutionary paper—on such thin paper— it was called *The Spark*. I swiped it so I could read it for myself. That's where I found the quote. But please don't go ringing all the bells about it. Don't even blab about it to Mama. They don't give me any peace as it is. 'You read too much, you're overdeveloped for your age, like an old man; you're going to get sick and die or go out of your mind,' until my ears are ringing. And Mama gets upset and looks at me with those sad eyes, as though I was doomed. And you know what, Kolya, let me tell you—" And Tosya put his warm, thin hand on Kolya's. "Sometimes I think that I am in fact doomed, some sort of freak."

"Quit it, Tosya. You're talking gibberish, you hear?"

Tosya was staring with such serious, sad eyes. His thin hands, with their unhealthy delicate quality, were such a painfully touching sight. He was so utterly fragile, not of this earth, it made Kolya's heart ache with sadness.

"Why do you say 'gibberish' to me? After all, I'm a product of my inheritance. You could knock my father down with a feather. I can barely drag my legs along. You all run, play, frolic, and *live*—but I? I'm a four-eyed cripple, Kolya. And I sometimes think I won't last long. After all, I know a few things. I can tell—but listen!" Tosya suddenly roused himself: "Is that album still around?"

"What album?"

"The one in Bessarabia. You remember, the one that fancy girl in Byeltsy gave you. You told me about it yourself. Klebonskay . . . Kle . . ."

"Klevanskaya? Yelena Vladimirovna? Yes, it's still in one piece. Almost completely intact. Why did you suddenly think of that?"

"I was looking at my notebooks, and it came to me all of a sudden: a leather binding, brown, with an imprint."

"Absolutely right. Yes, it's all in one piece. The only thing is, two poems have been added. My grandfather wrote them for me, for my edification."

"Interesting. They write in your album as though you were in college. And how touching, that your relatives—"

"I know them by heart."

"Well?"

"Oh, it's just trifles. Not worth hearing. Just a joke. Here's one of them:

Kolya, dear, beloved boy,
I will beat you with a stick.
But for me to beat you right,
You'll have to drop your pants a bit."

"Hmm, well, that one's for little kids. What about the other one?"

"Kolya, dear, these years too quickly
Into eternity shall vanish.
Other times will come for you,
Replacing this day and this minute.
May this happy life you have
Be a beacon for your future,
And may holy love—believe it—
Be your safest, surest harbor."

"Tell your grandfather he's no Byron. Certainly no Byron. Especially absurd is your past life as a beacon—years one to nine. Or is it ten? A beacon from behind? No, he's no Byron. I'm always amazed by people who write poetry and have no idea how weak their verse is."

"Tosya!" came a voice from the dining room.

Tosya ran out and brought back two glasses of tea, a little jar of jam, and two pastries: "I brought it out here. Let the fathers blab among themselves; we sons have our own business. Do you have anything against that, my friend Arkady?"*

"No. Except being written down for an Arkady."

"Right you are. By the way—"

While the boys were talking, a conversation of another kind was going on in the dining room.

"I invited you here, Ivan Antonych, for a specific reason. There are a lot of things one wishes to ask about. What's going on here in the capital where you live? What are the 'bards of the people' carrying on about?"

"Well, you know, Natasha, I . . . I mean . . . excuse me—"

"What's to excuse, 'beloved Jeannot.' Remember? That's what Sonya used to call you."

"Yes—remarkable girl she was—"

---

*"My friend, Arkady" was an expression used by the supersophisticated "nihilist" student Bazarov (on whom, see glossary) in addressing his naive young friend Arkady Kirsanov. Kolya objects to being cast as an Arkady while Tosya assumes the superior role of a Bazarov.

"Well now, forgive me please, Ivan Antonych, for reminding you—let's come back to the present. What are the politicians saying? What things do you hear, here in your city?"

"I'm ashamed to say I don't know anything at all. My work takes up all my time, and before that I didn't have a job, and we all went through the sufferings of the damned. Now I'm busy from morning till night. 'Earn thy bread by the sweat of thy brow.' That's the only way we're eating now, by the sweat of our brows. I read the papers, but not always. My circle of acquaintances doesn't include such people—not like when I was young— soon Kolya will be teaching me things along these lines, it seems."

"Too bad. Someone in the theatrical world told my husband that last summer he met Chekhov at Komissarzhevskaya's. She was on tour here in Moscow. Chekhov, he said, has gotten old, he's not well, tired, turning gray. They began asking him if he wouldn't write something for the theater. He said he was writing, but it wasn't the right thing, something different was needed now, we've outlived the old way, the long drawn-out way of doing things; our country has taken a sharp turn. Then he began telling them: it's not so obvious among you here in Moscow, but in the South a powerful wave is breaking, there is ferment everywhere among the people—he said he had visited Tolstoy, and Tolstoy sees it too, and he is a sharp-sighted old man. Russia is humming like a beehive. Just you wait and see, in two or three years you won't recognize Russia."

"Is that you talking, or Chekhov?"

"Chekhov. Why aren't you having lemon? How about pastry?"

"*Merci.*"

"*Merci* yes or *merci* no?"

"Yes, of course."

"Then please help yourself."

"Don't get upset, Natalya Dmitryevna. I'm still able to do that. So you say that according to Chekhov, 'a powerful wave is breaking' in the South? And you've just come from the South. The conclusion is obvious."

"How you twist things around."

"I have nothing to twist. I am nobody. *Continuez, madame.*"

"In the South everything really is in ferment. After the strike in Rostov there are unprecedented stirrings among the workers. I have the impression there's a smell of revolution in the air, a real one, you know. There is tremendous unrest. Even the peasants are no longer the same; there are rumors of rural conflicts from all over. Chernyshevsky's predictions, it seems, are coming true."

"Hey, do you remember how we used to sing, 'Let us drink to him who wrote *What Is to Be Done?*'"

"Those were idle dreams, Ivan Antonych. Today it's not 'Let's drink to'—today, it seems, action is being taken. And it's serious business. I'm judging by the wide circulation of revolutionary literature. Haven't you seen it?"

"How would it ever come my way?"

"We see it in Kishinyov. Both *The Spark* and *Revolutionary Russia*."

"What are those? I'm totally illiterate about such things."

"Actual parties have now been formed. The Marxists have their Social Democratic Party and the Narodniks have their Socialist Revolutionary Party."

"You mean Struve? And who do the Narodniks have?"

"My God, how far behind you've fallen! Struve is a turncoat. Left the movement. He's in Stuttgart, putting out his own publication, the official organ of the Union of Liberation. He's now the leader of the liberals; he's abandoned Marxism completely. He has an extensive network of supporters in the zemstvos. He's their man. And the Legal Marxists have ceased to be Marxists. Different people are now the leaders of the Social Democrats: Plekhanov and Lenin. Plekhanov's pen name is Beltov, and Lenin's is Vladimir Ilyin."

"The economist?"

"Yes, and the SR's—"

"What? What is that?"

"The Socialist Revolutionaries call themselves SR's for short. And the Social Democrats are called SD's. The SR's are called the *serye* (gray ones), and the SD's are called *sedye* (hoary-headed)," Natalya Dmitryevna explained, smiling. "Chernov. You probably know him. He writes under the pen name Gardenip."

"I've run across the name, it seems—a collection dedicated to Mikhailovsky, *Na slavnom postu* (At one's glorious post)."

"Yes, that's him. The South is flooded with party literature. Among the students the extreme radical parties are having colossal success. And the seeds are not falling on barren ground. What a shame that Sonya and Raspopin aren't alive to see this—"

"Yes, certainly. They'd be diving right in."

"The SR's are continuing the fighting traditions of the People's Will. On the other hand, though, they are much broader. And the Marxists are terribly intransigent, especially those around Lenin. Fanatics and dogmatics. For them the industrial workers, the 'proletariat,' are everything. Yet it seems to me sometimes that there is a kind of new truth behind them, something fresh, not from the old town of Suzdal. There's nothing pedestrian about them. They're an energetic and angry crowd. And anger is needed in this case; you can't get by without it. They are incorrigible debaters. But they march in iron phalanxes. A new kind of people, you know: they don't like fancy phrases, sitting around drinking tea, having parties, in the old way that we used to do. They don't have much respect for the old intelligentsia; they make fun of it fairly often. And among the workers they've had unquestionable success, as though cut to measure for them; and the latter stick to them so—hmm, do you want some more tea?"

"Sure, pour me a glass. But no sugar, please. I thank you."

"Look at me, going on and on like this."

"I'm grateful to you for it. It's all new to me."

"In Kishinyov the atmosphere is very tense. The chinovniks and police are trampling down the Jews and revolutionaries. Just you watch—a pogrom against the Jews is going to break out any moment now—you know the general situation in Bessarabia very well. Only, now the whole situation has deteriorated so badly that you probably couldn't even imagine. Lately it seems to me that we're sitting on hot coals. You can't keep tightening the screws endlessly; something's got to give . . . They're putting every trick to work; they shrink at nothing, nothing is beneath them. They openly make speeches calling for pogroms against the Jews, claiming that the Jews use Christian blood for ritual purposes, that they secretly torture and kill Christians to get their blood, that they're against the tsar because he's Orthodox and defends the Orthodox—the devil only knows what-all they say—'Beat the Jews' has become practically an official slogan in Kishinyov. It's the battle cry of all the 'patriots.' They're all being supplied and supported by Baron Levendal, head of the Okhrana (the secret police), and the Russian millionaire Pronin, a repulsive figure. And Krushevan—remember him? From the patriotic magazine *Znamya*?"

"I remember. How could anyone not remember?"

"Well, that's the one. And around them is an entire flock of chinovniks, police officials, detectives, and flatfoots. Their supply of money is bottomless, and they obviously have blessings from on high. They cruise through the taverns and gambling dens. In my opinion, some sort of dreadful St. Bartholomew's Night is being prepared—I don't know, maybe I'm wrong, but it looks very much like it—it's become very frightening. Government-organized police-state gangsterism—"

"Yes, Hertzen wrote that Russia is a 'frozen hell.' And Tyutchev spoke of the 'eternal Arctic pole.' That Arctic pole image comes off well. So everything has gotten frozen?"

"Apparently so . . . It's much quieter among you here in Moscow . . . Either we haven't yet had a good look around here or the southern waves really haven't washed up this far yet. But they will—"

Natalya Dmitryevna stopped talking. There was silence. The lamp shed its light softly on the tablecloth.

"The main thing is I have no solid faith. I cannot utter the commandment: 'I am the Lord thy God; thou shalt have no other gods but me.' And I don't know very well what direction should be taken. Aside from the most general one, a negative one, against brutal despotism . . . You know that by family origin, by blood, I'm Jewish. But let's take the question from a purely Russian point of view. I sometimes think society underestimates the anticultural character of the Romanov monarchy—honestly—after all, the best heads are cut off, the flower of the nation, as though by a mowing machine. If there's the slightest whiff or sign of genius or talent—put it on the chopping block! Everyone knows the facts, but if you stop and count them up? Pushkin—banishment, prohibitions, death. Lermontov—banishment. Chaadayev, whom Schelling himself considered one of the most intelligent people he knew—into a madhouse by order of the tsar. Polezhaev—tortured in the barracks. Remember his 'Song of the Captured Iroquois'?"

" 'I die. To the shame of the butchers I give up my body defenseless.' "

"Yes, his was an enormous talent. Chernyshevsky—sent off to hard labor. Pisarev—five years in the Peter and Paul Fortress. Turgenev—even Turgenev—sent to prison. Hertzen—prison and emigration. Ryleyev—hung. Radishchev—after being banished, was poisoned. And what a scientist the executed Kibalchich might have developed into! Today, Tolstoy is subjected to searches of his home. A world-renowned genius! And what about the outrageous recent incident involving Gorky?—a prison term for him goes without saying—he has been jailed already more than once."

"Are you talking about the Academy of Sciences?"

"Yes. And what fine men the members of the Academy are. Even Chekhov—the mildest of persons—got up on his hind legs! Did you read his letter to the president of the Academy, that ever so lofty liberal coquette?"

"Yes, I read it—"

"So there—talented and ingenious Russians are systematically destroyed by gendarmes, barons with German names. The Benckendorfs, Dubelts, Lebenthals, bastard offspring of the house of Romanov. Tell me, can a nation survive if it is constantly being decapitated? I'm not even speaking of the masses, the peasants, the workers—no, the kettle is going to boil over. And soon—"

Natalya Dmitryevna had gotten up and was pacing up and down the room, very much aroused. For a while Ivan Antonych said nothing, then: "But Natalya Dmitryevna, should you take all this so much to heart?"

"Yes, I'm not a corpse. Not yet. But actually I'm on the sidelines, Ivan Antonych—there's something going on with my Tosya, though. If he survives, he'll join the revolution. I haven't a particle of doubt about it. Maybe he'll be the expiation for my sins, philistine that I am. But at the same time I fear that—one's fate, in this walk of life, is virtually sealed. Very few survive, even in the event of victory—"

Ivan Antonych fell into reflection. In general he was a highly impressionable person, and his thoughts churned quickly in his head. His old friend had plunged him into a sea of issues from which he had been far removed, not because he didn't know about them in general or understand their importance, but because he always lived as one whose immediate involvement and concern was only with what was in front of his nose, his immediate surroundings, and the concerns of this immediate agenda engulfed him totally—everything else faded from his consciousness, and sometimes he waved extraneous thoughts away like annoying flies. Now suddenly it was all right in his face, had emerged out of the fog and assumed distinct features and definite shapes.

At that moment the everyday, the petty, and the ordinary, which had filled up Ivan Antonych's real life, grew murky and receded into the background, retreated into a kind of distance that seemed unreal. The balance of perspective in his consciousness altered, various planes and spheres of life changed places. That was why Ivan Antonych fell into a reverie.

"Hey, what time is it?"

"Quarter of twelve."

"Dammit all. I've got to get home. Lyubochka—it's a good thing I remembered—Lyubochka asked me to send you her respects and invite you to come visit us. You know our address. Bolshaya Gruzinskaya. Georgiyevskaya Square. Blokhin's. From the Zoological Garden you go down Gruzinskaya. When you reach the gates go straight ahead till you come to the outbuilding with the front garden. That is our Promised Land. Got to call Kolya now."

"Right away. Kolya! Tosya!"

The boys came out of their room.

"Time to go home, Kolyun."

"So, Tosya, you've got to come visit us, you hear? I'll be waiting for you every day . . . Natalya Dmitryevna, please see too it that Tosya comes as soon as possible."

"Kolya, come on, Natalya Dmitryevna has promised to come. You're so crude and boorish!"

"But, Papa, I was only—"

"Never mind, Ivan Antonych. It's only natural that Kolya wants to see Tosya, not me."

"No, and you too, you too."

"But mainly to see Tosya—what's there to be ashamed of in that?"

Kolya, confused, lapsed into silence.

Tosya whispered in his ear: "Don't go blabbing about *The Spark* now." Then out loud: "I'll come visit in the next few days. Maybe day after tomorrow."

But Tosya didn't come.

Two days later Ivan Antonych, arriving home from work by horsecab, said to his son: "Tosya unexpectedly died."

"How's that? What are you saying?"

"Yes. Meningitis, inflammation of the membranes surrounding the brain. I called from school—to ask why they hadn't come. The only thing Natalya Dmitryevna said was, 'Tosya died of meningitis.' She couldn't say anything more."

"I'm going right over there."

"You mustn't. You'll only cause the mother greater suffering. As it is, I don't know how she's going to get through this."

Kolya felt as though he'd been struck by lightning. He wanted to weep, to sob, to beat his head against the wall. In a stupor he looked around him, from side to side. He had just been talking with Tosya; he had just seen his fragile, delicate forehead, his clear eyes, his slender hands. He heard Tosya's soft voice . . . Oh Tosya! How can it be? Can it really be true that you are no more?

Tosya's remains lay on display in the coffin, his gentle face frozen in the colorless mask of death. Natalya Dmitryevna, her lips tightly compressed, was tending to her husband, who was lying down, nearly unconscious.

Chapter 18

The Romanov monarchy was heading toward catastrophe in foreign affairs as well as internally. On August 4, 1902, there took place in the harbor at Revel (Tallinn) a meeting between two emperors, Wilhelm Hohenzollern and Nicholas Romanov, which gave further powerful impetus to events that were coming to a head.

The imperial octopus had already insinuated its greedy tentacles into the Far East. Russia had seized large chunks of territory from China and was participating to the full extent of its capacities in the truly thievish expedition of the Great Powers against the Middle Empire. Their civilized, superbly armed corps under the command of the German field-marshal Count Waldersee, outdid themselves in suppressing the Boxer Rebellion, which was provoked by seizures of Chinese territory. They burned villages and cities and occupied the very capital of China, Beijing. The capture of Beijing, which took place before the count had yet arrived, was led by General Linevich and the Russian troops, who together with the Japanese, looted the city and destroyed the palace.

The uniquely voluble German Kaiser at that time—late June 1900—gave a send-off speech in Bremerhaven, from a high platform at the harbor, to his ever so Christian, thoroughly drilled and trained columns of troops. The speech was a call to arms against the "yellow peril." Raising high his right fist and belligerently thrusting out his well-developed chest, he shouted in a strong voice: "Show no mercy! Take no prisoners! Just as, a thousand years ago, in the days of Attila, the Huns left a distinct memory of themselves and of their power, a memory that has survived in legend and story to this day, even so, as a result of your actions, the name of the Germans must be remembered in China for a thousand years to come, so that the Chinese will never dare even to look sideways at a German!"

These ever so Christian powers imposed the most shameful treaties on China, stealing Chinese territory and planting the powder kegs of future conflicts. In passing, they put to the torch one of China's ancient national treasures, an encyclopedia of vast dimensions. And these cultured officers—Germans, Englishmen, Frenchmen, Russians, and others—returned home bearing stolen goods: pictures, precious statues, silks, china, gold, ivory, various ornaments, antique knickknacks, and coins, thinking of their actions as worthy of the Apostles rather than as coming under the heading of theft. Back home they would drink whiskey, beer, red wine, or vodka, depending on their nationality, and laugh merrily while trading recollections of the little Chinese girls whom they, when not engaged in martial exploits, had favored with their enlightened attentions.

Now, two years later, a conflict was brewing between Japan and Russia, and Wilhelm, who was possessed by a mania for a world government of duumvirs—himself, Wilhelm, and his beloved brother, the northern tsar, Nikki—hurried with his military and diplomatic staff to work on outstanding issues of great international policy. He was attracted to the Russian autocracy because of his obsession with the idea of a combined struggle against the hydra of revolution. He himself constantly dreamed about a coup d'état, about a bloodbath against the workers, about the destruction of that pitiful entity, German parliamentary government, about his own role as a great new Caesar, who, like St. George, would shatter the dragon of socialist revolution. As early as 1899, during the workers' strikes in Augsburg, he said to his friend, Philip Eilenburg, who subsequently became notorious for court homosexuality: "That's fine. Let them, let them! The moment will come when it will be necessary *to act* . . . Then I will stop at nothing, and even the ministry won't hold me back; it will simply fall if it does not go with me. Please, read the recently published collection of speeches I have given since accession to the throne. You will see clearly that at first in a friendly way, and then in all seriousness, I call the attention of the German people to the dangers that threaten them . . . *The government must act*; otherwise everything will go to ruin! If in a serious foreign conflict there emerges such a situation that half the army has to be mobilized inside our country because of a general strike, then we're *done for*! I have already found out how far my authority extends with respect to the constitution. The minister of war has told me that at *any time* I can declare a state of siege throughout the entire empire. One cannot expect an improvement in the situation until soldiers remove the Social Democratic leaders from the Reichstag and shoot them. We need a law by which it would be possible to banish every Social Democrat to the Caroline Islands . . . It will be necessary to carry out a *very* intense bloodletting . . ." And the Kaiser, offering wine, smugly smoothed his mustache.

Now he was going to a meeting with the Russian emperor, who feared revolution not one whit less than Wilhelm: Nikki had already been feeling its tremors continually.

It was a bright, lovely morning. At sea the air was crisp; light ripples furrowed the surface, and small reddish-green waves, streaked with the brilliance of bottle-green glass, splashed against the shore and receded, leaving a fine lace of white, faintly hissing foam. It smelled of seaweed, iodine, the fresh tang of salty sea spray. Fourteen huge naval vessels and fifteen torpedo boats awaited the distinguished guests. The white hulls of the *Varyag* and the *Retvizan* gleamed dazzlingly in the sun. The other ships sat blackly with gloomy hulls, the embodiment of the ponderous naval force of the empire, and their monstrous guns stood with muzzles gaping. The luxurious royal yachts—the *Shtandart* and the *Polyarnaya Zvezda* (Polar Star)—stood out with their appearance of elegance and gracefulness. There were several sailboats with flickering sails like frightened swans.

Above the battleships and cruisers flocks of seagulls hovered with their plaintive cries. They would first shoot upward, then drop to the water, snatching up their catch, then, rising again, remain motionless in the air, almost without moving a wing, just like Christmas doves of wax suspended on thread, and their snow-white wings glittered against the pale cobalt of the northern sky. On the ships the highest officials of the imperial Baltic fleet had gathered. A huge crowd of people swarmed on the shore: everyone wanted to watch the unprecedented spectacle. The harbor was thickly strewn with the curious: respectable bourgeois gentlemen, society ladies, craftsmen, laborers, white-collar workers, bureaucrats— people wearing bowlers, cloth caps, hats, peaked caps, multicolored dresses, and carrying umbrellas—everything blended together in this moving mass. Among their legs urchins darted and pushed, thrusting forward their astonished faces and trying to squeeze through to where they could see a little better. Policemen pompously kept order and chased away drunks.

Then, far off on the horizon, beyond Nargen Island, in the soft blue haze, there appeared the dingy, barely discernible puffs of smoke of the German squadron. The imperial yachts rushed off toward them, accompanied by the cruiser *Svetlana*, and the water began to froth up along the sides of the ships like small, white, agitated snakes.

Festive flags were raised and began to flutter on all the ships. Like steel sea monsters touched by a magic wand, they suddenly blossomed with the multicolored little stars of bright flowers, decorated themselves lavishly, putting on brilliant, festive garments. Two hours later the German squadron and the imperial yachts were already coming up to the roadstead: the *Prince Heinrich*, the *Nymphe*, the torpedo-boat *Sleipner*, and the Kaiser's yacht the *Hohenzollern*, white as snow—all moved with one accord toward the meeting place.

The air began to shake with the rumble of a cannonade. Covering themselves with a cloud of gunpowder smoke, the ships let their cannon roar with monstrous force—one might think a giant naval battle was taking place. The birds, flapping their wings, scattered and, deafened, landed on the water, preening their feathers in bewilderment. On the flagships and yachts bands blared, and the heavy copper sounds of trumpets and kettledrums went ringing skyward. The Germans played "God Save the Tsar"; the Russians, an anthem for the German Kaiser.

On the captain's bridge of the ships—on the battleships, on the cruisers—were positioned important, well-dressed people, in epaulets, silk ribbons across the shoulder, with silver aiguillettes, lavishly adorned with an entire iconostasis of stars, decorations, and medals. On the upper decks, arranged at attention, shoulder to shoulder, toes to the line, in snow-white uniforms with blue collars, one just like the next, there stood the tanned sailors with bronze faces and chests. It was as if they were frozen stiff, like the statues on the Avenue of Victory. The rest of the crew clung to the shrouds and hung in the air like wreaths of human bodies. A long-rehearsed "Hurrah" ripped the troubled air in uninterrupted rolling waves, now dying away, now roaring with new force.

Both rulers were on the imperial yacht *Shtandart*. With Wilhelm had come, among others, Prince Heinrich, Admiral von Tirpitz, the most talented of German sailing men, clever, hard, with a large beard and a stern glare in his piercing eyes; and the cunning diplomatic fox, the cautious and ingratiating Prince von Bülow, in his youth a volunteer hussar, a participant in the Franco-Prussian War, a lion of diplomatic salons, a brilliant conversationalist, who had also been ambassador to St. Petersburg—a man with elegant manners and excellent literary speech.

Wilhelm, of average height, with a military bearing, self-confident as always when there was no immediate danger, with theatrical excitement and the air of a person without whom not a single question could be decided, behaved ceremoniously, bestowing compliments on his beloved cousin, Nikki. The content of his remarks had been thought out in advance and even formulated in writing by the Ministry of Foreign Affairs. But the garrulous monarch more than once caused unforeseen difficulties for his diplomats. He would get carried away by his own eloquence, and it sometimes seemed that he, like a grouse in mating season, would not see or hear anything around him. He did not like to speak using a crib sheet. He could not tolerate instructions, and at one time because of this he had had a falling out with the "Iron Chancellor," Otto von Bismarck, subjecting him to disfavor. He was so imbued with megalomania that more than once the question of his normalcy arose in the narrow circles of the court camarilla, and his most august mother once uttered the prophetic words "Mon fils sera la ruine d'Allemagne" (My son will be the ruin of Germany).

Nicholas, on the other hand, was simply colorless. The merchant Bugrov, an Old Believer, defined him well in a conversation with Gorky: "That little piece of coal gives off no heat. He'll say ten words—seven are unnecessary, and three aren't his. His father wasn't a great mind either, but still he was a solid fellow, with a sharp sense of smell, a master. But this one is gentle, the eyes of an old woman . . . Ah, our little tsar is not great! . . ."

"Yes, beloved cousin!" Wilhelm hypnotized the tsar with his powerful eyes. "Firmness above all. Can the Japs really dare to encroach upon your great monarchy? A worldwide mission rests on your shoulders. The yellow peril continues to threaten Europe. I warned the nations long ago: civilization must be protected from these locusts."

"I'm with you, Willy, I agree completely."

"We showed the Chinese barbarians what the white race stands for. As early as 1900 I was saying that they deserved punishment and vengeance for their crimes of unprecedented impudence. Now, evidently, it is the turn of the Japanese: these monkeys fancy that they have entered into the family of civilized nations. They are nothing but imitators. More than once I have written to my good friend President Roosevelt that he must be on the alert. But that republic is not capable, obviously, of carrying out what only a sound monarchy can. It seems to me that our interests here coincide completely."

"I think so, too."

"It would be extremely dangerous if France, with whom you are in alliance, were to upset our relationship. France is a waning nation, with an unquestionable tendency toward decline; the blood of the slain king and nobles lies on that nation, which atheism is destroying."

"I also think that a quarrel between us can only benefit our enemies," Nicholas said quietly, and his face suddenly took on a kind of almost childlike expression of alarm. "Ce serait faire le jeu de la revolution" (That would mean playing into the hands of the revolution). "I don't think that our interests are in conflict anywhere—"

"Of course," Wilhelm joined in passionately, gesticulating with his right hand. (His left hand did not function well and, in order to hide this physical defect, he would slip it inside the front of his dress uniform in the manner of Napoleon, thus killing two birds with one stone: he both hid the defect and mimicked the mannerism of a great military leader, here forgetting about the "waning nation.") "We are united by the most solid bond: our role in the struggle against revolution. This is the chief danger of our century. And our sacred duty is to crush it. Socialism—that is the common enemy. And I wouldn't be who I am if I didn't smash the Social Democratic gang in my country. They are in need of a bloodletting. And soon it will be impossible to stand on ceremony there. It may be that a little bit later will already be too late. *Periculum in mora.*"

"I am also concerned about this problem—terrorists, labor disturbances, the Social Democrats, the Freemasons, and the Jews are becoming insolent—but I am sure that in the event of a conflict with Japan all truly Russian people will unite as one man around my throne. My people have fine old traditions, and in the end they will tear the troublemakers to bits. I do not want to force a war, but if Providence brings one upon us, I hope that the enemy will, with God's help, be punished as he deserves."

"I'm very glad, Nikki, that we share such identical views—"

"And so am I. But it seems to me—I'm even certain—that with firmness on my country's part the Japs won't dare to measure their strength against such a mighty power as ours. And this firmness is a law of my policy." In saying this, the tsar surprised even himself and peeked timidly into the other's eyes to see whether he believed in this firmness.

"So then, dear Nikki, we can conclude that you are *the Admiral of the Pacific*, and I am *the Admiral of the Atlantic.** Ha, ha, ha!" Wilhelm broke out in a loud, satisfied laugh and began to stroke his renowned mustache.

In using this English phrase, Wilhelm was engaging in word play. *Pacific* in English means "peaceful" (thus the Pacific Ocean is the "Peaceful Ocean"). And by naming Nicholas, foreseeing a war, the admiral of the "peaceful ocean," the Kaiser, who was pushing him toward military seizure of this "peaceful ocean," was laying bare the real sense of the conversation. Nicholas smiled sourly but uttered no objection.

It pleased Wilhelm to realize that he had inspired Nicholas to some extent, especially since he himself found any hint of instructions from any of the responsible leaders of "his" policy most unpleasant. To make the mighty emperor of all the Russias his mouthpiece seemed to Wilhelm to be the height of political accomplishment, the climax of his own personal power and greatness. He was not aware in the slightest that he himself was nothing but the mouthpiece of the Prussian landowners, who stank of sta-

*The italicized phrases are in English in the original text.

bles and potato vodka from a distance of ten versts. Nicholas saw clearly the hidden springs of Wilhelm's exhortations and, while outwardly assenting, felt within himself a definite resistance: indeed, a conflict in the Far East would, in the final analysis, mean risking *his* neck, not the Kaiser's. But he was impressed by the flattering speeches about his great historical role, and—not without some caution, which was connected with his lack of self-confidence, his timidity, and partially his cunning—he tried his hand at the game in which the one who gives up all his pieces wins.

Having parted company with Wilhelm, the emperor made an appointment for a short audience with Prince Bülow.

"Listen, Prince, how is your wife's health?" Nicholas asked as Bülow entered his cabin.

"Thank you, Your Majesty, she's feeling fairly well just now."

"Please, have a seat. I've had a talk with the emperor."

Bülow remained silent, respectfully waiting to see what would follow the traditional inquiry about his wife's health.

"I am worried," the tsar said slowly, choosing his words carefully, "by a certain nervousness on the part of my friend when he spoke about France. The interests of Russia and of Germany don't conflict anywhere. And our relations with France are in no way directed against Germany. And, what's more, you, Prince, know perfectly well that it is through no fault of Russia that a somewhat different configuration has emerged. I am just as averse to French atheism and republicanism as is your highly esteemed monarch. But it would be regrettable if a fissure were to be created in our relations, and if in general—"

Nicholas did not finish his sentence, glancing questioningly at Bülow, on whose face it was impossible to detect the slightest movement of his well-trained diplomat's soul.

"My opinion, Your Majesty, coincides completely with the opinion of Count von Bismarck, about which I have already once had the honor of reporting to Your Majesty—"

"Be so kind as to remind me," Nicholas said, although he remembered perfectly well what Bülow was talking about: he wanted to see whether the obliging prince would repeat the exact same thing or whether he would introduce some new nuance of political *imponderabilia*, the imponderable quantities to which Bismarck attached such significance.

"Very well, Your Majesty. Our great chancellor said that it is difficult to predict the outcome of a war among three states in terms of a military victory, but on the other hand one can say with complete certainty that three monarchies would have to pay the price—"

The emperor grabbed Prince Bülow by the arm and for a long time looked at him with seemingly unseeing melancholy eyes. Finally he said: "I am just as convinced of this as you are."

A half hour later Wilhelm was already walking about the deck, cheerful and excited, be it by the sea air, by the wine, or by his political exploits. Arm in arm he went with Nicholas, who, in this couple, personified, rather, the female principle. Having spotted Bülow, Wilhelm, without releasing his colleague, set off toward the prince and from afar shouted loudly, so that those present heard everything very well: "Do you know, Bernhard, what we have decided to call ourselves from now on? Emperor Nicholas will call himself *the Admiral of the Pacific*, and I—*the Admiral of the Atlantic*."

The tsar's face expressed obvious embarrassment at Wilhelm's joke. For a moment he was at a loss about how to react to his overly talkative "friend's" indiscreet outburst.

"It does not surprise me in the least, Your Majesty, if a monarch, who, despite his might, so highly values the blessings that peace provides, has adopted such an epithet," came the swift response from the adroit and quick-witted Bülow.

The tsar immediately came to life, his eyes lost their expression of dull speechlessness, and he unintentionally nodded his head as a sign of his complete solidarity with von Bülow's response.

Finding a moment when Wilhelm was alone, Prince Bülow carefully, in a roundabout way, stepping with his words like a cat on soft velvet paws, began to try to make his sovereign see the logic of not joking about such things; in various ways he tried to demonstrate to him that if the Kaiser's latest bon mots were to become widely known and make their way into the press, they would be taken as an expression of the emperor's extreme belligerence and would inflict substantial damage on the authority of the sacred person of His Majesty . . . The Kaiser heard these lectures out with a condescending, bored look and appeared to agree: deep down in his heart he recognized the truth of Bülow's arguments. But at lunch, after cold French champagne from bottles that had been lying in ice in massive silver buckets, he, like a capricious child, kept returning to this topic the whole time, to the obvious displeasure of the tsar, who would wince slightly, rolling little bread balls with his fingers.

After lunch, at three in the afternoon, the festive flags were lowered, the festive full-dress uniforms were taken off. The Russian imperial fleet prepared to show the German Kaiser its artillery skills, and the floating fortresses, having cast aside their flowery ceremonial attire, appeared in their prosaic and frightening steel nakedness. Both emperors were now on the cruiser *Minin*. Here also were Prince Heinrich, Admiral Tirpitz, fleet commander Grand Duke Aleksei Aleksandrovich, Minister of the Navy Tyrtov, admirals and officials of the imperial retinue. Wilhelm stood with his hands on his hips in the uniform of an admiral of the Russian fleet. He had been promoted to admiral several years earlier by Nicholas before a ceremonial dinner in St. Petersburg. Wilhelm was then so delighted at this appointment that he offered to kowtow to the tsar in celebration, and at dinner made a toast in which he "placed at his feet heartfelt, joyful gratitude for this unexpected appointment," thereby scandalizing his ministers to no small degree . . . Now he was wearing a Russian uniform, with a light-blue ribbon of the Order of St. Andrew across his shoulder, in a naval tricorn, and fancied himself a real commander. Nicholas, dressed in a German uniform, looked like a poor specimen in comparison with his self-confident, bellicose colleague, who with a managerial air, was casting hard, unyielding glances in every direction

The shooting turned out to be very successful. The targets fell one after another . . .

Wilhelm congratulated the emperor: "I would be very fortunate if I had in my fleet such talented admirals as your Rozhdestvensky."

The tsar beamed. He went up to the grand duke, who in reality was a puppet in someone else's hands and was notable for his highly frivolous character—despite his rank of admiral-general and his venerable age. The tsar embraced and kissed him, then did the same with Rozhdestvensky. And this large, massive, monumental man, with broad shoulders, a gray beard, and the piercing eyes of a wolf, suddenly bowed like a slave and kissed the tsar's hand. The Germans exchanged glances.

In the evening the sailors found out: the targets were set up in such a way that "the slightest breeze" would have knocked them over. The celebration lasted three days and nights. In the deep darkness of the night, in the middle of the sea, black as ink, danced the enchanting lights of the illuminated ships; their reflections coiled and flickered, breaking up in the invisible ripples of the sea. On the flagship *Minin* the monograms of the sovereigns were lit up in fiery designs, and the imperial crowns gleamed above them like bright, magical stars.

The time of leave-taking had come. The emperors embraced and kissed each other with kisses that excluded neither enmity nor perfidy nor betrayal; they were part of an obligatory ritual, like a dress uniform or a salute. As the *Hohenzollern* was approaching Nargen, it signaled the following message: "The admiral of the Atlantic wishes bon voyage to the admiral of the Pacific."

"Good-bye," was the restrained reply.

Later, Count Witte, one of the most intelligent of the tsar's officials, made the following entry in his diary: "I do not know if it was the influence of Kaiser Wilhelm—which was expressed, among other ways, in this signaled message—or if it was something else, but from that time on, especially during 1903, in dispatches sent to His Majesty's representative in the Far East, and in other documents, the thought was repeatedly expressed by the Sovereign that he wished Russia to have a dominant influence in the Pacific."*

*On Witte, see glossary.

Chapter 19

The *gimnaziya* that Kolya Petrov attended was getting ready for its centennial celebration. People were saying that as a mark of honor on this important occasion the school would be awarded the very lofty and ever so gracious title "Imperatorskaya" (the Emperor's), and several teachers at the school were already dreaming of flaunting medals: the Order of St. Anne, St. Vladimir, St. Stanislav—there were such "chasers after rank" at the *gimnaziya*, too. At any rate, from the highest spheres came the information that the governor-general of Moscow, the Grand Duke Sergei Aleksandrovich, would be coming to the ceremony, and all the authorities at the school—including liberals—trembled at the prospect.

The saying, "It is not the place that adorns the person, but the person that adorns the place," is highly relative in its applicability; in real life one's "place" (or social position) actually adorns the person to a considerable extent, even when essentially there is no person present. The "place" enters and fills the personal emptiness, and the common herd, educated in the spirit of religious deference to hierarchy, may well kneel to this emptiness, which has swollen to vast proportions solely because of its "place." In fixed and frozen hierarchies of the caste type, such hereditary fetishes maintain themselves on the strength of historical traditions, whose roots go deep into the soil of economic existence.

The governor-general of Moscow was like a feudal prince, having unlimited dominion in his own fiefdom. Tall and straight, like a cudgel stick—as though he had swallowed a poker—and long-legged, he walked as though on stilts. From his gray, murky, watery eyes there emanated an icy hauteur and cold indifference. His whole figure was belted up and buttoned up—the prince wore corsets that had been specially made for him.

His intellectual horizons were extremely narrow and impoverished. He belonged to the most extreme group of retrograde politicians and sought with all his might to keep Russia frozen in place with draconian measures. He had a special passion for the Orthodox Church and for plump, rosy-cheeked young fellows, mainly from the more youthful grades of the cadet corps, a passion that brought real torments to his wife, Yelizaveta Fyodor-ovna, the empress's sister by blood. For this reason his visits to churches and monasteries, together with various corps of cadets, visits during which Grand Duke Sergei would scan with eagle eye the assembled rows of cadets—all this occupied a considerable place in the performance of his official duties.

Secret vices, concealed sanctimoniously by piety and a religious cult, resulted in his surrounding himself with aides who ruled for him, indulged him, and knowing his offstage activities, were able to manipulate him. It is not surprising that they themselves were no pillars of virtue. At the start of the reign of Tsar Nicholas II, the right-hand man of Grand Duke Sergei was the police chief Vlasovsky, a habitué of fancy restaurants and a heavy drinker, a police official in the style of a Turkish *bashi-bazouk*, a bribe taker and a bully, crafty and sly, one of those chiefly to blame for the tragedy of the Khodynka, who evaded responsibility for that disaster thanks to the intercession of Grand Duke Sergei.

Now his favorite was General Trepov, a gallant horseman of the Guards. From head to foot he was the typical crude, loud-mouthed soldier, a man with black hair, frightening eyes, and wild mustaches, one of those who, in seeking to become a dictator, spoke of himself as a "clean and honorable sword," a guardian of the existing order for the nobility and men of the court, a good, straightforward fellow who dreamed of chopping off the head of the ascendant revolution with one blow of the axe.

This did not prevent him, incidentally, from being a sponsor and one of the main architects of the system of "police socialism," which he prop-agated with the permission of Grand Duke Sergei and the assistance of the notorious Zubatov, the truly diabolical great grandfather of all secret police officials and agents, who created workers' organizations for the express purpose of diverting workers from seditious revolutionary activity.

Trepov spoke in a soldierly way—in short, abrupt sentences—as though he were firing shots, and took arrogant pride in the bluntness of his opinions. Owing to his manly appearance he enjoyed the special favor of the Grand Duchess, and at the same time was the Grand Duke's pet, rendering him services both in government affairs and in more intimate connections.

Grand Duke Sergei had great influence in court circles and was one of the tsar's chief advisers: as the tsar's uncle and the husband of the tsarina's sister, he exerted whatever pressure was necessary, from his point of view, whenever appropriate. He was also one of the chief Jew haters, and the controlling threads behind the anti-Jewish pogroms often led, by way of the police organizations, directly to the hands of his Excellency, Grand Duke Sergei.

Nevertheless, in Sergei's eparchy, or diocese, there was great unrest. No matter how hard the snoops and bloodhounds tried to catch all the discontented workers in their net, success eluded them. On February 19 the Zubatov people brought out their brood for a patriotic demonstration at the statue of the tsar-emancipator. But on the same day, to the horror of the police, the Social Democratic workers organized a revolutionary demonstration, free of police control, on Tverskoi Boulevard. There were strikes at the Gakental, Bromley, Dobrovo-Nabgolts, and Guzhon factories. Disturbances broke out among the students, and the authorities went all out with mass arrests, which only spread the bitterness and hatred further. Besides that, directly under the authorities' noses, there sat the Fronde of the merchants and the liberal nobility: the princes Dolgorukov, Trubetskoy, Shospov, Golovin, and Stakhovich, the liberal and liberalistic zemstvos, which set the tone for the entire zemstvo opposition and had already begun to organize zemstvo congresses . . .

Grand Duke Sergei went wild and issued orders to "clamp down" and "mercilessly uproot." The agents of the Okhrana, the secret police, crawled out of their skins in their eagerness to comply. On Gnezdikovsky Alley, behind thick walls, interrogations went on, uninterrupted, through the nights. The Taganka and Butyrka prisons were filled to overflowing. Yet unrest continued to mount, and the hydra kept growing new heads . . .

On the centennial day the *gimnaziya* students were lined up in rows along the length of the main stairway. They had been drilled for a long time in advance. Baron Kiester, the gymnastics teacher, a foppish gentleman with a monocle—one of the Baltic nobility, the "Ostsee" aristocrats of German descent who had run their estates into the ground—had diligently instructed them on how to place their legs, hold their arms, and shout in unison: "We wish you good health, Your Imperial Highness." The students, to whom it had never occurred previously to be concerned with their extremities, shivered in deferential fear, but some of them, inclined toward protest, awaited the spectacle not without a certain curiosity.

Grand Duke Sergei showed up with his wife, and tossing his greatcoat to a janitor, who was bent over double in deference, hardly bothered to respond to the hurrahs and cries of greeting, but strode past and entered the assembly hall, accompanied by his adjutants and the school principal. The orchestra broke into "God Save the Tsar!"

Sergei stood through the prayers, then walked over to the principal, who was bright red from nervous tension, patriotic emotion, fear, and veneration, shook his hand, and said through his teeth: "Uh-h-h . . . I congratulate you—you had a student here, it seems, named Bogolepov, no?"

Minister of Public Education Bogolepov, who had recently been killed, actually had graduated from the First Moscow Boys School, and his portrait hung in a prominent place in the assembly hall.

"Why, of course, exactly so, Your . . . Your Imperial Highness."

"Again, I congratulate you . . . But the atmosphere in your school is . . . uh-h-h . . . not quite right—"

He clanked his spurs, saluted, turned on his heel, and marched back toward the stairway, his head held high, staring over the heads of the others, while all eyes were riveted on him. As the Grand Duchess Yelizaveta Fyodorovna passed, a barely perceptible aroma of delicate perfume trailed behind her, completely out of harmony with the Grand Duke's jangling spurs and jackboots polished to a luster.

Kolya stood on the stairs among the others, and as the representatives of the royal family passed him—Sergei at a distance of no more than half a yard—there suddenly entered Kolya's brain, piercing it like a needle, an absurd and naughty thought: What if I pinch him? Or punch him in the back? An icy chill swept over Kolya—he had come, it seemed, within an inch of acting on that thought, which had flashed into his mind like lightning.

The *gimnaziya* officialdom was in dismay. They looked at one another, perplexed. The principal's fat lower lip, red and moist, was hanging helplessly. There were tears in his eyes. One of the school officials, whose title was "inspector," was walking along with mincing steps, his face a plaster mask of seriousness. Those who had hoped for honors were moping. The radicals smiled ironically, as if to say: "That's what you get, idiots!"

Soon the entire school knew what the Grand Duke had said, and a noisy horde of students, waking from a frozen state of hypnosis, were laughing at the unfulfilled hopes of the *gimnaziya* officials. There was no chance now that the school would be named "the Emperor's." Those hopes had been given a first-class burial!

"Hey, Little One!" one of his classmates shouted to Petrov. "Let's do an imitation!"

"Huh?"

"A funeral."

"What for?"

"For disappointed hopes."

The students bunched together and began a noisy discussion of the proposal. Then they quickly unscrewed the tops of their school desks, used chalk to draw some imitation icon figures with halos round their heads, grabbed Kolya Petrov by his arms and legs, and began carrying him through the hallways as their "corpse." The boys with the "icons" went first, followed by the "choir," whose members, bursting with laughter, chanted "Eternal Memory to Disappointed Hope . . ." The monitors were caught off guard and slow to figure out what it was all about. They shrank back, clearing a path for the theatrical procession. On the whole, it was the most effective feature of the centenary celebration, if you didn't count the "main event"—that is, the incident with Grand Duke Sergei.

The atmosphere at the school really "wasn't right," not what the higher authorities would have wanted. There was ferment everywhere, and it unavoidably penetrated the thick bureaucratic walls of the *gimnaziya* building.

Even among the school officials the screws were being loosened: the teachers in one way or another had been infected by various tendencies, or at least moods. The principal in fact did not know in what direction to orient himself, which tuning fork to use to set the tone for the functioning of the school: the old tuning, the way of the reactionary Minister of Education Tolstoy,* with its terribly harsh standards, was no longer suitable, but what to put in its place? No one knew.

Discipline among the students declined with each passing day, and the boys—even in the younger grades—were starting to act up, willfully flouting all sorts of established traditions: at one point they floated a balloon during religious services in the assembly hall; it kept bobbing lightly about, bumping against the ceiling—pmm, pmm, pmm—so that a ladder had to be brought and an attempt made to catch hold of it, but it kept slipping away, while the mischief makers snickered; on another occasion, a chicken was let loose in the corridor, and it went rushing about like a house afire, cackling and sliding on the parquet floor, flapping its wings and inspiring universal merriment. At one point they nailed a teacher's galoshes to the floor after putting sparrow's eggs or some other trash in them, and the honorable pedagogue slid his feet right in, then looked around dumbfounded, unable at first to understand what was going on; another time, they sewed up the sleeves of the principal's overcoat, then waited to see what kind of face Iosif Osvaldovich would make when he began trying in vain to pull the coat onto his substantial figure . . .

*On Dmitry Tolstoy and his *gimnaziya* policy, see glossary.

Then they thought up the idea of having a betting pool on the teachers. It worked this way. A large bell hung in the corridor, to be rung when the first lessons of the day began. All the teachers headed for their classrooms and of necessity passed this bell. The students bet on who would reach the bell first; then, gathering in a crowd with excited faces, they would watch every move of the "horse" they had bet on:

"Look, look! Sikerdon has already passed Fedya by half a length—"

"Now Cuttlefish is ahead! So much for your Sikerdon."

"Well, so what? Did you bet on Byzantine Nose?"

"Hey, fellahs! Klistir's broken into a gallop—Cheech has dropped out—he's off his stride—and now they're approaching the finish line—"

"Hurray, hurray! Klistir came in first! Good for the German pepper sausage!"

"Klistir! Klistir!" The boys rushed to their classrooms at breakneck speed, shouting the latest news of the school "derby."

It was very hard to fight against this betting pool. The teachers decided that the inspector would go out alone. Then after him, at a respectable distance, the others would come along, like a herd of rams, with each one sticking to his neighbor, afraid of getting "half a length ahead." But that didn't help: from the start the students had been betting on "Fedya," and they greeted his victory with a loud rendition of "Fedya, our curly-headed boy." Then they began to bet on the others, and in the process they recalled an incident in which the principal had once lectured the students. (He was trying to disperse them after they had gathered in a crowd in a school corridor.)

"You can't all fit here—tell me, why can't you all fit here?"

When they stopped talking, not knowing what to reply, he triumphantly, as though pronouncing a magnificent truth, just discovered by himself, answered for them: "Because of the laws of phys-sics! Petrov cannot occupy the same space Ivanov is standing in."

Remembering this profound aphorism, the students took into account the slightest movements forward in space, and the betting pool flourished, arousing violent passions and even leading to small cockfights in the school's "water closet," which served as a clubhouse and smoking room, while at the same time dispensing its primary function.

Among Kolya's classmates various tendencies, not yet fully formed and not even fully conscious, were starting to define themselves—to put it more exactly, they were sympathies that had certain centers of gravity. A certain frame of mind, or mood, would take hold in daily life, flowing from the various social milieus in which the boys themselves circulated.

There was the aristocratic group, the individualists, a handful of sons of the nobility and big bourgeoisie—wealthy merchants, bankers, stock brokers, and Jewish bigwigs, who intently made their way into the most refined spheres. These boys aped their elders, pompously playing at being dandies and snobs. They wore trousers with straps, English boots with long socks, jackets of expensive light-colored fabric, fitted to the waist at well-known Moscow tailors' shops, and wide leather sashes that were considered chic. They always wore starched collars, had their hair neatly clipped, and characteristically parted it impeccably in the middle, with not a single hair out of place or protruding from their carefully slicked-down heads. They attended the school as though doing it a great favor. They kept to themselves. Often they carried French books with them, from Baudelaire to Maeterlinck and Rodenbach, and went about with a melancholy air, as though to show that they lived in a world of other dimensions—and they would read these books while concealing them under the lids of their school desks. They walked with an effeminate gait and loved to exchange remarks in French or English and talk about art; they were exaggeratedly "correct" about everything, as though everyday life to them was something to be held by two fingers at arm's length, squeamishly, with the pinky raised. They bandied about the names of Nietzsche and Solovyov but hadn't read them, not one whiff. Sometimes they would bring in reproductions of the refinedly sinful, ever so elegant chef d'oeuvres of Aubrey Beardsley or the drawings of Felicien Rops and would speak in prayerful whispers of Oscar Wilde. Among the latest Russian poets, they recognized only the Symbolists and showed off in front of one another by recounting the latest tidbits of news from the behind-the-scenes literary or personal lives of the Symbolists, thus making the subtle transition to specialized gossip.

The direct antipode of this group consisted of children mainly from families of the *raznochintsy* and intelligentsia. Under their jackets they wore peasant blouses, and they deliberately let their hair get shaggy, often not bothering to comb it. Some of the older boys even let their hair grow long. During lessons they secretly read Pisarev, Dobrolyubov, Saltykov-Shchedrin. They were enamored of Gorky, who became their veritable idol; they demonstratively spat on all authorities of any kind and made fun of any and all "Chinese ceremonies"; and they mocked the *belopodkladochniki* (the ones with white linings under their jackets), caustically remarking on the way they walked as well as the "ideals" they professed, gave them cutting but rather apt nicknames, such as "Australian wagtails," and sometimes got into lively discussions with them, usually on literary topics. They had a vague sense that the great flood of life would soon answer the question: "When will the real day come?" They were thrilled

by every demonstration of courageous protest, every word of denunciation, every heroic act of resistance against the established order, and even
mischief making had a certain value in their eyes—it could lead sponta-
neously, unintendedly, to "the erosion of the foundations," if only in trifling matters. They had insolent tongues in their heads, were never at a loss
for words, and loved to taunt their more sheeplike neighbors.

These were the "elites" of the class (in a certain sense). The majority still
lived as God had decreed for their souls: they read what they were supposed to, according to the school curriculum; they got into mischief at
school only because punishment was no longer a sure thing—or simply
out of excess energy and as a protest against boredom. There was also a
group of big boys, regular "bulls": the sons of large landowners of the
wilder sort and several lanky fellows from families of wealthy, highly
placed government officials; most were repeating a grade for the second
year. They were already going to houses of prostitution, talking about
cards, "girls," and the bottle, and they would boast about catching a really
bad case of gonorrhea, "with blood"—among them that was considered a
special sign of masculinity.

The first time Kolya experienced a form of oppression at the school was
when the following incident occurred. He and Sokolovsky undertook to
publish a school magazine—something completely innocent, with stories,
poetry, criticism, articles about life at the school, and drawings. (Kolya even
pictured the kind of cover the magazine would have, and for some reason
this imagined cover played a big role in his thinking.) They told a number
of friends about the magazine—and got support. They decided to acquire
a hectograph and buy paper. And they collected money, about ten rubles.

The next day, not long before lessons ended, the school inspector, with
a dry gleam in the lenses of his pince-nez, remarked in passing, but in a
serious tone: "You, Petrov, are to stay after class. I'll come by to see you."

Kolya stayed, completely unsure what this could all be about.

Soon Fyodor Semyonovich came in. He closed the door firmly behind
him and looked through the glass to see if there was anyone in the corridor, then suddenly knitting his brows—or more exactly, those places
where brows ought to be—asked a question: "Have you been collecting
money?"

"Yes."

"For what?"

"For a magazine, Fyodor Semyonovich."

"That is categorically forbidden—don't you know that?"

"For heaven's sake, Fyodor Semyonovich, it's completely innocent, just
a school magazine."

"Not under any guise—"

"But what is there to object to?"

"Why, don't you know—" The inspector leaned over, right against Kolya's ear, and continued in a whisper, "Don't you know that even for the most innocent thing—they can arrest you? And you heard what the Grand Duke said about our school? What do you want, not only to get yourself in trouble but the whole school?"

"Well, I didn't at all expect that anyone could see a magazine like this as—"

"But I'm telling you—it doesn't just depend on us—understand?—get rid of everything. Return the money. And I ask you, Petrov, in fact I insist—do you hear me, *insist*—don't bring the matter up again. If you were not our—if you were not such a brilliant student, I wouldn't be talking with you this way." Again the inspector leaned against Kolya's ear: "I rely on your discretion. There's nothing more I can add—understood?"

"Understood, Fyodor Semyonych."

"Will you do it?"

"I'll do it."

Thus it was necessary to say good-bye to the magazine, and thus Kolya received his first object lesson on a fundamental matter, forcing him to reflect on the question of "certain rights."

The winter went by cheerlessly. Kolya felt a lot of pain whenever he recalled Tosya, and he sometimes thought about death: what was the point of living if, no matter what, you had to die? There Tosya had been, such a talented, intelligent person. And now he was gone. As though someone had stepped on an ant. How stupid and absurd the whole arrangement was! At night Kolya would hide under the covers and try to imagine that he had died: there he lay, moving neither legs nor arms, seeing nothing, hearing nothing . . . No, it couldn't be nothing! Try as you might, some sort of little hole, a small opening onto the world remained, and you found yourself watching yourself . . . And what about sleep? Say I fall asleep and later on, wake up. What was there in the meantime? It was as though there had been no time . . . The devil only knew how strange it all was. After all, there was a time when I, too, didn't exist, wasn't that so? But other people had existed, and trees, and stars, and flowers, the sun and the earth. What was so strange about it, then, after all? But Tosya, Tosya! Just a little while ago he was alive, and now—nothing. No, there was no way to be reconciled with that, in spite of everything. It was impossible! When I go to the university, Kolya thought as he lay under the covers, I will have to study this business—no doubt about it. After all, there are as many polyps living as you could want. Reproduction by division—isn't that a kind of immortality? And in humans the sex cells pass on from generation to generation: the individual dies, but the race lives on. But why couldn't it be arranged that these cells constantly revived the individual human being, so that he would be reborn eternally from himself? Or is that just greenhorn nonsense? But why in fact would it be nonsense? . . . Then again, what would happen to the earth if nobody died? It would get filled up with people, like sardines in a can. But that's a thing that can be corrected. From Darwin's teachings it follows that all species of living beings are related. Both the fruit fly, which only lives for a day, and the crow, the elephant, and the parrot, which live for a hundred years.

The Origin of Species has a mass of examples showing that the present arrangement can be changed. That means that an organism can also be changed in such a way that it acquires greater longevity. But if that were successful, where would the limits be set? No, for sure, I'll have to study this . . . It's worth putting some effort into . . . But still, there's no bringing Tosya back. That's something that has been lost forever. On the other hand, what's the explanation for the way you feel sometimes, as though you had seen and experienced before what you are seeing and experiencing now, in every detail? Of course there's the doctrine of transmigration of souls . . . religious foolishness . . . superstition. Nevertheless, how do you explain it? It has to be dealt with. Why hasn't it been possible for so long to artificially create living matter? They got as far as urea and got stuck there. I'll have to study about that, too. I wish I could start at the university sooner. What about Fyodor Semyonych? He got really scared, it seems, over the magazine idea. Again, it's the system! You can't say a word. . . .

Another interesting thing is dreams that have a continuation: you dream something, then a year and a half later a continuation of that dream comes to you . . . And again, later on . . . You recognize all the places . . . What is that? And what about flying in your dreams? You move your arms and think how easy it is to fly . . . Is this a memory from the times of the Cheiroptera? Of pterodactyls and other remote ancestors? After all, their blood runs in our veins . . . The devil only knows how interesting it all is; and you never have time to learn everything you want before you die . . . Like Tosya . . . No wonder he talked about his own death, as though he had a premonition . . . On the other hand, in this case it's all very understandable—he was so weak, he himself spoke about his genetic makeup, he understood . . .

Under the covers it was dark and warm. Kolya tried to get control of his thoughts but they ran on one after the other, then dispersed, became vague, he could no longer grasp their meaning. It was warm. He felt so sleepy . . . Nothing really mattered . . .

And Kolya fell asleep

One of the clear frosty days of winter the Petrov boys and the tutoring students organized a big skating and sledding party in Blokhin's yard. The snow hill was iced over gloriously. The snow in the yard squeaked under-foot. Dark-blue shadows fell from the outbuildings. A cold sun shone in a light-blue sky. The trees in Makhova's park and the Armenian garden were covered with a lace of frost and stood still, as though in a spell, with not a single twig stirring. The windowpanes of the houses were adorned with frost-patterned colors. Breath came short. Steam rose from overheated mouths. Brightly reddened cheeks burned. Hands, wet with melted snow, ached from the cold. But a great bustling about and joyful laughter reigned in the yard. Urging one another on, the boys dragged the heavy sleds up the snow hill, then rushed down it, steering skillfully with their feet so as not to hit the corner of the house going around the turn . . .

Along the way someone would get shoved off the sled, and he would roll, laughing, head over heels into the snow, then would get up, shaking himself off and thoroughly cleaning his nose, eyes, and ears of the packed-in tiny snow crystals, which, when melted, would run down his face and, in icy rivulets, get under his collar.

Kolya and Andryusha were going down the hill on skates. The hill was very steep, and the boys would rush down it at a dizzying speed, keeping their balance with their arms. Volodya was steering a sled . . .

"Kolya, try to catch up!" Volodya shouted, pushing off with his felt boots, and the sled went racing off, sliding over the ice and leaping over bumps. Volodya, lying on his stomach in the back, with his legs stuck out, was "steering." The sled turned the corner and, gradually slowing down, nearly rammed into the fence around the Medyntsev's vacant lot. But it stopped.

"And here I am," cried Kolya. While making the sharp turn on skates, to keep from falling, he had held tightly to the other boys' backs.

"Well, let's go again!"

Grabbing the ice-covered rope and awarding one another friendly cuffs and blows, the boys went running and hopping back toward the snow hill. Coming up from behind the house, they saw Andryusha lying on his back, directly on the ice.

"Andryushka! What's wrong?"

"I fell!" he said with pain. "I hit the back of my head real hard."

He got up and took off his skates.

"You better go inside and lie down a while."

Everybody loved Andryusha—both his brothers and people outside the family. He was kind, extraordinarily capable, outgoing and affectionate.

Although he was only seven, he dreamed of going to the *gimnaziya*, and they called him "Yanchik, Yanchik, the *gimnaziya* student."

"Andryushka is starting to outclass Kolya," Ivan Antonych would say on occasions when, taking part in tutoring lessons, Andryusha would quickly solve problems that the other boys, twice his age, were wrinkling their foreheads over in vain.

Andryusha went in, but after a while he came out and began to skate again.

"I have a headache. But maybe it'll go away."

And it did go away. They all happily continued their sporting about; they played in the yard until late in the evening, with only a break for dinner; they made their way into the Armenian garden and stole a green trap with four triggers that belonged to the guard there. The guard guessed what had happened. But this trap had long been the object of their boyish dreams, so they paid for their stolen booty with forty pieces of silver (forty kopecks) and the matter was smoothed over to the satisfaction of all concerned.

That evening the boys were loudly horsing around in their rooms. Andryusha put a Viennese chair up against the back of his neck. And Kolya, on the fly, jumped and sat in it. Then suddenly he noticed that Andryusha's eyes had filled with tears.

At that moment Ivan Antonych walked in.

"What's wrong?" he said, seeing the tears.

"Kolya did something that hurt me—"

"I didn't mean to—"

And that was all there was to it.

That night as everyone was sleeping peacefully, a strange, inhuman cry broke out . . . Andryusha was writhing about on his bed, unconscious, crying out, shouting . . . Kolya ran to his side at the same time as his mother . . . Andryusha kept crying out . . . Kolya put his arms around his brother's little body, his warm, tiny little body . . . Andryusha kept shouting, twisting about . . . Everyone was up . . . Running around helter-skelter . . . They ran outdoors without coats to get ice . . . But he kept on shouting . . . Suddenly he stopped . . . Andryusha was no more.

The next morning he was lying on the table, like wax, his eyes closed, with his little aquiline nose, like a baby bird; one side of his face was dark, black and blue, up to the temple.

Kolya nearly went mad.

"What if I'm to blame? What if I killed him? The tears. But he had that fall earlier. But the tears . . . Oh, Lord. What am I to do?"

Kolya was beside himself. Priests came . . . And Manya Yablochkin, in her cat-fur cap. There was incense . . . Hyacinths . . . His mother was weep-ing . . . At the cemetery there was a snowstorm . . . the grave . . .

"Wee-eeping by-y the graveside . . ." People were singing . . . A raven swayed in the branches of a birch tree . . . The wind whipped up a fine pow-der of snow and sprayed sharp little needles of ice in people's faces . . . "E-eter-nal me-em-ory . . ." The coffin was lowered. Dear little Andrei . . . I fall on my knees before you . . . Say something, just one word . . . Dear one!

Kolya kept sobbing soundlessly. At night bad dreams oppressed him. He saw Andryusha, kissed him . . . Why, he was alive! . . . He hadn't died—that was just a dream, a terrible dream . . . Then suddenly Andryusha's eyes filled with tears and he kept staring and staring at Kolya with a look of inexpressible reproach . . . Kolya awoke in horror and confusion.

Weeks went by. The anguish did not go away. Kolya concealed his ter-rible doubts within himself, and was tormented inexpressibly.

His father was sitting by the window, deep in thought. Kolya came up to him.

"You know, Kolya, all of a sudden it's as if you . . ."

With broken sobs Kolya threw himself on his father's neck—the boy's whole body was trembling, even his shoulder blades jerking.

"Easy, Kolya, calm down. It isn't so, you know. You understand that yourself," his father murmured softly.

"Oh, Papa, Papa. Who will give me the answer?"

It was a question to which no one would ever be able to give Kolya the answer.

Chapter 20

At the apartment of the Molodtsov brothers, schoolmates of Nikolai Yablochkin, in one of the little dead-end alleys off the Arbat, preparations had been made for a decisive confrontation between Social Democrats (SDs)and Socialist Revolutionaries (SRs). All the windows in the large room had been covered with heavy claret-colored blinds so that nothing could be seen from the street. Sitting on the wide leather couch were Nikolai, Manya, and their friend Sokolov, a serious young man whose whiskers were just starting to sprout. The guests took seats on the chairs: the SR Lebedev, an eighth-year *gimnaziya* student; two girls, Mara and Sima, also SRs, with the ecstatic, radiant eyes of Madonnas; and Vasilyev, a first-year university student, wearing a red shirt under a double-breasted jacket, who had curly red hair and surprisingly rosy lips. He was the main force and the great hope of the SRs on that evening. The Molodtsov brothers, Ivan and Aleksandr, resembled each other greatly; they both had straight noses, handsome faces, and almost identical golden hair. They stood by the wall. Their sister, Margarita, who had graduated from the *gimnaziya* and whose nickname was "Queen Margo," sat in an armchair next to a large desk and mechanically leafed through the pages of a book left spread out on the desk.

"Well, what do you say? Shouldn't we start?" said Nikolai, frowning gloomily.

"Let's wait a little. Stepanov promised to come," Margo commented.

"All right. Only we have to set some sort of time limit. I propose ten minutes per speaker," Nikolai mumbled, snuffling and coughing.

"Do you agree, comrades?"

"We agree. We agree."

Not two minutes had gone by when a loud, jangling bell went off in the front hall. It was such a furious sound they all looked at each other in alarm. Margo calmly, like a peacock, glided off into the hallway, which was thickly hung with topcoats and greatcoats—the coatrack barely held them all. Laughter and wheezing could be heard, then into the room burst the busy, bustling, shortsighted Stepanov, whose nickname was "Tut-tut," because of his stutter.

"I'm a little late—tut-tut—it seems—tut-tut. Damn snowstorm," he spoke in a quick patter and rather thickly. "All present and accounted for?"

"Yep, we were just waitin' for you."

"Sorry, sorry—" He pulled out some sort of squat and heavy ancestral timepiece. "It's only been ten minutes. Not even an *akademische Viertelstunde* (one quarter of a school lesson). Excuse me, but why isn't Popov here?"

"We forgot to invite him. It's so annoying," replied Ivan Molodtsov, wrinkling his brow. "Why didn't you remind us, Margo?"

"I forgot just like you."

"Well, never mind. Next time we'll invite him."

Several people lit up almost at once, and the smoke began to coil around the room.

"Ugh, let's get started," growled Nikolai, gasping and coughing. He couldn't stand tobacco smoke, and smoke-filled rooms were beyond his endurance.

"Nikolai Mikhailych, don't sit there being such a grump," Margo addressed him with a smile, then added: "Unless I'm mistaken, it's time to begin."

"Listen—tut-tut—*zur Tagesordnung* (on the agenda)—I propose we choose someone to chair and keep order. And I nominate Margo."

"What? The Queen?" Vasilyev remarked ironically.

"Motivation," Stepanov went on, paying no attention to Vasilyev. "She, as everyone knows, is a woman—"

"Ha, ha, ha."

"Nothing funny about it. We should continue Chernyshevsky's tradition . . . Besides that, Bebel says—"

"Keep it short," Nikolai said dryly, between his teeth.

"Furthermore, she's very tactful, calm, and fairly impartial."

"Well that's different. All right. Let it be Margo," the SRs agreed, glancing at one another.

"She's *interesting*—," whispered one of the SR women to the other. The other silently nodded in agreement.

"Thank you for choosing me," pronounced Margo, not a bit embarrassed. "Nikolai Mikhailych, you have the floor."

"Gentlemen—"

"Not gentlemen, but comrades!" said one of the Madonnas offendedly.

"It's comrade for some people and mister for some others," snarled Nikolai.

"Oh, what a viper he is, a bespectacled snake," the SR woman whispered.

"In the first place, for theory, the Socialist Revolutionaries live on crumbs from the gentry's table. The whole international socialist movement is going through a split just now. The theoretical premises of opportunism, formulated with an enviable frankness by Bernstein, are essentially a rehash of the bourgeois critique of Marxism. They're the justification for reformist tactics that involve abandoning revolution, accepting posts in bourgeois ministries, transforming socialist parties into auxiliaries of the liberal bourgeoisie. In this dispute between Marxists and revisionists, only from the theoretical standpoint so far, the Socialist Revolutionaries stand almost entirely on the side of revisionism."

"That's wrong. Where did you get that idea?" the hot-tempered Vasilyev interrupted Nikolai.

"Comrade Vasilyev," Margo said quietly. "Please don't interrupt the speaker."

"Wrong? All right—"

Nikolai reached in his pocket and pulled out a crumpled and ragged copy of the SRs' *Vestnik Russkoi Revolutsii* (Herald of the Russian Revolution).

"In this article, 'The Worldwide Growth and Crisis of Socialism,' it plainly says that Marxism has emerged 'shaken' from the dispute with Bernsteinism, that is, with the liberal bourgeois and petty bourgeois politicians in the workers' movement, with the disciples of the bourgeois apologists. (The characterization isn't ours!) You can judge for yourself, if it suits you." Nikolai tossed the *Vestnik* on the table.

"But this is—"

"Ergo," Nikolai continued, "no matter how evasive the SRs are about it, they *do stand with the reformists against the revolutionaries.*"

"That's outrageous. What's he saying? That we, who used bombs—," Sima whispered, turning red as a rose, her eyes burning. She could hardly contain herself and looked questioningly at Vasilyev. He had buried his face in the *Vestnik* and did not notice the girl's flaming glances. The Molodtsovs smiled. Queen Margo sat like a statue.

"In the second place, despite all their noisy radicalism, the SRs haven't accepted, they don't recognize, they don't understand the basic theoretical and practical principle of revolutionary socialism, the principle that the class struggle and the dictatorship of the proletariat are the necessary conditions for a socialist revolution."

"We recognize the class struggle. But—"

"Just a minute there. You recognize it only halfway. You recognize it in such a way that you submerge the proletariat—the only consistently revolutionary class in capitalist society—into the general category of 'the people.' You strip the industrial working class of its distinctive characteristics and put it on the same level with the small property owners, that is, with the small shopkeepers, the peasants, and the intelligentsia, which is bourgeois democratic, however radical it may be. Thus you obscure the contradictions between the proletariat, which is deprived of the means of production, and the petty bourgeoisie, which possesses the so-called means of its own livelihood. You obscure the difference between those who sell their labor power and the small commodity producers, between the buyers and the sellers of agricultural products, between the representatives of socialized labor and the labor of atomized individuals—"

"We've heard this before—"

"Maybe so. What's more, you try in every way, in spite of the facts, to ignore the social differentiation among the peasantry, the class divisions and contradictions within the peasantry itself. You mix all together the landless laborers, the poor peasants, the middle peasants, and the rising, prosperous ones. You look at the peasantry as a formal category, as a 'social estate,' rather than from a class standpoint."

"But how can you deny the poverty, the suffering, the tears of the peasantry?" the girl with the blazing eyes suddenly broke in. "Don't you know that the peasants' bellies are swollen from malnutrition, that they're dying of starvation, that in many places they live worse than the workers? Have you no shame?"

"Comrade," Margo's deep contralto sounded reassuringly. "Put your name on the speaker's list, and you'll get the floor."

"Forgive me, I just couldn't contain myself."

"That's too bad," Nikolai cleared his throat. "Aargh . . . Guh," he said half choking. "If you used your head, maybe you'd see that your arguments aren't to the point. Poverty and tears are not the only criteria for determining the role of a class. Excuse me for using an extreme example, but impoverished gentry also weep, like Herman in Pushkin's *Queen of Spades.*"

"That's really cheeky! What cynicism!" Sima said softly into her girlfriend's ear. Vasilyev was jotting notes on a slip of paper with a fine-pointed pencil.

"We are well aware that some peasants live worse than workers—

machinists, for example. But tell me, if you please, don't the lumpen proletariat, Gorky's heroes, those who live by their wits, often live still worse. Still, you wouldn't claim that they are the hope for socialism. On the other hand, a lot of anarchists, including Bakunin, were not far from doing that. In ancient Rome, the lumpen proletarian masses were the instrument of Caesarism and not of socialism. But certainly they were poor."

"Nikolai Mikhailych, excuse me but you seem to be getting off the track," said Margo, looking at the speaker a little guiltily.

"Maybe so. I'll sum it up. The peasant masses will come into the revolution, into this bourgeois revolution, but as small owners. They are a very important, an enormous force, but they are still not a consistently socialist force. They are a revolutionary democratic force. Anyone who claims otherwise is deceiving himself and others. That is the job the Socialist Revolutionaries are doing, and they have to be fought.

"To go on. In the third place, it flows from this that the working class must take the leadership of the petty bourgeoisie. After shattering the tsarist system, basing itself on the poor peasants, the proletariat will lead the peasant masses toward socialism. But for that it is necessary to have a clear understanding of the proletariat and the small property owners, that is, to stand on the ground of the class struggle and to build a class party of the proletariat, and not some vaguely defined party of the plebeian masses in general, in which all cats are gray (*sery*)—pardon the pun!" (This could be taken to mean "all cats are SRs," since the Russian abbreviation for "SRs" is pronounced *sery*.)

The Molodtsovs, Manya, Sokolov, and Stepanov all smiled as one. Something like a smile even flashed across Margo's face.

"The SR program for 'socializing the land' is connected to this. You are creating illusions about an agrarian utopia within capitalist society. But this 'socialization' has as much to do with socialism as small property owners in capitalist society have to do with the proletariat, who are the gravediggers of capitalist society. Here also, instead of looking reality soberly in the eye, you paint a child's picture of paradise.

"Now, to conclude, a couple of words about terrorism as a method of struggle."

"Let's see what he's going to say here," the Madonnas whispered.

"The theoretical presupposition for terrorist tactics is a thoroughly bourgeois conception of 'heroes' and 'the crowd,' Lavrov and Mikhailovsky's 'critically thinking individuals' and 'inert masses.' Beltov* destroyed these presuppositions in his book."

*Plekhanov.

"You're making assumptions. That's a very sweeping assertion," Vasilyev remarked. Margo looked sideways at him.

"It's not hard to prove. You should take a look at Carlyle or Vladimir Solovyov. You'd find plenty to chew on there."

"Nikolai Mikhailych, I must reprimand you for rudeness," Margo said.

"That's from the standpoint of a charitable young ladies' institute," Nikolai spat out with irritation, and continued: "In preaching terror, the Socialist Revolutionaries preach the single combat of heroic individuals divorced from work among the masses that is aimed at preparing the way for a mass uprising. It's like children playing at being heroes. These are failed methods. Trying to breathe life into them is like trying to breathe life into mummies."

"You are spitting on the martyrs," Mara shouted hysterically.

"This is the limit," Sima said, virtually with tears in her eyes.

"We don't spit on people. We recognize the heroism of the People's Will fighters. But we also see their tragedy. In general—," Nikolai said irritably and then began speaking in a rapid patter, "in general it's time to stop replacing logic with gushing and arguments with emotion. We are discussing the most effective way to wage the fight against tsarism. The most eff-ect-ive way. Do you understand? This is not something for hysterics. The only serious thing is to work to prepare the masses, to enlighten them, to organize them for the uprising that alone can overthrow tsarism."

"If you please, are we against mass work?! It takes nerve, comrade, to deny—"

"You are sitting between two stools."

"That's not true!"

"Not true? Fine—"

Again Nikolai dug in his pocket and pulled out an elaborately printed proclamation put out by the SRs in connection with the assassination of Minister of the Interior Sipyagin. Fixing his myopic eyes on it, he read: " 'To deal with the crowd, the autocracy has soldiers; to deal with the revolutionary organizations, it has the secret police and the uniformed police. But what will save it from individuals or small circles that do not even have knowledge of one another and are ceaselessly preparing for attacks and carrying them out?' That's not badly put. Take a look." And he handed the proclamation to Vasilyev, who exclaimed: "Listen, comrades, it is all here in so many words and in bold type. We call for terror, not *instead* of mass work but precisely *for the sake of* this work—and in conjunction with it. Look!"

"I know. The road to hell is paved with good intentions. And what do you think is the meaning of this condescending reference to the 'crowd' and the 'revolutionary organizations'? To deal with these, it says, the autocracy has the means, while it doesn't have the means to deal with 'individuals.' Is this the line? At best, it is an indigestible salad. I have finished. The conclusions are self-evident."

Nikolai took out his pince-nez, wiped it, and then said, turning to Margo: "Margo, keep track of this, please, so that all this literature won't be forgotten, so that the maid won't get hold of it, or somebody else."

She nodded.

"Comrade Vasilyev, would you like to say something?"

"Yes."

"Please do."

"First of all, I want to say I'm not going to follow Nikolai Mikhailych's example; I'm still going to call him and other SDs 'comrade.' "

"How remarkably noble of you. I am touched and deeply moved," Nikolai muttered, looking at the Madonnas, thinking: Well, they are nice . . . Where do the SRs get these pretty girls? . . . But they all have their eyes turned toward heaven.

"Manya," he whispered to his sister. "They really are Virgin Marys, aren't they?"

"That's enough running on at the mouth. You're interrupting. Stop it."

"How was I? Was it all right?" again he spoke quietly to his sister.

"Not bad. A little dry, as always. But logical. Unfortunately you messed up at the end. But stop pestering me. It's awkward. Quit the whispering."

"So, comrades, I have to make one preliminary remark. Like all Marxists, Comrade Yablochkin based himself on a schema. The general schema of capitalist development—that's all there is. But what about Russia's special features? Where are they? He didn't mention them. They flew away."

"What *samobytniki*?* Good thing you remembered."

"Comrades, I am not defending the Slavophiles. I know that the old Narodniks were mistaken. In denying the possibility of capitalist development in Russia, V. V. and the others got athwart of the facts."

"Glory to God," grumbled Nikolai.

"Comrades, don't interrupt," said Margo sternly and looked directly at Yablochkin.

"Yes. They turned out to be wrong. But does that mean the Marxists were right about everything? By no means. That would be the greatest oversimplification. We face an autocracy, which doesn't exist in Europe. Among the peasantry here there is a collective form of organization, the

---

*Advocates of the Slavophile theory that Russia has a unique or exceptional (*samobytny*) path of historical development.

mir, which also doesn't exist in Europe. We have a working intelligentsia that loves the people, which, again, doesn't exist in Europe. In our country, literature is on the side of the people, our long-suffering, great literature, which is conscious of its duty to the people, a kind of literature that doesn't exist in Europe. Our students are not at all like the German *Burschen*, with their scars, their dueling swords, and their beer mugs, or like the Oxford and Cambridge lovers of rowing competitions. Our working class—"

"You mean there *is* such a thing after all? Thanks very much for that." Nikolai wouldn't let up.

"Our working class is closely bound up with the peasantry, which is also not the case in Europe. Comrade Yablochkin has obviously forgotten about all this. So, instead of life, he has a schema. That is the dead dogmatism of the Marxists. They don't see the flickering light of the great dawn, when the entire people—"

"Now he's just running off at the mouth," Nikolai muttered.

The Molodtsovs looked at Manya, as if to say, "Make that brother of yours stop."

"Precisely because our peasantry is not exactly the same as the Western European—"

"And who is right about Western Europe, Bernstein or the Marxists? You take everything from David and Hertz and the other types like them."

"Nikolai Mikhailych, I beg of you," Margo looked imploringly.

"Let him speak. We didn't interrupt you," Sima and Mara cried out in unison.

"Excuse me. I'll be as quiet as a fish."

"As long as it's not a shark, if you please," Sima put in.

"As to that, we'll see," Nikolai responded to her jibe. "But for now— *finis. Silentium!*"

"The critics of Marxism are right about a lot of things. But they draw wrong tactical conclusions from quite correct positions. That's the answer to your objections—now to get back to the subject. We base ourselves on specific conditions of development. Our thinking intelligentsia, which has given Russia so many ideas from brilliant heads and martyrs, which has sacrificed the lives of its noblest sons, is unknown to Europe. Even you know, perhaps, that today the Russified word *intelligentsia* is being used in Western European literature. This combination of the peasant collective organization, the *mir*, our peasant traditions—and I emphasize *our*—traditions, together with a special type of intelligentsia, gives rise to the three-in-one formula: the peasantry, the workers, and the working intelligentsia. Even Marx, in his letter to Vera Zasulich, did not exclude the possibility of another road for Russia. You, of course, would dismiss him as a Narodnik. It's not for nothing that he told Lafargue: 'If these people are Marxists, then I am no Marxist.' "

"Quite good, marvelous," whispered Sima and Mara. The Molodtsovs smiled, looking back and forth at Yablochkin and Stepanov.

"Engels wrote that Marxism is not a dogma. In his last writings, he said that he and Marx had underestimated the noneconomic factors. He said the theory had to be reworked. And what do you Marxists do?

"You have gotten your minds into such a straitjacket that you are like people quoting the Bible, and you don't want to know anything new. You have transformed your party into a barracks. You also think the same way. You have killed all freedom of criticism among yourselves and you want to extend this barracks to include everything and everyone. We humbly thank you. But the only response we can make to such invitations is a categorical no, and again no."

"Oh, you've frightened me!" Nikolai mumbled sarcastically.

"Hey, we're not inviting you to join us. We don't need people like that," Ivan Molodtsov couldn't restrain himself.

"Vanya, you're talking out of turn," his sister remarked reproachfully.

"So, I say that all your so-called principled invectives against our party fall on their face. You are insulting the party that is continuing the most heroic traditions of the Russian revolutionary movement, the party that is adorned by the shining stars of glorious names. These jibes are the product of dry dogmatism, naked schemas that do not take into account the special features of Russia's development.

"Now, let me turn to the question of terror. But before that a few words about the intelligentsia and 'heroes.' Isn't the Lenin that wrote *What Is To Be Done?* one of yours? Unfortunately I don't have the pamphlet at hand."

"We have a copy," Aleksandr Molodtsov shot back. "I'll find it right now."

"So much the better; you can check it. Doesn't your Lenin say that socialism is injected into the workers' movement by the intelligentsia? That without this intelligentsia, the workers' movement will get mired down in trade unionism. So, how can you—"

"Here's *What Is To Be Done?*" Aleksandr held out a copy of Lenin's pamphlet to the speaker.

"Now—" He started leafing through the pamphlet. "Here, I found it. Here it is. 'We said,' Lenin writes, 'that there can be no social democratic consciousness among the workers. It can only be brought in from the outside.' Do you get the full clarity of the formulation? It says quite clearly, only from the outside. Further on, it says, 'The history of all countries testifies that by its own forces alone the working class is able to develop only trade union consciousness—that is, a conviction of the need to unite in unions, to wage struggles against the bosses, to get from the government whatever laws are essential for the working class. The teachings of socialism arose from philosophical, historical, and economic theories worked out by educated representatives of the possessing classes, the intelligentsia. The founders of contemporary scientific socialism, Marx and Engels, on the basis of their social position, belonged to the bourgeois intelligentsia. Likewise in Russia, the theoretical teachings of socialism arose in complete independence from the spontaneous growth of the workers' movement. They arose'—listen to this!—'They arose as the natural and inevitable result of the development of the thought of the revolutionary socialist intelligentsia.'

"That seems clear, doesn't it?

"And yet you, precisely you, cannot put two and two together. Where, in these lines by Lenin, do you see your celebrated consistent class standpoint? You think a class that cannot develop its own ideology is a great thing, that it is a wonderful class point of view that has representatives of another class assuming the mission of theoretical and practical leadership.

"From this it follows that as soon as you want to ground yourself on the facts you suffer bankruptcy. You deny the role of individuals, yet you make a cult of your Lenin. You hurl thunder and lightning at the sins of intellectuals, yet you exalt the intelligentsia to the skies. You talk about the consistency of your class point of view, yet you destroy it. And instead of drawing appropriate conclusions from this—that is, looking for broader theoretical and practical bases—you repeat your dry, dogmatic propositions over and over . . . But forgive me, I have digressed a bit. There are undoubtedly exaggerations in the proclamation that Comrade Yablochkin has quoted here. If I am not mistaken, the party has noted this in its official publication."

"That's true. That's the usual method of 'qualifications,' qualifying everything you say," Nikolai said dryly from his seat. He was annoyed that the SR speaker had moved from the defensive to the offensive, and he, Nikolai, was mobilizing counterarguments he could use to "kick the SRs' teeth in" in the rebuttal.

"Not qualifications, but corrections. If you follow the effects of the terrorist actions, you will see that they stir the population. And this speeds up the mass movement and helps it. The heroic deeds teach people to sacrifice their lives for the great cause of liberation. History is not some inevitable process, as your doctrine teaches."

"Oho," wheezed Stepanov. "He's gone around the bend!"

"The masses need deeds and sacrifices. It is our party that keeps alive the sacred flame on the altar of Liberty."

Vasilyev shook his curls, wiped the sweat from his forehead with the sleeve of his jacket, and sat down. Sima shook his hand, and her eyes flashed. Nikolai eyed her with the look of a young wolf, as if to say, "What a fool!"

"Who wants the floor? I think the best is to alternate speakers according to tendency. That way, there will be more order. All right?" Margo asked, looking at everyone present.

"All right, all right," several voices rang out.

"Then I'm asking for the floor," Aleksandr Molodtsov said quietly. He was a very well read young fellow, a diligent student of ancient and medieval history and a serious student of philosophy.

"I would like," he began, "to go into the question of classes, especially the peasantry and the proletariat. To say that every country has special features of development is a truism. No Marxist denies that. If Comrade Vasilyev had read *What Is To Be Done?* attentively, he would have seen that Lenin took extraordinarily precise note of the peculiarities of Russian development. But when Vasilyev tries to show that the type of development in capitalist Russia differs from the type of development in other capitalist countries, that is the source of a great error. You, for example," Molodtsov gestured toward Vasilyev, "claim that there is nothing in Western Europe like the Russian intelligentsia. But that's not true. Take Germany before 1848. What are poets like Herwegh, Chamisso, Freiligrath? What are writers and commentators like Behrens? Philosophers like Bruno Bauer? Don't you know that in essence Bruno Bauer already had your entire ill-famed concept of 'critical individuals'? Even the wording was the same. If you were familiar with Marx's work *The Holy Family*, you would see how similar your exercises are to Bruno Bauer's 'critical criticism.' In his work also, you have spirit and matter, heroes and the crowd, critical individuals and the masses. And what about the French intelligentsia before and after the Great Revolution? You forget about them. Here also there are many similarities. Here also you exaggerate Russia's uniqueness (*samobytnost*).

"Then you exalt the exceptional quality (*samobytnost*) of the Russian peasantry, the existence of collective organization, 'the land is God's,' and so on. Don't you understand that all those are relics of the Middle Ages, features that at one time were seen everywhere? Don't you know the elementary facts about the medieval peasant wars, the peasant communistic sects—the Taborites, the Cathari, and others? You cite Marx's letter to Vera Zasulich. But you don't get the point of the letter. It says that it is possible that Russia can bypass capitalism and move on to socialism, if there is a socialist revolution in the West. But you yourselves have to admit that Russia long ago set out on the road of capitalism. And now it is subordinated to the laws of capitalist development. That theoretical possibility has already been lost; it no longer exists. After that, why refer to this letter?"

Aleksandr spoke quietly, calmly, with a firm voice. Everyone had listened attentively. No one had interrupted, and there were no grounds for interruption.

"Margo," Aleksandr continued, "was probably wrong to distract Nikolai from his thoughts concerning the ancient lumpen proletariat."

Margo blushed and made a vague gesture with her hand. Vasilyev grinned. The Madonnas also smiled.

"All right, hold on, what did I want to say?"

For a moment, Aleksandr was confused, all his thoughts had flown out of his head at one go. But quickly he got them by their tails, pulled them back, and continued in an even, calm voice.

"Yes. Yes, the Roman lumpen proletariat was poor. It lived on handouts from the state. But it could not be a force for transforming society. Why? Because it was not the bearer of a new mode of production. Don't you understand that the present-day proletariat is not just poor (by the way, your theoretical allies, the Bernsteinites, deny Marx's 'theory of impoverishment'). It is concentrated in production. It is educated, organized in, and unified by the mechanisms of capitalist production themselves. All the conditions of its social existence are original. And they give rise to a corresponding social consciousness."

"And what about Lenin in *What Is To Be Done?*" Vasilyev brought this up with a sneer and a snicker.

"I had not intended to take up that question, but since you have thrown down the gauntlet, all right. It's just that you understood Lenin very superficially, that is, you didn't understand him at all. In capitalist society, the proletariat is an economically exploited and politically repressed and culturally oppressed class. Therefore, without going outside the framework of capitalist society, it cannot by itself acquire the great achievements of science and critically rework them. That means that the ideologists of the working class come from other classes—"

"Aha!"

"What's this 'aha'? They go over to the side of the working class. They express its tendencies of development; they formulate them, basing themselves on the full development of science. They detach themselves from their previous social base and find another social base. They are not suspended in a void outside classes. They are not interclass intellectuals but exponents of the class interests of the proletariat. This is an expression of the fact that capitalism is doomed, and that inevitably the best minds perceive this. For them capitalism has lost all historical and moral credibility. This is not any violation of the class principle. This is not at all treating the intelligentsia as a body outside classes. On the contrary—

"If you please, let me get back to the subject now. Precisely because today's proletariat embodies the principle of socialized, collective labor, organization, solidarity, concentrated mass action, precisely because it is deprived of property, it is the only consistently revolutionary class. The peasantry does not have and can never have any of these features. The *obshchina* (village collective) has broken up. You don't want to see that. To a considerable extent, it has become an administrative mutual-protection arrangement. The peasantry is undergoing social differentiation and becoming proletarianized with striking rapidity. You lose sight of that. You want to conjure away these processes, but that can't be done. In our country we will have some sort of peasant war against the feudalist landlords and against their absolutist government. But the peasantry will overthrow the landlords and not be broken by them because they will find allies and leaders not in some Martin Luther or Götz von Berlichingen but in the industrial proletariat and its solid battalions. It has never happened that the countryside has pulled the cities behind it. The city is the great provider of forces that can organize and lead. The good fortune of the peasantry is that this leader and ally has arisen and is continuing constantly to grow. This is how the question has to be posed. That's all."

"Listen, comrades," Margo broke in, "it's already impossible to sit here because people have been smoking so much. I propose taking a break. You stay here for now. I'll set up tea in the dining room, then we'll air out this room. Put aside your cudgels for a minute. People have gotten a bit tired. It's all right, isn't it, if we have a break?" she asked, getting up. She was perfectly aware that the group's stomachs were already growling.

"Excellent idea," Vasilyev said cheerfully, blowing a smoke ring.

"I have no objections," said Nikolai. "The devil himself knows these smokers—cough, wheeze, cough—have really fouled up the place."

"Let's go, Margo. I'll help you." Manya left, arm in arm with her friend.

A quarter of an hour later, the whole group was sitting in the brightly lighted dining room, hungrily eating cheese and sausage sandwiches. "Now, mind you, no smoking here," Margo admonished, as she poured tea.

"So, what do you think about your Chernov? 'Peasants and Workers as Economic Categories.' In the magazine *Zarya* Lenin smashed all of them—Chernov, Bulgakov, David, and company—smashed them to bits," a voice was heard at one end of the room.

Another voice was quoting:

All, all, that threatens to bring death
Hides in itself for the mortal heart
Delights that are inexplicable.

Then it asked: "Is that what attracts you to terrorism? But you need to die intelligently, not for a pinch of tobacco."

Vasilyev could be heard saying: "Materialism in general is an antiquated conception. Modern philosophy strives to overcome every kind of metaphysics, including materialism." Chewing on a piece of kalach, he asked: "Pass the butter, please. Thanks, Comrade Margo. And hand me a glass—"

"You're just playing with terminology. That's another escape route into the bourgeois camp. Kant and the agnostics are now all the rage. This will pass, like the rage for lace-up English shoes."

"No, no matter what you say, Beltov with his contradictory nature of motion—"

"All right, if you like, let's debate that question, too—"

Then Nikolai's voice could be heard: "I suggest you concentrate on the process of consumption so that we can move on to the front of theoretical class struggle as soon as possible; it's already late."

"No, let them rest a bit," Margo objected. "Have you finished already?"

"Of course."

"Take a piece of candy. You have a sweet tooth, it seems."

"You're wrong. I don't smoke, nor do I have a sweet tooth."

Soon they gathered again in the other room. They took the same seats they had had before, as if each had reserved his or her fortified position.

"Fu. Damn it. Someone—tut-tut—has let the cold in," Stepanov grumbled.

"And so the honorable assembly continues. Who wants the floor? Remember your turn."

"Let me," Lebedev motioned agitatedly.

"Comrade Lebedev has the floor."

"I want to take the bull by the horns."

"It's interesting to note what long ears he has," Nikolai whispered to Manya. She waved him away with her hand.

"All of you have been too polite so far."

"All right. Getting down to it! I like that!" Nikolai shouted loudly, with a cough and a wheeze. "All right. Let's see. Let's listen."

"Right, you listen, Nikolai Mikhailych. You attacked us because we supposedly support reforms. But we, our party, in every step of our struggle have shown with our own blood that this is a slander. Yes," the young fellow continued in a terribly agitated way, "an unmitigated slander. And who is judging us? People who think that their role is to smooth the path, to clear the way, for capitalism—that is, for the Kolupaevs, the Razyvaevs, the Morozovs, and the Chetverikovs.* Yes, yes, that's it exactly. And yet you dare throw accusations at us!"

"A hot-headed fellow—tut-tut—he's got the bit in his teeth."

"Let me ask you, honorable Marxists, where is the development of your ideas heading? Who fired the first shots for the Marxists? Struve, Tugan-Baranovsky, Bulgakov, Berdyaev, and company. Where are they? They're completely in the camp of the bourgeoisie. They've gone all the way. That's dotting the *i*s and crossing the *t*s. Who wrote your party's first manifesto, esteemed opponents? Have you forgotten? It was your man Struve, today the leader of the zemstvo constitutionalists, the editor of *Osvobozhdenie* (Liberation), who has already forgotten completely about socialism. Before, the Marxists were the footmen of capitalism. Today, they have gone up in the world. From helpers, they have become bosses. Your socialism was worth an awful lot. So, do you think this evolution was an accident?"

"You're talking nonsense, Comrade—tut-tut."

"Enough of this fool," Nikolai spat through his teeth.

"No, it wasn't an accident. First you have to smooth the way for capitalism, and then—"

"That's the way Krivenko replied."

"And then join it, join the bourgeoisie. And, for you, that's not shameful. After all, it's more progressive than feudalism. And socialism is a long way off. That's why you don't want to see the socialistic aspects of the *obshchina*, of the *mir*, cooperation, the peasantry, the intelligentsia. That upsets your schema; that upsets your bourgeois belly. Yes, that's what I wanted to say."

"Are you through?"

"Yes."

"Who's next?"

"I am, if you please," Stepanov blurted out with a lot of huffing and puffing.

"I'm—tut-tut—not the greatest speaker. But, the devil take you—tut-tut—you, Lebedev, you talked nonsense. I can't believe my ears. What does smoothing the path mean? You haven't given that a thought. Should we fight against all the vestiges of feudalism or not? You don't even realize what you yourselves are doing. The fight against the autocracy is a fight

*Prominent Russian capitalists.

against the most important feudal institution, and overthrowing the autocracy means smoothing the path for capitalist development. On this basis, and within this process, then, our task is to organize the forces for a fight against capitalism. Oh, how clever—tut-tut—you have to be to understand that! When the Jacobins cut off Louis XVI's head in France, they thought that the reign of liberty, equality, and fraternity would ensue. They were as full of illusions as you are. We have no illusions. We don't need winged phrases—tut-tut—or dreams. We need sober work—sober, that is, not abstemious. You get the difference? We will overthrow tsarism, all right. But for us, that is—when the most difficult tasks begin for the further struggle for socialism. But the overthrow of tsarism is all you see. As for Struve, who was it that first exposed him? Lenin! True or not? Who's Bulgakov associating with now? The SR leader Chernov! All the arguments in his two-volume so-called work, *Capitalism and Agriculture*, are the same as Chernov's, just more detailed. Who's closer to Struve today? You, of course. The same general terms, national in general, human in general, cultural in general, popular in general, and—I'm losing my train of thought—"

"Are you through?"

"Yes—tut-tut—I wanted to say something . . . else. But all right, that's enough." Stepanov waved his hand and sat down.

"Why were you so brief?" Nikolai whispered to him. "You were just getting started, and you broke it off."

"Christ, I got sick of it. Anyway—tut-tut—you can't enlighten them. And what do I need them for? See what kind of specimens they are. Enough is enough."

"Who wants the floor now. Sima? Mara?"

The girls shook their heads no.

"Then, Nikolai Mikhailych, you wind up."

"Cough, I'm not going to—cough, wheeze, cough—beat my head against a wall. Stepanov said a lot of what I wanted to say. I'll try to be fairly brief. Besides, the place is all full of smoke again—cough, cough—

"I still haven't gotten a reasonable answer to my first question. I said that when the whole international socialist movement is split between the Marxists and the reformists, the SRs generally stand on the ground of Bernstein, David, and company, that is, on the positions of Brentano and the bourgeois critics of Marxism. There is no third way. The SRs haven't yet said anything about the Kropotkin anarchists or the French syndicalists. How did my honorable opponent reply? He said that they're right in theory, but they draw the wrong conclusions. No, excuse me, for them theory and practice are completely bound together. So, how can it be explained that in Russia today the SRs take a revolutionary position? They do take such a position, and I would not think of denying it . . .

"The explanation is simple. In the West, socialism is a serious question. In our country, what's on the agenda is smashing the autocracy and carrying out a bourgeois democratic revolution. As democrats, the SRs are revolutionary. And the West European reformists fully sympathize with the bourgeois democratic revolution. It's the socialist one they're afraid of. The same is true of the SRs. Their socialism is not revolutionary. Their revolution is not socialist. The best characterization of them is 'liberals with bombs.'

"Second—cough, cough—my opponent sought to enlighten us regarding the uniqueness of Russian development. Aleksandr offered quite effective examples showing all the limitations of the SRs' arguments. I'll say a few words about another aspect of the matter. The main peculiarity of our capitalism is that it is developing in the context of the autocratic rule of the landlords and serf owners. The landed property of these serf lords and their governmental power is the main reason for the particularly difficult and weak development of Russia. Therefore it is not only the working class that has an interest in bringing down the autocracy but the entire peasantry and even the bourgeoisie (which later on is inevitably going to get scared of the workers). This configuration of forces creates the illusion that 'the people' is a single entity. But we have to understand what this 'people' is made up of, the specific weight and interrelation of class forces within this 'people.'

"The peasants are not quite the same here as in the West. That's true. But my opponent hasn't had a word to say about my designation of them as petty commodity producers or about their differentiation. That's the Achilles' heel of the SRs' conception. And here, in fuzzing over the class contradictions, which will reveal themselves in their full force the day after the autocracy and the landlords are eliminated, lie hidden the roots of the SRs' potential reformism. When the liberals with bombs no longer need bombs, they will become simply liberals."

"Disgraceful!" Lebedev cried.

"Disgraceful, yes. But that's how it's going to be. I agree—cough, cough—that it's disgraceful."

"That's not what I was calling disgraceful—"

"I understand you perfectly well. But you don't understand simple irony—Aleksandr said the essential things about the peasantry and the proletariat, and about the Vera Zasulich letter, too. A couple of words about terror. You see, now we're at the start of 1903. I have drawn up a summary, for 1902, of so-called mass disturbances. It won't hurt to read it out loud."

Again Nikolai dug in his pocket and pulled out a little oilcloth-covered notebook filled with his fine small handwriting. Sticking his nose into it, he began to read:

" 'January 22: Demonstration by workers and students in Kiev; clash with the police. February 2–6, strike by the workers at the Bryansk factory. February 8, students beaten up at the People's Center in Petrograd. February 9, student mobilization in Moscow; mass arrests. February, disorders in Finland, in connection with a call-up order. February–March, strikes, demonstrations, and clashes with the army in Batum. February 19, demonstration by Social Democratic workers in Moscow against the Zubatov people. February 19, demonstration in Rostov-on-Don. March 3, demonstration of workers and students in Petrograd, clashes with police. End of March, peasant agitation in Kharkov and Poltava provinces. March, demonstrations in all the cities in Finland. March 26, disorders in the Botkin factory in the Urals. April 18, demonstration in Finland against the new military regulations. May, mass May Day demonstrations in Baku, Sormov, Nizhny Novgorod, Saratov, Odessa, and a number of other cities. May 9, disturbances at the Tikhoretsk station. Summer months, peasant agitation in Saratov, Tambov, Novorossisk, and Stavropol provinces; agitation in Guriya. June 28, strike by railroad and engineering workers in Kiev. September 13, strike in the rail shops in Krasnoyarsk'—"

"Why are you reading all that?" Lebedev burst out.

"Read it! Read it! It's a very interesting picture overall," several voices said.

"Why am I reading it? You'll soon see. Funny you're not interested in this kind of 'prose.'

"November, Finnish congress and resolution on civil disobedience. November 2–23, strike in the rail shops on the Vladikavkaz lines, strikes in the plants and factories in Rostov-on-Don, mass rallies, demonstrations, use of armed force by the government. November 17, workers beaten up at the Tikhoretsk railway station. November 21, demonstrations in Tiflis. December 9, strike in Batum.'

"And now, gentlemen, I will just say that 1903 is showing an enormous increase in such mobilizations. Why did I read all this out? Shall I tell you in strictest confidence?" Nikolai gaily flashed his pince-nez. "All right, I'll tell you. You do know, don't you, that in light of all this, only a blind person could fail to see what is the nub of revolutionary politics today. A vast mass movement is awakening and growing. It requires agitators, propagandists, organizers, bold and consistent leaders. It is growing without the stimulation of any terrorist attacks or individual fireworks and sensations. It is a more serious and decisive business, and it determines the line. Being distracted from this work by 'heroic single combat' means disorganizing the mass movement. Here, gentlemen, you have to make a choice; you can't sit between two stools. Now, have you understood why I dwelt for such a long time on material that is so boring to you?

"Now, a word about this barracks thing. An opponent used barracks to scare us. I'm not at all scared of the word. There are barracks and there are barracks, just as there are soldiers and there are soldiers. We are building our party, if you please, not as a collection of different species of birds, crabs, and fish, but as a party of those who share the same conception, as a fighting party. Yes, as a combat party. Because revolution means civil war; an armed uprising is war. Such a war has to be prepared for, and the party has to be a combat party. If this is not to your liking, what can be done about it? That means that you prefer chatter to serious business. As for our brutal intolerance, and the cries about 'freedom of criticism,' let me imitate my opponent and quote Lenin's *What Is To Be Done?*

"Hand me the pamphlet, Margo . . . Here's what Lenin writes about the subject: 'We are proceeding in a tight file along a twisting and difficult path. We are surrounded on all sides by enemies, and we nearly always have to move under their fire. We joined together, on the basis of free choice, in order precisely to fight our enemies and not to retreat into the neighboring swamp, whose inhabitants have reviled us from the start because we separated ourselves off into a distinct group and chose the path of struggle and not the road of conciliation. And here we have some of our own people shouting, "Let's go into the swamp." And when people start to shame them, they respond by telling us what backward people we are and aren't we ashamed of denying them the freedom to show us a better road! Yes, gentlemen, you are free, not only to show us a better road but to go wherever you like, even into the swamp. We even find that your proper place is in the swamp, and we are ready to offer you whatever help we can to move you there. Just let us go, don't hang onto us, and don't debase the great word *freedom*, because we are also free to go where we want, free not only to fight against the swamp but also against those who want to turn toward the swamp.'

"That should be enough for you. *Schluss* (I'm done)."

"The meeting is over."

The SRs got up. The others did, too.

"Comrades, don't rush! Leave one at a time, except for the girls."

"Manya, I'm going with the Madonnas. You don't object, do you?" Nikolai asked.

"What's that to me? But it seems you've come of age in this respect, too, eh?" Manya remarked, and it was not without amazement that she glanced at her brother.

"In revolutionary times, a year is worth decades," he answered with a laugh.

The street was quiet. In the alley, footsteps echoed hollowly. Snow was falling in large flakes. They fell silently, swirling out of the darkness and forming circles around the street lights. They formed a soft, white, crumbly featherbed that covered the sidewalks, the stones, the coach, and the back of the dozing, not entirely sober driver.

Chapter 21

Minister of Internal Affairs Sipyagin was assassinated on April 2, 1902, by the student Balmashov, who was soon executed by verdict of a military court in gloomy Schlüsselburg fortress. In place of Sipyagin the tsar appointed an experienced gendarme with much police experience, Vyacheslav Konstantinovich Plehve, who as far back as the 1880s had specialized in hunting down members of the People's Will organization (Narodnaya Volya). He was an old wolf of a policeman, "a cavalry sergeant-major by education and a pogrom organizer by conviction," as he was subsequently characterized by the liberal-leaning Prince S. D. Urusov. A careerist, a cynic to the core, not inhibited by anything and stopping at nothing, Plehve promised the tsar to put an end to the "hydra of revolution" in three months, which made the tsar very happy: he was impressed by such resoluteness and such vigorous strength of will—and at the time of the conversation with Plehve he almost believed that this sharp-fanged Cerberus would indeed slash the throat of rising sedition.

The tsar appointed Plehve mainly out of fear. But this fear was given conscious form, a justification wrapped up in lofty words about the good of Russia, responsibility to history, etc., by the tsar's adviser, Prince Meshchersky, the publisher of *Grazhdanin* (The Citizen), one of those unsavory adventurers who always cropped up at the emperor's court and amassed for themselves political capital with deft, underhand strokes, with gossip, denunciation, blackmail, refined groveling, and Byzantine flattery and servility. Under both Alexander III and Nicholas II, Meshchersky received, by direct order of the sovereign, eighty thousand rubles from the state treasury annually. He often wrote letters to these tsars with his political advice and received letters from them in which the autocrats addressed him with the familiar form of "you," a special sign of monarchical favor.

About him he kept certain selected objects of Socratic love, whom he called his "spiritual sons," beginning with a handsome trumpeter of a king's infantry battalion and ending with various young officers, who alternated with one another. In behalf of these beloved objects, Prince Meshchersky interceded with various ministers, and in the case of refusal would write libelous diatribes about them: any bureaucrat could be found to have committed sins; there was no great difficulty there.

Many, even in the court circles, considered Meshchersky a filthy man and hated him, but at the same time they feared him and trembled before him, knowing his connections and suspecting that he had some sort of hold on certain highly placed people and was blackmailing them. Of course this admirer of classical Eros was a true patriot, and *The Citizen* once expressed its patriotic sentiments in the following political maxim: "When everyone's thought regarding the holder of power is 'He might cut off my head,' then there is both submission to authority and tranquillity."

So it was precisely to this man, more than to any other, that Plehve was indebted for his advancement to the post of most powerful minister in the Russian Empire. Plehve was of Polish origin—therefore he could not tolerate anyone but Russians. Plehve himself believed in neither God nor the devil: he was not foolish. But, having received the appointment, he immediately set off by special train from St. Petersburg to Moscow, and from there to the Troitse-Sergiyeva Monastery to kiss the relics of Saint Sergius of Radonezh, who from the earliest times was honored by the tsars of Muscovy and the emperors of all the Russias: this was sure to please the tsar, the tsarina, and Grand Duke Sergei Aleksandrovich, whose ancestral estate was adorned by this renowned and wealthy religious institution.

Kissing the relics was all the more necessary for Interior Minister Plehve since a journey to Kharkov was his immediate next step: his task there was to approve on behalf of the government the brutal thrashing of peasants carried out by the Kharkov governor, His Illustrious Highness Prince Obolensky, and at the same time to visit A. A. Lopukhin, prosecutor at a regional appellate court, who had been displaying great talents at police work. Not long before, a wave of agrarian disturbances had rolled across southern Russia; arson had licked here and there at manorial estates; and peasants, choked by the shortage of land, had begun to talk about the land of the gentry.

The disturbances had been suppressed, and Prince Obolensky had established order, personally traveling to the villages that had rebelled in order to be present when the inhuman corporal punishment was administered: it even gave him a certain pleasure to see the red peasant blood flow from under the torn shirts.

"You won't live to see this again, scum! Lunkheads! Mutineers! Next time I'll hang you by your ribs . . . Just thank God that this is all . . . You got off easy—"

Some of the flogged peasants were lying flat on the ground, others were standing silently, with boiling ferocity in their eyes: the tears of the mice are poured out for the cat.

The tsar's interior minister went next to the scene of the fighting. He praised Prince Obolensky for his honorable defense of the throne and recommended him for an award: the prince received the rank of adjutant-general and the office of governor-general of Finland.

Sitting in the Kharkov governor's well-guarded home, Plehve ordered that Lopukhin be summoned: he had things in mind for this man.

Lopukhin was of old boyar stock. Family tradition traced the genealogical thread back to the semimythical Kasogian prince, Rededya, of the medieval epics. Peter the Great's wife Yevdokia, the last of the empresses of Russian blood, bore the family name of the Lopukhins, and although her cruel and willful husband had divorced her and sent her to a convent, family tradition honored her memory as a representative of the clan. Now the Lopukhins had become scarce, and their former grandeur was no more; still, Aleksei Aleksandrovich had inherited more than a thousand desyatinas of land. He graduated from the university and quickly began to advance up the ladder of official service. Fairly well educated, with an excellent command of languages, he had great self-control, was vain and ambitious, a lordly aristocrat and a sybarite; moreover, he belonged to a category of young careerists for whom wide prospects had opened, especially because, while loyally serving the autocracy, they were well received in liberal circles, too: Lopukhin sentenced peasants to savage punishments and at the same time was a very close friend of Professor Sergei Trubetskoi, a liberal prince, one of the pillars of the zemstvo movement, an admirer of Vladimir Solovyov, and a specialist in Plato and the Gnostics. The gendarmes were delighted with Lopukhin, as were the secret police: he always worked things out with them in advance.

Neat, clean-shaven, with close-cropped hair and wearing a pince-nez, through which he peered with his somewhat slanting eyes, he placed himself before the stern gaze of Minister Plehve. Plehve sat in the office, at a desk, frowning, stroking his thick walruslike policeman's mustache, and rolling the whites of his big, bulging eyes.

"How may I be of service, Your Excellency?"

"Have a seat, Aleksei Aleksandrovich. Please." And then: "Let's dispense with titles—"

"As you wish."

"Do you smoke? Please—"

He clicked open a massive cigar case of silver with gilt trim . . . The window to the garden was open . . . A sunbeam rested on the bronze candlestick; now it pierced the moving, dissipating rings of smoke, revealing the pale, scentlike quality of their blueness . . . In the garden there were apple trees blooming, and a light puff of breeze occasionally carried in a petal, delicate and light, that would fall spinning to the mirror-smooth parquet floor . . . Birds chirped . . .

"So here's the thing, Aleksei Aleksandrovich. I would like to know your opinion concerning the agrarian disturbances—your candid opinion—"

"Yes sir—"

"That the prince has flogged the mutineers—that is outstanding—such things cannot be left unpunished, and firmness was necessary here—wouldn't you say?"

Plehve glanced at Lopukhin's small figure from under his brows: "Of course. I completely agree with you—"

"But this does not end the matter. Preventive measures are also needed . . . I am now responsible for the tranquillity of both the dynasty and the whole empire—but prophylaxis requires both an accurate diagnosis and an accurate determination of the causes of the disease . . . Pa . . . What do doctors call it? I've forgotten . . . I'm getting old—"

"Pathogenesis."

"Exactly. So I wanted to ask you, Aleksei Aleksandrovich, to set forth your views on all these questions . . . But please, with no constraints—otherwise all this will be of no value to me. You of course understand that I have official material in abundance—"

And Plehve pointed his short finger at a tightly packed leather portfolio, swollen like a mountain, with silver clasps and monograms, that was lying on the desk.

"It goes without saying that our conversation today is strictly confidential. And so, that is what I request of you."

Plehve fell silent and fixed his gaze on Lopukhin with a questioning expression.

Lopukhin began to think quickly. Why was Plehve having this conversation with him? What would its consequences be for him, Lopukhin? . . . Knowing his environment very well, he understood that there was an ulterior motive; that Plehve was testing him; that he needed him, Lopukhin, not merely as a source of information . . . Indeed, the minister would now replace his staff: a new broom sweeps clean. Some heads would fall, some would rise . . .

And the young careerist sensed that something good was in the air; he sensed it with all his being.

He gave Plehve a serious, committed look, as if he had fallen to thinking and was collecting his thoughts . . .

A bumblebee flew in through the window and, buzzing, knocked against the upper pane, now rising with a deep buzzing sound, now falling helplessly . . .

"I must first remark, Your Excellency, Vyacheslav Konstantinovich, that your question to a certain extent has caught me by surprise—and therefore I ask you to pardon the unsystematic nature of my statement—"

"That's not important," Plehve answered.

"Next, my critical observations are personal observations that do not touch on the fundamental bases of our state system . . . I must emphasize this in order to avoid any possible misunderstandings—"

"You have absolutely nothing to worry about in that regard, Aleksei Aleksandrovich—"

"Yes, sir . . . It seems to me that we must recognize the disturbances that have taken place as being by no means random but rather as deeply symptomatic. They are the first signs of a great agrarian movement or, to dot the *i*'s and cross the *t*'s, of a spontaneous revolution . . . The causes are rooted, as far as I can judge, in the general conditions of our life; they are many, and the chief among them, in my opinion, are—"

Plehve turned heavily in his chair and leaned his elbows on the desk. Lopukhin paused . . .

"Please, continue. You have my full attention."

"The main pathogenic factors are the ignorance of the peasant population, the ignorance and darkness which provide sufficient support for all kinds of plotters who dream about the laurels of Pugachov and Razin; the terrible impoverishment of the peasantry, the destruction, the starvation, the conditions of material life in general—I would be able to give you a detailed statistical picture for a number of our provinces . . . Sheer indifference on the part of the authorities toward the material and spiritual needs of the peasantry; finally, the petty supervision of village constables, district policemen, land captains, police chiefs, governors, etc., often directed against the vital and essential interests of the peasant homestead and the individual peasant, beginning with the interests of his property . . . The local authorities are far from being imbued with the idea that the autocratic monarchy should to a considerable extent rely on the conservatism and devotion to the throne of the many millions of peasants; that the destruction of this traditional trust and devotion to the dynasty is fraught with innumerable consequences; that, finally, the peasants and petty bourgeois should develop their own economy in order to pay and to have the means to pay more and more taxes, because the needs of the state—I am speaking of financial needs—will inevitably grow. That, so to speak, is a law of nature. Our administrative machinery is not adapted to the carrying out of the tasks that have arisen, and here, Vyacheslav Konstantinovich, certain reforms are needed. Without them—"

"Without them—revolution is inevitable. I fully agree with you. It is approaching both from the city and from the countryside, and if the urban strikes unite with a Pugachov rebellion, then the situation may take a threatening form—"

"Exactly—"

"And what would you say—I fully share your diagnosis—to the idea of the creation of a kind of substitute for a constitution?" asked Plehve, watching for changes in expression on Lopukhin's face.

"I do not share the point of view of a constitutional monarchy. But what form of substitute do you wish to speak of?"

"For example, in the form of a drawing of public organizations—the zemstvos, the dumas, etc.—into the work of the State Council. Indeed, these loudmouths are also a factor and a source of discord—if we throw them a bone—and then control the matter of elections—what do you think?"

"I think that that plan is rational. But at the same time it is essential to rationally bring up the matter of punitive measures, of the suppression of discord . . . Political wisdom has long pointed to the need for both threats and bribery—this is perhaps highly regrettable from the point of view of abstract humanism and the ravings of some Tolstoy—but for us, who are responsible for the fate of the country and of the monarchy—"

Plehve jumped up from his chair, then lowered himself again.

"Aleksei Aleksandrovich, I am extremely glad that you broached this topic first. On this point, I feared, there would be disagreement between us. Now I see that you understand perfectly the whole complexity of the situation, which requires combined methods of pressure from us. Reforms—prudent reforms—do not preclude, but rather presuppose, relentless suppression of revolt and all manifestations of the anarchistic movement—"

"I think so, too."

Neither spoke for a moment. In reality Plehve was in no way contemplating any type of reforms whatsoever. But in keeping careful track of Lopukhin's correspondence, the old gendarme was well aware of the young prosecutor's flirtation with the constitutionalist liberals. He had a longstanding habit of using such people mainly for their connections; they would meet him halfway—his many years of police experience told him that. Therefore he played with Lopukhin, completely sure of coming out of this game the winner. Lopukhin, for his part, was picturing his forth-coming brilliant career and was already prepared to do anything, as long as he could ensure himself a stable position in the promising future open-ing before him. He pricked up his ears and waited.

"Then allow me, Aleksei Aleksandrovich, to draw the practical conclu-sions from our frank discussion—"

Plehve raised his head a little and looked Lopukhin straight in the eyes. Lopukhin remained silent.

"I," continued the minister, "am offering you the post of Director of the Department of Police—what do you think of that?"

Lopukhin thought quickly . . . Director of the Department of Police—one step to Minister of Internal Affairs . . . Plehve is old . . . Moreover . . .

"I accept, Your Excellency—"

"Then allow me to congratulate you—I am very, very glad."

Plehve got up from his chair and held his hand out to Lopukhin. Lopukhin also rose, and the handshake sealed the deal that had been made.

Having thus recruited a new department director, Plehve, for the sake of appearance, requested heaps of memoranda on reforms and left them to ripen in large, neatly compacted files. His business—the business of smothering the life that was bursting forth—he decided to put on a firm foundation, concentrating it in the hands of an aficionado and artist, a person who seemed to have been born for police investigation, provoca-tion, and torture chambers, Zubatov. At the sight of him, Zubatov would never have given the impression of an experienced police hound. He looked more like a typical Russian intellectual—in his outward appear-ance, in his mannerisms, even in his habits. A small beard, straight brown hair combed back, a little jacket—he seemed a rare bird indeed among the blue police uniforms, the jauntily twirled mustaches, the spurs and epaulets, the clean-shaven chins, and the clang of sabers. By this time he had risen from the rank of small-time informer to that of chief of the Moscow Secret Police Department. Ambitious and imperious, he stood several heads above his dull-witted colleagues: he used ideology to justify the practice of his work as an executioner, and as a practitioner he had a wide range. He was the real father in Russia of police socialism, in which snatches of Western European ideas about a so-called social monarchy, of official Slavophilism, of Tikhomirovism, and of the main traditions of the Third Section were amazingly intertwined.

As a counter to the mass working-class movement he set up police orga-nizations for the workers, and sometimes even supported economic strikes; he encouraged discussion of the everyday needs of the workers, depicting the revolutionary ideology as an ill-intentioned product having nothing in common with the true interests of the workers, who were being looked after by the father of the people, the autocratic monarch, who stood above all classes and strata.

Zubatov even brought in professors to give lectures: the lame financial expert, professor I. Kh. Ozerov—who verbally even flirted with Marx—was one of the active agents of Zubatov's policy in Moscow. In Odessa Zubatov installed "Doctor of Philosophy" Shayevich. In St. Petersburg, as in Moscow, he had a whole blossoming "working-class" society, where professors, gendarmes, generals, and priests stopped in, suddenly inflamed with a great love for their little brother.

In vain certain capitalists and bureaucratic luminaries, like Witte, grumbled, warning that this was playing with fire, that the movement would overflow the police barriers, that the escapades of the secret police would turn against them, that the police could not both provoke strikes and manage them . . . Zubatov continued his policy, laboring to construct the ideal of a police bridle on the whole working-class movement.

At the same time he feverishly reformed police techniques: he introduced the photographing of those who were arrested, Bertillon's tables with the classification of distinctive marks; dactylography, where revolutionaries hiding under someone else's passport were identified by their fingerprints; he created cadres of trained detectives and provocateurs. He instructed police officers and secret police scoundrels himself, explaining how it was necessary to confuse people, deflecting suspicion from police agents and directing it onto honest people. "You, gentlemen," he would say, "must look upon your collaborator as upon a beloved woman with whom you are in a clandestine liaison. Care for her like the apple of your eye. One incautious step, and you will disgrace her." He especially valued the provocateurs among the terrorists . . .

Soon after the assassination of Sipyagin, on the direct recommendation of Plehve, the old provocateur Yevno Azef, a disciple of Zubatov, became the head of the armed wing of the Socialist Revolutionary Party. Thus the chief figures of the police world were arranged in their places.*

*The police agent Azef, as head of the SR terrorist organization, was soon to be responsible for the assassination of Plehve himself (in 1904) and of Grand Duke Sergei Aleksandrovich (in 1905). The exposure of Azef, in 1908, created a scandal for the tsarist regime—as one part of the government was revealed to have engaged in violence against another. The Azef scandal also discredited the SRs' policy of terrorist actions carried out by "heroic" individuals.

Chapter 22

After the death of Andryusha, Kolya Petrov could find no peace. He experienced a severe emotional crisis: a bottomless abyss seemed to have opened before him and he was walking at its very edge. The whole world had lost its luster, all colors had turned pale, all sounds were muffled: a deathly pallor lay over everything, filled with nameless dread and inexpressible sorrow. It was as though Kolya's soul had tumbled against the world, and since then, to his mind, the world had ceased to exist, had become insignificant, unimportant, unworthy of notice; or else, it had been filled to the brim with a terrible poison and was staring at Kolya with transparent deathly-green eyes. Dream, fantasy, delirium, reality—they all got tangled up and mixed together in a confusing whirlwind of painful images, questions to which there were no answers, riddles and problems that could not be solved. Kolya grew wan and thin and began to seek solitude. Anguish and melancholy gnawed at him every moment. He would go off by himself into the Armenian garden, sit right down on the snow, and be lost in thought . . . He made his way out onto the streets, through which he would wander aimlessly, talking to himself, spreading his hands and gesticulating, pointing at passersby, who, hurrying along, would suddenly turn and stare, stopping for a moment, then hurry off again, busy with their own affairs . . .

Kolya was indifferent to everything then: pedestrians, horsecab drivers, carriage shafts that nearly ran into his face, street kids who would yell things at him; he withdrew completely into himself and lived in his own dreadful inner world. Functioning automatically, he went to school, answered his teachers automatically, wandered down the corridors automatically, and everything around him—the hustle and bustle, the teachers, the lessons, his friends—seemed to reach him through a thick layer of water.

"Our Petrov seems to have gone off his rocker—"

"Hey, Little One, what's wrong? Can't you see past your navel?"

"Leave him alone. His brother died."

"Aha—well, the hell with him then—but shouldn't we shake him out of it?"

"We've tried. Nothing works."

And they left Kolya in peace.

Nevertheless, Kolya knew no consolation. Everywhere he went he seemed to see Andryusha's eyes, filling up with tears, reproachful . . .

Lord, but how to bring back the past? Kolya saw his brother's thin little arms, his little nose, felt the native warmth of his fragile body, the eternally close tie between them. The more tenderly he felt that tie and the more vivid and immediate the feeling of closeness with his brother, the virtual oneness of their flesh, the more painful, terrible, monstrous did the gnawings of conscience become . . .

Was everything else really worth just one of Andryusha's little tears? What was the use of any action, virtue, heroic deed, act of atonement when you could not bring back the past? Dear little Andryusha, Andreichik! My God, what I wouldn't give to have you not die. I'd give my life. Without a moment's hesitation. So that there wouldn't be those reproachful eyes. How I would love you, protect you, watch over you . . . hug you around your little neck . . .

Sometimes for Kolya everything, all the values in the world, became concentrated in just one of Andryusha's little tears, and it seemed that the ultimate depths of being were hidden there. This was something he felt, rather than thought. The concepts were vague and confused, but he found himself completely enveloped by some direct and powerful feeling, which consumed him with its universal sorrowfulness: But how could this be? Suddenly snapping out of it, he would ask himself that question. *That* is gone, it no longer exists, that time is past . . . Face the facts: Andryusha is gone and his tear does not exist . . . Yet I see his eyes before me . . . What in the world is this? Am I to blame? . . . It's impossible to figure out . . . Lord, what agony! No, I can't live like this, and there's no point . . .

One night Kolya couldn't sleep. He lay there thinking, with his eyes wide open. He kept thinking the same thing over and over. Somewhere a mouse was bitterly scratching at a floorboard. The moon shone in through the window, pale and cold. The clock on the wall beat out a rhythm with its pendulum: *ti kto ti kto ti kto* (who are you?) . . .

"Who in fact am I? And what am I? And why?"

Kolya tried to sleep. Impossible. The thoughts kept coming on, crowding into his head and tearing at his heart. This had to stop!

Cautiously Kolya got out of bed. There was no one around. Not a sound. Everything in the house was quiet. Only the clock kept insistently asking: *ti kto? ti kto?*

Kolya tied two towels together, made a noose, tied the end to a handle high up on the window . . .

Do I have to? . . . Yes, I do . . . The sooner it's all ended, the better . . . Not to see anything . . . Not to hear . . . Not to know . . . Not to suffer . . .

And the moon kept shining.

Who are you? What are you? Who are you? What are you? . . . Kolya's heart was pounding, troubled and aching.

He stuck his head in the noose and jumped. It was as though two powerful, implacable hands had seized his throat. He couldn't breathe! And suddenly a hot blessed stroke of lightning passed through his heart, and everything went black.

He came to, lying on the floor: the end of the towel on the window handle had come untied and had not strangled him completely.

The moon was shining as before, cold and dispassionate. Just as implacably and steadily the clock kept ticking. Had it happened? Or not? Kolya remembered everything and couldn't believe it, and believed it . . . He got up quickly and sat on the bed . . . For a second something like the joy of being alive flashed through him, and the sensations of life, his body, his consciousness, the mattress beneath him, the moonlight, the sound of the clock suddenly filled him with a kind of surging wave of courage . . . Then a feeling of exhaustion swept over him; he was deathly tired: he began to yawn, his mouth stretching wide open; it seemed to him that his jaws would be dislocated by these immense yawns . . .

What stupidity, he thought, observing himself. Death was so close, and here I am yawning, yawning like an animal . . . God, how I want to sleep!

Kolya curled up in a little ball, seeking oblivion; he fell asleep and slept the sleep of the dead.

Days of new thoughts and reflections set in. One conclusion was clear to Kolya: it was necessary to love people, to take care of them. Otherwise the saying would prove true: if we don't safeguard what we have, we'll soon weep for what we've lost. Kolya became more serious, he stopped joking at his friends' expense, became sensitive to others to a painful extent, delicate almost to the point of eccentricity. He was afraid of hurting people's feelings or making them angry—never mind causing anyone pain . . . At the same time he felt a deep-seated need to somehow generalize all these fleeting thoughts, to arrive at some stable certainty, to discover the real meaning of life . . . He sorted through the fragments of various outlooks on life that he had come across one way or another, but he couldn't find—how many people have been tormented this way!—the answer to his naive questions.

There was Pisarev's "rational egoism." What about that? It was brilliant, entrancing. Seemingly, almost scientific. Proud and sober.

But what about the heroes who had gone to their deaths, the martyrs of science, and people like Caius Mucius Scaevola and Plutarch's heroes? And what about the Boers? The revolutionaries? Uriel Acosta? No, there was something lacking here after all. What kind of rational egoism could there be when the ego itself was up for grabs?

The Bible says, "Greater love hath no man than this, that he gave up his life for a friend."

Of course it's all nonsense that Christ was God. But he was a leader of the poor in his day . . . And aren't there really some good ideas there? . . . Of course, but is it possible to love all people? Didn't Christ himself drive the money lenders out of the temple? Why should we love them, the scum? And then there was the commandment calling for poverty, the denial of earthly things. Wasn't Heine right in his "Winter's Tale"? Didn't that commandment lead to monasticism and asceticism, fools like Simeon Stylites, the burning of witches, and devil knows what else? . . . On the other hand, why love only people? What about animals? Some scientists, including some who don't believe in God, claim that there is more difference between a European and a Hottentot or Bushman than between a Bushman and a chimpanzee. After all, the great apes are the cousins of human beings. And all living things are related. Everything is related. Francis of Assisi used to say: my brother the wind, my sister the night. Well, suppose that's just nonsense served up with Lenten butter: the deification or humanization of nature. Religion. The hell with it. What about the Buddhists who preach love for all living things, for animals, flowers, a blade of grass? Where do you stop along this path? Should you caretake a flea, be afraid to swat a mosquito, as some Hindu sects teach? Or just not eat meat—"corpses," as Tolstoy put it . . . There was no understanding it . . . It was all so mixed up . . .

Maybe the answer was the *ataraxia* of the ancient Greek wise men? Impassivity, indifference. But they were more like *non*rational egoists: each one going along with his own separate virtue, and no one else being warmed or cooled by it. Its only value was that you could point at yourself and say: "Ah, how good I am, how wise I am, how virtuous." This was nonsense, plain nonsense . . . Wasn't it just like Tolstoy's nonresistance to evil? Just sit there, do no evil, but don't touch anybody either.

Suddenly Kolya recalled reading somewhere that Turgenev's housekeeper had once said to him: "Ach, Ivan Sergeyich, one shouldn't be sad—

man soll nicht traurig sein. Life is like a fly: der most unlikable inksect! But vass can ya do? Ya got to put up mit it!" That "inksect" was good, thought Kolya . . . Only it was more like horror, hell, than an "inksect" . . . And you don't actually have to put up with it . . . It's impossible to put up with . . . What was that quotation from Marx that Tosya read out loud just before he died? . . . Clear as a bell . . . Got to find it . . . Read it again . . .

Once Kolya was sitting quietly, all by himself, reading Dostoyevsky. Suddenly he came upon a passage that shook him to the core. It was a passage in *Podrostok** in which Dostoyevsky described how people of the future would feel after they had lost their faith in God and the immortality of the soul and were going without the consolation of their thousand-year-old faith:

"Human beings, thus orphaned, would immediately begin to press against one another more closely and lovingly."

As Kolya read this his heart contracted . . .

"They would seize one another by the hand, understanding that now they alone constituted *everything* for one another! The great idea of immortality would have disappeared and would have to be replaced, and all the great abundance of former love for what had been immortality, would now be turned by everyone to nature, to the world, to people, to every little blade of grass. They would fall head over heels in love with life and the earth, and to the extent that they gradually came to realize their own transitory and finite nature, they would love no longer with the love they had felt before, but with a new and special love.

"They would begin to notice and discover in nature such phenomena and secrets as they had never previously imagined, because now they would be looking upon nature with new eyes, the way the lover looks upon the beloved. They would wake up and hasten to kiss one another, in their hurry to love, knowing that their days were short, that that was all that remained to them. They would work for one another, and each would give to all, all the fortune each possessed, and that alone would make them happy. Every child would know and feel that anyone on earth was like a mother and father to him. 'Tomorrow may be my last day,' each would think, watching the setting sun, 'but even though I die, all of them will remain, and after them, their children'—and this thought, that the others would remain, all full of love and trepidation for one another, would replace the idea of meeting beyond the grave. Oh, they would hasten to

*Podrostok (literally, "a juvenile" or "teenager"); the last novel Dostoyevsky wrote before *The Brothers Karamazov*. It has been translated into English in several versions under different titles, e.g., *A Raw Youth*, *The Adolescent*, and *The Accidental Family*.

love, in order to stifle the great sorrow in their hearts. Each would be proud and daring in his own behalf, but toward one another they would become shy and tentative, each would have a trembling concern for the life and happiness of the other. They would become gentle with one another and would not be ashamed, as people are today, but would freely caress one another, as children do. When they met they would give one another looks that were deep and full of meaning and comprehension, and in those looks there would be love and sorrow."

Kolya read this passage straight through, unable to tear himself away. He felt feverish in the head. He had found it! And with no God. How good it was and how vivid!

Dostoyevsky had touched Kolya's most sensitive strings, and they all began to sound, and already he could hear miraculous, unearthly music descending upon the earth . . . But how could that be? . . . The doubts and torments began again . . . All that was in the future, when people would be better . . . But now . . . Before Kolya's eyes there suddenly arose the Arakcheyevs, the Saltychikhas, the butchers and executioners, the menacing, imposing figures of tsars and kings, merciless oppressors . . . No, it was still necessary to cleanse the earth of them . . . "Who does not know both sorrow and anger / Does not love his native land." Isn't that so, really? And the words of Marx that Tosya had quoted before he died came back to Kolya again . . . Besides that, everyone's talking and writing about Kant . . . Have to take a look, see what that's all about . . .

Kolya had long since stopped asking grown-ups about anything; he tried to search out the answers on his own. He looked things up in the Brockhaus and Efron encyclopedia at the school library, digging up all sorts of elaborate wisdom. But when he got to Kant, he couldn't understand a thing, not a single thing: "transcendental idealism," "numena," "phenomena," "antinomies," "categories"—they all danced in his head like mysterious monsters. He grasped some of what Kant said about "man as an end in himself" and the "categorical imperative." But this categorical imperative looked to him like a cold piece of intestine, which you could fill with whatever you wanted—there was nothing living or vital here, nothing that would give a living answer to living questions. Or maybe, Kolya thought sadly, it's just that I don't understand. Maybe my own intestine is too frail, maybe I'm not up to it—and the pages of the book seemed to him an elaborate code he would never be able to decipher.

For the Christmas holidays Kolya decided to visit his Uncle Georgy. Sorrow had eaten at his soul, like rust. Everything reminded him of his tormenting secret. He wanted a change of scenery, if only for a while, to have some relief, to collect himself after all the suffering he had experienced. He was recovering, but his recovery was slow and he sensed that.

At school with Kolya was a boy named Borya (Boris) Balashin, with whose mother Kolya's Uncle Georgy lived, in her house, without benefit of churchly mysteries, and this pleased Kolya immensely, inspiring tremendous respect in him for his uncle, whom he defended furiously against the attacks of his virtuous grandmother, Agniya Ivanovna, and even against chance remarks dropped by his own mother, Lyubov Ivanovna. Borya was a boarder, living in the school dormitory, and like almost all pupils of closed government educational institutions, he saw it as especially daring to engage in the specific forms of debauchery practiced at the *gimnaziya*, though they were small in caliber. In general he was kind by nature, though not especially gifted nor very highly evolved. Traveling with him were two other *gimnaziya* students, the sons of an impoverished local landowner named Glotov. It was in their company that Kolya set forth

Along the way, late at night, the students began to whisper conspiratorially. Kolya was dozing.

"Got a glass?"

"Yep."

"And a corkscrew?"

"Damn it, I forgot the corkscrew—well, I'll ask the conductor for one."

"Won't that be a problem?"

"Nonsense. I'll give him ten kopecks, and everything'll be fine. What are you? A fine lady? Or maybe just stupid? Just came in from the village?"

"All right, all right. Do what you know—"

Kolya opened his eyes. The Glotovs were unwrapping a bottle of vodka and a bottle of port. Right in front of them lay slices of sausage, bread, a few apples, and pickled cucumbers.

"So, you woke up?"

"Well, I wasn't sleeping—"

Borya triumphantly returned with a corkscrew. It was almost dark in the railroad car. The conductors were economizing on candles, and burning in the only lantern was a fat little stump of a candle, with wax stalactites floating around it on all sides.

With a blow of his hand Borya dashingly popped the cork of the vodka bottle, while the older Glotov boy opened the bottle of port with the corkscrew. The unsettled vodka, now foaming with bubbles, was decanted into tea glasses, and they drank it down at one gulp, gasped, and bit into the *zakuski* (snacks to accompany vodka).

"What about you, Kolya? Aren't you gonna?"

"Not vodka."

"Pour the wine, then—for our scholar . . . How does that thing in French go, Misha? About 'it must be drunk'?"

"Uhh . . . *le vin est tiré, il faut le boir.*"

"There ya go. *Le vin est tiré*—so don't go making faces."

"All right. I'll have some port."

Kolya felt ashamed for several reasons—because they were drinking somehow like criminals, on the sly, trying to hide the fact; because he didn't have enough independence and character of his own, but instead went along with them like a puppy on a leash; and because, finally, this thief-in-the-night type of drinking was completely at odds with the complicated sufferings that had filled his life in recent times.

From not being used to it his head began to swim after just half a glass of port, little jets of fire ran through his body, and he felt himself nodding . . . Borya and the lamp were spinning before his eyes . . . Kolya pulled his greatcoat over his head, and soon he was dreaming: flapping his arms he was flying over forests, ravines, fields . . . The wind was blowing in his face . . . He felt free and at ease . . .

"Kolya! Hello, hello," Georgy Antonych greeted him when they arrived the next morning. "Haven't seen you for so long. How are things? Let's go have some tea . . . How's your father? And Lyubov Ivanovna? Why do you look all sour? I almost didn't recognize you."

"I don't know. I'm not sour. Everything's fine at home, nothing special. You aren't terribly angry, are you, that I showed up at your door without any warning?"

"What are you saying? For heaven's sake, I'm ever so glad to see you! The only thing is, unfortunately, I have to run."

Anna Ivanovna Balashina came into the dining room. She was a full-bodied blond woman of about thirty-five, with fairly regular features, blue-eyed, with slightly too much powder on.

"This is my nephew Kolya, Anna Ivanovna. Please treat him well—I have to run—but where's Boris?"

"He'll be coming along later. He lay down and fell asleep," said Anna Ivanovna, and she darted a look at Kolya.

She proved to be a rather well-educated woman of quite radical views. Her radicalism came in part from the burdens of her previous family life; her former husband, an officer, had not wanted to grant her a formal divorce. From Emilia Andreyevna, her mother, a very intelligent German woman, she had inherited a strong temperament and will, although she herself was noted for her fiery temper: it was said in the town that she had once fired a gun at Georgy Antonych out of jealousy, but missed him—the bullet had whizzed past his left ear and buried itself in the wooden wall. Kolya, too, had heard this story, and therefore he watched her, not without curiosity: there was nothing to indicate such fiery passions, other than a strangely severe crease, or frown line, over the bridge of her nose, a certain restraint in her speech, and a guardedness in all her manner, down to the gestures of her chubby, pink hands.

"If you're finished, Kolya, let me take you and show you your room."

"All right. Thank you."

Anna Ivanovna led him to a well-lit room with a large window. The whole floor was covered with—pears! The room had the very specific, pleasant aroma of an orchard in autumn, a smell of leaves, fruit, and earth. Out the window the world was white with snow, the windowpanes were patterned with frost, and a fat, curlicue icicle was visible just outside the window, glistening in the cold winter sunlight; because of the conditions outdoors the strong autumnal smell inside seemed especially comforting.

"Please excuse us, Kolya, because of the pears."

"What do you mean? It's very pleasant. Really. It's a wonderful smell and they probably taste great, too—"

Thus Kolya settled in for the winter holidays at his uncle's. That first day went by sluggishly: he kept nodding off, his whole body felt tired and achy, and his head hurt. In the evening he and Boris decided to go to the circus. An old brick building, either a tavern or an inn, had been turned over for use by the circus. It was down by the river, where motley crowds of people were strolling, children riding sleds down the steep bank, boxing matches being organized out on the ice, people shouting, shrieking, fooling around, having fun. Kids and grown-ups, the beau monde of this provincial town, elegant ladies, guys and gals, shop hands, and peasants from neighboring villages—all were bumping into one another, running around, or proceeding with measured tread, each according to his own fashion. At the corner of the building was a slightly tilted, old, wooden lamppost, with a kerosene lamp winking its yellow eye nearsightedly against the dark blue of evening. Pasted to the lamppost was a colorful promotional poster with the circus program. And at the entrance stood a loud-voiced fellow wearing an unusual sort of outfit with a stovepipe hat on his head, and he kept shouting in a frenzied voice:

Let the first bell ring.
The show's about to start.
Come in, come in! You're all invited.
You there, passing by. Please stop!
Take a look at the wonders we have.

All you fine ladies and flirts,
Peasant women and gossips,
Tiny, little old ladies,
Soldiers in the service,
And whiny old grandfathers
All bent over and bald,
Come right up from the back rows,
Push your way up to the cash box!
Buy a ticket. Just ten kopecks.
And in you go to the circus!

"Ugh, the flies and mosquitoes are eating him alive!" a man in a sheep-skin commented, shaking his head.

"Yah, but what's he gonna do. Has to shout, you know: he's invitin' the public in."

A youngster, stumbling as he ran, called out to his friend: "Fedka, lend me five kopecks, will ya? I'm five kopecks short—pay you back on Sun-day—better yet, lemme borrow six kopecks, huh?"

"Not from me, you don't! How about you let me have seven?"

"Skinflint!"

A peasant in a long sheepskin coat was standing by the lamppost and reading syllable by syllable:

"Eq-quil-lib-brist—now whut the heck would thet be?"

"Devil only knows."

"Com-mic-cal ent-tree—now thar's somethin' fer ya—who the hell they writin' fer, the bastids!"

"So what are you guys, here to be carpenters?"

"Yah, carpenters—but we cain't unnerstan' a damn thing—"

"Well, ask the guy in the fur coat—over there, in the glasses."

"Ah, the hell with all of 'em."

"Say, whut're all the people here fer?"

"Circus."

"Ugh, one-eyed cannibals, what kind of a paper they've pasted up!"

Boris and Kolya pushed their way through the crowd and went into the circus. They were overcome immediately by the musty odor of manure and horse sweat. People in winter clothing were sitting and standing around. The performance had already begun, and you could hear the snap of the whips, the clowns slapping one another, and the shrill cries of the red-haired one. There were sword swallowers; a trained dog who could count up to ten; a monkey that had gone all mangy, wearing glasses with a newspaper in its hands, sitting on a chamberpot—and all this inspired unfeigned delight, even rapture, among the spectators. The audience loudly applauded the especially successful presentations. The air was very close, suffocating, and this suddenly reminded Kolya, with extraordinary vividness, of that strange night when only by chance he had come free of the noose. All at once the whole circus—the audience, the clowns, the dressed-up goose, the lap dog dancing on its hind legs—swam off into the distance. Kolya's thoughts were far, far away . . .

"What's the matter, have you fallen asleep. Look! Listen!" Boris whispered directly into the whorl of Kolya's ear.

Two men were standing on the stage: one was dressed as a Frenchman, the other as a building superintendent or town policeman or village constable: what he was wearing was either a uniform or it wasn't, but you couldn't find fault with it; the idea was obvious.

Kolya, snapping out of it, began to listen. The circus performers were taking turns in a comic monologue:

"In French we say *le savon*."
"In Russian, 'soap.' "
"The French say *mille pardons*."
"The Russians, 'in your snout!' "
"In French they say *royale*."
"But we say 'accordion.' "
"The French say *etoile*."
"But we say 'matryoshka doll.' "
"The French all say *salat*."
"But we say *zakuska*."
"In French they say *promenade*."
"But we say *kutuzka*" (the lock-up).

The crowd burst out laughing. There was a round of applause.

"In French they say *societé*."
"In Russian we say *shaika*" (gang of thieves).
"In French they say *liberté*."
"But we say *nagaika*" (the whip).

The turbulence of the crowd kept increasing. Soon the whole "auditorium" was hooting and clapping furiously. The actors continued, unruffled.

"For the French it's always *fromage*."
"For us it's the bottle."
"In French they say *voyage*."

"In Russian, 'internal exile.' "

"In French they say *dilettante*."

"But we say *liubitel'* (lover or amateur).

"The French say *intendant'* (police official).

"We say *grabitel'* (plunderer or robber).

At this everyone went wild. Hats, caps, gloves flew in the air. "Bravo!" "Well done!" "They're really lettin' 'em have it." "Yeah, right up the left nostril."

A police official approached the master of ceremonies and, after whispering something in his ear, took him behind the curtains.

The crowd muttered but then quieted down. A few isolated shouts were heard.

"What savagery! What do they want?"

"Down with the herrings," someone called out in a hoarse young voice.

After a few minutes the emcee came out, white as a sheet.

"We beg your forgiveness. Due to circumstances beyond our control, the show is closing down. We ask . . . the respected public . . . to disperse quietly."

"Goddamn Herods!" muttered a peasant woman with a wool shawl over her head.

"They didn't like it—the truth hurts," a shop hand responded.

"This arbitrary rule is scandalous!" the lenses of a pince-nez flashed.

Nevertheless, the audience dispersed. The next day the circus, in its entirety, was expelled from the town. To make up for it, there arose a veritable mountain of rumor and discussion concerning the incident, and the winged phrases about "plunderers," "gang of thieves," etc., flew in all directions. Of course the audience didn't understand what the "Frenchman" was saying but it had an excellent grasp of the Russian epithets, and that was quite enough to stir up hundreds of people, who cuttingly ridiculed the powers that be—not going all the way to the top, to be sure, but no longer constrained by the holy terror which previously the average person had displayed even toward an ordinary watchman.

The scene at the circus made a powerful impression on Kolya. For the first time he saw with his own eyes "how 'it' is done." Yes, he thought to himself, when he was alone, we'll have to wait a while with this idea of universal love. No use throwing kisses at police officials. The sons of bitches! Kolya was swept away with increasingly intense feelings of protest—he wanted to do something, to head in some direction. But what to do? Where to go?

For the time being he went with Borya into the woods early in the morning, Borya having brought along his double-barreled shotgun. It was a mild and cloudy winter's day. The evergreen forest was gloomy. Their skis slid smoothly over the snow. It was quiet in the forest. Only now and then a soft crackle was heard, and suddenly a pile of snow would fall from the spreading bough of a spruce tree, sticking to the virgin snow cover and sending out a fine spray of icy particles. There were tracks on the snow: a hare had jumped here—two and one, two and one. And here a field mouse had stitched its little threads. Over there were the tracks of an ermine or weasel. "Si, si, si," tiny goldcrests were peeping as they hopped from branch to branch with their tiny wings trembling. Softly a lump of snow spilled from a bush someone had brushed against, and all at once, a twig would show, black and quivering, against the whiteness all around. A gray-ish-brown tree creeper flew down to the base of a birch tree, down by the roots, and began circling the trunk, with its tail up, steadying itself occasionally with its wings.

Bang! A puff of smoke. Boris had fired . . . On the snow lay a little gray-brown lump. Kolya picked up the dead bird. It had been shattered by bird shot, but this badly torn little ball still held the warmth of a life that had disappeared.

"What the hell did you kill it for?"

"Well, what was it?"

"A tree creeper."

"I wanted to test the sights on my gun."

Silence.

Kolya was thinking his own thoughts, the same ones as before. What was the difference between this little bird and a human being. None. There had been life—now it was gone. And what about our descendants? As Dostoyevsky pictured them?

The human race, too, will perish some day. And so will the Earth, our dear old planet, and its corpse, on which all life has ended, will drift through endless empty space until it is drawn by some gigantic force of gravity into new orbits or plunges against the fiery breast of some mighty radiating sun. And yet out of all this chaos new life will eventually arise, as it arose before . . . My, but it was good to be alive.

"Kolya, what's wrong with you, have you gone nuts? You're gonna trip on a stump and go right down into that ravine! Ha, ha, ha. You've gotten sort of tetched."

"You'll get tetched yourself," Kolya growled, turning his skis sharply.

They arrived home damp and sweaty. It seemed stifling hot inside. They took off their jackets and lay down.

"Kolya."

"What?"

"Let's have a drink."

"Enough of you."

"Come o-on!"

Boris slid off the bed. (They were both in Kolya's room, to keep each other company.) Borya dragged his friend into the dining room by the scruff of his neck. In there, following ancient custom—it was Christmas, after all—the table had been set; on it were small carafes of vodka and homemade fruit liqueurs, and there were wines: port, Madeira, sherry. A large ham lay on a plate, and there were smoked whitefish, sardines, sprats, and marinated mushrooms of various kinds: white ones, brown ones, saffron milk caps, milk agaric; the *kulebyaka**pie was covered with a napkin; little tender, pimply gherkins were lying in a covered dish. Enjoy, blessed belly!

Borya swept up a glass of *zubrovka* (vodka flavored with "buffalo grass"), crammed his mouth full of *kulebyaka*, shoving a bit of caviar in there, too, using his fingers, and began to sing a parody of a church song.

Be sanctified, be sanctified

As you bake, blessed pie.

May you be mounted by

Three jugs of blancmange.

"What about you? At least have some port. I'll pour it for you."

"Just a little. Hey, what are you pouring in the glass?"

"Doesn't matter; it'll all fit. It'll all end up here," Boris, laughing, patted himself on his lean tummy.

Kolya took a drink of the sweet port wine and cheered up.

"That's enough—take the good things a little at a time—let's go outside."

"Again? We just got in."

"Come on."

They ran out without their coats to ski some more, on racing skis this time. There was a slight roaring in Kolya's head; he began to play the fool, threw snow around, sang, whistled piercingly, with two fingers, like Solovei the Bandit, fell over backward with his arms spread out, making the imprint of a human body deep in the snow, and all the while he was thinking, what a strange thing a human being is, how strange that he, Kolya, cheered up by half a glass of wine, had for the moment spilled all troubling thoughts out of his mind, like mushrooms from a sack.

"Kolya! Boris! Are you totally insane? What are you doing, running

*kulebyaka—a large pie with many ingredients (meat, fish, vegetables, etc.).

around in the freezing weather without coats? Are you tired of living? There are more efficient methods than that if you wish to use them."

"But we were only—"

" 'We were only'—'we were only'—into the dining room, march! Drink some hot tea with cognac."

"We'll do that, with pleasure. With cognac and with pleasure," Borya rumbled, settling himself at the table.

"That's a plagiarism," Kolya smirked. "Or close to it."

"Why?" Georgy Antonych asked, his pince-nez gleaming by the light of the lamp, and when he looked over the tops of his lenses now and then, it gave him an unusually serious look. He was smoking a cigarette—puff, puff, puff—and blowing smoke rings.

"Because there's a well-known play on words, Uncle Zhorzh: 'The rain was under way and so were two students / One in an overcoat and one to the university / One was called Ivan; the other had been called to a name day party.' "

"Where did you get these bits of wisdom?"

"From school—and you know—"

Kolya began to unload, as though from a sack, his whole store of witty sayings of every kind, for which "Uncle Zhorzh" had a great fondness. Anna Ivanovna came in, with her mother, Emilia Andreyevna, a dried-up little old lady with a large wrinkled forehead, gray hair tied in a bun, intelligent gray eyes, and a stern mouth, which could be represented exhaustively, it seemed, by a single thin line.

Everyone laughed cheerfully at Kolya's stories, and he was charging along like a horse without a bridle: he was so wound up by their outing, the skiing, the wine he had drunk, and the obvious success of his storytelling that, without realizing it, he crossed the traditional boundaries of decency and, administering a final shock to respectable society, began to recite Baudelaire's "Carrion."

"*Schrecklich! Das ist doch eine Schweinerei—und Sie—*" (Dreadful! That is sheer swinishness—and you—), Emilia Andreyevna addressed Kolya, "*so jung und so verdorben*" (so young and so depraved).

She rose from the table and demonstratively walked out.

An awkward silence ensued. All his ardor had left Kolya in an instant, he sank down, and a lump formed in his throat. He didn't know what to do. He never had any intention of offending Emilia Andreyevna. He had only spoken with her once but was impressed and amazed by how intelligent and well-read she was. And now—crash!—he had fallen on his face, completely by surprise. He felt very bitter and angry at himself . . .

[The manuscript breaks off here.]

Afterword

STEPHEN F. COHEN

Knowing how Kolya's life will end three decades later, readers may wonder about the fate of other members of his family still alive when the novel breaks off.

Bukharin's mother, Lyubov Ivanovna, hoped that her eldest son would use his precocious academic abilities to become a biologist and continued to worry about his radical nonconformity. Though pleased when he enrolled in Moscow University, she was dismayed by his role as a revolutionary student leader, by his decision in 1906 to join a Marxist party, and even more by his three arrests in 1909 and 1910. She saw Kolya for the last time in 1911, when he fled administrative exile and, traveling through the Moscow underground, went abroad. Bukharin returned to Russia only in 1917, two years after his mother's death.

All three of Lyubov Ivanovna's surviving sons were consumed by the revolution. The youngest, Pyotr, whose birth is just mentioned in the novel (chapter 14), died in 1918 fighting with the Red Army in the Russian civil war. Little more is known about him.

Only Vladimir ("Volodya"), the second son and little Kolya's constant companion, lived a long life, but much of it was unhappy. Educated as an engineer, he became one of the first Soviet "Red directors," quickly reviving a provincial cloth mill devastated by revolution and war. Though never a Communist Party member, Vladimir was always, it is said, a "staunch non-Party Leninist." (Lenin urged him to join the Party and assume larger managerial responsibilities, but he declined for family reasons.) Vladimir moved his family back to Moscow in 1927, living for a time with his brother in the Kremlin. He was arrested not long after Bukharin's trial in 1938 and spent the next eighteen years in jail, labor camps, and exile. In 1961 Vladimir Bukharin—by now, Uncle Volodya to his martyred brother's two children—was officially exonerated and given a Moscow apartment and pension. He died in 1979 at age eighty-nine.

Thus by 1938 the novel's father Ivan "Antonych" (Ivan Gavrilovich) had lost all his children. When the family's final ordeal began to unfold in 1936, he was living with Bukharin, Anna Larina, and baby Yuri in the Kremlin. The old man's grip on Stalinist realities diminished as they descended on the household. "What's going on? . . . My Kolka a traitor? What nonsense! . . . It can't be that he won't return!" Frail and bedridden, he was nonetheless thoroughly searched when the NKVD came in 1937. After Anna's arrest, Ivan Gavrilovich somehow retrieved Yuri from an orphanage, but he couldn't manage for long. (Stalin, ever thorough, had terminated his pension.) He died in 1940, never able to read the loving portrait written by his first son.

Kolya's cousins—the "Yablochkin" (Lukin) children Nikolai, "Manya" (Nadezhda), and "Vasya" (Mikhail)—fared no better under Stalin. They, too, were arrested soon after Bukharin's trial, and all three died in a Moscow prison in 1940. Little is known about Mikhail, except that he was tortured into giving false testimony against his sister. Nikolai, director of the Academy of Sciences' Institute of History at the time of his arrest, died in prison of abuses he suffered there. He was posthumously exonerated and restored to the pantheon of Soviet Marxist historians in 1957, but without any mention of his famous and still stigmatized cousin.

Nadezhda's fate, in keeping with Russia's long tradition of women's suffering and courage, was especially horrible. She had gone abroad with Bukharin in 1911, as his wife, and despite their traumatic breakup in the early 1920s, remained his dear friend to the end. Long afflicted by a progressive spinal disease, by the mid-1930s, when she too was living with Bukharin's new family in the Kremlin, she could not even stand without a special plaster corset.

Once Bukharin's persecution began, Nadezhda—Nadya, as he called her—defended him repeatedly in reproachful letters to Stalin and, even after his trial, openly at a Party meeting. When the NKVD finally came for her on the national holiday of May 1, 1938, they stripped her of the corset and flung her on the floor of an overcrowded cell. Despite great physical pain during her nearly two years in prison, she refused to confirm any of the criminal charges against her beloved Kolya, which Stalin's men still demanded even after Bukharin's execution. On March 8, 1940, in a brief prison trial presided over by the same Ulrikh who had announced Stalin's verdict against Bukharin, "Manya" was sentenced to death, and the next day dragged or carried out to be shot.

Letter to Anna Mikhailovna Larina

What follows is the only letter ever found of the several Bukharin wrote to his wife, Anna Mikhailovna Larina, from prison. When finally retrieved fifty-four years later, it was for her a lacerating emotional experience and for all of us conclusive proof that he had written four manuscripts in Lubyanka, including this novel. The letter is reprinted with permission from Anna Larina, *This I Cannot Forget: The Memoirs of Nikolai Bukharin's Widow* (New York: Norton, 1993).

Dear Sweet Annushka, My Darling!

I write to you on the eve of the trial, and I write to you with a definite purpose, which I emphasize three times over: No matter what you read, no matter what you hear, no matter how horrible these things may be, no matter what might be said to me or what I might say—endure *everything* courageously and calmly. Prepare the family. Help all of them. I fear for you and the others, but most of all for you. Don't feel malice about anything. Remember that the great cause of the USSR lives on, and *this* is the most important thing. Personal fates are transitory and wretched by comparison. A great ordeal awaits you. I beg you, my dearest, muster all your strength, tighten all the strings of your heart, but don't allow them to *break*.

Do not talk carelessly with anybody about anything. You will understand my position. You are the person closest, dearest to me, only you. In the name of everything good that we have shared, I beg you to use all your strength and spirit to help yourself and the family *endure* this terrible phase. I think that father and Nadya should not *read the newspapers* during the days in question: let it be *as though they are asleep*. But you will know best what to do and what to say so that it will not be an unexpected horrible shock. If I ask this of you, believe me when I say that I have come to it through great suffering, and that everything that will happen is demanded by bigger and greater interests. You know what it costs me to write you such a letter, but I write it in the deep conviction that I must act only in this way. This is the main, basic, and decisive factor. You yourself understand how much these short lines say. Do as I ask you, and keep a grip on yourself—be *like a stone*, a statue.

I am very worried about YOU, and if they allow YOU to write to me or to send me some reassuring words about what I have said above, then THIS weight would fall somewhat from my soul. I ask you to do this, I beg you, my dearest friend.

My second request is an immeasurably lesser one, but for me personally very important. You will be given three manuscripts:

a) a big philosophical work of 310 pages (*Philosophical Arabesques*);
b) a small volume of poems;
c) the first seven chapters of a novel.

Three typed copies should be made of each of them. Father can help polish the poems and the novel. (A *plan* is attached to the poems. On the surface, they seem to be chaotic, but they can be understood—each poem should be retyped on a separate sheet of paper.)

The most important thing is that the philosophical work not be lost. I worked on it for a long time and put a great deal into it; it is a very *mature* work in comparison to my earlier writings, and, in contrast to them, *dialectical* from beginning to end.

There is also that other book (*The Crisis of Capitalist Culture and Socialism*), the first half of which I was writing when I was still at home. Try to *rescue* it. I don't have it here—it would be a shame if it were lost.

If you receive the manuscripts (many of the poems are related to *you*, and you will feel through them how close I feel to you), and if you are allowed to pass on a few lines or words to me, *don't forget to mention my manuscripts*.

It is not appropriate for me to say more about my feelings right now. But you can read between these lines how much and how deeply I love you. Help me by fulfilling my first request during what will be for me a very difficult time. Regardless of what happens and no matter what the outcome of the trial, I will see you afterward and be able to kiss your hands.

Good-bye, my darling,

Your Kolka
January 15, 1938

P.S. I have the small photograph of you with the little one. Kiss Yurka for me. It's good that he cannot read. I am also very afraid for my daughter. Say a word or two about our son—the boy must have grown, and he doesn't know me. Hug and kiss him for me.

Glossary

This glossary includes many, though not all, of the names and terms that appear in Bukharin's memoir-novel. It is partly based on the endnotes, or commentary, in the Russian text, *Vremená*, with a foreword and commentary by Boris Frezinsky (Moscow: Progress Publishers, 1994).

Not listed are most of the better-known Russian writers and artists, as well as radical literary and social critics—including Chernyshevsky, Dobrolyubov, Pisarev, Radishchev, and Chaadayev. Most standard reference works have information on such figures, and in this novel Bukharin himself describes and discusses many of them in interesting and informative ways. An excellent source on many of the painters and collectors Bukharin mentions is Suzanne Massie, *Land of the Firebird* (New York, 1980).

Alkonost See Sirin and Alkonost.

Avvakum (1620–1682) archpriest and leading spokesman for the Old Believers, dissenters in the Russian Orthodox Church; persecuted and finally executed for refusal to recant; his autobiography remains a powerful account of suffering endured for loyalty to one's convictions.

Azef, Yevno Fishelevich (1869–1918) agent of the tsarist Okhrana (secret police), who became a leader of the Socialist Revolutionary Party (see note to chapter 21, p. 318).

Bakunin, Mikhail Aleksandrovich (1814–1876) Russian revolutionary, at first a Narodnik, later the founder of anarchism; joined International Workingmen's Association, in which he had many disputes with Karl Marx and from which he was expelled in 1872.

Balmashov, Stepan Valerianovich (1881–1902) student member of the Socialist Revolutionary Party; assassinated Minister of Internal Affairs Sipyagin, for which he was hanged.

Barbizon school A group of French painters (Theodore Rousseau and others), who worked at the village of Barbizon near Paris, ca. 1830–1870. They played an important part in the development of realistic landscape painting.

Barkov, Ivan Semyonovich (1732–1768)   Russian poet, author of frivolous works.

Bazarov   Main character in Ivan Turgenev's novel *Fathers and Sons*; he epitomized the radical young "nihilists" of the 1860s, who rejected all authorities, in contrast to the moderate idealists of the 1840s (the "fathers").

Belinsky, Vissarion Grigoryevich (1811–1848)   one of Russia's foremost literary critics in the first half of the nineteenth century; a Westernizer; favored realism and social responsibility in literature.

Benckendorf, Aleksandr Khristoforovich (1783–1844)   chief of gendarmes under Tsar Nicholas I, beginning in 1826.

Berdyaev, Nikolai Aleksandrovich (1874–1948)   Russian religious philosopher; formerly a Marxist, he became an émigré after the Russian revolution; Bukharin's speech in Paris, April 3, 1936, "Fundamental Problems of Contemporary Culture," was largely a polemic against Berdyaev's views.

Bernstein, Eduard (1850–1932)   a leader of the German Social Democratic Party, headed the movement that began in the mid-1890s to revise Marxism, to favor reform rather than revolution.

bogatyr   One of the mighty warrior-heroes of medieval Russian epics.

Bogdanovich, Ippolit Fyodorovich (1744–1803)   Russian poet; his long narrative poem *Dushenka* (1778), based on a plot from classical antiquity, was stylized to imitate a Russian folk tale.

Bortnyansky, Dmitry Stepanovich (1751–1825)   Russian-Ukrainian composer, especially skilled at choral works.

Brehm, Alfred Edmund (1829–1884)   German zoologist and explorer, author of a popular six-volume work *The Life of Animals*.

Bugaev, Nikolai Vasilyevich (1837–1903)   professor of mathematics, father of the poet Andrei Byely.

Bulgakov, Sergei Nikolaevich (1871–1944)   economist, religious philosopher, and theologian.

Chernov, Viktor Mikhailovich (1873–1952)   one of the founders of the Socialist Revolutionary Party and a leading SR theoretician and propagandist.

David, Eduard (1863–1930)   one of the leaders of the German Social Democratic Party; favored revision of Marxism to advocate reform rather than revolution.

Danilevsky, Nikolai Yakovlevich (1822–1885)   writer, sociologist, and natural scientist; ideologist of Pan-Slavism; promoted a quasi-scientific racist theory of Slavic "superiority," justifying expansion of Russia as a great power; polemicized against Darwinism.

Devrien Editions   A publishing house founded in St. Petersburg in 1872 by the Swiss businessman A. F. Devrien; it put out books for young people and major works in the natural sciences; the books were noted for their great scientific value and high quality of production; in 1917 the business was moved to Berlin.

Domostroi   Book of instructions for running a patriarchal household and maintaining a strict patriarchal way of life; cf. Sylvester.

Dubelt, Leonty Vasilyevich (1792–1862) from 1835, chief of staff of the special "Third Department" of the gendarmes under Tsar Nicholas I.

gimnaziya in nineteenth-century Russia a government-sponsored elite secondary school (inspired by and supposedly modeled on the gymnasia of ancient Athens). After 1866, under Minister of Education Dmitry Tolstoy, increased emphasis was placed on classical education with the result that more than 40 percent of class time went to instruction in Greek and Latin, one purpose being to discipline students and distract their attention from current affairs. In the late 1800s graduation from a gimnaziya was virtually the only means of admission to a university.

Grand Duke Sergei (1857–1905) son of Tsar Alexander II, governor general of Moscow (1891–1905); assassinated by the Socialist Revolutionary Ivan Kalyaev.

Grot, Yakov Karlovich (1812–1893) Russian philologist, member of the Academy of Sciences; author of a two-volume book of research on the Russian language (*Philologicheskie razyskaniia*, 1st ed., 1873).

Hertz, Friedrich Otto (born 1878, date of death unknown) Austrian Social Democrat, economist; supported revision of Marxism; emigrated to England in 1938.

Ioann Kronshtadtsky ("Father John of Kronstadt") Full name, Ioann Ilyich Sergeyev (1829–1908); a priest of the Russian Orthodox Church, archpriest of the Andreyevsky Cathedral (St. Andrew's) on the island fortress of Kronstadt near St. Petersburg. Notorious for the extreme conservatism of his political views; a supporter of anti-Semitic, fascist-like gangs, the Black Hundreds.

Kaigorodov, Dmitry Nikiforovich (1846–1924) popularizer of the natural sciences in books with such titles as "Conversations on the Russian Forest," "From the Kingdom of Greenery," and "From the Feathered Kingdom."

Khodynka Disaster that occurred on the field of Khodynka in Moscow on May 18, 1896, as part of celebrations of the coronation of Nicholas II. Owing to careless planning by the authorities, overcrowding and panic occurred as huge throngs turned out to partake of the monarch's largesse; more than thirteen hundred people were killed, most being trampled or crushed to death.

Kholodkovsky, Nikolai Aleksandrovich (1858–1921) Russian zoologist, entomologist, and translator of poetry.

Kibalchich, Nikolai Ivanovich (1853–1881) a revolutionary of the People's Will organization; executed for his part in the assassination of Alexander II; also an inventor, he developed a design for a jet-propelled flying machine.

Klyuchevsky, Vasily Osipovich (1841–1911) historian, member of the Russian Academy of Sciences, author of *A Course in Russian History*.

Korsh, Valentin Fyodorovich (1828–1883) Russian philologist and literary historian, edited a "Universal History of Literature" (*Vseobshchaia istoriia literatury*), published in fifteen volumes (1880–1883).

Kostomarov, Nikolai Ivanovich (1817–1885)   Russian-Ukrainian historian and writer.

Kotlyarevsky, Ivan Petrovich (1769–1838)   Ukrainian writer; his verse "epic" *Aeneid* (1798) gave a comic depiction of the life of various segments of Ukrainian society.

Krushevan, Pavel Andreyevich (1860–1909)   journalist, founder of the anti-Semitic newspaper *Znamya* (Banner); deputy to the State Duma from Kishinyov.

Kukolnik, Nestor Vasilyevich (1809–1868)   Russian writer.

Lafargue, Paul (1842–1911)   French socialist; member of the International Workingmen's Association; married Karl Marx's daughter, Laura; author of numerous books and pamphlets.

Lavrov, Pyotr Lavrovich (1823–1900)   philosopher, sociologist, and essayist; one of the leading ideologists of the revolutionary Narodnik movement.

Legal Marxists   A number of Russian academics (notably Peter Struve, Mikhail Tugan-Baranovsky, Nikolai Berdyaev, and Sergei Bulgakov) who in the 1890s applied elements of Marxism to criticize the Narodnik theory of a separate, noncapitalist path of development for Russia ("peasant socialism"). In opposition to the Narodniks, and in temporary agreement with the Social Democrats, they saw capitalism as inevitable and progressive for Russia. Because their criticisms of the tsarist regime were muted, the authorities allowed them to publish and function legally. In the early 1900s they turned against the Social Democrats and Marxism.

Leontiev, Constantine (1831–1891)   Russian writer and literary critic; one of the leading Slavophiles.

Linevich, Nikolai Petrovich (1838–1908)   Russian general, headed the Allied military expedition sent to suppress the Boxer rebellion in China, 1900–1901.

Lokhvitskaya, Mirra Aleksandrovna (1869–1905)   Russian author of erotic verse.

Lopatin, Lev Mikhailovich (1855–1920)   Russian philosopher and psychologist; editor of the journal *Voprosy filosofii i psikhologii* (Problems of Philosophy and Psychology).

Lopukhin, Aleksei Aleksandrovich (1864–1928)   director of the tsarist Department of Police, 1902–1904; under the impact of the 1905 revolution, he made public materials showing the government's involvement in anti-Jewish pogroms, for which he was placed on trial and exiled to Siberia. His memoirs about the Department of Police were published in 1907.

Meshchersky, Prince Vladimir Petrovich (1839–1914)   editor of the newspaper *Grazhdanin* (The Citizen); advocated return to the old order preceding the abolition of serfdom and other reforms of the 1860s.

Mikhailovsky, Nikolai Konstantinovich (1842–1904)   sociologist, literary critic, and social commentator; a leading spokesman of the Narodnik movement.

Narodnik (Populist)   Member of the movement to "go to the people (*narod*)" that arose in Russia in the 1860s and 1870s. One wing of this movement formed the People's Will (Narodnaya Volya), a conspiratorial terrorist organization that in 1881 assassinated Tsar Alexander II.

Nemirovich-Danchenko, Vasily Ivanovich (1848/49–1936) author of numerous novels and ethnographic studies.

Nikita Pustosvyat (died 1682) leading writer and speaker for the Old Believers; the epithet Pustosvyat, meaning "Empty Saint," was applied to him by supporters of the official church; his full name was Nikita Konstantinovich Dobrynin. After being condemned by a church assembly in 1667 he recanted and was allowed to remain at liberty; later, in 1682, he spoke out again for the Old Believers, and was arrested and executed.

Nordau, Max (1849–1923) German author of works on philosophy and psychology; one of the founders of Zionism.

Plehve, Vyacheslav Konstantinovich (1846–1904) minister of internal affairs and chief of the corps of gendarmes; assassinated by a Socialist Revolutionary.

Posrednik Publishers An educational publishing house founded in St. Petersburg in 1884 on the initiative of Leo Tolstoy; in 1892 it moved to Moscow; its books were produced at the printing plant of I. D. Sytin; it continued to exist until 1935. (Posrednik means "intermediary" or "middleman.")

Rededya According to a medieval Russian chronicle, prince of the Kasogians (Adyges), who in 1022 engaged in single combat with Prince Mstislav Vladimirovich of Tmutorokan, and was defeated.

Romanov, Sergei Aleksandrovich See Grand Duke Sergei.

Rossolimo, Grigory Ivanovich (1860–1928) one of the founders of pediatric neurology in Russia.

Rozhdestvensky, Zinovy Petrovich (1848–1909) Russian admiral; commander of the Russian fleet defeated in the Russo-Japanese war of 1904–1905; regarded as a petty tyrant and satrap of the tsar.

Russkiye Vedomosti Newspaper of liberal orientation, favoring reform in Russia; published in Moscow (1863–1918).

Russkaya Mysl Monthly magazine of liberal orientation, with literary and scientific as well as political content; published in Moscow (1880–1918).

Saint Sergius of Radonezh (1314–1392) founder of the Troitse-Sergieva Monastery (Trinity Monastery of St. Sergius); canonized by the Orthodox Church.

Saltykov-Shchedrin "Nikolai Shchedrin" was the pen name of Mikhail Yevgrafovich Saltykov (1826–1889; Russian author of satirical works). His *History of a Town* in particular satirized the officials of the tsarist civil service, the "chinovniks." He himself served as such an official.

Sergei Aleksandrovich See Grand Duke Sergei.

Shulyatikov, Vladimir Mikhailovich (1872–1912) Marxist literary critic. During and after the 1905 revolution, he was also a leader in the Moscow Committee of the Russian Social Democratic Labor Party. Shulyatikov, according to a grandson writing in a Soviet newspaper in 1988, had a close association with the young Bukharin when the latter was a rising figure in the party (1907–1912), and it is odd that Bukharin would make a seemingly cutting reference to the "sorry fame" gained by Shulyatikov's book *Justification of Capitalism in Western European Philosophy*.

Sipyagin, Dmitry Sergeyevich (1853–1902)   minister of internal affairs; used harsh measures to suppress worker, peasant, and student disturbances; assassinated by the student Balmashov.

Sirin and Alkonost   Symbolic figures in old Russian manuscripts, and in revived form in the art of Viktor Vasnetsov and others. They were depicted as large birds with human heads, personifications of morning and evening, joy and sorrow, life and death. Their names are distortions by old Russian chroniclers of two names from Greek mythology, Halcyon and Ceyx, a wife and husband whom the gods transformed into birds.

Slavophiles   A group of Russian writers and public figures, especially from the landed gentry, who beginning in the 1830s and 1840s glorified and idealized the "unique" (*samobytny*) Russian and Orthodox heritage, including the Russian peasant commune, declaring "true Russian principles" to be superior to the rationalism, individualism, and legalism of the West.

Solovyov, Vladimir Sergeyevich (1853–1900)   Russian religious philosopher and writer.

Solovyov, Sergei Mikhailovich (1820–1879)   historian; member of the Russian Academy of Sciences; author of the multivolume *History of Russia since Ancient Times*.

Struve, Peter Bernardovich (1870–1944)   economist, philosopher, historian, social commentator, and theoretician of the Legal Marxists.

Sylvester (died 1566)   Moscow churchman; adviser to Tsar Ivan the Terrible; author of the best-known edition of the *Domostroi*.

Timiryazev, Klimenty Arkadyevich (1843–1920)   natural scientist, Darwinist, specialist in plant physiology and the biological bases of agronomy; popularizer of science; welcomed and supported the Bolshevik revolution of 1917.

Tirpitz, Alfred von (1849–1930)   German admiral; as secretary of state for naval affairs (from 1897) he directed the buildup of a powerful German fleet.

Tolstoy, Count Dmitry Andreyevich (1823–1889)   extreme conservative in the court of Tsar Alexander II; became minister of education in 1866, tightening government control of the schools, discouraging advancement of students of low social background, and placing emphasis on classical education in the gimnaziya. After the assassination of Alexander II, in 1881, Count Tolstoy became minister of internal affairs and chief of gendarmes and helped set the tone for the reactionary policies that prevailed under the last two tsars, Alexander III and Nicholas II. See also gimnaziya.

Trubetskoi brothers   Sergei Nikolaevich (1862–1905), religious philosopher and social commentator; and Yevgeny Nikolaevich (1863–1920), religious philosopher and legal expert, active in public affairs.

Tugan-Baranovsky, Mikhail Ivanovich (1865–1919)   economist, historian, Legal Marxist.

Vasnetsov, Viktor (1848–1926)   Russian painter, one of the first to incorporate national historical and folk traditions in his art.

Urusov, Sergei Dmitryevich (born 1862, date of death unknown)   governor of Bessarabia in 1903–1904; as a deputy to the State Duma in 1905, he exposed the tsarist government's involvement in anti-Jewish pogroms; after 1917, joined the civil service of the Soviet government.

Vorontsov, Vasily Pavlovich (1847–1918)   economist and social commentator; ideologist of the liberal wing of the Narodniks.

Waldersee, Alfred von (1832–1904)   Prussian general; headed the German expeditionary force sent to China in 1900–1901.

Witte, Count Sergei Yulyevich (1849–1915)   Russian statesman; served as minister of finance, 1892–1903, introducing major economic reforms; as prime minister in 1905–1906, he negotiated peace with Japan; the Russian original of his memoirs, written in the period from 1907 to 1912, is in three volumes; an English version is *The Memoirs of Count Witte*, translated and edited by Sidney Harcave (Armonk, N.Y., 1990).

Yakubovich, Pyotr Filippovich (1860–1911)   Russian poet and translator; a revolutionary of the People's Will organization; arrested in 1884 and sentenced to hard labor; author of *V mire otverzhennykh. Zapiski byvshego katorzhnika* ("In the World of Outcasts: Memoirs of a Former Hard-Labor Convict"), published in 1898 under the pseudonym L. Melshin.

Zabelin, Ivan Yegorovich (1820–1908/1909)   Russian historian; director of the Historical Museum in Moscow.

Zasulich, Vera Ivanovna (1849–1919)   Russian revolutionary, at first a Narodnik, later a Marxist and close associate of the founder of Russian Marxism, **Georgy Plekhanov** When the Russian Marxists split in 1903 and after, she was one of the Mensheviks (minority) who opposed Lenin and the Bolsheviks (majority).

zemstvo   From 1864 to 1917, an institution of local self-government, a kind of local assembly or board, established for rural Russia as part of the reforms that accompanied emancipation of the serfs. The zemstvos had limited powers, including responsibility for local health services, schools, and roads. Many of the liberal intelligentsia, professionals, and enlightened gentry were active in the zemstvos, seeing in them a hope for moderate reform rather than a fundamental challenge to the tsarist system.